THE HERMETIC LINK

10821786

Hermes as origin Father in the dome of Sienna.

THE HERMETIC LINK

FROM SECRET TRADITION TO MODERN THOUGHT

JACOB SLAVENBURG

IBIS PRESS
Lake Worth, FL

Published in 2012 by Ibis Press
An imprint of Nicolas-Hays, Inc.
P. O. Box 540206
Lake Worth, FL 33454-0206
www.ibispress.net

Distributed to the trade by
Red Wheel/Weiser, LLC
65 Parker St. • Ste. 7
Newburyport, MA 01950
www.redwheelweiser.com

Copyright © 2012 by Jacob Slavenburg

Originally published in Dutch in 2003 as *De Hermetische Schakel*
Translated into English by Greteke Lans
Final editing by Kyle L. Proudfoot
Ibis Press editor Laurel W. Trufant, Ph.D.

All rights reserved. No part of this publication may be reproduced or transmitted in any form or by any means, electronic or mechanical, including photocopying, recording, or by any information storage and retrieval system, without permission in writing from Nicolas-Hays, Inc. Reviewers may quote brief passages.

ISBN 978-089254-167-6

Library of Congress Cataloging-in-Publication Data

Book design and production by Studio 31
www.studio31.com

Printed in the United States of America

Table of Contents

Preface

Ich ein böser Geist?
Ich bin der beste Geist von der Welt!
("Me a bad Spirit? I am the best Spirit of the World")
—(Papageno—*Die Zauberflöte*)

My father was a born storyteller. Night after night, I listened as a child to myths, fairytales, and legends, which he adapted with great enthusiasm in such a way, as far as I was concerned, that it seemed as if they took place in our own village. There was one fairytale in particular that I wanted to hear over and over as a youngster: *The Genii in the Bottle*. Much later, I encountered it again in the Brothers Grimm stories. A young student walks through the forest and arrives at a big oak. All of a sudden he hears a voice calling out in a muffled tone: "Get me out, get me out!" The student starts searching at the roots of the tree until he finally discovers a glass bottle in a tiny hole. He picks it up, holds it to the light, and observes something inside resembling a jumping frog.

At the most crucial moments in the fairytale, my father always had the habit to leave it up to me to determine how the story should continue: "Shall we let the boy open the bottle or shall we go to bed?" At such a moment, I always felt like a magician. Of course, the cork was removed each evening and an awe-inspiring genii escaped from the bottle and disappeared between the trees. He called out: "I am the mighty Mercurius; whoever lets me free, I am bound to break his neck!" (Looking back, it turned out that my father had been directly quoting the words of the Brothers Grimm.) With a clever trick, the student returns the genii into the bottle, but then, promising the student great favors, the genii once more begs him to be released (my father looked at me again, and I risked it again!). Mercurius suddenly appeared as the great benefactor of humanity. The student received a cloth and was told: "If you move one end of it over a wound, it will be cured; if you move the other end over steel and iron, it will transform it into silver."

No matter how commandingly my father had called out "I am Mercúúúúúrius," he did not have the remotest idea that the magic cloth was a gift from the great Hermes-Mercurius, the God who has blessed our civilization with his medical science, especially alchemy. We both intuitively grasped that the fairytale encouraged us in some way to re-open the bottle and that the spirit needed to be released. In far by-gone "enlightened" centuries, a disappointed alchemist apparently had hidden this spirit, imprisoned in a bottle under the ground, waiting for better times to come. Moreover, my father announced, to my great surprise, that this Mercurius lived not far from us in a big mountain—of all places, in Bergeijk! He ruled there as the underground King of the Hobbits and was named Kurië. The farmers in the district Kempen recited the tale over and over, telling how, during the night, honest folks were rewarded and the dishonest punished by this (Mer)Kurios and his Hobbits. Once again duality!

The Brabantian seminarians, in the province of Brabant (Netherlands) during the beginning of the 20th century, composed the well-known song about the "Hermenieke van Bergeijk." Within it, they spoke of the death of the pastor who let the "barley beer of Kyrie" flow, but had no knowledge of the ancient legendary background of this sage, since the phrase "barley beer of Kyrie Eleison" does not mean anything anymore.

These seminarians were no longer taught that Hermes-Mercurius was born as the son of the Heavenly Zeus and the Earth-born nymph Maya in an underground cave in Arcadië, and that Zeus, knowing his son belonged to two worlds, Hades and Olympus, appointed him as the great mediator, the guide, the message, the Messenger. Hermes is at home beneath the earth with the dead, as well as above the earth with the living, as well as in Heaven with the Gods. He is the winged spirit who flies wherever he pleases!

Jacob Slavenburg is well versed in all of this. In his book, he shows us in an elaborate way how we should search for the historical roots of this Greco-Roman God in Egypt, where his original name was Thoth some 5000 years ago. When the Greek Herodotus visited Egypt in 450 B.C., he observed that this Thoth resembled the well-known Hermes, and from then on both Gods melted together in one God called Hermes-Thoth. Later, the Romans called him Mercurius. Slavenburg points out repeatedly that the writings ascribed to Hermes—the *Hermetica*—have their roots in Egypt. Based on legends and myths and historical texts, he shows that people in the world of antiquity possessed a deep conviction that the fountain-sources of the wisdom of our civilization flowed from the land of the Nile.

Almost all of the great "civilizers" took a trip to meet the Egyptian priests to be initiated by them: Orpheus, Pythagoras, Plato, but also Joseph, Moses, and Jesus! The evangelist Matthew allows the flight of the "holy family" to the safety of Egypt and, in verse 2.15, allows God to declare triumphantly: "Out of Egypt I have called my Son!" Slavenburg holds tightly to this line of thought and does not neglect to point out that sometimes great experts in the field of the *Hermetica* are hardly aware of this Egyptian frame. Therefore, it is no mere coincidence that the great mythical incarnation of Hermes-Thoth—the Thrice-Great Hermes, Hermes Trismegistus—was an Egyptian living in Alexandria, in antiquity's cosmopolitan syncretistic city *par excellence*. This was also the root of Judeo-Hermetic Christianity, sadly enough buried a couple of centuries later—not in a bottle beneath an ancient oak, but rather in a jar in the Egyptian dessert. It came rather as a surprise to me when I read the Nag Hammadi texts—supremely authentic hermetic texts that turned out to be indispensable additions to the *Corpus Hermeticum*. Again and again, these hermeticists indicate that Egypt was their Motherland, even up to present times. If the Freemasons at the end of the 18th century in Vienna wanted to put on stage their alchemical-hermetic philosophy of life in *Die Zauberflöte*, then, according to them, this scene could only take place in the land of Isis and Osiris.

Anyone who realizes that, by definition, the treasure of hermetic thought is spread over many dimensions simultaneously, from Hades to Olympus, anyone who has acquired knowledge of the many mainstream and underground hermetic streams during a time span of 4000 years, anyone who comprehends correctly that a hermetic point of view challenges all conceptual narrow-mindedness—that person can only have great admiration for the tour de force of Jacob

Slavenburg that we find in this book. Besides his usual lucid writing, two aspects stand out for me in his book. On the one hand, he describes a total overview of the history of the hermetic *Gnosis* (as far as I know, this is the first time this has appeared, especially in the Netherlands); on the other hand, he illustrates this wide panorama with many examples that sparkle like jewels.

A total overview usually ends up in an abstract summation—you miss the trees for the forest. The reverse is also often true—you are pointed out so many trees that you lose track of the larger picture. Slavenburg never loses sight of the forest, but stands still every time to show us beautiful examples of trees, shrubs, and even flowers. He recites abundantly—to his heart's content (literally)—so that the reader becomes aware of and feels the living beating heart of the Arcadia of Hermes.

What do we mean by the "hermetic concept of life"? What makes a text a "hermetic"? Is Hermeticism a type of religion, like Judaism, Christianity, or Islam? After reading this book, it becomes clear to me that this is not the case. The term "hermetic" refers to a specific state of consciousness, which can occupy a place in all three traditions; and, as this book indicates, it has already achieved its place in all three, and always had! A hermeticist is someone who, in a specific way, looks at everything that exists between Heaven and Earth and lives accordingly!

The place *where* you are initiated and the tradition *in which* you are initiated are not *per se* hermetic; but the fact *you are initiated* is typical for the hermetic framework. Initiation always means, one way or another, crossing a threshold. It is Hermes, who is never stationary, who can be of great service to us. He is the winged, androgynous guide leading us from one plane to another and constantly helping us step over boundaries. A hermetic theory is essentially a theory of transformation. The most beautiful texts in the *Hermetica* are those in which a human is taught and guided to climb from heavenly sphere to heavenly sphere, up to the seventh—yes...even up to the eighth and ninth—heavenly sphere. Above all, Hermeticism encompasses the art of "hermetic Gnosis," an ability, a gift of Hermes, to discover and unveil within ourselves the hidden wisdom.

This unveiling does not take place by means of concepts, but by means of symbols.

This book of Jacob Slavenburg is called *The Hermetic Link*. A perfect title. The essence of Hermes is correct—as the connecting link between Heaven and Earth, between Spirit and Matter. As above, so it is below; as below, so it is above. Is this not the first postulate of the *Tabula Smaragdina* of Hermes Trismegistus?

And this book is, of course, by itself a link within the centuries-old wisdom tradition. Thoth, himself, can be proud of this contribution to his library!

—Tjeu van den Berk

Introduction

An old Egyptian legend tells a story about a carefully sealed *Book of Thoth* that contains the ancient wisdom of the entire universe. Another saga speaks of the archetypal mother figure Sarah finding a grave near the Palestinian city of Hebron. When the grave was opened, it seemed to contain the still-intact body of the sage Hermes Trismegistus. On the writing table in front of him lay an open book full of universal wisdom.

Who was Thoth and who was Hermes Trismegistus? The latter is most likely a mythical figure from ancient Egypt, more or less equal to the Egyptian God Thoth. After the capture of Egypt by the Greeks in the 4th century B.C., a connection was made between Thoth and the Greek Hermes.

Wisdom writings have been attributed to Hermes Trismegistus as well as to Thoth, and they have been handed down. The legends seemingly hold a symbolic truth. Many were literally and figuratively buried under the sand—just like the once magnificent cultist center of Thoth named Hermopolis. There indeed appear to have been many, many manuscripts, which have been periodically rediscovered, sometimes pulled right out of the sand.[1] The manuscripts that are preserved, together with the discoveries of the last decennia, are very fascinating. The *Hermetica* (hermetic writings) contains a comprehensive account of what everyone should know. It answers questions about where we come from, who we are, and what our future will be.

When I read these documents for the first time, fifteen years ago, I had a strange experience. It felt as if a kind of nostalgia for something very beautiful and grand—something that had always been present in the background—was now being realized. Through it, I have become a happier person. Nevertheless, my knowledge needed to mature in order for me to be able to convey the history of the *Hermetica* as accurately as possible.

As a result, this book represents the outcome of the search for the legacy of Hermes Trismegistus. It is the first book that reflects the history of the Thrice-Great Hermes and the hermetic tradition from ancient Egypt to the present, a period of about 5000 years.[2] It starts with a visit to the city of Hermopolis—literally dug out of the sand—and ends with a tentative breakthrough of (what we call) scientific thought and its search for the "Universal Theory"—the "Hermetic Link" that, in the first instance, connects extremely diverging topics.

The first part of this book covers the myths surrounding the figures of Thoth, Hermes, and Hermes Trismegistus. From the 4th century B.C., the hermetic writings have been known primarily for magic, alchemy, astrology, healing arts, and botany—and their miraculous interconnections. At a later stage, the more well-known philosophical treatises were added, such as the *Corpus Hermeticum* and *The Divine Revelation (Asclepius)*.

In the Interlog, it becomes clear that, when these texts were hardly known anymore in the West, Arab scholars devoted profoundly deep studies to them. Via the Middle East and Spain, they eventually reached the Old World again.

The rediscovery of the hermetic writings during the Italian Renaissance created a previously unknown movement. From this period on, the new fame of Hermes spread over western Europe and shaped the intellectual climate for at least a century. Part II of this book deals with this climate and the fascinating history that followed.

In contrast to ancient history, there survives an abundant amount of material about the development of the hermetic intellectual heritage during the Renaissance and afterward. It is impossible, within the scope of a single book that illuminates a history of more than 5000 years, to be exhaustively complete. This is not my intention. I aim rather to present a clear and recognizable line of thought that illustrates the uninterrupted progress of the hermetic tradition up to the present. After all, the history of Hermes seems to be our own history.

—Jacob Slavenburg

(And then Isis spoke to her son Horus:)

For 'tis not meet, my son,
That I should leave this proclamation ineffectual,
But [rather] should speak forth what words
[our] Hermes uttered when he hid his books away.
Thus then he said:

"O' holy books,
who have been made by immortal hands,
by incorruption's magic spells...
free from decay throughout eternity
remain and incorrupt from time!
Become unseeable, unfindable
for every one whose foot shall tread the plains of this [our] land,
until old Heaven doth bring forth meet instruments for you,
whom the Creator shall call souls."

Thus spake he; and, laying spells on them by means of his own works,
he shuts them safe away in their own zones.
And long enough the time has been
since they were hid away.[3]

Prolog

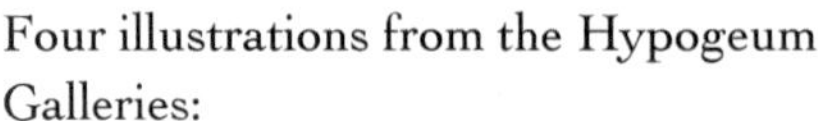

Four illustrations from the Hypogeum Galleries:
In the subterranean vaults of the necropolis of Hermopolis, Thoth was worshipped as a baboon (above left and right) and as an ibis (above). The remains of a hundred thousands mummified ibises are being stored in the catacombs (middle right) of the necropolis. At right is a sign hanging at the entrance to the necropolis.

O' Land of Egypt, O' Land of Egypt.

Your Gods will become a myth
out of long forgotten times.
Your divine liturgies,
your deeply impressive ceremonies
and holy revelations,
will be for the descendants
incomprehensible hieroglyphs,
which are chiselled out of stone,
and admired by tourists.[4]

An Early Adventure

On a very early morning on a late December day in the year 2001, I stood among the ruins of the once great city of Hermopolis. This is the city of the God Thoth—the birthplace of Thrice-Great Hermes.

The journey had not been without problems. Bloody attacks on tourists some years prior had made traveling freely impossible. It was mandatory to travel accompanied by a military escort. This also had certain advantages. My wife, two friends, and I were able to observe the sight peacefully, without the presence of tourists. At five o'clock in the morning, we had already left the Middle Egypt city of el-Minya. In front of us, a jeep full of soldiers armed to the teeth led our vehicle; another followed. Within the city limits of el-Minya itself, the escort was strengthened by a police car with a flashing light. Blue beams across the Egyptian night.

At seven o'clock, when it was becoming light, we trod through the still-cold sands of the desert to one of the strangest places I have ever encountered. In front of us, a hired guide; behind us in file formation, nine or ten Arab guards of the archaeological site armed with carbines. We descended into a kind of crypt that turned out to be a necropolis. At first sight, it reminded me of the catacombs in Rome or Malta—long stretched-out corridors with alcoves. In antiquity, there must have been close to two million mummified ibises stored here.[5] Several remnants of them were displayed. I had read about them once in a work by Herodotus from around 450 B.C.[6] and now I saw them with my own eyes![7] Mummified baboons had also found a final resting place here. In a sort of subterranean temple, we suddenly found ourselves face to face with Thoth, in the form of a baboon. We observed a fascinating wall painting of a Baboon-Thoth. In an alcove, somewhat farther, a picture of him; this is a holy place.[8]

The expedition continued to the grave of Petosiris, a famous high priest of the Thoth and Hermes cult. On our way, we walked along the ruins of a small temple dedicated to Thoth. The spot is magnificently located; it is in the desert at the edge of the not-too-wide fertile ribbon of land that stretches along the Nile from Cairo to Aswan—a resting place similar to the holy sites at Abydos and Dendera.

The place where I stood about an hour or so later lies in the middle of fertile land. This was not the site of a "Death Cult," just the dug-up remains of a most rigorous vital religion. Here, the great Thoth temple stood that stored the old wisdom scriptures. They must have been consulted and recited from time to time. The spoken word in Egypt had a magical power. Participants not only heard the text; the words themselves released something. They were connected to images that arose from within.[9] And Thoth was ultimately the divine aspect of the Word, the *Logos*—God of the script, the master inventor of magic.

Hermopolis Magna covers a far-reaching area containing the remains of old city walls and numerous old temple ruins, even a Christian church. Goats and sheep graze between the rubble. Women with colorful shawls stride along carrying pails of water balanced on their heads. Children from the nearby village, Achmounein, play here. Only the small open-air museum is empty; no one is looking for anything there. And yet, meter-high statues of baboons stare out over the old city. They are remnants of the destroyed Thoth temple, the central point in this previously renowned holy city.

We were not given a long time to explore this historical site. The convoy had to go on, as we had to catch the train to Aswan. Along picturesque and colorful tracks, through villages with improvised houses and limestone streets, and across a green palm-tree landscape, we drove at top speed back to el-Minya. The sun shone brilliantly. The same Sun once worshipped in the ancient city of Hermopolis. Ruins of an old temple of Ammon stood as silent witness—a supreme God with two divine eyes—one is the Sun; the other the Moon. This is symbolized by Thoth, in whose temple ruins I had just walked. But, who was Thoth?

Part I
The Secret of Hermes

Hermes is the name of a noble race,
just as Manu and Buddha.
He simultaneously represents
a human, a caste, a divinity.
Hermes as a human is the first,
the greatest initiator of Egypt;
as a caste he is the priesthood,
the keeper of the occult traditions;
as a God, the planet Mercurius,
whose sphere corresponds to
a string of enlightening principles
and godly initiators.
In short,
Hermes rules the Heavenly spheres
of divine initiation.
In the spiritual hierarchy, all such matters
are woven together by a secret unification
as if connected by an invisible thread.
The name Hermes is a talisman,
which binds them together,
a magical sound which conjures them…[10]

CHAPTER 1

THE ETERNAL FIELDS OF REED AND THE EYE OF HORUS

In a far bygone and gray day, in the honorable old Kingdom, there lived a remarkable God—*Djehuti* or *Thoth.* Thoth, as a God should be, was omniscient. As a God of creation, he meticulously maintained law and order. As a God of the cosmos, he recorded accurately all cosmic appearances and phenomena. As a God of knowledge, he left behind 36,525 writings for his descendants,[11] although some sources are rather more modest and speak of forty-two books.[12]

As a God of wisdom, Thoth was also the inventor of script, by which people were able to write things down. This is something with which King Ammon, according to Plato, was not too pleased.[13] In addition, Thoth was a legendary healer. In this capacity, he placed the torn-out eyeball back into the eye-socket of Horus, the equally legendary son of the divine couple Osiris and Isis. Naturally, Thoth had divine ancestors. Sometimes, as a Moon God, he is called "the writer of Re," or even the "second eye of Re."[14] Re himself was the great Sun God; his reflection was the Moon. Thoth was also considered to be the "heart of Re" and was also known as the "tongue" of the deity Ptah. He created by means of the divine Word, the *Logos*. Thoth was also the inventor of magic and many other sciences.[15]

However, Thoth's knowledge even extended to an ability to peer deeply into the most inner being of humanity. "He knows what lives in the heart," we find in a text in the temple of Karnak.[16] Thoth is thus the father of the *Gnosis*.

THE MIRACULOUS THOTH

The cult of Thoth was already known in Egypt prior to the construction of the pyramids and cultic centers dedicated to him existed in the pre-dynastic period. The Feast of Thoth was already celebrated in ancient times and texts from the 3rd Dynasty report a temple of Thoth.[17]

In the oldest tradition, Thoth appears as a lunar God. An inscription in a temple of Ammon praises the Moon as "ruler of the stars, who divides the seasons, months and years."[18] Thoth healed the eye of Horus on the day of the full Moon. This is not without significance, since the full Moon was associated with the overflowing of the Nile and the very necessary fertility of the flooded land.

The origin of Thoth's cult can be traced to the delta of the Nile, the perfect sanctuary of the ibis, for the ibis appeared as the Nile was about to flow beyond its banks, depositing its fertile silt. In the Prolog, I spoke of the necropolis in Hermopolis where an estimated two million mummified ibises were laid to rest.

In Sakkara, archaeologists have unearthed buildings in which the ibis of Thoth—the Moonbird of the Night—and the hawk of Horus—the Sunbird of the Day—have been entombed together, although not in mummy form.[19]

Since the early ages, the city of Hermopolis Magna[20] in Middle Egypt was definitely the principal center of the cult of Thoth.[21] During the 1st Dynastic period (3100–2686 B.C.) the Baboon-God Hez-Oer (of Hedj-wer) was worshipped at this location. During the Middle Kingdom and afterward, Thoth was personified not only as an ibis, but also in the form of a baboon.

Thoth in the image of a baboon during the ritual for the dead.

Baboons worshipping the Sun.

A god in the image of a monkey may sound strange to our ears. However, an Egyptian could ultimately hope to become a baboon, since baboons were considered the ideal worshippers of the Sun God Re. In fact, I witnessed a touching fresco on the grave of Ramses IX showing a number of baboons joyfully delivering an ode to the upcoming Sun. In the British Museum in London, a relief can be seen of three baboons standing upright greeting the Sun, which in Old Egypt was associated with the music of the spheres.[22] Whoever could comprehend the god-like language of the baboon had access to the religious knowledge.[23] Even a pharaoh was, in the most favorable scenario, only an imitation of a baboon. In the *Egyptian Book of the Dead*[24] we find various hymns pertaining to the baboon, like this one:

> *. . . I have celebrated in song and worship the (Solar) disk,*
> *and I have joined the jubilant Baboons,*
> *since I am one with them.*[25]

And:

...O', these four baboons, who seated forward in the barge of Re,
who offer justice to the Overlord,
who choose between the weak and the powerful,
who rejoice the Gods with the breath of their mouths,
who make divine offerings to the Gods and funeral offerings to
the blessed souls, who live in justice,
whose hearts are free of malice and lies and
whose abhorrence is Sin...[26]

The Transition

Another aspect of Thoth is that of peacemaker. He intervenes during conflicts between Gods and pharaohs and carefully guards the harmony between the cosmos and its Earthly counterpart, Egypt.

However, Thoth is also the "Thought of Re."[27] Without Thoth, this thought could not possibly become manifest. Thoth is also speech, "the Word of Ptah." Here too, he manifests what lies latent in the intelligence of the deity and reveals it. By his breath, he creates manifest things. In this sense, he is the *Logos*.[28]

In religious literature, Thoth, as a lunar God, acts as a God of transition from one state to another, just like the new and full Moons. It is common knowledge that the Egyptians were convinced of life after death.[29]

After an Earthly death, the deceased had to justify himself to Osiris, God of the Underworld. The human heart, seat of intellect and feeling, was weighed against the feather of *Maat*, representing truth and justice. Thoth acted in this role as divine scribe. On many papyri, he is portrayed with a writing tablet, as a symbol for hearing and seeing. Very accurately, he records the verdicts of the scale. One text found in one of the king's graves in Thebes says it was Thoth himself who "probes the bodies and examines the hearts."[30] Quite often, we see the monster Ammit, devourer of the dead, standing next to Thoth. Ammit patiently waits for its prey, a heart burdened with sin. It was of great importance to avoid being devoured

Thoth, as God of Script, records the results of the weighing of the soul.

by means of an extensive litany to confess accurately all sins. The pronouncement of each sin was followed by a denial made by the deceased. This magical ritual, called the Declaration of Innocence, could protect the departed from a miserable end.

However, even after this, the trials were not at an end. The departed one had to know the forty-two names of the god figures perfectly. They appeared in their fear-inspiring form, one by one, in front of the inner eye. Like passwords, the departed had to speak out the names of these "guardians."

There were even more magical formulas to prevent the deceased from suffering a second death. In certain traditions, a "Letter from Thoth" granted the deceased the right to pass through the portal between the two worlds protected from a second death. Thus, Thoth was also considered the guide of the dead. He could assist deceased souls during their dangerous journey through the Underworld.[31]

Often, the departed were given amulets—for example, a heart-shaped scarab with magical warding signs like the names of all the guardians whom the soul had to pass. Magic was, afterall, an "invention" of Thoth, and especially spoken magic was, as we saw, considered extremely powerful. As for the rest, the pronouncement of words alone was a magical action. According to the ancient Egyptians, the intonation of words held a special power. This we find again in the hermetic writings.[32] At the beginning of the dangerous journey, a ceremony called the Opening of the Mouth took place. Symbolically, this was performed by the Gods, especially Thoth, who in this way blew new life into the departed. This was performed during the burial ritual by a priest who touched the mouth of the mummified corpse. In the Old Kingdom, this ritual was only performed on pharaohs; in the New Kingdom, it was also done for ordinary mortals.

The final destination of the soul, having passed all guardians, was the symbolic union with Osiris, Lord of the Underworld, but also God of fertility and new life. The departed one has now actually become a God—or, as we read in one of the many sarcophagus texts:

Whether I live or die, I am Osiris,
I enter and appear within you,
I dissolve in you, I grow in you...[33]

The liberated and reborn soul was allowed to sail away with Re, who rode along the banks of the Nile daily, and at night continued his journey through the Underworld to regain strength. Its home lay in the Eternal Fields of Reeds, a string of unparalleled fertile islands in the Underworld, where, after the rich harvest, souls could feast on "Earthly" pleasures like eating, drinking, and love-making.

Legends

Two aspects of Thoth are important enough to put under the magnifying glass. There was first his function as messenger of the Gods. It was primarily due to this stature that the Greeks unified him at a later date with Hermes, also messenger of the Gods.

So we observe that Thoth is often represented as guide to the other Egyptian Gods. For example, according to an inscription in the temple of Hatsheput, in one delicate situation involving Ahmose, wife of Pharaoh Tuthmosis I, Ammon-Re predicted that a Queen would rule over the whole of Egypt. Together with Thoth, he started out for the palace of the pharaoh and took possession of Ahmose, who is supposed to have shouted in supreme delight: "Hatsheput," which became the name of the daughter who was conceived in the lap of Ahmose during this event. And indeed it was she who, at a later date ruled the Empire as the first woman pharaoh.

The second hermetic aspect of Thoth on which I want to focus briefly was his function as guardian of the ancient wisdom. According to ancient records, Thoth had composed a book of magic con-

Upper left: Water carriers now walk where once Hermes strolled.
Upper right: One of the meter-high baboons once decorating Thoth's temple (1370 B.C.)
Bottom: Ruins of the large temple of Thoth in Hermopolis Magna.

Above: Remnants of the temple of Thoth situated at the necropolis of Hermopolis.
Below: Temple grave of Petoris, High Priest of Thoth.

taining all the wisdom of the cosmos. In a legend, an old priest told Prince Nanufekiptah that there was an iron chest buried on the bottom of the Nile. In this chest, there was a copper chest containing more chests: the first was made from juniper-berry wood, the second from ivory, the third from silver, and the last from gold. In this golden chest, the *Book of Thoth* was to be found. However, the chests were kept under the closest surveillance by monstrous snakes and scorpions. This fact, nevertheless, did not discourage the prince. By means of magical formulas and rituals and an inexhaustible battle with the constantly regenerating serpents, Nanufekiptah took possession of the book. After reading out loud the first incantation, he was able, to his great joy, to understand the language of the animals, birds, and fish. After the second incantation, the Gods of the Sun, Moon, and stars appeared in front of him in their true form.

The wrath of the Gods was horrendous. There followed a series of violent trials that resulted in the prince being drowned in the Nile and buried with his so-desired book.

The learned son of Pharaoh Ramses II, Setne Chamus, after hearing the story, was determined to secure the *Book of Thoth* for himself. He found the grave of Prince Nanufekiptah. Just as he was about to get hold of the book, the spirit of Nanufektiptah stopped him. They both agreed to play a game of chess to decide the ownership of the book. Setne lost the first game, unfortunately, and Nanufektipath made him sink to his knees on the earth. He also lost the second game, after which he sank deeper, up to his groin. By the third game, he had sunk to his ears. However, with the help of amulets given to him by his powerful father, Setne managed to escape the grave with the book.

Still, Setne could not avoid his punishment. Against the will of his father, Pharaoh Ramsesses II, he kept the book and recited from it to many people. One day, he became mesmerized by a lady of matchless beauty, after which a hunger took possession of him equal to that of a wolf. He was willing to give up everything to be with her, if only for one hour. He donated all his possessions to her and even killed all his children, thereby giving the object of his adoration the assurance that her newly acquired fortune would not be challenged. But when the *moment suprême* arrived, the beauty disappeared like a ghost into the night, and Setne remained behind totally naked and feeling foolish. It was in this deplorable state that his father found him, imploring him again strongly to return the book. Fortunately, it all turned out to have been a bad dream. Setne Chamus returned the book to the grave of Nanufekiptah and sealed it carefully.[34]

The Book of Thoth

Besides these legends, there are also other sources that mention the *Book of Thoth*. The German Woldemar von Uxkull, during the 1920s, wrote an intriguing book about an Egyptian initiation based on a reconstructed version of the so-called *Book of Thoth*.[35] More actual references are given by Clemens of Alexandria, a Christian Church Father from around the 2nd to 3rd century B.C. He speaks about forty-two books kept in Egyptian temple archives. This is not improbable. In the Ptolemaic Horus temple at Edfu, a catalog of books was found chipped out on the inner wall of a room where they were stored. Some of these books have been attributed to Thoth.[36] Egyptian holy books were copied in scriptoria, so-called *pir-ankh's* (homes for the living).[37] These "homes for the living" were, however, much more than just scriptoria[38] Here, the healing arts were exercised and taught.[39]

Clemens distinguishes the following treatises:

> A Hymn to the Gods, a book called About the life of the King with four astrological volumes (the order of the fixed Stars, the position of the Sun, Moon and the five Planets, about the conjunction of the Sun and Moon phases and the points of time of the ascending Stars), ten books on Cosmology and Geography (especially pertaining to Egypt and the Nile; about the construction of temples and the measurements and required material for these temples); ten books about the worshipping of Gods (such as offerings, ways of worship, holy songs, prayers, processions, festivals and so on); ten priestly books (pertaining to the laws and the Gods and the Priest training) and six medical volumes (about the anatomy of the body, diseases, organs, medicine, eye-diseases and woman sicknesses).[40]

Just recently, a stirring event happened. Two German professors spent several years studying fragments of texts with the title *Book of Thoth*. Parts of this *Book of Thoth* were found in Berlin, Paris, Vienna, Florence, and Copenhagen. The structure of the texts shows great similarity to what we later encounter in the *Hermetica*;[41] the deity reveals knowledge and insight to a disciple. In the *Hermetica*, in almost all instances, it is Hermes Trismegistus himself who announces the wisdom to his son, Tat, and specifically to Asclepius.

We see the same form in the *Book of Thoth* researched by the Germans:

Book of Thoth:
May his foot be at rest,
May he have girdled himself against the darkness,
May he with full assurance walk into the light...[42]
May he, in possession of these teachings,
observe the stars and constellations of the sky at night.[43]

Afterward, the road lies open to the disciple to comprehend the teachings from the Book of Insight, the Book of Power, the Book of Annals, the Book of Djed's Column, and the Book of Interpretation. From then on, he drinks in the Book of Collective Prayers and the Book of Worshipping the Omnipotent, and takes knowledge of the Book of Secrets. Thus he becomes a disciple of the servant of Thoth.[44]

In a preliminary reaction to these discoveries, the French expert of the *Hermetica*, Jean-Pierre Mahé, draws a parallel between the above fragment and the *Treatise of the Eighth and Ninth Heavenly Sphere*.[45] In the passage, Hermes teaches his pupil that the only ones capable of reading what has been written in "this book" are those who have arrived, by experiencing each phase of development, on the Path to Immortality. Only then will they come to understanding.[46] The pupil, prior to this, had already acknowledged his progress, together with the pre-knowledge that he acquired "from the books," and had surpassed his shortcomings.[47]

In the *Book of Thoth*, the pupil asks Thoth:

Reveal to me the source of the fountain-source of all Wisdom,
so I may from the sweet water drink.
The vulva waits patiently for instruction,
may I enter her abode.
See, my mouth has been opened,
may someone pour milk into it.[48]

Thoth answers that he will instruct the pupil and gives him some counsel:

Beware of tomorrow!
Be upright!
Be persistent in the lessons!
See plenty!
Do plenty!
Listen plenty!
Point your heart towards God!
Keep yourself to the Law![49]

Station of Departure—Egypt

The Egyptian character of the *Book of Thoth* is emphasized by the pledge of the disciple that he will protect the *ba* and that he will be like an ape (baboon). Also, there is talk about the Underworld. Moreover, in the Parisian version of the *Book of Thoth*, Thoth asks the disciple to call out the names of the forty-two vultures.[50] This resembles the incantations in the *Book of the Dead*.

Both professors, therefore, come to the conclusion that the newly found fragments of the *Book of Thoth* are "essentially Egyptian": "It is a Book of Thoth, not a Book of Hermes."[51] Also, "if the Book of Thoth cannot be the father of the known-to-us hermetical writings, it must be one of its grandfathers."[52]

Mahé sees in the *Book of Thoth* a very close predecessor of the Greek *Hermetica*.[53] There are also differences, however. The refining transformation taking place in the regions of the Underworld, so customary to the Egyptians, we can trace back to the *Book of Thoth*. This, however, is in contrast with the liberating ascension through the heavenly spheres as this is normally described in hermetic literature.[54] Mahé, too, sees this problem. However, he states, the Underworld also has a place in the *Hermetica*,[55] even though he states that this is exceptional.[56] On the other hand, we notice that the discovered sarcophagus texts, dating from the period of the Middle Kingdom, contain "geographical maps" of the Heavens in conjunction with the Underworld.[57]

Even more amazing is that Thoth, in the *Book of Thoth*, is named Thrice-Great (great, greater, greatest). As we shall see, the epithet Thrice-Great (*Trismegistus*) belongs to Hermes. Mahé notes that the epithet *Trismegistus* is used in the *Book of Thoth* as well as in the *Treatise of the Eighth and Ninth Heavenly Sphere* whenever there is a question in the dialog regarding enlightenment and transformation processes. In most cases, the term appears in the form of Songs of Praise.[58] Mahé describes the *Book of Thoth* as "far the closest Egyptian document to the Greek philosophical *Hermetica*."[59]

It certainly has not been proven—at least yet—whether the recently (re)discovered fragments of the *Book of Thoth* are excerpts from the legendary forty-two books of Thoth mentioned by Clemens of Alexandria, or whether they only show similarities to it. It becomes more and more clear to me that the hermetic tradition, discussed in this book and to which this book is dedicated, is a treasure with its source in ancient Egyptian literature. Thoth became Hermes at some point. Therefore, let us see who Hermes actually was.

CHAPTER 2

HERMES—A PHALLIC DEITY

On a night in early summer in 415 B.C., the streets of Athens were disturbed by a violent outburst. A group of late partiers attacked phallic statues of Hermes that were placed here and there around the city. Some were totally destroyed, others heavily damaged. In politically orientated Athens under the rule of Alkibiades, this act of vandalism was taken very seriously. It led to a comprehensive court case that went into history as the *Hermokopiden* trial.

A Greek phallic *herme.*

PHALLIC PILLARS

Which statues are we talking about here? Fortunately, owing to the Greek historian Herodotus, these statues had been described earlier, albeit in a different context. After his visit to Egypt,[60] Herodotus reported that the names of almost all Greek Gods stemmed from Egypt.[61] However, he added: "the Greeks build their statues of Hermes with a raised lid, which they did not learn from the Egyptians."[62] This tradition can be traced to the mysteries of Samothrace,[63] in which, as in pretty much all ancient mysteries, the fertility element played a role. According to researcher Karl Kerényi, one of the most well-known facts about the Samothrace mysteries was the disciple's awakening to the male aspect of fertility—an awareness that continued to affect the individual outside the rituals.[64] Kerényi also connects Hermes with Hekate, saying that they are two aspects of the same great (Mother) Goddess. Moreover, Hekate, like Hermes, was a winged messenger (in some myths, a witch), and, just like Hermes, she was a guide of souls. At crossroads throughout Greece, there sometimes stood *hekataia* with three-sided pillars that were a counterpart to the four-sided *hermen*.[65]

These hermen—which, as the name already tells us, were dedicated to Hermes—were straight-sided pillars adorned with a bust of a bearded Hermes. This is in contrast to later-dated iconography, in which Hermes was usually shown as a slender, beardless youth. The front side of the *herme* was decorated with a strong erect male phallus. In Athens, but also in other Greek cities, these hermen were placed on the agora, but also in front of private residences and estates, temples and gymnasia, and on graves. But they appeared primarily along important roads, at city boundaries, and at intersections and crossroads—like traffic signs today. The Greeks believed these hermen brought luck.

The Cow Thief

The name Hermes can be found at a much earlier date in various palace archives of the late Bronze period, like the one at Knossos.[66] Just as with many Gods in the Greek pantheon, we are dealing here with a gradual evolution. In Arcadia, in the second millennia B.C., Hermes had been traditionally honored as the "good shepherd," God of the country-side. In this role, he also appeared accompanied by a ram.[67] His shepherd's crook was later transformed into a herald's mace. We will return to this shortly.

The most common myth, although not necessarily the oldest, indicates that Hermes was an off-spring of an extra-marital relation between Zeus and the nymph Maya, daughter of the Titan Atlas. Noticeably, Hermes himself will later grow into the prototype of the "secret lover."[68] Greek mythology is full of stories describing Hermes' amorous relationships and the children resulting from these escapades.

According to the Homeric *Hymn to Hermes*,[69] the birth of Hermes took place in a cave on the mountain Cyllene in Arcadia, the same region where he was worshipped as a good shepherd. On the first day of his life, the precocious and very advanced little boy slips away from behind his mother's back and sneaks out of the cave in search of adventure.

Quite soon, he discovers a herd of cows and decides to steal them. When he finds out that, in fact, this herd belongs to the God Apollo, the temptation to steal them is heightened. The clever young Hermes cuts out shoes from tree bark and ties them with braided blades of grass underneath the cows' hooves to avoid leaving any tracks. After a long search, Apollo apprehends the culprit and little Hermes is taken to Olympus to appear before the Heavenly tribunal. Much against the will of his father, Zeus—who did not believe his son could have been so naughty—the boy finally confesses. As far as he is concerned, Apollo may have his herd back. But two cows, as is appropiate, must be slaughtered and offered to the twelve Gods.

> "Twelve Gods?" asks Apollo, since he counts only eleven!
> "Who is the twelfth then?"
> "At your service, Sir." speaks the little lad modestly.
> The twelfth God had manifested himself.

In his birth-cave, immediately after his adventure with the cows, the young Hermes fabricates a lyre from a tortoise shell with strings made from cow guts. It is the sweet-sounding music he produces from it that gives away his whereabouts to the spies sent by his step-brother Apollo. After the court trial described as the *Hermokopiden*, Hermes makes peace with his illustrious step-brother. Apollo receives the much-desired lyre as a peace offering. Peace is signed and, at Olympus, Zeus, after some reprimanding words about property rights, looks down proudly at his most gifted small son.

The supreme God gives him a herald's staff with two white ribbons, a red cowled hood, and winged sandals. The speed which he can achieve with these will be useful to him in his new function as messenger of the Gods. In addition, he was also given the task of promoting trade and offering protection to all travelers.

In the Homeric *Hymn to Hermes*, we read that the clever Hermes taught the Gods on Olympus the art of making fire by means of rapidly turning a "fire-stick." According to Robert Graves,this invention for creating fire was allotted to Hermes because the turning of the male drill into the female block suggested a phallic magic.[70] According to Graves, the white herald ribbons attached to the staff received from his father were later mistakenly construed as serpents.[71] These two serpents bend around the staff, the *caduceus*, in the form of an eight.[72] Today, the (sometimes double) figure-eight is seen as the DNA strand.[73] According to a tradition from the 6th century B.C., when the *caduceus* was still a simple shepherd's staff, it also served as a magic wand by which people were brought into sleep and dreaming. The Homeric *Hymn to Hermes* confirms Hermes' image as a guide of dreams.[74]

Messenger of the Gods

The general portrayal of Hermes found in classical literature is of a capricious God. He is clever, sly at times, and possesses the gift of eloquence. He can use this to deceive, which makes him popular as a patron of trade and thieves. In the Homeric *Hymn to Hermes*, he is called the Prince of Thieves.[75] Before he delivers Pandora to Epimenides, he endows the beautiful lady with a crystal-clear human voice.[76] The gift of the word can also be interpreted as the power of Creation. Plato calls Hermes a talented orator and even compares this aspect of him to the *Logos*.[77]

But above all else, Hermes is the messenger of the Gods. He is usually portrayed in Greek-style traveling attire: a short mantelet, a wide-brimmed hat, and sandals. The hat and sandals are decorated with wings by Zeus.

Hermes was the one who fetched Paris when the Trojan prince was appointed arbitrary judge during the disastrous beauty contest that took place the night prior to the siege of Troy. Hermes assisted Ares in the battle against two Titans and saved the young Dionysius by pulling him out of the consuming fire.

Hermes guides the *femme fatale* Pandora to Empitheus.[78] But it is also Hermes who acts as a courier for Persephone on her historic journey to Eleusis, where the virgin is reunited with her mother.[79] The Greek Hermes' function as messenger of the Gods is identical to that of the Egyptian Thoth. However, it also included a function as guide of departed souls.

Guide of Souls

Hermes called upon the souls of lovers.
In his hands he carried the pure golden staff
where he can by own choosing bewitch the eyes of human

Hermes as psychopompos, Guide of Souls, with Orpheus and Eurydice.

but can also wake the sleeping.
He winked for them to come along and
softly peeping they followed him.
Such as bats, all squeaking, peeping and
flitting criss-cross in the dark,
like one which has lost its grip on the rocks,
falls below, such was the sound made by the dark ones,
when they went after Hermes across the narrow paths of dissolution.
They went past the streams of Oceanus and the portals of the Sun God
and the Land of Dreams and finally reached the flower sown field
where the dark ones lived, the shadow images of the deceased.

So begins the last book of the *Odyssey* by the blind bard Homer, with Hermes as *psychopompos*, guide of the souls to Hades.[80] And thus he is sometimes depicted, as in the very touching relief in which he is present at the seperation of Orpheus and Eurydice before he accompanies the latter to Hades.

Grave texts and other epigrams also show the importance of Hermes as a guide of souls:

> Hermes, with his winged feet, has taken you by the hand, accompanied you to Olympus, and made you luminous among the stars.[81]

As stated, this image of Hermes coincides with one of the functions of Thoth. The Greek Hermes is also associated with the Moon and surgery.[82] The Roman historian Diodorus of Sicily, in his *History of the World*, shows even more similarities between Hermes and Thoth. According to him, it was Hermes who composed the alphabet and was also the inventor of astrology, the musical scales, and measures and weights. He wrote an account of the Greek Hermes.[83]

In the next chapter we will see how close these similarities are.

Chapter 3

An Egyptian Hermes or a Grecian Thoth?

This book is not about Egyptian or Greek Gods, but rather about centuries-old wisdom. It is about the wisdom of Hermes Trismegistus, written down in the hermetic writings called the *Hermetica*. Garth Fowden, in his standard work *The Egyptian Hermes*, makes a distinction between "technical *Hermetica*" and "philosophical *Hermetica*."[84] The first he classifies as the magical, astrological, and medical tracts; the second is comprised of the philosophical and religious writings. Comparable distinctions are made by several other researchers.[85] At the least, this is confusing, primarily because there is a great difference inherent in the character and origin of these various disciplines. To be perfectly clear: Whoever Hermes Trismegistus may have been and however many writings may bear his name, we are dealing with a multitude of writers in different time periods. To prevent the confusion from getting any larger, I will call all hermetic texts *Hermetica*.

The Thrice-Great Hermes

Who is Hermes Trismegistus, in whose spirit so many authors entrusted their revelations of wisdom to paper? Is he Thoth, the Egyptian God of Wisdom? Is he a glorified Greek Hermes? Is he a God or a god-like human, as Plato asked himself?[86] We do not know for sure.[87] In the 3rd century B.C., Manetho, the Egyptian high priest-historian of Heliopolis, was the first to tell us who Hermes was—and even he talked about several Hermes. The first was Thoth, who seems to have recorded the ancient wisdom on *stellas* (stone tablets) prior to the deluge. After the deluge, these were translated from the "Holy Script" by Agathodaimon, son of the second Hermes, for the benefit of his son, Tat. At least this is how several researchers have interpretated the introduction to a letter by a temple priest that was described by Syncellus, a Byzantine monk living in the 7th century A.D.[88] After the introduction by Syncellus containing this description, another letter follows, considered by the majority of researchers to be falsified. They prefer to talk about *pseudo-Manetho*. Considering that there is a lacuna in the manuscript of Syncellus, this intrepetation is not unexpected. The English classicist Waddell interprets the text as follows:

> Thoth, the first Hermes, chisseled the text in "Holy Script" onto stone slabs.
>
> They were translated after the deluge (this would have to be done by the second Hermes, Hermes Trismegistus.)
>
> The son of this Hermes, Agathodaimon (literally, Good Spirit), wrote the text up in books, which were preserved in the holiness of the temple—this being done for the benefit of his son, Tat, among other reasons.

In short, the lineage is:

Thoth (the first Hermes)
Trismegistus (the second Hermes)
Agathodaimon
Tat

Jean-Pierre Mahé follows a different classification:

Thoth
Agathodaimon
Trismegistus
Tat

Trismegistus, the second Hermes, becomes therefore the grandson of Thoth, the first Hermes.[89]

Fowden does the same, leaving open the possibility that, considering the uncertainty of the punctuation of the Greek text, Agathodaimon is the translator. Other treatises circulating in hermetic circles have been attributed to him.[90]

Peter Kingsley gives the best translation so far. Egyptian religious traditions were originally transcribed in hieratics, in this case:

> ... by Thoth, the first Hermes, and proceeding after the deluge translated from the Holy Script in Greek and deposited in the Egyptian holy temples in the form of books by the second Hermes, the son of Agathodaimon, father of Tat.[91]

Our Hermes is also here the grandchild of Thoth (the first Hermes). So we also read in the hermetic manuscript called *Asclepius*:

> Hermes, my grandfather, whose name I bear, as you know, still lives in this fashion (in his statue on his grave) in his birthplace which is named after him, and in Greek called Hermopolis...[92]

And the father of Hermes was Agathodaimon,[93] also mentioned in the well-known texts. It is quite possible that a collection of *logia* (citations) did exist that were written in the name of Agathodaimon.

We are almost certainly dealing here, as far as the tradition of hermetic wisdom is concerned, with a legend. However, not all legends are true in the literal sense; they often serve as metaphors for a deeper reality that hides behind the material-historical facts. You could call it metaphysical. Fortunately, pseudo-Manetho is not our only source. The Neoplatonic philosopher Iamblichus, living in 300 B.C., mentions old hieroglyphic texts of Thoth that were translated into Greek by an Egyptian priest.[94] In this work, *The Mysteries*, he also writes that Plato and Pythagoras had read the stellas by Hermes during their stay in Egypt, with the assistance of an Egyptian priest.[95]

In the hermetic text *Korè Kosmou*, we find a similar hint. Isis tells her son Horus:

> And the things he (Hermes) knew, he wrote down and hid them thereafter. Instead of speaking, he kept cautiously silent, so one would search for it in the young centuries of the world.[96]

The typical Egyptian character of this tradition has become even clearer after the discovery of the hermetic treatise at Nag Hammadi, *The Treatise of the Eighth and Ninth Heavenly Sphere*, where Hermes Trismegistus speaks to his initiated disciple:

> O' my Son, it is proper to inscribe this book on turquoise stellas in hieroglyphs, because the consciousness shall be the foreman of it. This is why I command this doctrine to be engraved unto stone and you will place it in my holy temple, where eight guards will protect it with the ninth being the Sun. The male guardians, on the right side have a frog-like face and on the left, the female ones have a cat's face. Also place a square milk-stone at the foot of the turquoise tablets and write the name on the sapphire tablet in hieroglyphic signs. O' my Son, you will place these, when I am in Virgo and the Sun is placed in the first part of the day; for fifteen degrees will have then passed me by.[97]

Meanwhile, the surname of Hermes, *Trismegistus*, appears for the first time during Hellenistic times, although prior to that there were similar surnames added to Thoth.[98]

In early Islam, the name Trismegistus (thrice) was interpreted quite literally to mean the three manifestations of Hermes. The first Hermes lived in Egypt prior to the flood and built pyramids there. The second Hermes lived after the flood in Babylon, but immigrated to Egypt. The third Hermes wrote about various sciences and trades after the flood.[99]

Who is Hermes Trismegistus? Once again, we are not sure, for much seems to point to a mythical figure. If he really lived, he was not a God, but a human. Figuratively speaking, he was the grandson of a God.[100] In Gnosticism, this implies that he was human, although most definitely an enlightened (fully spiritual) human, a Buddha—and as such, a God.

Colored Markers

When people in Florence, Italy during the 15th century rediscovered a part of the *Hermetica*, then translated it and published it in book form, most thought these were the writings of a Hermes

Trismegistus who had lived 1000 years prior to the Christian era, and was, therefore, a contemporary of Moses. This is literally seen in the cathedral in Siena, Tuscany, where an inscription on a magnificent mosaic floor is witness to this tradition.[101] This Hermes would have also been the mentor of Pythagoras. I will return to these claims and to this utterly fascinating period later.[102] The Egyptian wisdom had, according to the tradition of the Renaissance, spread to Greece and influenced the whole of the Middle East.

However, the high caliber of the Egyptian content of these writings, generally referred to as the *Corpus Hermeticum*, led to controversy when it was determined more than a century later by means of textual research that this composition could not have been written prior to the beginning of the 2nd century B.C. The Egyptian dream seemed to have passed by. It seems reasonable, therefore, that the new wave of research into the *Hermetica* in the 19th and 20th centuries emphasized the Greek character of these writings. The popular French publication of the *Corpus Hermeticum* by Nock and Festugière, for example, showed that the *Corpus* contained "extremely few" Egyptian elements.[103] This point of view was accepted without question, despite the sharp-witted analysis of Stricker: "The Hermetica is Egyptian in essence, Grecian in form."[104]

I just wrote: It is understandable that the new wave of research in the 19th and 20th centuries emphasized the Greek character of these writings. In one respect, this was due to the classicists' adoration of all that was Greek. Classical-orientated generations had grown up with the idea that antiquity itself was Greek, with other marginal cultures contributing. On the other hand, they evidenced a rigidly prejudiced attitude toward theology when they dealt with these types of writings, and many tried to explain them from a Christian point of view. Let's once and for all clearly state: Christianity has tried to—if not in all ways, nevertheless in many ways—erase or at least correct the record of antiquity with markers in Christian colors. There was great indignation in the West when the Taliban in Afganistan destroyed centuries-old Buddha statues prior to the fatal events of September 11th, when airplanes impacted New York's World Trade Center. This indignation seems justified to me. But Christianity, definitely in the first few centuries of its existence, did the same. It is, for example, utterly perplexing to observe how Coptic Christians hacked away, in a scrupulous fashion, at magnificent reliefs in innumerable Egyption temples whose decoration they considered "heathen"! Whatever they were, I am inclined here to see "heathen" as a pagan name. This is an appreciation that Christianity definitely did not have.

Hermes—Greek or Egyptian?

It seems to me meaningful, while continuing our research, to first study the manifold qualities of the "service-oriented" Gods, the Egyptian Thoth and the Greek Hermes.

Let's put their associated attributes next to each other once again:

> Thoth, one of the first Gods of the Egyptian pantheon; the consciousness, the heart, *Gnosis* and the second eye of the Sun God Re, the *Logos* of the God of Creation, Ptah; God of wisdom; God of the script; God of magic; God of alchemy; God of harmony in the cosmos; God of the calendar; messenger of the Gods; guide of souls; in later times, God of oracles and dreams.
>
> Hermes, one of the last Gods of the Greek pantheon; God of the rustic country-side; according to Plato, the *Logos*; God of (clever) speech, communication, trade, and the guild of thieves; messenger of the Gods; guide of souls to Hades; and according to a later source, also inventor of astronomy, the musical scales, measurements, and weights.

Even a quick glance at the hermetic treatises shows us that these writings reflect much more accurately the characteristics of the Egyptian Thoth than those of the Greek Hermes. Whether only the identical function as messenger of the Gods, certainly not prominent with Thoth, is responsible for the assimilation of Thoth-Hermes, or whether there could also be other unknown factors, we do not know. Thoth in the Sinai, together with the Goddess of Love, Hathor, was worshipped and there his name was equivalent to the epithet of Min,[105] frequently shown on temple walls with a strongly protruding lid.[106] Could this be considered a similarity with the phallic Hermes from ancient times? Another similarity—although in my opinion, a far-fletched parallel—is the function as God of Thieves. Thoth apparently, as classifier of the year (and namer of the first month), seems to have "stolen" a few days.[107] This hardly qualifies as a key similarity. It is also notable that Plato speaks of Thoth as the inventor of script and does not identify this with Hermes.[108] Thus, their similarity is not so clear. The last word on this subject has not been written yet.

Around the end of the last century, a more pronounced attitude regarding the God's Egyptian vs. His Greek characteristics became prevalent in reaction to the work of French Dominican priest Festugière. This came from another Frenchman, Jean-Pierre Mahé, in his two-part work: *Hermes in Upper Egypt*.[109] The tone was set by Garth Fowden in his *The Egyptian Hermes*. According to Fowden, the Hellenistic Hermes was Egyptianized by his assimilation with Thoth. Egyptian aspects are found more prominently in Greek magical papyri than what he calls the philosophical *Hermetica* (such as the *Corpus Hermeticum*).[110]

While Fowden remains overly cautious, modern scientists dare to pose more radical propositions along the line of the Casaubon-Festugière interpretation.[111] Roelof van den Broek suggests that new discoveries—like the one at Nag Hammadi in 1945 and the recently surfaced *Hermetic Definitions*—will lead to a more positive evaluation of the Egyptian background of the *Hermetica*.[112] Peter Kingsley is even more certain. The claim of Greek hermeticists that they are carrying on the authentic Egyptian Wisdom seems to him completely justified.[113] The hermetic tradition reaches to the very root of Western culture and civilization.[114] The origin of the Greek hermetic corpus is shown in the Egyptian temple practice of counseling dream oracles.[115] The Protestant Casaubon (16th century) was probably correct with his dating of the writings published in Florence more than a century prior, but his comments about the contents were far removed from the truth.[116] Iamblichus had written: "the texts published under the name Hermes contained indeed hermetical teachings, even though they contained a lot of usage of philosophical terminology. This is because they were translated from Egyptian into Greek by scholars familiar with Greek Philosophy."[117]

Above, I have given a simple comparison between Thoth and Hermes. Therefore, I can wholeheartedly agree with Peter Kingsley when he concludes it should be clear that the world of Hermes Trismegistus has nothing in common with the antiquated Greek Hermes, but rather everything to do with Thoth. Thoth, due to the ignorance of researchers in connection with Egyptian literature, is presented as a cliché.[118]

However, what do these writings actually contain? More about this in the following chapters.

CHAPTER 4
UNITY IN DIVERSITY

On a wet day in December, I found myself in the Bibliotheca Philosophica Hermetica of my friend Joost Ritman in Amsterdam. Employees of the library had arranged a beautiful exhibition whose theme was Creation. The most important reason I was here on this afternoon, however, finding myself next to early prints and centuries-old manuscripts, was that Joost Ritman had arranged a meeting for me with Wim Zitman.

A SPECIAL ENCOUNTER

Wim Zitman has written a fascinating book, one that makes you wonder when you glance at it quickly, whether it is not all a little far-fetched. At moments like this, I usually develop a typical curious scientific attitude, questioning the reason why new insights had not been discovered before by reputable and respectable science, and why we were not informed. But at the same time, I know the answer. Beyond the fact that not all scientific literature is easily accessible for interested parties who have not been weaned on scientific terminology (the result of such professional research is often printed strictly in extremely dry articles in professional magazines and so will only reach a small circle of insiders), there is something else—something much more essential. Established scientists usually reason from specific axioms. Their contribution to science is to formulate proposals that are based on these axioms. But what happens if these axioms turn out to be wrong? Most want to hear nothing of this. Only a few have the courage to investigate the validity of the axioms themselves.

Mind you, this does not mean there are no solid axioms. You have to start from somewhere. And not all the sensationalism from other corners—from scientists not attached to reputable institutions, from journalists, or from dedicated amateurs (in the best sense)—turns out to be true when scrutinized in the light of day. Quite often, we encounter amateurism in the worse sense. And sometimes it results in a brilliant discovery.

Let us go back to Wim Zitman's book, *The Constellation of Horus*.[119] In this book there is a more detailed study of the theory of Bauval and Gilbert regarding the placement of the pyramids corresponding with the constellation of Orion, alias Horus. Zitman assured me in our conversation that their theory is not incorrect *per se*, but that there are gross mistakes made in the application of it. He indicates that the cosmic correspondences can be found in relation to many more pyramids besides the one at Gizeh. Photos of the starry sky and the holy Egyptian sites seem to be identical at the marked points! It was as if I heard Hermes say: "Don't you realize Asclepius, Egypt is an image of the Heavens?"[120]

Zitman told me about much more—about incorrect time calculations, ancient astrology, cultural time periods, and old myths that enfold a sublime truth. A very instructive afternoon.

By reading his book, you can come to the conclusion that there is nothing coincidental. Nothing appears to be placed randomly. The buildings of the many temples along the Nile alone appear to be in the placement of a "divine" plan. This sounds vague; but it is quite the opposite. The strength of Zitman's book is that its content can be tested on the sound principles we have come to appreciate in science. The Egyptian king-priest structure has been witness to an unbroken line originating in the far, far past history of its initiation rites. And the god-like Hermes, the all-knowing priest, king, healer, and guide of souls, is a shining example and messenger of that tradition.

The Temple of the Cosmos

Through my study and translation of the Nag Hammadi manuscripts, it became more and more clear to me that, in ancient times, the cosmos played an important role in the life of humanity. I also encountered this prominence in the *Hermetica*. Many times, there is talk about a "path along the stars" by which the human soul travels along the planets and signs of the zodiac—the departed after death, the mystic during life. Such a journey has not only an outer meaning, but also a strictly inner one. I knew this already from the earlier *Merkawa* mysticism of the ancient Jews[121]—a mystery religion of Mithras that also acknowledged a Path of Initiation along the seven planets.[122] And I found the same symbology in the holy books of the Mandeans.[123]

We can hardly comprehend the intensely deep religious meaning of these concepts. Their cosmology can be quickly reduced down to a form of astrology. Festugière even goes so far as to say: "the Hellenic Astrology is a concoction of an enticing philosophical study, a foolish mythology and unapplicable learned methods."[124] And the eminent French researcher of archaic astrology, Franz Cumont, questions out loud how in heaven's name this absurd teaching could have been started, developed, and spread among the superior intelligentia, let alone persist century after century.[125] Such a devaluation of an ancient science is understandable from a detached standpoint. But humanity in those days was not an onlooker; it was a participant. Our development, which has emphasized the rational, has forced us to act as onlookers. We view the heavens only by means of telescopes. We name; we calculate; we can be filled with awe at the sight of the glory of the stars and filled with our "enlightened" Western world. Yet we truly remain outsiders.

In antiquity, people experienced the cosmos in every fiber of their bodies. Stars were Gods, and Gods had a far-stretching influence on life on Earth. Communication with the Gods was simultaneously communication with the stars. This cosmic involvement, in which humanity is assigned a microcosmic version of the same powers as those of the macrocosm, is a highlight of the hermetic tradition.

In *Asclepius*, we read an intriguing pronouncement made by Hermes Trismegistus:

> Don't you know, Asclepius, Egypt is the image of the heavens? Better said, it is the working arena of Heaven and all the Heavenly powers. When we make speak the truth: Our land is the temple of the Cosmos.[126]

The ancient Egyptians were experienced students of the stars. So-called priests-of-the-hour, situated on top of holy temple roofs, observed the phenomena in the sky and charted them. It is not inconceivable that there is a correlation between heavenly bodies and terrestrial holy places.[127]

Cosmology

> The Egyptian Cosmology is founded on coalescent scientific and philosophical principles with the integral unity of the Cosmos as its thesis. The whole Egyptian civilization was grounded on a thorough and extremely exact knowledge of universal laws... For the ancient Egyptians there existed no perceptible difference between the sacred and worldly actions... Each act, how sober or earthly it might be—ploughing, sowing, harvesting, brewing, building ships, going to war, playing, the devising of a system of measurement and weights—were all seen as a terrestial symbol for certain divine activity...[128]

As we discussed in the preceding chapter, modern researchers have given preference to making a distinction in the *Hermetica* qua character. This customary differentiation into categories usually consists of the following divisions: magic, alchemy, and astrology, along with botanics and the healing arts, philosophy, theology, and sometimes also natural science. But this makes us prone to do injustice to the perception of the people who wrote, read, and were inspired by these writings. The splitting up of these categories is a sign of the time in which we live. With our dependence on the *ratio* (reason), which led to the (historical) Enlightment, we have split up subjects that were cohesively bound together in the consciousness of humanity for centuries. Astronomy was equal to astrology; chemistry was equal to alchemy; theology was equal to philosophy. And everything, including magic, was a part of natural science.

The big questions that concerned humanity were, in essence, cosmological. To ponder about our place in the cosmos was called philosophizing. The assignment of abilities and attributes to specific powers and energies in this cosmos was called theology. Calling upon these energies was called magic. The contemplation and continuous repetition of living through and experiencing of Creation was a form of natural science. The observation of the spherical heavens and the feeling of being intrinsic to them were called astronomy and astrology. The research about the interconnection of these cosmic elements was called alchemy. And the driving force behind it all—the deepest knowledge of God, the cosmos, and humanity—was called *Gnosis*, esoteric knowledge. This is exactly the key principle of the *Hermetica* in all its great diversity and many divisions.

The Dutch professor Roelof van den Broek stated very clearly, as early as 1980, that *Gnosticism* means, in the first place, an experience—not actually theology or philosophy, but a practical experience that makes use of philosophical and theological codes.[129] Once again, the distinction between theology and philosophy is a late development coming from the Enlightment, with its emphasis on a strictly materialistic empirical scientific model. *Theosophy* would be a better word for Gnosticism, if we do not limit it to the distinctive Theosophical Movement that emerged in the late 19th century.

Looking at it more closely, the writings attributed to Hermes show similarities that surpass barriers erected by empirical science. We also encounter cosmological and magical components in the so-called "philosophical" treatises (think of the magical formulas in *The Treatise of the Eighth and Ninth Heavenly Sphere*[130] and the astrological elements in *Poimandres*[131]). On the other hand, we find an abundance of Theosophy in the "technical" papers.

Here, we shall first occupy ourselves with the cosmic image in the *Hermetica*, since, in my opinion, it contains the key principle of classical hermetics. Besides the term "cosmology," I shall use the term "astrology," because a specific category of the hermetic writings is named *Hermetica Astrologica*. In essence, there is no difference between cosmology and astrology. You could call astrology the practical application of a cosmological conception. Later in history, astrology actually stood independent, firmly on its own, and was sometimes totally separate from the original cosmic concept on which it was founded. In the hermetic cosmic-astrological writings, there are also connections made to medical, magical, and alchemical themes. Thus, for example, the "law" of alchemy, the *Tabula Smaragdina*, is saturated with cosmology. However, what was truly the essence of this cosmological astrology?

CHAPTER 5
HERMES AND ASTROLOGY

The relationship of humanity to the cosmos is the central theme in the oldest manuscripts dedicated to Hermes. The ancients knew a great quantity of astrological writings, of which not many were preserved; moreover, those that were preserved were, in practically all cases, later editions. Of most documents, there are only fragments known in private collections or commentaries of writers at a later date. Regardless, what was preserved is still without any doubt very impressive.

THE ENSOULED COSMOS

The surviving documents describe the influence of the planets, the zodiac signs, the astrological Houses, and the divine decanates on the life of humanity and the world. By planets, the ancients meant the five planets known then—Mercury, Venus, Mars, Jupiter, and Saturn—and the Sun and the Moon.

> Seven stars varying in their orbit, circle around the threshold of Olympus while Eternity walks hand in hand with them. The Moon, shining brilliantly at night, terrifying Cronos, the loving Sun, the "Goddess from Paphos" who carries her wedding bed with her, courageous Ares, the magnificently-winged Hermes, and Zeus, the prototype from whence Nature sprung. These stars whose seed was spread in part upon the race of humanity, and so do they influence us: The Moon, Zeus, Ares, the Paphian (Aphrodite), Cronos, the Sun and Hermes. And so is our Fate determined to receive from these ethereal spheres: Tears, laughter, anger, propagation, intelligence, sleep and strong desire. The tears are Cronos, propagation is Zeus, intelligence is Hermes, courage is Ares, sleep is the Moon, desire is the Goddess Cytherea, and laughter is the Sun.[132]

The zodiac signs, even in non-astrological circles, are still known far and wide, although we now acknowledge twelve. The first sign of the horoscope is Aries, then Taurus, Gemini, Cancer, Leo, Virgo, Libra, Scorpio, Sagittarius, Capricorn, Aquarius, and Pisces. We will come back to the significance of the astrological Houses. The divine decanates[133] are zones of ten astrological degrees. The zodiacal circle has 360 degrees. Since there are twelve Houses, each encompasses 30 degrees. These are, once again, divided into three divine decanates. In total, there are thirty-six groups of these decimals.

All of this implies the hypothesis that the cosmos is ensouled and that the cosmic energy fields are the Gods and Goddesses. Their forces empower all the astronomical planets, including the Sun and the Moon. They creep into the skin of these planets, so to speak, and, at a later stage, give them their names. So in astrological literature, there is no difference between the deity and the planet.[134] This is why astronomy and astrology, in this time and for a long time thereafter, were one and the same thing. Knowledge about the celestial bodies, the orbits they followed, their distance from each other, the angles they formed, their brilliance in the sky—all were considered as imparting knowledge of the Divine Plan. And since humanity experienced itself as a living part of the cosmos, this knowledge could help humanity understand more about itself and the surrounding world.

"As above, so below" is, indeed, the most famous hermetic axiom! As a product of the cosmos, humanity knew—in itself, and also in its natural body—the same cosmic energies present in the world. To learn about these energies could make for a better life. We find this very explicitly referred to in the many medical-astrological discourses, in which each human organ represents an astral godliness, a star, a planet, and a zodiac sign.

The ancient literature with astrological content, according to Wilhelm Gundel, covers a period from 300 B.C. to 600 A.D.[135] These survive for us, as said before, primarily as fragments. However, there are certain important monographs preserved intact. In later periods, these old "handbooks" were referred to regularly and quoted. During the Roman Empire, we see an increase in astrological material, although many of these texts have not yet been published by the scientific press.

The core of the astrological literature of the Roman Empire lies in the Hellenic culture (Ptolemaic period). This is also the time from which the famous astrological plaque discovered in a temple at Dendera dates.[136] Yet, it is not surprising that some writings arise from an even earlier date, going back even as far as the pharaonic epoch. The first authentic astrological texts probably date from the 30th Dynasty (circa 400 B.C.), or even earlier.[137] In the literature, there is mention of several pharaohs who were actively involved with astrology.[138]

Most of the composers of the *Astrologica* are anonymous. Their compositions were later recorded and edited into essays, collected writings, and compendia. The most important examples of this group of manuscripts are the hermetic astrological corpus and the so-called *Nechepso-Petosiris compendia*,[139] which I will cover later.

It is, however, not only Egyptian melodies that resound in our ears. We find many references that point to the Egyptians as the forefathers of the ancient wisdom, however there are also the Babylonians, Chaldeans, Syrians, and Jews.[140] It is clear that the more matured form of both the Greek and the hermetic astrology relies, on the one hand, on Babylon, and, on the other, on Egypt. In conclusion, it is Hermes Trismegistus who is seen as the inventor and founder of astronomy/astrology.[141]

The *Horos Skopos*—Observer of Time

But first to Babylon. From 1400 B.C. on, the Babylonian priests divided the heavens into a quantity of sections. This developed, during the 5th century B.C., into the twelve signs of the zodiac as we know them from the Hellenic-Alexandrian era. This is still the convention.[142] The zodiacal divisions originated from the composition of the time calendar, in which the lunar and solar calendars were harmonized.

Babylonian astrology was not primarily concerned with predicting events. It stood primarily on the principle of synchronicity. As such, it sought a connection between a heavenly occurence (primarily the Moon) and an event on Earth. Only later did astrology develop a predictive and individualistic character. The oldest known personal horoscope (in Babylonian-Assyrian script) dates back to the year 410 B.C.

A similar development occurred in old Egypt. It was the so-called priests-of-the-hour who, late at night on the rooftops of temples, recorded and charted the heavens. They paid specific attention to the intensity of the stars that shone brightly on their arrival and brightest at their zenith, and then grew dimmer in proportion to their descent and disappearance. In time, the insight grew that, if the birth of a human coincided with a certain rising star, there was a connection with the star. Besides stars, however, the significance of other astronomical constellations and zodiacal signs came to be considered as well.[143] The rising sign at the time of birth was therefore considered important in the personal horoscope (*horos* = hour/time, *skopos* = observer). Even now, this point is still called the *Ascendant*.

Beyond the Ascendant (with its opposite, the *Descendant*), the Mid-Heaven (the *medium coeli*) was fixed at the time of birth.[144]

Almost all researchers agree that the hermetic *Astrologica*, the most significant basis for ancient astronomy, is unmistakably Egyptian.[145] One of the oldest—and sadly only partially preserved—texts is the *Salmeschoiniaka*,[146] which describes the time of transition from universal astrology to individualistic iatrological astrology.[147] The origin of this writing is not quite clear. Supporters for a Babylonian origin translate its title as the *Book of Images*, while defenders of its Egyptian heritage name it the *Book of the Great Creation*.[148] In this document, we find the most important star Gods and Goddesses (the planets as deities), as well as the doctrine of the divine decanates. The latter refers to a distinct Egyptian element that we find applied in cures for many diseases, in the rise and fall of stars and their significance for the future, and as a classification of the astrological Houses.[149] Another transitional manuscript is the *Panaretos*, but this text has not survived.[150] We encounter much of this astrological material in the absolutely central piece of work, the *Liber Hermetis* (*Book of Hermes*), but more about this later.

The Song of the Thunder

The archaic astrological treatises are very diverse. The oldest ones often treat the *thema mundi* and show a kind of world horoscope.[151] Ancient writers even had a proposition for how a birth horoscope of the Earth would look at the time of Creation. This is what we read in Firmicus Maternus in his *Mathesis* from 337 A.D.:

> [According to the Ancients] who saw, following in the steps of Asclepius and Anubis, who were by Mercurius' [Hermes] vital godly power initiated into the secrets of Science, the birth horoscope of the world looks like the following: The Sun stands in 15º Leo, the Moon in 15º Cancer, Saturn in 15º Capricorn, Jupiter in 15º Sagittarius, Mars in 15º Scorpio, Venus in 15º Libra, Mercurius in 15º Virgo and the Ascendant in 15º Cancer (the sign of Hermes).[152]

The old treatises *Brontologion* and *Peri Seismon* can also be linked to the *thema mundi*. *Brontologion*, the doctrine of thunder, is of Greco-Egyptian origin and treats the significance of thunderstorms in various months of the year. For the month of January, it announces:

> When there is storm and lightning (in January) during the day, the land will not be destroyed by a tyrant; the earth will (surely) not bear any fruit; the Nile will not lack of water; Egypt shall control its own masters; even the people of the West, too, shall live without worries and in prosperity. However, if it surely occurs during the night (the storm), the people of the West will (still) live without worries and in prosperity, but there will (certainly) be radical changes taking place; several Kings will be at war; in the West certain men will be honoured; there will be war in the lands (Egypt); many will perish at sea, the weather will continue to be fair.[153]

Not only could thunder, lightning, and the accompanying hailstorms have a disastrous effect on the harvest, many feared even more the highly destructive earthquakes. *Peri Seismon* is a treatise in poetic form that sketches the aftermath of an earthquake in various months of the year. A short citation from a literally and figuratively prosaic hermetic version of the original poem is as follows:

> April. When the Sun stands in Aries and the earth trembles during the day, those who stand close to the Kings will defend themselves against ambushes; the neighbouring cities will suffer from

> great misery and violent acts; a famous man will perish and the people in his court will be endangered; down-pours will take place, fruits of the earth and from the trees will (surely) ripen; if the earth heaves at night, there will be disagreements among the people and they will go in uprising against the high-placed tyrant, soldiers of the despot will abandon him, they will go in opposition and rebel against their own King; there will be difficulties and revolutions among the people, the tyrants of the West will perish, there will be down-pours; the seed will multiply. In Egypt there will be starvation and in the Nile there will be water depravation.[154]

After April, the beginning of the old Egyptian calendar, follow more prophecies and similar descriptions of the other months.

A Priest of Hermes

When I visited the beautifully decorated funeral tomb of the high priest Petosiris in Hermopolis a while ago, I did not know that, soon afterward, his "spirit" would appear again in my written study on the hermetic roots of astrology. I am talking about the so-called *Nechepso-Petosiris compendia*. Nechepso was pharaoh during the 26th Dynasty (677–672 B.C.) and Petosiris was his most important priest. Petosiris is also definitely known, as stated, in the Hermes cult. In the astrological literature, Petosiris is even equated with Hermes.[155] The manuscripts attributed to them, however, predate them. In the 2nd century A.D., an astrological compilation must have been assembled that was then attributed to these authors. So we see them cited again in the writings of Vettius Valens (200 A.D.). Prior to this, Necheposis and Petosiris were not mentioned together, but separately.[156]

The connections with Hermes become even clearer from notations in the text—questions like whether Nechepso and Petosiris had been taught by Hermes in epiphanies (appearances from the "other" world).[157] The spiritual character of the revelations is also found in a text in which Nechepso speaks himself:

> It came to me, while I looked the entire night up at the heavens, there resounded a voice; my body was embraced with a sky-blue garment, which symbolized the darkness.[158]

Vettius Valens must have had a very detailed astrological reference book inscribed with the names of Nechepso and Petosiris lying in front of him on his writing table. The fourteenth book is, in fact, an extensive astrological-medical dissertation about twenty-five healing celestial stones to be used in combination with certain planets. This book was discovered in the 1st century by none other than the learned Doctor Thessalos; it was consulted in the library of Alexandria. Galen also knew the teachings of Nechepso from a book of the divine decanates in which names, images, stones, and plants of the thirty-six divine decanates were described for all ailments.[159] The influence of such a compendium is, therefore, difficult to estimate. Even the great astronomer-astrologer-geographer Claudius Ptolemaeus, in his classic astrological work *Tetrabiblios* used the *Nechepso-Petosiris* as a source. A very enticing detail of this is the term—used by many classical astrologers, but also in modern astrology—the occupied *Rule of Hermes*[160] that we find in the ancient wisdom of Petosiris, high priest of Hermes, to whom it was dedicated.[161]

The *Liber Hermetis Trismegisti*

The French priest-scholar André-Jean Festugière, in his extensive study of the hermetic writings, names the *Liber Hermetis* as the most important witness of the astrological *Hermetica*.[162] We are now fortunate to possess a practically complete edition from the 3rd century B.C.[163] The original Greek version, probably even more extensive, is unfortunately lost. The Latin translation available to us is quite old and must have been made prior to 480 B.C.[164] The book contains thirty-seven chapters; in modern print with a reasonably large format, it consists of about 100 pages.[165]

What is immediately apparent is the comprehensive description of the divine decanates and their rulers, a teaching most likely finding its roots in the pharaonic era.[166] We know that there were lists of divine decanates, complete with descriptions, kept in the Egyptian temples.[167] The divine decanates are discussed in an interesting dialog by Stobaeus:

> "Since you have promised me in the General Discussions to give me an explanation about the thirty-six divine decanates, I ask of you to explain them and their affects."
>
> "O, Tat, I do not want to exclude anything from you. It could very well become the most important and prominent discourse. Contemplate everything carefully.
>
> I spoke with you about the Zodiac, which one also calls the signs of the Zodiac, about the five planets, the Sun, the Moon and the circle of each of them."
>
> "You did such, Trismegistus!"
>
> "So, I want you now to create a proposition of the 36 divine decanates. If you keep the previous points in mind, this explanation will be the easier to comprehend."
>
> "I remember them in my consciousness, Father... Do these (divine decanates) have an influence on us as human?"
>
> "Very much, my son; if they influence the Heavenly bodies, how could they not influence us, collectively and individually?
>
> Everything which collectively cascades over Humanity, comes from this power; for example, and understand what I say, power-taking by kings, uproars in cities, famine, epidemics, floods from the sea, earthquakes, none of these things, my son, occur without their influence."[168]

It is interesting, next to this so-called philosophical text, to include a small part of the first chapter of the *Liber Hermetis*:

> *About the First Form of Aries*
>
> The first divine decanate shows itself in the form of Mars. His name is Aulathamas. It is the image of a weaponed person; he stands in human-like fashion, on feet with (truly) clawed nails and he holds with both hands above his head a double-edged axe. This (divine decanate) rules the World-Ocean.

About the Second Form of Aries

The second divine decanate shows itself in the form of the Sun. He carries the name Sabaoth. This one has the face of a sparrow-hawk and as a sign of royalty, a lotus unfolds from the top of his head; at the ends of the flower petals are stars of a golden splendour. He carries in his right hand the Hydra (water serpent) symbolising "life." In the left hand he carries a scepter, with a sparrow-hawk on top; the divine decanate himself is clothed in a linen garment upon a turtle, which is entirely covered with a net. This one rules over the area of the Bactriers.

About the Third Form of Aries

The third divine decanate shows itself in the form of Venus. Her name is Disornafais. This one is imaged as a woman standing upright, dressed in a straight-hanging linen garment covered with laces and filled with golden colors and roses. Her head wears the king's crown. On the middle of her body, next to her navel, there are green emerald studs. She carries a staff, with a four-headed serpent on top. In the middle, there are two side-faced and two backwards-faced heads. This one rules over the land of the Lidiers.[169]

As we can see, each description begins with the form of the planet ruling over the divine decanate. They are, with Aries, respectively Mars, the Sun, and Venus; with Taurus, they are Mercury, the Moon, and Saturn; with Gemini, they are Jupiter, Mars, and the Sun, and so on, up to and including Pisces.[170] Then follows the name of the divinity hidden behind the form of the planet. The description of the godhead is most fascinating. At first reading, I thought immediately of tarot cards. They are just like images out of a dream, full of symbology. They stand, certainly, for people of that era and are recognizable archetypes. The last part of the description of the divine decanates is interesting as well, indicating which geographical area is influenced by the specific sphere.

In the second chapter of the *Liber Hermetis*, the signs of the zodiac are separated into male and female: Aries is male; Taurus is female, and so on—always alternating. This division, which is still practiced by present-day astrologers, we also find in the *Tetrabiblios* of Ptolemy.[171] In fact, much of what is described in the *Liber Hermetis* we find in later-dated handbooks like Ptolemy's. So we read in a chapter about the conjunctions (connections) of the Sun and other planets:

> The Sun in conjunction with Venus at night position, liberates from evil, as Jupiter does.[172]

Or, in a chapter about marriages:

> When Venus stands in Capricorn, in a section known for shamelessness and change, Saturn and the Moon are in opposition to her, the Lord of the domain is Saturn and Mars stands in the house of Venus, then the wife will sleep with her step-son…[173]

The chapters that delve into the astrological phenomena of the *loci* (Greek, *topoi*)—called Houses in astrology—are remarkable. The division of the horoscope into twelve sections, called Houses, is a so-called *mundane* division. The division, starting at the Ascendant, accounts for the daily turning of the Earth on its axis. The Houses symbolize the development of humans throughout life. In the classical sense, the first House (the Ascendant) stands primarily for life, the second for property, the third for brothers, the fourth for parents, the fifth for children, the sixth for slaves, the seventh for marriage, the eighth for death, the ninth for travel, the tenth (Mid-Heaven) for career and honor, the eleventh for friends, and the twelfth for animosity.[174] But, there are still many more significations.[175] In the *Liber Hermetis*, we also find detailed descriptions of the significance of planets, for example, pertaining to births. A small example for illustration:

> When the Moon is rising and Saturn is at Mid-Heaven in opposition and Mars is descending, an insignificant child will be born by a servant or a slave; the mother will then die before the father… and the child will at birth have a scar on the left eye.[176]

The Degrees of Life

The longest chapter in *Liber Hermetis* is the twenty-first, which deals strictly with the influence of the fixed stars situated on the degrees, the so-called *monomoirai*.[177] Every astral phenomena of a specific zodiacal sign is dealt with meticulously. An example:

> In the first to the third degree of Taurus, we find the constellation Pleiades. This is also sometimes called "Life." This degree is quite obscure, since she stands on her own and is multi-facetted. In this position, she has significance for farmers and mariners...
>
> In the third degree and sixth minute, Gorgon is rising, possessing the characteristics of Saturn and Jupiter.
>
> In the fourth degree and sixth minute, the head of Perseus is rising, who (also) has the characteristics of Saturn and Jupiter.[178]

Thus it is conclusive that these astral phenomena (astronomically fixed stars, constellations, and planets) are, in reality, divinities. Gundel calls them Gods of Destiny[179] and associates them with an old Egyptian belief that several Birth Gods are present in the birth chamber to predict the just-born infant's destiny. The fairy-tale "Sleeping Beauty" has its roots in antiquity.

The rising sign, the Ascendant, was given an especially important role. Naturally, the God of the Mid-Heaven and the combined influence of planetary deities in the degrees at the time of birth were also given attention. An illustrative example of this is found in one of Hermes Trismegistus' teachings given to Asclepius:

> Now every single class of living thing, Asclepius, of whatsoever kind, or it be mortal or be rational, whether it be endowed with soul, or be without one, just as each has its class, so does each several [class] have images of its own class.
>
> And though each separate class of animal has in it every form of its own class, still in the selfsame [kind of] form the units differ from each other.
>
> And so although the class of men is of one kind, so that a man can be distinguished by his [general] look, still individual men

within the sameness of their [common] form do differ from each other.

For the idea which is divine, is bodiless, and is whatever is grasped by the mind.

So that although these two, from which the general form and body are drived, are bodiless, it is impossible that any single form should be produced exactly like another—because the moments of the hours and points of inclination [when they're born] are different.

But they are changed as many times as there are moments in the hour of that revolving Circle in which abides that God whom we have called All-formed.

The species, then, persists, as frequently producing from itself as many images, and as diverse, as there are moments in the Cosmic Revolution—a Cosmos which doth [ever] change in revolution. But the idea [itself] is neither changed nor turned.

So are the forms of every single genus permanent, [and yet] dissimilar in the same [general] form.[180]

In the *Corpus Hermeticum*, we find similar teachings:

Now bodies matter [made] are in diversity. Some are of earth, of water some, some are of air, and some of fire.

But they are all composed; some are more [composite], and some are simpler. The heavier ones are more [composed], the lighter less so.

It is the speed of Cosmos' Course that works the manifoldness of the kinds of births. For being a most swift Breath, it doth bestow their qualities on bodies together with the One Pleroma—that of Life.[181]

And they selected out the births of men for gnosis of the works of God and attestation of the energy of Nature; the multitude of men for lordship over all beneath the Heaven and gnosis of its blessings, that they might increase in increasing and multiply in multitude(...) that they might know the fates that follow good and evil [deeds] and learn the cunning work of all good arts.[182]

And in a letter from Asclepius to King Ammon, we read:

> For on each one of us being born and made alive, the daimons take hold on us—those [daimones] who are in service at that moment [of the wheel] of Genesis, who are ranged under each one of the Stars.[183]

The different degrees, the divine decanates, and the positions of the stars in various signs, as indicated by Hermes, decide the outer characteristics. Moreover, through clever use of this knowledge, it seems possible to influence the process. In a text that has come to us in four different manuscripts, the *Secret Method of Hermes Trismegistus*, the Thrice-Great teaches us:

> For each important decision, one should consult the position of the astrological signs and the orbit of the planets, so one will succeed and not fail at one's own endeavours. If one, for example, questions in concern for a conception, what is going to be born, if such will possess a human or an animalistic character, will be male or female, will be two-footed, four-footed or winged, or will have to live in danger, and once born, if it will be fed or not, and the same for any other occasion, then use the following method...[184]

In antiquity, they were well acquainted with the *katarchen horoscope*, known in modern astrology as *horary astrology*. At the beginning of an important enterprise, a horoscope was made of the moment of conception—in other words, the moment the plan was born or the moment the first step toward realization of the plan was taken. In ancient literature, there are many examples of questions about births: Will it be a boy or a girl? Is the child going to live? Will he become a king or not? However, they also tried to get answers to many other practical questions in this way. In this, not much has changed over the years.

CHAPTER 6
HERMES AND THE HEALING ARTS

As a child of these times, I have read several popular books about stones, plants, and herbs. Even outside New Age circles, a widespread belief exists that certain stones belonging to your zodiacal sign are good for rheumatism, can stop your headache, or can lessen the danger of the radiation from your computer monitor. Especially in tourist areas in our country and abroad, there are many shops and booths where the beneficial impact of precious stones is openly praised.

Just as important is the quite common belief in the healing action of herbs and plants. Only a decade ago, not far from my city, a farmer's wife created a furor with her shockingly simple diagnoses. Although most radio and television stations in this country stay far away from anything pertaining to esoterism or occultism, this lady was invited to perform—season in and season out—at Bussum in Utrecht, and so she became quite a sensation. Her books were often sold out and reached sales figures that would make even bestselling authors' mouths water.

It also may come as a surprise to many when they discover that the belief in the active healing power of stones, plants, and herbs was not discovered by Dr. Albert Vogel, but is thousands of years old. Proof of this is found in the hermetic writings!

IMHOTEP-ASCLEPIUS

In ancient times, we find more than just predictive astrology; we find practical astrology focussed on leading a healthy and happy personal life. The individual astrology in the *Hermetica*, according to Gundel, is strongly associated with healing astrology,[185] and thus with operative healing.[186] Health was also greatly valued in those

One of the numerous statues of Asclepius at the ruins of Greek cities.

days and healing has, for a long time, had a strong sacred character. Which brings us to Thoth-Hermes:

> All medical treatments were ordained by the Gods and coded in Secret Books by Thoth, known by the Greeks as Hermes Trismegistus. These books were kept in medical colleges at the temples of Sais and Heliopolis. They were only meant for the Initiated, in other words, priests. According to verbal tradition Thoth had invented the Arts and Science. He also possessed the secrets of the Gods and knew how to cause and cure a disease...[187]

During the 19th century, there were extremely important Egyptian medical papyri found that dated back to the Old Kingdom (3300–2360 B.C.), the time of the first eight dynasties, whose rulers built the pyramids of Cheops, Cheffren, and Mycerinus. It is even possible that some of the recipes from these papyri belonged to Imhotep.[188]

Who was Imhotep? Imhotep[189] is generally considered to be the architect and builder of the step-pyramid of Djoser, built during the 3rd Dynasty (2667–2648 B.C.). Wisdom writings are attributed to him, just as they are to Thoth, for he was highly respected for his great knowledge. Two thousand years after his death, this priest-architect-physician was raised to godhood, quite a rarity for non-royal individuals in Old Egypt. Imhotep became the God of the art of healing and was associated with the Gods Thoth and Ptah. The cult center of Imhotep in Saqqara, the *Asklepion*, became a pilgrimage center for the sick. Many worshippers left behind a mummified ibis as a devotional offering in the large subterranean catacombs nearby. As we know, the ibis is a symbol for Thoth, which shows how closely these two were interwoven with one another. Outside of Saqqara, Imhotep was also honored at Karnak, Deir el-Bahri, Philae, and Deir el-Medina.[190]

The name *Asklepion* showed the later connection of Imhotep with Asclepius, son of Apollo. The name was actually overlaid on top of the Egyptian Imhotep. Asclepius had numerous sanctuaries throughout the whole Greco-Roman world. These were part of an old tradition of the art of healing in caves under the holy temples[191]—a custom we know was followed during the priest-king era in Egypt, with its *pirankhs* and healing chambers in the temples. It is interesting to see the constant association between Thoth and Imhotep, and later between Hermes and Asclepius. Where Asclepius, in the "philosophical" treatises, acts as the dialog partner of Hermes, he is, in the magical papyri, still wearing his physician's white coat.

About the Divine Sympathy[192]

In the astrological *Hermetica*, healing is linked with divine energy, personified in the astral phenomena. A beautiful example of this is found in the *Liber Hermetis*, which we discussed earlier. In the chapter dealing with the divine decanates, there is a part of the body associated with each count of 10. We read, for example, under the sign Virgo:

> The first divine decanate of Virgo wears the face of the Sun. The name is Zamendes. He causes stomach-aches...
>
> The second divine decanate of Virgo wears the face of Venus. The name is Magois. She influences the liver...
>
> The third divine decanate of Virgo wears the face of Mercurius. The name is Michulais. He influences the spleen. His whole body resembles a grave (mummy). He rules over the region of Meroe and Elephantis.[193]

Not only the divine decanates, but also the astrological zodiac signs, represent a certain part of the body. According to the French researcher Auguste Bouché-Leclercq,[194] we find in the ancient astrology the following links: The head corresponds with Aries, the neck with Taurus, the shoulders and arms with Gemini, the chest with Cancer, the sides with Leo, the lower abdomen and bladder with Virgo, the buttocks (which, in sitting, keep the body balanced) with Libra, the crotch with Scorpio, the thighs with Sagittarius, the knees with Capricorn, the legs with Aquarius, and the feet with Pisces.

This is not just a summation for practically orientated astrologers (in general, present-day astrologers still use this division); it also has a deep religious background. From the hermetic point of view, one human, as the microcosmos, consists of the same substance as the macrocosmos, representing the deities in parts of the body—yes, even God. So we can read in *The Holy Book of Hermes to Asclepius*:

> Aries is the head of the world, Taurus the neck, Gemini the shoulders, Cancer the chest, Leo the shoulder blades, the heart and sides, Virgo the stomach, Libra the buttocks, Scorpio the crotch, Sagittarius the thighs, Capricorn the knees, Aquarius the legs and Pisces the feet.[195]

Illustration of the influence of the signs of the zodiac on the human body. It reads: "View of the Celestial Influx on the Body of Woman, as illustrated in Culpepers Family Physician, and Sibleys Occult Sciences." With sub-text: "Illustration of the influence of the signs of Zodiac on the human body."

The heavenly human, the image of God, is built up out of the above-mentioned elements. A very old idea, which we also find in ancient Jewish mysticism before the time of Christ, is the concept of *kabod*—the "enjoyment" of God.[196] The terrestrial human has the same "characteristics" as heavenly Man and is, as it were, an imprint of it.

Besides the divine decanates and zodiacal signs, the planets, of course, also influence the body. So we read in the *Iatromathematica of Hermes Trismegistus to the Egyptian Ammon* (subtitle: *Mathemathical prescience of bed-ridden diseases*):

> The human, my dear Ammon, is called by learned men, a Universe, since he resembles completely the nature of the world. Indeed, at the moment of his conception, he receives from the seven planets a complexity of rays influencing each part of the body. The same occurs at time of birth based on the position of the twelve zodiacal signs. Thus falls, as said, the head under Aries, and the senses of the head are subdivided among the seven planets: The right eye falls to the Sun, the left to the Moon, the ears to Saturn, the brain to Jupiter, the tongue and uvula to Mercurius, scent and taste to Venus, the arteries to Mars. If now, at time of conception, or of birth, one of the celestial bodies stands in a malevolent position,[197] the result will cause a weakness in the part (of the human) which corresponds with the heavenly star...[198]

The instructions given in these writings are not without conditions. Knowledge of the constellation and the person helps the physician find the correct medicine. When he has ascertained which heavenly body is causing the disease, he is able, according to its nature, to prescribe appropriate recipes and medicine. Then he can choose a *sympathetic*, or even an *antipathetic*, solution. In the first instance, he will prescribe a solution (plant or herb extract) that harmonizes with the sphere of the malignant cause to strengthen the inner healing force. In the second instance, he will propagate a solution with an opposite influence as a counter-force to the malignant cause. It is evident we have, hereby, landed upon the field of therapy.

Hermes as Therapist

In the *Holy Book of Hermes to Asclepius* based on the above-mentioned compilation of the *Anthroposis*, the heavenly human is given further explanation:

> Well now, each of the zodiacal signs has power over its own part of the body and causes in the area sickness. If you wish to avoid the suffering, which is connected with the divine decanates, engrave on stone the forms and shapes of the divine decanate itself, place the plant belonging to this divine decanate under it, make a talisman of it and wear this as a powerful and luck-bearing support for your body.[199]

The *Holy Book of Hermes to Asclepius*, which was bestowed on the renowned Roman physician Galenus,[200] is one of the many hermetic writings wherein, analogous to the *Liber Hermetis*, a division is made of the divine decanates and their influences. The protection against evil influences is simple: find a sympathetic stone, engrave the image of the divine decanate on it, place a sympathetic part of a plant or extract under it, make of this an amulet (often a ring), wear it and remember not to consume food that is antipathetic to the divine decanate.

What were these stones and plants that were *sympathetic* with the specific divine decanates? The *Holy Book of Hermes to Asclepius* gives an answer, as can be seen in Table 1 on page 84.[201]

Recipe Books

In other hermetic "botanical" writings, more elaborate details are often given on how to prepare plant extracts from which a drink is brewed. The best time for this to happen is given by the texts as well. So we read, for example, in *From Hermes about the plants of the twelve zodiacal signs*, how certain plants have to be prepared "when the Sun stands in Aries or if the Sun, in the constellation of the plant one is cooking in the horoscope of the moment, makes a triangle with the Moon."[202]

Another striking note in this hermetic "recipe book" is:

> Plant of the Sun: Chicory... Mix this (plant) with rose-oil until the juice turns into salve. This ointment is meant for heart patients, frees them of their illness and reduces even fevers... Mixed according to the same recipe, but now with pure virginal oil, it stops headaches. If a human, while turning east-wards, smears this on his face and calls upon the Sun to be merciful to him/her, he/she will receive round about the same day the (called upon) benevolence.
>
> For heart patients and sufferers of indigestion experiencing a sick stomach, who can take food but not be able to digest it, one prepares an elixir of the root (with the following ingredients):
>
> - eight drachma stalks of wheat
> - two drachma croci
> - fourteen drachma honey
> - six drachma flowers from the mastic shrub
> - twenty-four drachma chicory root.
>
> Pound all of this fine in a pestle with very old honey; then make pills of it, weighing approximately one drachma; give to heart-patients a dosage of one pill, dissolved in water; and to patients with indigestion the same dosage, dissolved in the best possible wine.[203]

Plant extracts were not used only for diseases, but could also serve other purposes. So we read in an old hermetic text:

> The plant belonging to the Moon is the peony; in Italy it's called Moon-plant. Pick them when the Moon is in the sky, recite the (prescribed) prayers, call on the Angels and also the hours, the months, the wind and the sign of the Moon—which is Cancer.
>
> If you wear a cock's comb on your head, this plant will give you the following advantages: All business preoccupying you will be resolved quickly, and in all your enterprises your direction will be correct.[204]

Besides healing or bringing about prosperity, parts of plants can also influence fertility or prevent it, and were used for menopause

Table 1.
Correspondences of the Astrological Signs and Decanates

Sign/ Decanate	#	Affliction	Remedies: Stone	Remedies: Plant	Amulet	Forbidden food
Aries	1 2 3	Head Sleep, nose Ears,larynx, teeth	Porous Babylon-stone Starstone Bostrychiet	Isoprene Wilde ruit Lamsoor	Iron ring Golden ring Own choice	Pig's head Crane's meat Ramspens
Taurus	1 2 3	Throat Tonsils, neck Mouth, throat	Moonstone Libido-enhancing stone Hyacinth (topaz)	Cyprys bulbs Dictaam Ox tongue	Own choice Gold/silver ring Gold/silver ring	Sea eel Eel Ditto
Gemini	1 2 3	Shoulders Upper arms Hands	Diamond Panchrous Bloodstone	Orchid Cinquefoil Rosemary	Own choice Own choice Own choice	Electric eel Scaros (seafish) Fowl
Cancer	1 2 3	Intestines Lungs Spleen	Dryiet Jasper Euchaiet	Artemesia Peony Sphairites	Own choice Own choice Own choice	Pig's stomach Of a dog... Not indicated
Leo	1 2 3	Heart Midriff Liver	Agate Selenite Heliet	Lion's paw Chrysanthum Not indicated	Own choice Gold ring Own choice	Kind of Sparrow Eggs Beans Tuna
Virgo	1 2 3	Stomach Intestines Navel	Coral Dendriet Euthlizon	Cat's eye Sweet wood Soort wikke	Own choice Own choice Own choice	Pig's liver Crane's meat Colt's meat or Bear's meat
Libra	1 2 3	Back seat Bladder urine duct Anus	Jaspagaat Sardon Emerald	Polium Duivenkruid Verbena	Own choice Own choice Own choice	Duck and bitter almonds Blackberries Pork chops
Scorpio	1 2 3	Genitals (exit) Crotch Testicles	Hermatite Pyrite Egyptian sardios	Bingelkruid Scorpion tails Peony	Own choice Own choice Own choice	Not indicated Not indicated Testicles
Saggitarius	1 2 3	Thighs Bones Hips	Frygische stone Amythist Aerizon	Sage Andractitalon Centaur	Own choice Own choice Own choice	Moorhen Zeerog Chicken brains
Capricorn	1 2 3	Knees Elbows Lids, elbows	Ofiet Amethyst Anankiet	Lion's paw Anemone Cameleon	Own choice Own choice Own chouice	Eel Sea eel River crab
Aquarius	1 2 3	Shinbone Knee, slintbone Splint bone, knee	Knekiet Magnetstone Medersteen	Asarum Little scarlet Thyme	Own choice Own choice Own choice	Barley bread Pork chop Donkey's meat
Pisces	1 2 3	Feet Feet* Feet*	Beryl Perileukios Hyacinth	Verbena Rosemary Camille	Own choice Own choice Own choice	Lion's meat Mutton Goat's head

* This does not appear in the *Secret Book Of Hermes*, but it does in the *Liber Hermetis*

and hot flashes as well. As we saw, the influence of the divine decanate was checked, including the plants and stones that sympathize with it.

Not only do the divine decanates have their own plants, but planets rule over certain botanics as well, as is put into words in the *Book of Hermes Trismegistus to Asclepius about plants belonging to the seven stars*.[205] There are also hermetic texts that show the link between the twelve signs of the zodiac and healing plants. There must even have existed complete hermetic herb books.[206]

In many of these texts, there are references made to the time of planting or harvesting of seeds and plants—even to the moment of the day, the phase of the Moon, and the geographical area. The biodynamic agriculture of Rudolf Steiner knows, therefore, illustrious predecessors!

Hermes and the Letter *Sympatheia*

On a memorable day in 4th century B.C. in far-off Babylon, a certain Harpokration—originally from Alexandria, the city of philosophers and Gnostics—went in search of wisdom and met an old grey man. He appeared finally to have met his Master—someone who was capable of initiating him into the mysterious secrets of the All. After a series of lessons, the old man took him to a holy place—an unusual place surrounded by magnificent towers. In the center, on top of a high ziggurat, stood a temple that was accessible only by mounting 365 stairs. On top, there appeared to be a pillar erected inside that holy place. At one time, according to the locals, it had been brought from Syria and solemnly consecrated for the treatment of the sick from the surrounding area.

What interested Harpokration were primarily the numerous inscriptions on this holy pillar. So he read a superb poem about the soul that is captured on Earth by destiny, but is destined after death, once freed from the body, to meet God.[207] On this same pillar was engraved a section of the *Kyranis*. The *Kyranis* forms, with the *Koiranides* and the *Kyranides*, one of the most influential collections of hermetic medical-astrological-magical texts.[208] With the assistance of the old wise man, Harpokration translated the inscriptions from the strange composition of characters in which it was written.

This story is full of symbology. How many beautiful legends exist relating to holy writings chiseled in stone that are found in the most unexpected places? The text that Harpokration, or whoever, left behind is, however, not a legend; it is as real as life. In one of its manuscripts, we read the preface: *Therapeutic handbook, originating in Syria, put on paper by Harpokration for benefit of his own daughter.*[209]

The original text of the legacy that Harpokration recites dates back to the 1st century A.D.[210] It's about a hermetic revelation bear-

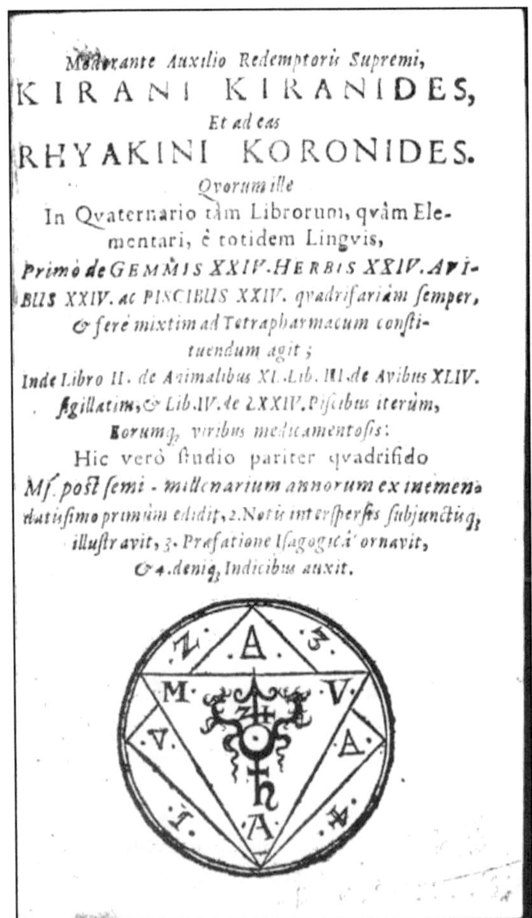

Moderante Auxilio Redemptoris Supremi,
KIRANI KIRANIDES,
Et ad eas
RHYAKINI KORONIDES.
Qvorum ille
In Qvaternario tàm Librorum, qvàm Elementari, è totidem Lingvis,
Primò de GEMMIS *XXIV.* HERBIS *XXIV.* AVIBUS *XXIV. ac* PISCIBUS *XXIV. qvadrifariàm semper, & ferè mixtim ad Tetrapharmacum constituendum agit;*
Inde Libro II. de Animalibus XL. Lib. III. de Avibus XLIV. sigillatim, & Lib. IV. de XXXII. Piscibus iterùm, Eorumque viribus medicamentosis:
Hic verò studio pariter qvadrifido
Ms. post semi-millenarium annorum ex inemendatissimo primùm edidit, 2. Notis interspersis subjunctisque illustravit, 3. Præfatione Isagogicâ ornavit, & 4. deniq; Indicibus auxit.

Title page of a Latin publication of the hermetic *Kyranides.*

ing the intriguing title: *Received from the angels, a gift from the unforgettable God, the God Hermes Trismegistus, to be shared with people gifted with understanding.*[211]

The text makes a connection between apparently independent issues—a bird, a fish, a plant, a stone—based on the first letters of their names. Since, as was believed, God gave names to the things, nothing is coincidental. For all creations whose name begins with the letter A, there is a certain form of energetic *sympatheia* (coincidence). This, of course, applies to the other letters of the alphabet as well. It is interesting that now there are, even in the description of the astrological divine decanates, these comparisons standing under the sign of the healing arts.

The same applies in the *Koiranides*, a separate section of the *Kyranides* that forms the *Abridged medical book of Hermes Trismegistus, assigned to his pupil* Asclepius*, based on the science of* Astrology *and the natural animalistic influence.*[212] Here, we also find the interconnection between animals, plants, stones, and metals based on the letters of the alphabet. And here, likewise, the therapeutic value stands central. The recipes often consist, as we saw before, of wearing an amulet that contains components of the described phenomena.

According to Festugière, the analysis of the *Kyranides* proves that the *Hermetica* occupies an important place in the medical-magical literature of the so-called *Physika*,[213] which originated in the 2nd century B.C. in Egypt. How could it be otherwise? Hermes was an Egyptian.[214]

Ode to the Peony

Historians are often faced with a nearly impossible task. To dig up the past is not so difficult. However, to sense the way people lived and experienced situations and understand what kind of feelings these experiences called up is much more difficult. Sometimes, texts can help with this. They familiarize us with another way of looking at things instead of seeing them only from today's point of view.

Just now, we discussed the "discovery" of (a part of) the *Kyranides* by Harpokration. Below, I will show you a large section of one of these texts that is categorized in the *Kyranides*. It concerns the peony, "as can be read in the *Kyranides* it is a sacred flower."[215] The peony, we read further, is a plant traditionally associated with Cancer. Cancer also represents motherhood; that is why quite a lot of recipes are for (pregnant) mothers. The citation I show here is longer than usual, to give you the opportunity to go with the text—to experience it, as it were.

After an introductory sentence, the manuscript begins directly with the practical side.

Here is the recipe:

> Search for the peony at the setting of the Moon. She should be planted in a noticeable place, open on all sides. You can best do this when the Sun enters Virgo. She grows best in the vicinity of the mountain Haemus, the hills of Taormina, on the slopes of Great Babylon, in Tracia, opposite Gadar and on the shores of the Egian Gulf. She also grows in other vicinities, but then she does not have the same power as in the places mentioned. This has to do with the lay-out of the land, the destiny assigned to zodiacal signs and the radiation of the stars.

You best proceed in the following manner:

> ... After you have removed one seed from the closed peony-pod, roll this one, together with another seed from the opened fruit, in seven leaves of the same plant, all in top-condition, and stick them in the ground on an elevated spot, there where it seems to you the best. When a root has formed and evening has fallen, you will find her (again). Protect her against storm, winds and changes of weather.
>
> Now, leave your house on the day of the Moon, at the start of the first hour; in other words, when the Moon descends and the Sun has not yet risen, in a clear state of mind. Take with you a seal's skin, blessed at the time of death... Then write these signs on the skin and wrap it with authentic raw silk around the plant's roots. During these actions, recite this prayer ...

A prayer follows, in which God is called upon in his many manifestations and names.[216] The petitioner prays that this plant (the peony) will provide protection against high fevers, demons, witchcraft, the evil eye, evil influences, and plotting, and that it will serve as a remedy against afflictions of the breast, chest, liver, spleen, stomach, and loins. It is also used for assistance against wind and darkness, migraine, gout, and arthritis; against diseases of crops; and, last of all, to regain good humor or memory, and to stimulate regular menstruation. After this prayer, another much shorter prayer follows, and the practical part continues:

> Return (after these prescribed prayers) for a total of seven days back to this spot, to check if everything is in order. Each day, before sunrise, recite the prayers as you go there. Go now there on the following day... on the first hour from home and take with you a never-used caramite stone whose strength is known and has been proven, also a siderite and beryline stone. Move incense clock-wise around the plant, reciting the two prayers.
>
> When you have dug a circle around the plant, thereby exposing the roots, pull her out carefully and treat her properly in the way which will be shown to you, and you will notice she has become sacred.
>
> When you cut her in pieces now, the root, the stems, the leaves and the bud, the closed and open seeds, you will see the parts will contain more power than in all the above mentioned instances. It is said, God revealed this flower to Hermes Trismegistus as a medicine for mortals to sooth their pains and since he wrote it down in the holy books of Egypt, it will be useful in life.
>
> Everyone in possession of a part of the root, if he has engraved on it the names of the incomparable Very Great God, does not have to be afraid of demons; in such a case, there will be no witchery. When you engrave the following letters, you do not have to be afraid of poison nor for any other evil. Since, it will... reduce fever; it will push back the evil eye, as well as witchcraft and plotting. This plant will give its carrier, comparative to others, pleasure and fulfil his prayers.

If someone suffers from epilepsy and you hang this root around his neck, you will cure him of every attack.

If someone is possessed by a demon, burn part of the root and the demon will be chased away; this is then a divine act.

If you take a small fibre of the root and you crush it finely on the day and hour of Venus, then mix it (with water) and let a couple drink it, when man and woman hate each other, then soon they will be in love again.

Everyone who puts the root under his pillow, will not have anymore bad dreams.

Everyone who possesses her, has an excellent remedy for the spleen.

In the home where she is kept, no demon will appear, nor any magical influence will take place.

Anyone who was poisoned and drinks it, will stop experiencing bad after-effects.

The seed, dissolved in high quality honey, is beneficial to the body and even for cattle.

The woman, who eats the root of this plant, has enough milk for nursing.

It is also a good antidote for snakebites…

When a man becomes crazy and he has smoked a small part of this plant, he is cured.

Crush some of the root to a fine powder at the time of birth of a child and mix it with milk; it will bring happiness to the mother's breast…

During conception take the unsprouted seed of this plant, wrap it in a cloth of real silk and have the woman keep this against her lower abdomen, in this way she will conserve the sperm.

Prepare of the plant's juice a medicine, which once drunk cures all inner and outer chest-ailments, of the "two parts," in other words, liver and spleen, navel area, especially the lower body, and the kidneys. Here follows the recipe:

- juice of the peony, 1 ounce
- juice of a pomegranate, 1 ounce
- styrax calamite, 5 ounces
- root of the theogoon, 1 ounce

When all of this is mixed, the wet and the dry, place it in a glass bowl, taste some of it if necessary and administer a ½ ounce as a drink (diluted) with wine. Read yourself, while the patient is drinking it, seven times the prayer out loud and the patient is cured.

Also make of the root an amulet, to keep orchards, fields and gardens, healthy... You won't be bothered by hail, mildew, rain-downfalls or storms...

If someone loses his voice and cannot speak anymore, prepare a small fire of this root, say "phrièl" and you will cure him.

If someone is suffering from amnesia, let him/her chew a bit of this root and while he/she is drinking the juice, speak the name, "Raphael." You will help him/her to instantly get his/her memory back.

If a woman suffers from a halt in her menstruation give her an ounce of the juice of the root to drink. When the words "apha, khama, maï, alla, phaza, tamana" have been spoken, you will cure her. She will get a really strong menstruation. You can stop this flow again, by giving her a drink from another juice, now without repeating the words.

Take a branch of the plant and write on it: "Ghenemptri gargar."

Carry it with you and by doing so every enterprise will be successful, your path will be correct and easy, and you will receive honour wherever you will be or go; people will rush up to you as if you were a God.

If someone carves the words "arkeu ili" on the leaves and puts them on the threshold of the door where thieves might enter the house, they (the thieves) will be blinded and lose their way.

The fruit of the peony is wholesome for enhancing conception or preventing it. This medicine turns barren women fertile and those who have had children barren: Take a seed of the opened fruit and roll this in a seal-skin, paste this on your stomach during the three-month's moon cycle after the waning of the Moon. In this way the woman will not conceive. One also needs to carve these signs on the seal-skin. If you want to try it, then experiment on an animal or a bird and it won't have an offspring.

A plaster made of the seed will chase away throat-sores; infected or difficult to heal wounds will be cleansed and its tissues repaired.

Here is the recipe:

- seeds of the peony, 1 litre
- juice of the stems, 1 ounce
- extraction of sage, 2 ounces
- root of the memakham, 2 ounces
- wax, 1 ounce
- goose fat, 1 ounce
- terebint, 1 ounce

If you have prepared this melange, keep it with you, and when need arises use it. While making the melange repeat the words: "Ao, io, ion, eloï, oikham, khiak, zampri, ripha, kham."

If a woman, while delivering, experiences severe pains and there is danger, take an opened seed of the plant, put it in oil and smear this on the loins and lower abdomen, she will deliver her child painlessly. Be hygienic during this treatment.

If someone knows of these medicines, do not hand them to others except your son, and keep them secret as a treasure.[217]

The Religious Experience of Doctor Thessalos

In antiquity, medical science was no "trick." It was a holy experience. In the above ode to the peony, purity of mind is constantly stressed. With total attention to every detail, the petitioner can lift, as it were, a small part out of the total harmony, treasuring it very dearly. It was a patient research, and sometimes it didn't work. Sometimes, a more accurate tuning-in to the cosmos, as well as further study, was needed. An illustrative example of this is the experience of the legendary physician Thessalos, who lived in the 1st century A.D. This learned Alexandrian wrote, in a letter to Emperor Claudius,[218] about his discovery of a book by Nechepso, in which he found twenty-four ways to cure all bodily diseases by means of stones and plants, each influenced by a sign of the zodiac. But although Thessalos did his utter best, trusting to the information in the book of his great idol, these experiments were not successful and he became desperate.

Partially because his colleagues laughed at him and drove him out, he left Alexandria and traveled to Diospolis. This old capital of Egypt, now called Thebes (Luxor), boasted a large number of temples. Thessalos describes here his first impressions:

> One finds, indeed, high priests, friends of the written word and learned men of many sciences. My affection for the high priests grew deeper the more time passed by, and one day I asked them if they still possessed some operative energy of magic. I noticed most of them became quite indignant at my audacity to hope about such. One of them, however, who had gained my confidence because of his serious way of living and his high age, did not betray my affection. He assured me he had the power to create visions by means of a water-filled basin.[219]

Thessalos invites the priest for a walk. They reach a forest, where a deep silence reigns. Here, he dares to announce his wish to the priest. He tells him what has happened to him and assures him that, if it is not possible for him to make contact with a deity to obtain clarity, only death remains. The priest promises to help and commands him to fast for three days. In gratitude, Thessalos kisses the hand of the priest and profusely thanks him, upon which he bursts out crying from happiness with tears streaming down his cheeks, "since it is a law of nature that unexpected happiness creates more tears than misery does. . . ." Thessalos can hardly wait until the end of the third day, but finally it arrives. At sunset, he hurries to the priest, who has prepared a chamber for him. "On my behalf, projecting ahead, without having told the priest, I had taken paper and ink with me to make notes." The priest asks him if he wishes to speak with a spirit of a deceased person or a deity. "With Asclepius," he answers, and he asks if he may be left alone with the deity. It is apparent from the priest's face that he does not like this, nevertheless he grants the request and instructs Thessalon to sit down with his face toward the throne upon which the deity will sit. Then, with mysterious words, he proceeds to invoke Asclepius and leaves the room, locking the door with a key.

The deity appears. At the magnificent appearance, Thessalon hardly dares to speak; his soul is touched to the greatest depth by the beauty of Asclepius. But at last he asks him why he has not succeeded in his experiments with the recipes of Nechepso. Asclepius answers him, saying that Nechepso possessed great magical power. He was gifted with great wisdom and he understood the relationship between stones, plants, and stars. But he did not know the exact moment and places where the plants had to be planted.

Then Asclepius entrusted to Thessalos more detailed instructions for the gathering of medicinal plants:

> Amongst the plants mentioned below, use those from Egypt, Arabia, Asia, Syria, and some from Italy. Since these regions are warmer than others. No plant, which the earth brings forth, can grow without being drenched by pneuma, spirit. In the coldest regions, the pores of the plants are narrowed and this stops the spirit from entering them in sufficient amounts—this is in contrast with the above indicated regions where the heat open the pores and allows enough vital air to enter. So they can fill themselves with energy and create better effects. If you cannot obtain plants from these regions, but still need them, use those from other regions. Be careful in picking them: It should be exactly on a star-ruled day of the week and falling under the plant's constellation; not only on the day but on the exact hour of the star which rules the plant. While you pull the plants out of the earth, utter the indicated prayer below at the precise moment. When you have done such, throw in the created hole which was created by pulling out the plant, a kernel of wheat or barley.[220]

All of this shows love and care for humanity as well as for Nature, which is considered a reflection of the divine cosmos. Hermes Trismegistus is the bridge between Heaven and Earth.

Chapter 7
The Ring of Hermes

The hermetic treatise the *Virgin of the World*[221] tells us that the Egyptian priests had received three arts from the Gods: philosophy, magic, and the art of healing: "By means of Philosophy and Magic they sustained the soul, by the Art of Healing they saved the body, in case of illness."[222]

Philosophy and magic fall here under the same category. The difference between "philosophical" and "technical" *Hermetica* adhered to by many scholars up to now is, in my eyes, debatable.

Antique Fashion Trend

In the time described here, there was no definite barrier between the "philosophical" and the "technical" aspects of the *Hermetica*, for everything experienced by humanity in this era was linked with everything in the natural world, so independant issues were difficult to separate. The magician was a philosopher and was held in high regard. In an old magical papyrus, we read: "He will be of service to you in an appropriate manner, O' blessed Initiate in Magic."[223] In antiquity, magic was ever-present. Fritz Graf begins his fascinating dissertation on ancient magic with the remark that contemporaries of Plato and Socrates placed voodoo dolls on graves and thresholds. Cicero laughed when told by a colleague that he had lost his memory due to a magical spell, and Pliny the Elder declared that, in his lifetime, everyone was afraid to become a victim of witchcraft.[224] And then there was, of course, one of the greatest classics ever: *Methamorphosis* (*The Golden Ass*) of Apuleius of Madaura,[225] wherein a young man is transformed by magic into a donkey.

According to the voluminous Dutch dictionary *Van Dale*, the art of magic means witchcraft. In a more detailed description, it defines it as: "All those actions in which humans try to gain power over the energies in the world (Nature) around them (incantations, etc.)."

Our word "magic" has its root in the Greek word *magos*, which appeared for the first time in texts during the 6th century B.C. Originally, it was not a Greek word, but was of Persian origin, where in the old times, priests were the *magoi*, specialists in religious matters. Socrates' pupil Xenophon would later call them "technicians in divine matters."[226]

The word "magic" has been unpopular for a long time, since it has been associated with Black Magic. Magic has gained in reputation; however, thanks to the occultists of the 19th century[227] and, in the last decade of the last century, we notice a strong increase in interest for magic in the sciences[228] primarily due to the mapping out of the Greek magical papyri.[229] In popular literature, magic is often confused with other esoteric subjects like the Kabala, astrology, and alchemy. In all these works, Hermes is given rather short shrift. Even Dumas spends only one and a half pages on hermetic magic in his enormous 600-page book on the history of magic, wherein we find nothing about hermetic magic except a mention of the *Tabula Smaragdina* and the *Kybalion*.[230]

Hermes as a Magician

We have already encountered magic in the preceding chapter. Invocations to the Gods and the preparation of amulets are clear signs of magic. Up to now, we recognized in this an interconnection with the art of healing. This seems to be an important link. But magic could (and can) be used for practically all affairs—for all-round welfare, happiness in love, success in business, and much, much more.

Magic was a day-to-day affair in ancient times. Magical incantations, amulets, and other practices all were common knowledge. Spells or incantations existed for everything and for every occasion. Life, in those days, meant more than just survival; it meant being on your guard through the observation of the deified stars and their constellations, careful behavior toward sowing and harvesting, trying to eat pure food, praying for happiness, and exorcizing evil. We already saw examples of these in the previous chapters.

The origin of hermetic magic, of course, lies in Egypt (how could it be different?). The Egyptian magical texts are old, very old. They appear from the Middle Kingdom, around 2000 B.C. Some are dated earlier. And Thoth, as inventor of magic, plays a role of the utmost importance in these texts. Here we read a spell used against the evil eye:

> Sekhmet's arrow is in you, the magic of Thoth resides in your body, Isis curses you, Nephthys punishes you, the lance of Horus pierces your head...[231]

Another incantation discusses the use of medicines against maladies of the extremities:

> ...To me belong the salutation of the Lord of the ALL, to ban (bad) influences of a God or a Goddess, of a male or a female deceased... Those (sayings) are part of me, they are in this head of mine, in this world of mine, in these shoulders of mine, in this flesh of mine, in these extremities of mine. (They are there) to punish the Slanderer, the chief(-demon) who causes this disruption in my flesh and the pain in my extremities; when something my flesh, my head, my shoulders, my body, my extremities enters I pay obeisance to Ra, since he has said: "It is me who will defend him against his enemies." And his guide is Thoth; he changes the script into words. He makes compilations. He gives useful information to scholars, to physicians who follow his ways, to free someone whose God wishes he stays alive. And I am such a one, whose God wishes he stays alive...![232]

Exclaiming the magical formulas, the victim crawls, as it were, into the skin of the deity: "I am a messenger of Thoth, who comes to offer protection."[233]

Greek Magical Papyri

In Greek magical papyri, we also frequently encounter Thoth-Hermes. Hermes is called the first of the magicians, the father of Isis.[234] Here too, the magician sometimes crawls into the skin of Hermes, as this excerpt from the *Ring of Hermes* describes:

About the making of a scarab:

> Take a scarab, engraved as is described below, put him on a writing-desk for papyrus and lay under the table a clean linen sheet and small olive branches. Scatter these and place in the middle of the table a tiny incense-jar and burn in it myrrh and kyphi. Keep close to it a small turquoise vase, filled with oil of lilies, myrrh or cinnamon. Lay the ring, after having it cleansed from all impurities, in the oil, burn the incense of myrrh and kyphi and let it rest for three days. Lay it, afterwards, on a pure spot. Keep for the blessing pure bread and seasonal fruit handy. While burning another offering on twigs of a wine-stalk, return the ring back to the oil. Rub the oil on yourself at daybreak and recite, while facing the Sun, the spell which is written underneath here.

The engraving of the scarab:

> Cut a scarab out of precious emerald, bore it through and put a golden string through it. Engrave on the bottom of it (an image or name of) the Holy Isis. When you have consecrated it, in the way described above, use it. Days which are favourable for this ritual, counting from the waxing of the Moon, are the 7th, 9th, 10th, 12th, 14th, 16th, 21st, 24th and 25th. Be peaceful on the other days.

The (above mentioned) spell which needs to be addressed to Helios (the Sun) is:

> I am Thoth, discoverer and creator of magical tools and letters. Come to me, you underneath the earth, awaken yourself before me, large demon, abysmal Noun. I am the famed Heron, egg of the

> ibis, egg of the falcon, egg of the sky-diving phoenix, with under my tongue the sludge of Em...[235]

The text continues. What primarily concerns me here is to show how people in those days got a grip on all kinds of matters. In the Greek magical papyri, there are many divergent examples of this, among them:

> When you enter a city, gather up the pebbles on the road which lies opposite the gate, as many as you wish, and keep in mind you take them with you as a means to stop your headache. Attach one to your forehead and throw the rest behind you, without looking, back behind you.[236]

Hermetic magical texts are quite divergent in subject. Many of them contain extensive praises to Thoth-Hermes, like the papyrus in which Hermes is asked to get an (incubation) dream—something that happened frequently in antiquity. In such a dream, the deity appeared and gave insight on certain circumstances in the life of the mystic.

Hermes, Lord of the World, who lives in the heart,
O' circle of the Moon, round and square,
Inventor of the words of speech,
Counsellor of the case for Justice,
Draped in a cape, wearing winged sandals,
transporting you from tenuous skies
to the deepest abyss of Earth.
Guide of the Spirit, eye of the Sun, thou art powerful,
founder of the word which leads to expression.
Thou who gives joy with your light to mortals
beneath the earth (in Tartarus), those whose life has ended.
Prophet of fate and divine dream,
thou who, day and night, gives out oracles
and who cures the pain of mortals with your medicines![237]

Hermes Dolls

In the so-called *Love Spell of Astrapsoukos*, Hermes is called by many names. The text starts, as usual, with an invocation, followed by practical instructions on how to create an amulet:

> Come to me Lord Hermes like the foetus in the wombs of women. Come to me Lord Hermes, who gathers food for Gods and men. Come to me, Lord Hermes and hand out to me your favours, supply me with food, give me victory, and (also) prosperity, happiness in love, a beautiful encounter and the strength of all men and women. Your names in Heaven are: LAMPHTEN OUOTHI OUASTHEN OUOTHI OAMENOTH ENTHOMOUCH. These are the names in the four Heavenly Quarters. I also know what your forms are: In the East you have the form of an ibis, in the West a baboon with a dog's face, in the North a serpent and in the South a wolf. Your plant is the vine, being an olive-tree there. I also know your wood-structure: Ebony. I know you Hermes, who you are and where you come from and what your city is: Heliopolis. Come to me Lord Hermes with many names, who knows the hidden things beneath the heavenly pole and Earth. Come to me Lord Hermes, be well humoured, beneficiary of the world. Listen to me and make me attractive to all forms in this populated world. Open my hands for anyone giving out gifts and induce them to give to me what they contain in their hands. I also know your strange (non-Greek) names: PHARNATHAR BARACHEL CHTHA, these are the names the barbarians call you... Protect me always against witchery, deceit, any form of slander and wicked tongues, any demonic madness, every enmity against Gods or people. May they give me prosperity, conquest, success in business and wealth. For I am you and you are me. Your name is my name and my name is yours. For I am an image of you. If something should happen to me this year, this month or this day, then it will happen to the great God ACHCHEMEN ESTROPH whose name is engraved in the prow of the holy ship. Your real name is engraved in the holy column in Hermopolis, there where you were born. Your true name is OS(E)RG(A)RIAG-NOMAPHI. Such is your name in fifteen letters, a number equalling the days of the waxing Moon; and the second

name with the number seven, equals with him who rules the world with the exact number 365 which equals the days of the year. Truly: Abrasax. I know you Hermes, and you know me. I am you and you are me. Accomplish everything for me and bring me face to face with Fortuna and Agathodaimon, now, now, fast, fast.

Take a piece of olive wood and make of it a small sitting baboon with a dog-face, wearing the winged helmet of Hermes and with a sheath on his back. Write the name of Hermes on a sheet of papyrus and stick it in the sheath. Write in ink of myrrh what you do and what you wish, and after you have covered it, burn some incense and put it where you want in the middle of the working area.

The name which is written sounds like: PHTHORON PHTHIONE THOYTH. Write next to it the great names: IAO SABAOTH ADONAIE ABLANATHANALBA AKRAMMACHAMAREI, 365. Grant the working area success, favour, wealth and happiness in love, as well as for me, the Gods, and the working area, now, now, fast, fast.[238]

Here an amulet to Hermes is made. We see this in many other papyri as well: "Draw on a piece of linen with quail-blood, as accurate as possible, the God Hermes standing up with an ibis head."[239]

The calling of names is pre-eminently a magical action. As we saw before, the pronunciation of a word is loaded with certain energy. We see this again in another hermetic magical papyrus, whose subject is the initiation of a boy:

Place an iron candlestick in the eastern side of a clean room. Place there a lamp not colored (by lead) and light it. Let the wick of the lamp be of new linen. Also use a small incense-vase. Then burn some incense on vine-slivers. The child shall now be innocent and pure.

Formula: PHISIO IAO AGEANOUMA SKABARO, SKASABROSOU ASABRO, I beg of you on this day, today, at this moment now, the light and the son will shine over this boy, MANE OUSIRIS MANE ISIS, ANOUBIS, servant of the Gods, accomplish this child to go into a trance so he may witness all these Gods, who are all present at these prophecies. Appear before me in this oracle, O' magnanimous God,

Hermes Trismegistus! Let him appear, he who has created the four heavenly regions and the four foundations of Earth, RESENNEETHO BASENERAIPAN THALTHACHTHACHOTHCH CHINEBOTH CHINEBOTH MIMYLOTH MASYNTORI ASTOBI. Come to me, who art in Heaven; come to me, thou who was born from an egg. I know by ENTO TAPSATI LEGENISTHO ELEGE SERPHOUTH MOUISRO LEGE the two Gods who are with you, Tath. The one God is called So, the other Aph; KALOU KAGOEI SESOPHEI BAINCHOOOCH.

The formula to be pronounced: Come to me, Spirit who rises through the sky, during this session with the lamp, which I am performing now, called upon with secret symbols and unpronounceable names and enter this boy's soul, so he may receive an immortal form within a powerful and unspoiled light; since I call upon you in my song: IAO ELOAI MARMACHADA MENEPHO MERMAI IEOR AIEO EREPHIE PHERERHIO CHANDOUCH AMMON EREPNEU ZONOR ALACHAL PERECHAEL SERENOPH DOUNAX ANAXIBOA EREBE BO BEROBIA ANESIODEU IAOA ENIOEAL EMERO MASAIADA.

Come closer to me, O' Lord, carried by immaculate light, without deceit and without fear; materialize before me and your medium, the boy, MARMARIAU ANAPSICHALAO PEOE NIPSEOUA AIETY HARENNOTHESW ANEROPHES ITHYAMAREM OSIER ANAPSICHYON PSYELEMICHALES, manifest!

Repeat such three times. When the child says: "I see your Lord in the Light." say then: "O' holy HYMERI EIGESOU ENTO TERIOUA MENE SOMIOO ALAMAOR CHOCHENEMETOR," and then he will answer...[240]

Magical Love Spells

In contrast to the magical text from the *Ring of Hermes* and the papyrus with the hymn to Hermes as Lord of the world, we find a somewhat strange manuscript. It appears to be an incantation for shy men to marry the women of their dreams. The remarkable thing about it is that it advises *not* to wish for what you so passionately desire. With the correct actions and formulae, the opposite of what you actually wished for will happen. You should, it tells us, put a ring on a sheet of papyrus, and cover it within and without. Make a drawing of the ring and between the outer and inner circles, write the magical formula. In the inner circle, after the notation of the holy names of deities, write what you do *not* wish for—all of this for the time span in which the ring is concealed. On the same papyrus, add a drawing, as illustration, to the inner circle, where you can read: "Let whatever I wish, not take place; and let her not get married forever."[241]

Some of the magical papyri are, indeed, intended to bring together loved ones. One of these describes Isis complaining to her father, Thoth the Great (whom she addresses as Ape Thoth—Thoth as Holy Baboon), about the infidelity of Osiris and his sexual affair with her sister, Nephthys. Isis' application of magic makes Osiris come back to her. We find the same story, although less pronounced, in Plutarch's *On Isis and Osiris*.[242] This magical papyrus supplies three formulas for unfortunate partners that act in a similar way: one for a man to attract a woman, one on how a woman may catch a man, and one for a man to catch a woman. Here is a short piece of the last fomula:

> When a large amount of phlegm is formed within your mouth when you speak, understand she appears to be in trouble and wishes to speak to you. When you yawn repeatedly, she wants to come to you. But if you sneeze two times or more, she is in good health and will return to her home. If you have a headache and cry, she is in peril or even dying.
>
> Rise to Heaven and stimulate the High, after the noble. Descend to the abyss and stimulate Thoth, after Nabin. Stimulate the heart of these two bulls, Hapi and Mnevis. Stimulate the heart of Osiris, after Isis. Stimulate Ra, after the light. Stimulate the heart of N (name of grandmother of the desired woman), who delivered N, whom (again) N delivered.
>
> Say these things in the name of the woman. But if you discuss this woman, say the reverse of what you are doing during your incantation when you arouse the feminine after the male:
>
> When she drinks, when she eats, when she makes love with another, I shall bewitch her heart; I will bewitch the heart of her, I will bewitch her breath, I will bewitch her three hundred and

> sixty-five[243] bodily parts, I will bewitch her inner being… wherever I wish to do so; until she comes to me and I know what lives in her heart, what she does and what she thinks, fast, fast, now, now.[244]

This kind of magical text appears to have quite a different character than the rich content of "philosophical" *Hermetica*. First, it appears that all these affairs belong to the lives of human beings, whether or not they are on the path to a mystical life. Therefore, they definitely have a particular religious connotation. Second, we encounter these magical texts in many forms outside the *Hermetica*, even in early Christianity. In Christian magic of the 1st century B.C., we find abundant and powerful profane magical spells next to devotional petitions. One of the earliest researchers, the German scholar Reitzenstein, found no great joy in collecting these spells (but you must have something for the sake of science...).[245] In Coptic Christian papyri, we see angels (i.e., Gabriel) as well as Egyptian Gods (Ammon and Thoth) being invoked, just as we see in modern publications of Christian magical texts.[246] And, as stated, we find spell formulas for love—even one for men to obtain a male lover![247]

The Christian magical texts are not always as "Christian" as you may expect. Here's one about a certain Maria who, with the help of Jesus, wants to humiliate her rival, Martha, even unto death:

> Maria: Michael, Gabriel, Souleël, you should carry her off as an ulcerating tumor. Raise in fury, humiliate her until a painful death, to prevent the marriage and to punish her, she who brings forth worms. My Lord, Jesus Christ, you should deliver her to her end, yes, Jesus Christ, you should take away her hope, so no one will come to her aid.[248]

The Power of Vowels

In the first magical papyrus, a collection published by Preisendam,[249] a ritual is illustrated that creates a manifestation of a (benign) demon "who will clarify everything for you and be your companion, dine with you and sleep with you."

For the practice of the ritual, you need two of your own fingernails, all of the hair from your head, a falcon, milk from a black cow mixed with Athenian honey, incense, old wine, and a roll of papyrus paper, on which the following should be written with myrrh:

A EE ÉÉÉ IIII OOOOO UUUUUU ÓÓÓÓÓÓÓ.

Then the text continues:

> Write this down in two forms:
>
> A
> E E
> É É É
> I I I I
> O O O O O
> U U U U U U
> Ó Ó Ó Ó Ó Ó Ó
>
> Ó Ó Ó Ó Ó Ó Ó
> U U U U U U
> O O O O O
> I I I I
> É É É
> E E
> A
>
> Take the milk with honey and drink it before sunrise and something divine will enter your heart...

The recital of vowels and writing them down in a certain order appears repeatedly in magical texts. We come across exactly the same vowels in an outline similar to the one above in the *Leidense Wereldschepping* (so named after the storehouse of this manuscript in the Museum of Antiquity in Leiden), where according to Reinhold Merkelbach, the seven vowels stand for the seven planets.[250] In

Maria's Prayer,[251] in the collection of Christian magical texts, we find a similar magical formula:

A	A	A	A	A	A	A
E	E	E	E	E	E	E
É	É	É	É	É	É	É
I	I	I	I	I	I	I
O	O	O	O	O	O	O
U	U	U	U	U	U	U
Ó	Ó	Ó	Ó	Ó	Ó	Ó

The sequence here is the same, but in this case it does not go up from one to seven; it is a continuous sequence of seven expressed in seven tones. Very similar to this is a citation in the Nag Hammadi text, the *Holy Book of the Great, Invisible Spirit*, also called *The Gospel of the Egyptians*. Here we read:

> ...the Father of the light of everything, He who was born out of silence, while He rests in silence. He whose name is concealed in an invisible symbol, (out of which) an occult, invisible mystery was born.[252]

i	i	i	i	i	i	i	i	i	i	i	i	i	i	i	i	i	i	i	i	i	i
é	é	é	é	é	é	é	é	é	é	é	é	é	é	é	é	é	é	é	é	é	é
o	o	o	o	o	o	o	o	o	o	o	o	o	o	o	o	o	o	o	o	o	o
u	u	u	u	u	u	u	u	u	u	u	u	u	u	u	u	u	u	u	u	u	u
e	e	e	e	e	e	e	e	e	e	e	e	e	e	e	e	e	e	e	e	e	e
a	a	a	a	a	a	a	a	a	a	a	a	a	a	a	a	a	a	a	a	a	a
ó	ó	ó	ó	ó	ó	ó	ó	ó	ó	ó	ó	ó	ó	ó	ó	ó	ó	ó	ó	ó	ó

Long before the writing down of magical texts, the Greek philosopher Pythagoras spoke about being in touch with "the harmony of the spheres." Each of these spheres knows its own tone, its own color. This is exactly what we encounter in all of these writings.

Each God has its name and number. By reciting particular vowels, we move into the vibrational sphere of a particular divine (planetary) energy field.[253] This is how the sound uttered by the baboons (symbol of Thoth) made at Egyptian sunrise must have resembled "the tone" of this "sphere." Peter Kingsley describes, in his book *The Dark Places of Wisdom*, how particular sounds and tone scales represented the Gods and were used during the initiation.[254]

The above indicates, as well, that vowel series appear in various different forms—not only in magical texts, but in sacred theosophical writings. In one of the most magnificent hermetic texts, *The Treatise of the Eighth and Ninth Heavenly Sphere*, we find a similar succession of vowels as part of a mystical prayer that is a preface to initiation into the most profound secrets of the universe:

O', power of the mighty,
which is raised above the royal dignities,
more imposing than the honorated,
Zoxathazo
a
òò
ee
òòò
èèè
òòòò
èè
òòòòòò
ooooo
òòòòòò
uuuuuu
òòòòòòòòòòòòòò
Zozazoth.

Lord, grant us wisdom with your power, radiating over us; so we ourselves may describe the perception of the eighth and ninth (Heavenly Sphere).

> We have already reached the seventh sphere, being devout, acting by your law and fulfilling your will at all times.[255]

In the prayer of giving thanks at the end of this Nag Hammadi text, we again encounter a similar saying:

> O' thanks. After all these things, I want to thank you by singing to you a Song of Praise. Since you have given me life. Since you granted me wisdom. I praise Thee; from the bottom of my heart, I evoke thy name:

a

ò

ee

ò

èèè

òòò

iii

òòòò

ooooo

òòòòò

uuuuuu

òòòòòòòòòòò

òòòòòòòòòòò

You are one with Spirit.

With divine adoration, I offer you my hymn of praise.[256]

Religion, philosophy, and magic are intricately linked together here.

CHAPTER 8
THE EMERALD TABLET

Only a year ago, it was silent in the meadows around my home. A ghastly silence. Accustomed as I was to fetching the paper out of my mailbox in the morning and always greeting the cows with a well-meant "Good morning, ladies," I experienced a strange discovery looking at the unoccupied dike. The foot-and-mouth epidemic had hit the countryside hard. But not only the countryside. What repeatedly shocked me was the mere mention of the word "removing," which had been used to describe the destruction of the herds. Even after the pig plague and crazy-cow disease, I still had not gotten used to this word, much less the horrific television images of the claws of heavy equipment holding dead spiritless pigs and cows.

"Removing." Clearing. Making things tidy—a job I find difficult to do myself, because so many items possess a sentimental value for me because they possess a history. But in this case, we speak of animals, living animals, over which we humans seem to think we are lords and masters based on an inscrutable wisdom—as if they were only things. And the wisdom is, indeed, impenetrable, since the ground, the foundation, appears to be knocked out of it.

All this passed through my mind as I tried to find ways to explain that the ancient alchemy of the past was not some kind of child's play, as modern science regards it to be.[257] During the century of "Enlightment," a quarter millennia ago, a split happened that resulted in the eminent science of chemistry evolving out of "an obstinate superstition," the alchemy of the past. Premises held for many centuries were no longer considered valid. And indeed, seen from a technical point of view, the new science meant a huge step forward. In her thesis about a famous alchemist, Dr. Helen de Jong writes:

> From the year 1780 onwards, due to new insights, the role of Alchemy was played out. The difference between Alchemy and

> Chemistry is while Alchemy differentiates matter based on the quality, in which fire, earth, air and water make a compound, Chemistry thinks in quantity and weights. One should consider Alchemy as the first qualitative phase of the modern quantative chemistry.[258]

But there is also something peculiar at hand. We do not notice it anymore, since we are brought up in "enlightened" thinking and have become familiar with the materialistic scientific model. For us, matter is matter. Things are things. We maintain a certain objective distance from things; because of this, we can deal with them mercilessly. This is the great difference between modern science and the era prior to the Age of Enlightenment.

We know from anthropologists that ancient Indian tribes would not saw a branch off a tree without asking permission to do so. Such respect for the living and what looks like dead matter was very common in antiquity, because everything was ensouled by the Divine and the One. We have seen this very clearly in our study of the astrological, medical, and magical formulas in the preceding chapters.

The *Lapis Philosophorum*

If we can assume that things were not considered utterly (souless) matter, it becomes clear that the investigation of matter was coupled with a sense of respect and handled with great carefulness. This also applies to the research of metals as it was practiced in ancient Egypt. Along with China, Egypt is one of the birthplaces of alchemy. Plutarch tells us, in his fascinating legend *On Isis and Osiris*, that the ancient name of Egypt is *chemia*:

> The bull, being kept in Heliopolis called Mnevis and offered to Osiris, is black... Egypt has identical black earth, resembling the blackest part of the eye, chemia. One can compare it with a heart; since it is warm and moist and enclosed by the southern parts of the populated world it borders to, just as the heart is situated on the left side of man.[259]

What speaks for itself is the Greek origin of *chemeia*, meaning "the production of precious metals" (silver and gold). The prefix *al* shows Arab influence, since alchemy was very popular there (*al-chemeia* = the chemistry).

Does alchemy really imply the making of gold and silver, or at least endeavouring to do so? This wide-spread misconception has to do with the unrestrained growth of alchemy in the late Middle Ages and the time thereafter, when every self-respecting monarch employed one or more alchemists to transform simple metals (i.e., lead) into precious ones (i.e., gold). And in those times, there were "alchemists" who occupied themselves solely with the material side of this art. However, much more was happening. The ultimate goal of the true alchemist is to find the *Lapis Philosophorum*, or Philosopher's Stone. The Philosopher's Stone, in its highest conception, is equal to the God Principle. Earlier we saw hermeticists, and not them alone, who ultimately wanted to accomplish a real blending of the initially unconscious, divine aspect of humanity with God in his completeness, expressed in the word ALL. So we read in *Poimandres*: "This is the good end for those who have gained Gnosis—to be made one with God."[260]

Next to immortality of the spiritual body, there was mentioned a second, lower aspect of the Philosopher's Stone—physical immortality, the "universal panacea" (complete medicine) or the "elixir of life" (*aurum potabile*, drinkable gold). The third, even lower, aspect of alchemy is "transmutation"—the transformation of metals. This outer, expressive form of alchemy became the most well known, as I pointed out above. But here lies a hidden spiritual-alchemical meaning as well. For, just as the hermetic axiom says "As above, so below," the investigation of "below" may lead to insight into "above." Handling metals, as well as working with minerals and plants, meant dealing with divine powers.

Keeping this in mind, we can understand the transmutation of simple metals into precious metals as something similar to the inner purification process—purging away the mortal appetites (selfish passions and desires) and transforming them into higher attributes, resulting in total spiritualization, or what is known as self-realization in modern psychology. I am using this modern word, which was not mentioned in classic antiquity, on purpose because, in our time specifically, alchemy has been pulled out of the deepest abyss by psychoanalyst Carl Gustav Jung.[261] His great acute mind realized what he called the "individuation process" that had been expressed in alchemical treatises centuries ago.[262]

We will see various outer aspects of alchemy frequently in the following pages. As mentioned, alchemy has been very popular for centuries, and was often identified with Hermeticism. In this chapter, we will limit ourselves to the earliest links between alchemy and the *Hermetica*—in other words, to Hermes as alchemist.

Hermes as Alchemist

The oldest Western alchemical text known to us is a papyrus text dating to 200 B.C. The title is very meaningful: *Physika kai Mystika* (Physics and Mysticism). The writer is the Egyptian Bolos Democritus[263] from Mendes. He was, according to alchemists of a later date, initiated into the mysteries in the temple of Memphis by "the Great Ostanes." His written work, *Physika kai Mystika,* is more than a chemical and metallurgic recipe book, as were many composed before his time that belong to physics. In the work, Bolos proposes that everything originates from one primordial substance. All of Nature is ensouled. If you are capable of transferring the soul—or spirit, as it is often called—from the one substance into another, you are able to see the change in it—the color, for instance, would literally and figuratively change. Bolos started out with four substances, which he called "bodies" (which, in the light of our premise, is not surprising). These were copper, iron, and pewter, plus two basic colors—gold and silver. He identified lead as a base, a kind of *prima materia* from which all the other metals could be derived. In the process, the colors changed, indicating the various stages of transformation—from black, to white, to yellow, to red.

After Bolos, a series of writings appear under the names of rather diverse characters like Hermes, Agathodaimon, Isis, Cleopatra, Maria the Jewess, and Theophilus. The general consensus in these early writings is that alchemy originated in Egypt and that Hermes was its founder.[264] Hermes is quoted frequently in the oldest alchemical literature, a trend that continued in Arab and medieval texts. Following are just a handful of these alchemical writings from the beginning of our age:

> The great Hermes says: It is the Sun which produces all things.[265]
>
> Hermes has said, indeed, what concerns smoke, in a passage relating to magnesium: Let it burn in a furnace containing peels of the red cobathia. For the white cobathia turns the "body" white.[266]

Indeed, he mentions somewhere: Virginal ground you will find in the tail of Virgo.[267]

Others state, water is dualistic, produced out of two composed elements... the same can be said of the world whose number is One, nevertheless composed out of more elements. Hermes declares the unity of things despite being manifold, is still One.[268]

The early alchemical literature sometimes yields interesting aphorisms dedicated to Hermes, like this one:

> If the body is not spiritualized and the spirit not embodied, the expected result will be nihil.[269]

Or:

> One is the All, by which it is All: For if the All is not the One, the All is nothing.[270]

These aphorisms indicate that hermetic alchemy is not purely a silly notion driven by a fierce passion to create gold. Rather, it is permeated by spirituality. In the *True Book of Sophè*, an anonymous manuscript probably from the 1st century A.D., we read:

> The true book of Sophè, the Egyptian, and of the Hebrew God, Lord of the Powers, Sabaoth—since there are two Sciences and two Wisdom traditions, one Egyptian, the other Hebrew—is more permanent than divine justice. For this most sublime Science and Wisdom pertaining to everything has its root in primordial Time;

> no Master has produced her, she is autonomous. She is immaterial and does not do research on submerged bodies in matter or on ordinary transistories, since she operates independently, not influenced what-so-ever by change. Now you possess it as a gratuitous gift. For surely, they who save and purify the divine soul, imprisoned in the elements and where divine breath is contaminated by the dross of the flesh, we see within the symbol of Chemistry, the essence of the creation of the world; such as the Sun, flower of fire, just as the heavenly Sun as well as the right-eye of the world, such is copper if it is by purification brought into blossom, an earthly Sun. It is king on Earth, just as the Sun is in the heavens.[271]

In this fragment, we can clearly recognize the contours of the "philosophical" *Hermetica*, which we will discuss extensively in the following chapters.

Secret Teachings

It is quite obvious that the spiritual and esoteric character of alchemy led to a kind of secrecy. Magic in antiquity was a very common phenomena for young and old, rich and poor, Greek and "barbarian," Christian and "heathen." The art of alchemy was passed on from father to son, from teacher to disciple. So writes Bolos of Mendes:

> After I had learned things from the here-mentioned Master (Ostanes) and I had become aware of the diversity of matter, I practised making alloys of (forms of) Nature. But then our Master died before finalizing our initiation...[272]

His master died from poisoning caused by an alchemical experiment to separate the soul from the body. This is probably why Bolos warns people "who wish to prepare a remedy for the soul as a way of escape from suffering, without having a well thought-out plan and just following an irrational impulse without being aware of the damage they might create in doing so."[273]

Throughout the centuries, references to secrecy appear frequently in the alchemical literature. On the one hand, the chance of persecution was never absent and, on the other, the esoteric character of the art of alchemy did not easily bear public airing. Moreover, it also required a particular intellectual (and spiritual) development to handle this matter.

The manner of secrecy was diverse. Bachmann and Hofmeier name three methods in their *Secrecy of Alchemy*:

1. Using pseudonyms (i.e. Bolos of Mendes alias Democritus).
2. Employing cryptography through coding: Various signs and transposition into letters and numbers.[274]
3. Magical script: Writings were drawn on material, unreadable without certain applications done first (milk and onion juice were often used, which stayed invisible until heated up).[275]

It is possible that these methods appeared only in later times. Indeed, some later etchings show the alchemist with one hand elevated and one hand covering his mouth. Moreover, there is a fourth method that made reading alchemical writings extremely difficult and still does—writing in allegories. With this in mind, we can now turn to the "Constitution of the Alchemists," the *Tabula Smaragdina*.

A Cave at Hebron

It is quiet in Hebron and outside of it. No opportunity arises to visit the cave where Sarah, wife of the patriarch for Palestinian Muslims as well as for Christians and Jews, made a special discovery. In an open coffin, she found the physical remains of the Thrice-Great Hermes. Despite the fact that he had been dead for several centuries, his body did not show any signs of decomposition. His incorrupt hands held a tablet firmly pressed against his chest—a tablet of precious emerald. On the writing table lay something legible. This something was the *Constitution of Alchemy*. This is the only true part of this legend.[276]

Other sources point to Alexander the Great as the discoverer of the Emerald Tablet. Still others say it was Noah who discovered the

Hermes in his burial tomb with the Book of Wisdom.

Tabula Smaragdina and kept it from the flood in his ark.[277] The most recited story is the one found in Hugo de Santalla's translation from Arabic in the 12th century B.C. of the *Book of the Secret of Creation*, in which Balinus, alias Apollonius of Tyana, talks about his discovery of the grave of Hermes:

> In my city of birth a stone statue was standing on a pillar of gold, on which was written: "Look upon me, I am Hermes, the Thrice-Great in wisdom; I have placed this miraculous sign for everyone to see, veiled with my wisdom so no-one would come near it except a wise Sage as I am."

On the front was written in archaic script:

"Whoever wants to know the secrets of Creation and acquiring more knowledge about the manifestations of Nature, search under my foot."

But the people did not understand what was meant and looked under his foot; they did not find anything.

In such a time, I was weak of mind due to my youth; however, when my spiritual nature matured, I read again what was written on the front of the pillar, contemplating on its significance and I started to dig under the pillar. And behold, I arrived at a subterranean chamber, filled with darkness, no sunbeam entered it although the Sun stood high above it and there were ceaseless blowing winds. It was as if someone had enchanted the winds, as if one had built a house for the wind swirling around continuously and growing in strength. Due to the darkness, I did not have a chance to enter the chamber, and due to the strong wind, not a flicker of light would stay lit. I was powerless and my sorrow great, finally sleep overcame me, when I contemplated with a worried heart the difficult situation I had arrived in. Then an old grey-haired man appeared in front of me having the same posture and body as me; he spoke to me:

"O' Balinus, rise and enter the chamber so you may reap knowledge of the secrets of Creation and manifestation of Nature."

I answered:

"In this darkness I cannot see anything, and a flame will not stay steady because of the strong wind."

Upon which he answered:

"O' Balinus, place your light in a glass container, so you can protect it from the wind and not let it be blown out, thus you obtain light in the darkness!"

After such, I regained my happy composure for I knew I had reached my goal and I said:

"Who are you, to bestow upon me this benevolence?"

He answered:

"I am your own sensitive perfected Self."

After such, I awoke full of joy, placed a light in a glass container, as my spiritual Self had advised me and entered the chamber. And behold, I saw an old man, sitting on a golden throne holding in his hand a plate of green emerald on which one read:

"This is the description of Nature."

In front of him was a book with written words:

"This is the secret of Creation and the Knowledge regarding the cause of all things."[278]

Balinus (Apollonius) carries the book with him and learns the secrets of Creation. He ends the story by saying that his fame was due to the knowledge he acquired.[279]

The plate of green emerald is the *Tabula Smaragdina*. According to one of the publishers and commentators on the text, Julius Ruska, the Emerald Tablet had just as great a value for medieval alchemists as the stone tablets of Moses had for the Jewish people.[280] Our own Dutch professor Gilles Quispel calls it the "Charter of Alchemy."[281]

We don't know how old this writing is. Discovered in 1923, the surviving manuscript is in Arabic, but further research shows it to be of Greek origin. The discoverer, Eric John Holmyard, dates it much earlier than this (around the beginning of our calendar), while Ruska is clearly more cautious. Gilles Quispel, in his erudite essay about the Emerald Tablet, links it with the Nag Hammadi texts from the 2nd century, like the *Gospel from Filippus* and the final edition of the *Gospel of Thomas*.[282]

Here we will discuss the Emerald Tablet because of the notable influence of the "philosophical" *Hermetica* in the work, which will be discussed in following chapters. (I will return in a later chapter to the utmost importance of the Alexandrian Zosimus of the 4th century A.D. for the development of alchemy.) This is not the case in the *Tabula Smaragdina* or Emerald Tablet. Still, there are interesting similarities.

Opposite Page: Symbolic illustration of the 7 steps of Zosimus. At the base of it, one sees a citation from the *Tabula Smaragdina:* "His father is the Sun, his mother is the Moon; the wind carried him in her lap and his nourisher was the Earth."

Sol pater, Luna Mater,
ventus portavit in ventre ſuo, terra eius
nutrix eſt.

Why I Am Called Hermes Trismegistus

After all the round-about motions, it is time to delve into the very text itself:

Where, beyond doubt, surely and actually true;
such which is above, is equal to what is below,
and such which is below, is equal to what is above,
to penetrate the wonders of the One;
and so as all things originated from the One,
by conquest of the One,
so all things were created by this One through adaptation.
His father is the Sun, his mother is the Moon;
the wind carried him in her bosom
and his nourisher was the Earth;
he is the Father of each perfection,
of the final completion of the whole world.
His energy will be complete
when it returns back to the earth.
You will separate earth from fire,
the fine from the gross,
carefully and with great sensitivity;
it rises from the earth to the heaven,
and descends back to earth,
and receives the energy of all energies
which will control every volatile substance
and which will penetrate all solid matter.
So the world was created.
Out of these all miraculous diversities came forth,
of which this is the method.
This is why I am called Hermes Trismegistus,
since I possess three parts of the wisdom of the whole world.
Complete it is now, what I have said about the labour of the Sun.[283]

The hermetic character of this text is clear—and not only because Hermes more or less undersigned it. It was very common in antiquity to use the name of a known figure in attributing one's own work. The New Testament contains a number of letters attributed to Paul that the good man never wrote nor dictated and that, in fact, were written almost a century after his own work.[284] No, we cannot go by mere attribution. But in the words "Such which is above, is equal to what is below, and such which is below is equal to what is above," we recognize the very essence of the *Hermetica*—"As above, so below." In the *Spirit of the All* from the *Corpus Hermeticum*, "such which is above" is called divine and "what is below" is subject to change.[285] The rest is really only an elaboration on the same theme, although not everywhere as clear. In this sense, it is a hermetic, but even more so an alchemical, text. Hidden things are shown.

What other kind of understandings are there? And what is exactly meant? These are questions that have occupied alchemists of all times. They investigated "secret" texts searching for a hidden message or practical advice concealed behind the allegory.

The text is, further, one great Ode to Creation: "The wonders of the One." Great joy literally shines in it. From out of this nucleus of Creation—Neoplatonists and hermeticists called it the One; Christians called it God—came expansion and emanation. "And so as all things originated from the One," for the One, like the Sun, is the engine.

The alchemical character of the text is inherent in the passage about the Sun (fire), the Moon (water), the wind (air), and the Earth (earth). These are the four basic elements of classical science. Sun and Moon stand for day and night, for positive and negative, for male and female, for action and reaction. Sol (Sun) and Luna (Moon) in *coniunctio* (combined) is a frequently used alchemical symbol for unification. Pictures of this dating from the 16th century are very popular. They often decorate the covers of books dealing with alchemy or androgyny.[286]

The typical alchemical element that stands out the most is the separation of fire and earth, of the fine from the gross. About the ascension to Heaven and the descending to Earth, which follows in the text, there is a beautiful citation in the *Corpus Hermeticum*, where we read:

> For thus the Demiurge—I mean the Sun—eternally doth order Heaven and Earth, pouring down the Essences, and taking Matter up, drawing both round Himself and to Himself all things, and from Himself giving all things to all.
>
> For He it is whose goodly energies extend not only through the Heaven and the Air, but also on to Earth, right down unto the lowest Depth and the Abyss.[287]

In *Asclepius*, we find other references:

> All things descend from Heaven to Earth, to Water and to Air. This Fire alone, in that it is borne upwards, giveth life; that which [is carried] downwards [is] subservient to Fire.
>
> Further, whatever doth descend from the above, begetteh; what floweth upwards, nourisheth.[288]
>
> That, then from which the whole Cosmos is formed, consisteth of Four Elements—Fire, Water, Earth, and Air; Cosmos [itself is] one, [its] Soul [is] one, and God is one.[289]

We read in the old hermetic alchemical records that Hermes revealed that "it is the Sun who creates all things"; elsewhere, the Sun is called the "flower of fire." This also gives us a clue to its Egyptian origin with its rich Sun symbology. This is crystallized, as it were, in this line from the *Tabula*:

> Complete it is now, what I have said about the labour of the Sun.

CHAPTER 9
ALL IS ONE

It was a moment of disorientation. On the red-painted wooden floor of the dead and gone New Age Centrum *De Kosmos* on the Prins Hendrikkade in Amsterdam, a select number of highly learned ladies and gentlemen were ready to give lectures about... Hermes Trismegistus. The then seventy-four-year-old Professor Gilles Quispel was the central figure of this special occasion. At the initiative and with the cooperation of the famous Bibliotheca Philosophica Hermetica, he had organized this challenging congress. And the result was clear: Hermes was put permanently on the map in the Netherlands.

HERMES IN AMSTERDAM

Something else significant happened at this international congress. From the hand of Roelof van den Broek and Gilles Quispel, commissioned also by Bibliotheca Philosophica Hermetica, there appeared an impressive Dutch translation of the *Corpus Hermeticum*. This publication was followed some years later by a translation of *Asclepius*, this time by Gilles Quispel himself. And shortly thereafter, there appeared the so-called *Fragments of Stobaeus* and the *Hermetic Definitions*. These key hermetic works are now available in the Dutch language.

Together with the *The Treatise of the Eighth and Ninth Heavenly Sphere* found near Nag Hammadi, these writings are generally considered to encompass the "philosophical" *Hermetica*. Beyond the fact that I question the division of the larger work into tiny sections, these works brought to light another misnomer—they are not necessarily philosophical, but extremely religious. Even Hermes gave this commentary to Asclepius:

> For I will tell thee, as though it were prohetic-ly, that no one after us shall have the Single Love, the Love of wisdom-loving, which consists in Gnosis of Divinity alone—[the practice of] perpetual contemplation and of holy piety. For that the many do confound philosophy with multifarious reasoning.[290]

Asclepius even called the existing (Greek) philosophy *kretology*. "The Greeks, O king, have novel words, energic of 'argumentation' [only]; and thus is the philosophising of the Greeks—the noise of words."[291] We will see that "naked" philosophy was not known by the hermeticists. The reasoning mind was seen as a theurgical tool by which we could learn about the over-seeing God to free our souls from its material bondage.

Now we speak of Asclepius. *Asclepius* is the most extensive hermetic treatise that survives in one piece.[292] The *Corpus Hermeticum* contains seventeen more-or-less independent treatises, but the same can definitely be said of the *Fragments of Stobaeus*. Let us therefore, first have a look at *Asclepius*.

A Talk in the Temple

Four men got together in a temple and started a profound debate, called in the olden days *Logos Teleios*, or *Complete Teachings*. Unfortunately, the Greek version of the *Teachings* has not been preserved and we have to settle for a rather vague Latin translation. Some citations (in Coptic) from the *Asclepius*, also found near Nag Hammadi, show how flamboyant the text was originally.

The *Teachings* are "complete" in so far as Hermes supplies insight into the Creation of the world, the cosmos, and humanity, and explains the word "spirit" and what relation the soul has to humanity and the cosmos. There are "young" and "old" souls. It further explains who or what God really is, and how He is compared to other divine beings and demons who guide men. And finally, Hermes speaks of life and death.

The dialog gives a rather one-sided point of view, in the sense that Hermes is extensively the speaker. Once in a while, Asclepius does make a remark and asks about matters that are not altogether clear to him. Despite the seriousness of the matter, the dialog has a rather easy-going and very warm character. To illustrate this, I will show a part from the very beginning. This begins with a salutation by Hermes:

> God, O Asclepius, hath brought thee unto us that thou mayest hear a Godly sermon, a sermon such as well may seem of all the previous ones we've [either] uttered, or with which we've been inspired by the Divine, more Godly than the piety of [ordinary] faith.
>
> If thou with eye of intellect shalt see this Word thou shalt in thy whole mind be filled quite full of all things good.
>
> If that, indeed, the "many" be the "good," and not the "one," in which are "all." Indeed the difference between the two is found in their agreement—"All" is of "One" or "One" is "All." So closely bound is each to other, that neither can be parted from its mate.
>
> But this with diligent attention shalt thou learn from out the sermon that shall follow [this].
>
> But do thou, O Asclepius, go forth a moment and call in the one who is to hear.
>
> (And when he had come in, Asclepius proposed that Ammon too should be allowed to come. Thereon Thrice-greatest said:)
>
> [Trismegistus] There is no cause why Ammon should be kept away from us. For we remember how we have ourselves set down in writing many things to his address, as though unto a son most dear and most beloved, of physics many things, of ethics [too] as many as could be.
>
> It is, however, with thy name I will inscribe this treatise.
>
> But call, I prithee, no one else but Ammon, lest a most pious sermon on a so great theme be spoilt by the admission of the multitude.[293]

After the men have gathered together, the actual treatise starts. Once in a while, Hermes amiably corrects Asclepius: "Dost not thou see Asclepius, that all has been explained to thee as though to one asleep?"[294] Sometimes the question of Asclepius is so urgent that Hermes has a "consultation" with God:

> Rightly thou questioneth, O [my] Ascelepius! And we pray God that He bestow on us the power of setting forth this reason; since

> everythings depends upon His Will, and specially those things that are set forth about the Highest Whole, the Reason that's the object of our present argument. Hear, then Ascelepius![295]

After this penetrating debate between the four, Hermes ends with a remark about exchanging spiritual nourishment for a more physical kind:

> And now it hath been told you on each several point -as man hath power [to tell], and God hath willed it and permitted it.
>
> This, then, alone remains that we should do—bless God and give Him praise; and so return to taking thought for body ['s comfort].
>
> For now suffiently have we been filled with feast of mind by our discourse on sacred things.[296]

God Is All-Complete in the Fertility of Either Sex

As in almost all hermetic writings, the unity of everything is also the main theme in *Asclepius*. Although different Gods, planets, spirits, demons, humans, animals, plants, and stones exist, everything is created from the One and, as such, is connected with everything else. God originates a "second God," the cosmos, and creates thereby humanity. It is the golden hermetic triangle: God, cosmos, humanity.[297]

> God is the Maker of the Cosmos and of all the things therein; at the same time He ruleth all, with man himself, [who is] the ruler of the compound thing; the whole of which man taking on himself, doth make of it the proper care of his own love, in order that the two of them, himself and Cosmos, may be anornament each unto other; so that from this divine compost of man, "World" seems most fitly called "Cosmos" in Greek.
>
> He knows himself; he knows the World as well. So that he recollects, indeed, what is convenient to his own parts. He calls to mind what he must use, that they may be of service to himself; giving the greatest praise and thanks to God, His Image reverenc-

> ing—not ignorant that he is, too, God's image the second [one]; for that there are two images of God—Cosmos and man.[298]

In short: "God is Himself, the Cosmos is in God; human is in the Cosmos."[299]

Within this, great contextual refinement takes place. The cosmos brings forth many forces and itself is borne out of *Aion*, Eternity. It is wise to keep this trinity in mind in order to better understand the not-so-simple hermetic texts. Cosmos and humanity will be dealt with a bit later. God is first in line.

> Indeed, I have no hope that the Creator of the whole of Greatness, the Father and the Lord of all the things [that are], could ever have one name, even although it should be made up of a multitude—He who cannot be named, or rather He who can be called by every name.[300]

Actually, says Hermes, he should be called by all names!

> For He, indeed, is One and All; so that it needs must be that all things should be called by the same name as His, or He Himself called by the names of all.
>
> He, then, alone, yet all-complete in the fertility of either sex, ever with child of His own Will, doth ever bring to birth whatever He hath willed to procreate.[301]

Asclepius is slightly shocked by this statement.

> Thou speak'st of God, then, O Thrice-greatest one?[302]

Hermes explains to his surprised listeners that, not only is God androgynous, but all that lives is as well. Each is capable of being both, he says; they "...are full of the drive to propagate. And the blending of these two, or better said, their union is beyond comprehension."[303]

And then Hermes uses an unusual comparison:

> I don't have to tell you how great and imposing the power is of this mystery: Everyone, from own experience knows what I mean when he looks at himself and contemplates the sex union between man and woman, which is a symbol of this mystery... At the moment suprême when by repetitive friction we have come so far that the vagina has absorbed the sexual part of the man with great lust and hides it within her, and the two melt together... At that moment the woman absorbs the energy of the man, and as a result the man has an explosion of seeds and receives the passivity of the woman. And they perform this wonderful and irresistible mystery of this true union in private.

The man receives from the woman and the woman receives from the man in complete equality. The heavenly union knows not only her Earthly image; the experience of the bodily union makes it possible to understand something of the cosmic unity. For humanity is made in the image of God and of the cosmos. And so the hermetic circle is once again complete. The above citation is not from the Latin translation of *Asclepius*, but from a fragment discovered near Nag Hammadi, in Coptic script.[304]

The Cosmic Chain

God, capable of being both male and female, gives birth, as it were, to Eternity (*Aion*), out of which flow the cosmos and a great quantity of entities. Or, in the words of Hermes:

> ...There are spiritual Gods who are in charge of all existing phenomena; below these are cosmic Gods who are being ruled by such a God of origin; these cosmic Gods can be seen and reflect their dual origin from spirit and matter. They create all the visible world with each other's help. Each one of them illuminates the region he rules... Mortals are being ruled by mortal beings, who look like them (the daemons).
>
> This is how the Cosmos is put together. Layers of the Being lock into each other from below to above. This is how everything is connected and influences each other, and in such a way, the immor-

tal Gods are linked to all which is mortal and invisible things are connected with invisible beings, all by one chain.

The whole obeys to the highest Ruler, who is the Master, so it does not form a diversity but rather one Unity. Since everything depends on the One and flows forth from it, despite the fact human thinks things show great differences, since human observes them separately. But if human observes the connection between them, they are actually one.[305]

By the way, not only is the sky filled with flocks of angels, good and bad; underneath the earth as well there are active forces, called, in modern esoteric teachings, elementals and elementaries:

Even a kind of living being exists, soulless, however possessing a sense of feeling, expressing itself as expansion when all goes well and contraction and injury when things go bad. With these, I mean the living beings underneath the earth nourishing themselves with roots and stumps. Representatives of this kind are spread all over the world.[306]

Humanity Is a Great Miracle

In the *Hermetica*, humanity is considered, not as the insignificant sinner we see in the teachings of some Christian Church Fathers, but as the image of God, actually a God. As is written in *Poimandres*, a person who has obtained *gnosis*, insight into things, and who has realized his true Self, has become a God.[307] He is akin to the Gods, the above-mentioned energy fields; he is, when he has received *gnosis*, even superior to them:[308]

...He (Human), God has privilege, he alone has received insight and Gnosis. From the beginning, He has bestowed these gifts in great measure with the intention human would be able to control his passions and surpass his shortcomings, as God wills. So he has made the mortal part of human to become immortal. This is why human has become good and immortal by God's hand. He created two natures (physeis), the mortal and the immortal. And so it hap-

> pened, God wanted human to become a more evolved being than the Gods: For the Gods are only immortal, humans in contrary are mortal and immortal. This is why human, as an immortal, is akin to the Gods. They know of each other's doings, with certainty. The Gods know what a human is and humans know what is godly.[309]

Most fascinating is the hidden speculation that God did not create humanity directly, but that he is of the same Being. The Earthly human is the reflection of the heavenly human, who is made by God.

> But All-Father Mind, being Life and Light, did bring forth Man co-equal to Himself, with whom He fell in love, as being His own child; for he was beautiful beyond compare, the Image of his Sire. In very truth, God fell in love with His own Form; and on him did bestow all of His own formations.[310]

This (heavenly) human, *Anthropos*, is the prototype of the Earthly human. "What is Human? The immortal idea of each human," claims one of the *Hermetic Definitions*.[311] We recognize in this reflection the Jewish esoteric concept of the Adam Kadmon,[312] as well as Platonic speculations about the divine world of thought reflected in material form. In an earlier chapter about the hermetic art of healing, we noticed that the same astrological attributes were used for both the heavenly and terrestrial human.[313]

And this is why Hermes can without worry exclaim: "O, Asclepius, human is a great miracle!"[314]

As title for this chapter, I chose *All is One*, the hermetic constitution. In *Asclepius*, this is emphasized over and over by Hermes. The cosmos, flowing out from the Eternity of God is an ensouled and immortal organism for whom death does not exist. Or in the words of Hermes:

> Well now, if the Cosmos is an organic unity, having always been alive in the past, alive in the present and alive in the future, then nothing will actually die in the Cosmos. Each part is alive and is as it is, in a Cosmos forever being One, ensouled and eternally alive: Therefore, in the Cosmos, there is no place for death. It has to be filled to the brim with life, to be able to live forever.[315]

Chapter 10

The Hermetic Body

The temperature is more than thirty-eight degrees Celsius. We have escaped Florence and are in search of a cool place in the hills. The car is actually the coolest place with the air conditioning on full-blast. The hills around Florence are rather steep. We have driven to the hospital Careggi. Not far from here is the villa that Cosimo de' Medici donated to Marsilio Ficino as compensation and thanks for the translation he made of the *Corpus Hermeticum*.[316] We stop at least seven times to ask the local people, but nobody knows anything about it. They have never heard of Marsilio Ficino. Villas? Yes, there are enough of them. Villas of the Medici? Yes. But nothing about the villa used by Ficino as he completed his historic task.

Via narrow one-way roads, we finally drive past the villa, which, as private property, is not accessible to us. The location is magnificent. And indeed, it is somewhat less warm here than in the old city. We visit other Medici villas not far away—wonderful architecture, beautiful gardens, and a fascinating view of the city of Florence, with its red-colored Brunelleschi dome and its elegant Giotto bell tower. And, of course, the Arno, a silver ribbon winding between green hills, pine trees, and cypress fragrant with wild thyme. I think fleetingly that I am in paradise. Is there any better place to recover Hermes from oblivion than in this city of the Renaissance, whose name means "reincarnation"? For more than 1000 years, the *Corpus Hermeticum* had been hidden. Have the Heavens now become old enough, as Isis told her son, Horus, to bring forth worthy souls to rediscover the holy books of Hermes, which have withstood the teeth of time?[317]

The *Corpus Hermeticum*

What is the *Corpus Hermeticum?* A collection of hermetic discourses with various connotations. They were written during the first two centuries A.D., and are more Grecian (less Egyptian) than *Asclepius* and most of the *Fragments of Stobaeus*. This does not mean, however, that an older Egyptian tradition does not exist. To paraphrase Stricker, they are Egyptian of content and Grecian by form.[318]

The name *Corpus Hermeticum* is actually somewhat misleading, for it implies that this collection of *libelli* (books) is the complete handed-down hermetic work. This is most certainly not the case. This is why, in scientific circles, they sometimes talk about the "old" *Corpus Hermeticum* and the *Corpus Hermeticum Novum*. The old *Corpus* encompasses the recently found works *Asclepius*, the *Fragments of Stobaeus*,[319] and the *Corpus Hermeticum* rediscovered in the Renaissance. The *Corpus Hermeticum Novum* contains the three hermetic texts found at Nag Hammadi, the *Hermetic Definitions* (originally known only in Armenian, but recently discovered in Greek), fragments of a *Treatise of the Soul*, Viennese fragments, and some loose material.[320]

For clarity's sake, we will maintain the established term *Corpus Hermeticum* as referring to the Greek treatises translated by Ficino in Florence.

By the way, Ficino delivered a translation of only fourteen discourses, while seventeen appear in more modern publications. After Ficino's translation, more publications appeared in the following decennia, also outside Italy. In some of these, the fourteen *libelli* were augmented with three or four fragments of Stobaeus. The humanist Lodovico Lazarelli added to Ficino's fourteen books an original manuscript, the *Definitions Asclepii*, published in 1507 by Symphorien Champier.[321] This was included, and can still be found, as the sixteenth and seventeenth discourses. (Of the now missing fifteenth discourse, only some of the earlier Stobaeus fragments remain.) Much later, another discourse was added, which was then called the eighteenth.[322]

Greek Herdsman or Egyptian *Gnosis*?

It may be coincidental, but the last three discourses of this work are the least interesting from a hermetic point of view.[323] The first fourteen books are very impressive. The *Corpus* starts with a treatise called *Poimandres*. This was also the name Ficino used for his complete publication of the fourteen codices under the name *Pimander*.[324] Poimandres was traditionally translated as "herdsman" (from the Greek "shepherd") until Peter Kingsley wrote an article in 1993 that shook the tree of science pretty hard when he stated that the name is not Greek at all, but pure Egyptian: *P-eime-nte-Re* ("knowledge (*gnosis*) of Re").[325] This emphasized the Egyptian influence of the *Hermetica* and also the Greek *Corpus Hermeticum*. The *Poimandres*, which we will soon discuss further, contains a direct revelation of divine consciousness to Hermes Trismegistus. There is, in the *Corpus Hermeticum*, another treatise that reflects a direct revelation to Hermes—the eleventh discourse entitled *Mind unto Hermes*. The other books are composed of instructive lectures from Hermes to his pupils, in particular to his son, Tat, and sometimes to Asclepius. Most discourses are almost entirely monologs interrupted once in a while by a question, and dialogs in the Platonic style.[326]

We will try—by means of the *Corpus Hermeticum* where it is illustrative, and aided by the *Asclepius*, the Stobaeus fragments, and other hermetic writings—to give an idea of the thinking and life of the hermeticists at the beginning of our calendar. At a later stage, we will determine if these thoughts are time-related or universally valid.

The Gnostic *Hermetica*

As *P-eimente-Re* already implies, *Poimandres* is a typical Gnostic manuscript. But this actually pertains to the whole *Hermetica*. The word "gnostic" is derived from the Greek word *gnosis*, meaning knowledge or insight. The classical assumption is that someone who has gnosis knows how things fit together—has insight into the more profound background of God, the world, and humanity. Those with gnosis know where they come from, who they are, and what their destiny will be. Gnosis cannot be learned at school or universities (although this knowledge can help to create order in the mind); gnosis is primarily an experience of consciousness. This is why gnosis is really of all times and of all cultures. It is the deep inner knowing that has guided people since time memorial.

Primarily within Christianity, gnosis has had a bad reputation for centuries, since Church Fathers considered it "heresy," a deviation from the normal pattern. They wrote colossal works "against the heresy" of the gnosis.[327] Yet, in the 19th century, interest in gnosis started to grow again. And when in 1945, in Egypt at Nag Hammadi, a vase was found containing fifty or more hermetic texts, it led to a great revival of interest in the phenomenon of gnosis.

The reason why gnosis was considered threatening in various religious traditions (not only in Christianity, but also in Islam) has to do with its teaching of salvation. Those who possess gnosis, insight into all things, are capable of transforming themselves into better human beings. They do not need mediators in the form of priests or intercessors like saints. This "personal salvation," as it was scornfully called (and still is) in certain circles, stands opposite to the thought that humanity is by nature sinful and can only hope for salvation by means of religious rules or by believing in the sacrifice of Jesus Christ. Within this paradigm, God weighs the pros and cons in his mind and is therefore considered to be completely different and apart from humanity. The Gnostic (and hermetic!) opinion is that human beings can become Gods. This is—although mostly unconsciously—considered within religious circles to be blasphemy.

It seems as if, within Gnosticism, humanity is equal to God. Nothing is less true. Practically all Gnostic and hermetic writings speak with great reverence of the One—whom they hesitantly dare to call God—because no name justifies the majestic power of the Nameless One by whom everything is, was, and will eternally be.

The great difference lies in the way of thinking about and experiencing humanity in relation to God. In the usual Christian theology, God is *other*—a totally different entity; in Gnosticism, God is in All, including humanity. Everything comes from God and carries something of the Divine within His/Her being. I use the term His/Her on purpose, since God, certainly in the *Hermetica*, is experienced as androgynous.[328] The One is not He and not She, but goes beyond this illusory duality.

Gnosticism, therefore, is not to be learned, although schools of initiation have always existed that helped humanity find a path to self-realization. Let us be very clear: in Gnosticism, self-knowledge is knowledge of God. "He who knows himself, knows the All," says one of the *Hermetic Definitions*.[329] "He who thinks he knows the All, but not himself, completely lacks understanding," says Jesus in the *Gospel of Thomas*.[330] By knowing your own deepest self—or, better said, by experiencing it—you get to know the All and also God. For, as Hermes teaches his son, Tat, "even if what is inside of you is invisible, how else could He (God) as He really is become visible before your eyes?"[331]

Before we go deeper into the content and spiritual meaning of the hermetic writings, it is wise first to study the background and environment in which these writings were formed. "Egyptian in content, but Grecian by form" means that Egyptian thought patterns and traditions have been poured into a Greek mold. You could almost say that, in the first two centuries of our calendar, Thoth has been put into a modern jacket. A century ago, many scientists—starting with Causaubon, but particularly Festugière—stared themselves blind looking at this new jacket. All the attention paid to this specially measured suit resulted in the Egyptian Hermes becoming ultimately invisible. Let us pay attention first to the outside cover, and then look at the underlying content.

City of Many Streams

One place that is inseparably connected to the *Hermetica* is Alexandria, which was, at the beginning of the 1st century A.D., a metropolis. The city probably counted almost a million inhabitants—an incredibly large population for its time. Situated on the Nile delta, it was a very accessible city. We know that the Greeks always chose their strongholds with great care. For we tend to forget that, although this city is situated in Egypt, the Greeks founded it in 332 B.C. Although primarily populated by Egyptians and Greeks, many Jews lived there as well—some estimate as many as three to four thousand. Of course, there were also Romans. And then there were the tradesmen from the East.

Alexandria enjoyed a rich commerce with Asia from as far away as India that also left many traces in the culture. It was inevitable that the thought patterns that we identify as "the wisdom of the

East" would become known in certain Alexandrian circles. There must certainly have been Eastern writings kept in the famous Alexandrian libraries.[332] A teacher of Clemens of Alexandria, Pantaenus, was active as a teacher in the East long before he became the predecessor of Clemens as head of the *Academia* (Christian catechismal school).[333] Unfortunately, we do not possess a written legacy of Pantaenus.[334] We do have those of Clemens, his pupil, who, probably following his tutor's example, is the first Westerner to mention Buddha in his writings.[335]

Roelof van den Broek, in his captivating article about Hermes and his community in Alexandria,[336] tells us that the authentic Egyptians lived in the suburb of Rakotis, where a large temple to Serapis was situated. Serapis had been elevated to "God of the State" under the reign of the Ptolemies, the Greek rulers of Egypt after the conquest of Alexander the Great. In this *Serapeion* there was an enormous, easily accessible library. There were also cells where people could withdraw for a time to devote themselves to the deity.

In the 1st century B.C., the philosopher Eudorus of Alexandria had breathed new life into Plato's teachings, although with additions of elements from the *stoa*. Philo of Alexandria became very successful with these. In a recently published book, Dutch scholar Henk Spierenburg shows that Philo was acquainted with the Kabalistic tree of life, only known in literature later, during the 14th century.[337] Spierenburg shows that the six human principles that Philo mentions in his book agree exactly with those in the Eastern *Vedanta*.[338]

A bit further in this book, I will show the correspondence between the seven-fold constitution of humanity put forward by the Alexandrian hermeticists and the theosophical teachings based on the Eastern wisdom. This fascinating, mutually beneficial influence between East and West was at first considered impossible by materialistically orientated science, but it is gradually coming to be generally accepted. Even Van den Broek considers it a possibility now.[339] It would indeed have been quite inconceivable that, in a cosmopolitan city like Alexandria that was exposed to and greedily absorbed so many diverse wisdom traditions, the Eastern writings would not have been studied. If the greatest library ever known in the West had not been lost to us, we would certainly have visible proof of this.

In "that swelling tidal pool of esoteric religions," as American scholar Bentley Layton called it,[340] Gnosticism thrived. The illustrious Valentine was an Egyptian and the same was true of the legendary Basilides. They lived and worked during the 2nd century B.C., the period of the completion of specific sections of the *Hermetica* (certainly the *Corpus Hermeticum*). A century later, we see Plotinus giving instruction in the same city. The very influential founder of Neoplatonism was a student of Ammonius Saccas, who worked during the day as a carrier of bales in the harbor of Alexandria and at night was a gifted and inspiring teacher. In his audience, besides Plotinus, was a certain Origines. This Christian teacher, successor of Clemens at the Academia, can easily be called one of the greatest Christian thinkers and mystics of all time. All of this was possible and indeed occurred in Alexandria, in the land of Egypt, as Hermes so sadly meditates:

> O' Land of Egypt, O' Land of Egypt. Your Gods will become a myth out of forgotten times. Your divine liturgies, your deeply impressive ceremonies and holy revelations, will be for the descendants incomprehensible hieroglyphs, which are chiselled out of stone, and admired by tourists.[341]

An Introduction to Alexandria

Many Gnostic wisdom teachings became well known through the mystery schools in which they were used.[342] There must have been hermetic mystery schools in Alexandria.[343] In this community, "The Way of Hermes" meant "climbing up" to a higher form of consciousness. The teachings of Hermes Trismegistus must have occupied a central position. What we see immediately is that several levels of teachings existed: for laymen, for advanced practitioners, and for the initiated. Typical iniation literature is found in some books of the *Corpus Hermeticum*[344] and especially in the *Treatise of the Eighth and Ninth Heavenly Sphere*. The teachings for the laymen embrace a part of the known *Hermetica*, including the already mentioned astrological, medical, magical, and alchemical material.

It is an established fact that a sort of introductory course existed as a kind of stepping stone to a "higher" level—a kind of propedeuse, shall we say. In the literature, this basic course is called the *General Teachings*. We find repeated references to these so-called *General Teachings* in the *Corpus Hermeticum*,[345] but also in the Stobaeus fragments[346] and in very small sections of at least ten of the hermetic treatises called the Viennese fragments.[347]

In accordance with the Egyptian practice of living chambers,[348] libraries must have been present in the hermetic circles in Alexandria. We have the written testamony of Clemens of Alexandria, in which he mentions forty-two books of Hermes that were stored in Egyptian temple archives,[349] as well as books dedicated to Asclepius. In a letter to King Ammon, he appears to have written:

> Hermes, my master, in many a conversation, both when alone, and sometimes, too, when Tat was there, has said, that unto those who come across my books their composition will seem most simple and [most] clear; but, on the contrary, as 'tis unclear, and has the [inner] meaning of its words concealed...[350]

In the *Treatise of the Eighth and Ninth Heavenly Sphere*, Hermes refers to the books that candidates for initiation had to read before they were ready for the "higher work": "...it is by loving it, you remember the progress which you experience due to the wisdom in the books."[351]

The disciple answers thus: "O' my Father, the progress I booked so far and the pre-knowledge I gained from the books, supercedes the shortcoming I once possessed... I understand now only the beauty which I gathered from them."[352]

Completely in accordance with the information Clemens offers, Hermes asks the disciple after the initiation: "O' my Son, write this book destined for the temple of Diospolis in hieroglyphs and call it the 'Eighth reveals the Ninth.'"[353]

The ritual is empowered with the writing of an oath on the book "so whoever reads the book will not misuse the name or (misuse it) against the law of destiny."

The oath goes like this:

I swear,
by Heaven and Earth
and Fire and Water
and the seven powers of Nature
and the demiurgical Spirit
who is therein,
and the sleeping God,
and the Self-awakened
and those who have been raised by him,
whoever wants to read this holy book,
will respect the things Hermes has proclaimed.[354]

Reading the "holy" books must have been considered a sort of propedeuse to the forthcoming initiation.[355] Moreover, the reading of the books had to prevent the disciple from "flipping," or suffering negative consequences during the mystical experience, as happened once in a while with mystics who showed up completely unexpected and unprepared.[356]

A Universal School of Wisdom

Garth Fowden writes, in his interesting study about the Egyptian Hermes, that, in hermetic circles, various levels of teaching and spiritual revelation existed side-by-side: "There is no reason whatsoever why we cannot imagine Initiates in the technique of Astrology and Alchemy would sit together at the foot of a disciple of Hermes with others who were eagerly awaiting for more in-depth spiritual knowledge."[357]

We just spoke about the introductory course, the *General Teachings*. In these lectures, references are often made to astrology, magic, and alchemy. The manuscripts we know where references are made to the *General Teachings* elaborate further on these subjects.

Exactly how the hermetic circles (in the modern approach to the *Hermetica*, it is common to talk about "lodges") looked in practice is hard to reconstruct. A number of elements are traceable. The word "lodge" *avant la lettre* is meaningful—like the modern lodges of Rosicrucians, Freemasons, and Theosophists—when we take into account that the teachings are given at various levels (possibly along with initiation rituals). In all probability, the Alexandrian hermetic circles may have provided an opportunity for the spiritually advanced to stay in residence temporarily. Some treatises suggest that the teacher (Hermes) would embroider on his revelations of the day before:

> I gave the Perfect Sermon (Logos) yesterday, Asclepius; today I think it right, as sequel thereunto, to go through point by point the Sermon about Sense.[358]

And a day later:

> Hermes. My yesterday's discourse (logos) I did devote to thee, Asclepius, and so 'tis [only] right I should devote today's to Tat...[359]

Sometimes a disciple refers to a teaching of the previous day:

> O' my Father, yesterday you promised me you would guide my consciousness into the eighth and after such allow me to enter the ninth. You said this was the order of tradition.[360]

Aside from these written references—for after all, the time line is vague—we have no proof that, far away from Alexandria on the banks of Lake Mareotis, a community that was a counterpart of the Palestinian Essenes settled that was in possession of the *Therapeutics*. Philo describes these in his *Vitae contemplativa*. We already discussed that the Serapeion contained cells where one could retreat for a short or extended period of time. We also know that, in the ancient initiation rites, mystics sometimes stayed within the walls of a convent for a long time. Therefore, it seems plausible to assume that this was also true in hermetic circles.

And so, the contours are beginning to show themselves. In Alexandrian hermetic circles, various rooms must have been set aside for different purposes—most likely a reception area for obtaining information about hermetic Theosophy, a place where one could pay homage to Thoth-Hermes, and another where "practical" hermetic writings were found. Surely there was a location for the (weekly?) gatherings of advanced disciples. They likely came together after the advanced teachings of the day and possibly after admitting new "brothers" into the circle to consume a holy meal. It is important here to note the similarity to the earliest Christian communities.[361] And there was an "inner group," those who delved even deeper into the secrets of Hermes. In this group, the higher initiations would take place, as we will describe next. The highest initiations, according to classical custom,[362] would have taken place one to one—between a disciple and a teacher who instructs and, as the case may be, provides guidance toward an ecstatic vision.

The bond between members was expressed in the "holy kiss" given prior to a meal, but also before and after a prayer.[363] This kiss also sealed the vision to which the disciple was guided by the teacher, as we will see later.

CHAPTER 11
A DIVINE REVELATION

Once, when mind had become intent on the things which are, and my understanding was raised to a great height, while my bodily sneses were withdrawn as in sleep, when men are weighed down by too much food or by the fatigue of the body, it seemed that someone immensely great of infinite dimensions happened to call my name and said to me:

"What do you wish to hear and behold, and having beheld what do you wish to learn and know?"

"Who are you?" said I.

He said, "I am Poimandres the Nous of the Supreme. I know what you wish and I am with you everywhere."

"I wish to learn," said I, "the things that are and understand their nature and to know God. O' how I wish to hear these things!"

He spoke to me again. "Hold in your Nous all that you wish to learn and I will teach you."

When he had thus spoken, he changed in form and forthwith, upon the instant, all things opened up before me; and I beheld a boundless view. All had become light, a gentle and joyous light; and I was filled with longing when I saw it. After a little while, there had come to be in one part a downward moving darkness, fearful and loathsome, which I experienced as a twisting and enfolding motion. Thus it appeared to me.

I saw the nature of the darkness change into a watery substance, which was indescribably shaken about, and gave out smoke as from fire, culminating in an unutterable and mournful echo. There was sent forth from the watery substance a loud inarticulate cry; the sound, as I thought, was of the light.

Out of the light came forth the Holy Word which entered into the watery substance, and pure fire leapt from the watery substance

> and rose up; the fire was insubstantial, piercing and active. The air, being light, followed the breath, and mounted up 'till it reached the fire, away from earth and water, so that it seemed to be suspended from the fire. The earth and water remained in their own place mingled together, so that they could not be distinguished, and they were kept in motion by the breath of the Word, which passed over them within hearing.
>
> Poimandres spoke to me and said:
>
> "Have you understood what you have seen and what it means?"
>
> "I shall come to know it," I said.
>
> "That light," he said, "is I, Nous, your God, who was before the watery substance which appeared out of the darkness; and the clear Word from Nous is the Son of God."
>
> "How can this be?" said I.
>
> "Know this," he said, "That which sees and hears within you is the Word of the Lord, and Nous is God the Father. They are not seperate from each other, for their union is life."
>
> "Thank you." I said.
>
> "But perceive the light and know it," said Poimandres.[364]

So begins *Poimandres*, the first book of the *Corpus Hermeticum*. Hermes is meditating when his consciousness overflows in the Consciousness of the All. He sees unspeakable things. He is allowed to throw a glance into the birth chamber of Creation. In a split second, he experiences the creation of the cosmos, the world, heavenly humanity, and terrestrial humanity.

> And I began to preach to men the Beauty of Devotion and of Gnosis: O ye people, earth-born folk, ye who have given yourselves to drunkenness and sleep and ignorance of God, be sober now, cease from your surfeit, cease to be glamoured by irrational sleep.[365]

After this vision, he is commissioned to become a guide for others. A holy duty.

The Cause of Everything

It is understandable that Marsilio Ficino published his work in the 15th century under the name of *Pimander,* for in this so attractive first book of the *Corpus* lies the nucleus of hermetic thought. But not more than this. In the following pages, we will try, by means of exact citations, to reflect the thought patterns of the *Hermetica*, starting with the golden triangle: God, cosmos, and humanity.

As was stated before, the hermetic literature speaks only with the greatest respect and reverence for God, or whatever He may be called. Numerous lyrical hymns are sung to Him/Her.[366] God is the Supreme Good. Everything is in God. God is the cause of All:

> Her. God, therefore, is not Mind, but Cause that the Mind is; God is not Spirit, but Cause that Spirit is; God is not Light, but Cause that the Light is...[367]

For God is the All and the All emanates from him, and everything is determined by his Will. He, who is All, is good, beautiful, wise, original, self-conscious, known only by himself and no-one else. Without him nothing would ever exist and will never be. For everything is from Him, in Him, and by Him. From Him come all different and many types and forms of attributes, great quantities, immeasurable distances, and all forms manifesting themselves.[368]

> When someone asked Hermes what God is, he answered:
> "The maker of the All,
> the all-knowing Consciousness,
> for eternity."[369]

Hermes tries many times to explain metaphorically to Tat (and Asclepius) what God really is, sometimes in a form-giving manner:

> And, thus, think from thyself, and bid thy soul go unto any land; and there more quickly than thy bidding will it be. And bid it journey oceanwards; and there, again, immediately 'twill be, not as if passing on from place to place, but as if being there.

And bid it also mount to heaven; and it will need no wings, nor will aught hinder it, nor fire of sun, nor æther, nor vortex-swirl, nor bodies of the other stars; but, cutting through them all, it will soar up to the last Body [of them all]. And shouldst thou will to break through this as well, and contemplate what is beyond—if there be aught beyond the Cosmos; it is permitted thee.

Behold what power, what swiftness, thou dost have! And canst thou do all of these things, and God not [do them]?

Then, in this way know God; as having all things in Himself as thoughts, the whole Cosmos itself.

If, then, thou dost not make thyself like unto God, thou canst not know Him. For like is knowable to like [alone].

Make, [then,] thyself to grow to the same stature as the Greatness which transcends all measure; leap forth from every body; transcend all Time; become Eternity; and [thus] shalt thou know God.

Conceiving nothing is impossible unto thyself, think thyself deathless and able to know all—all arts, all sciences, the way of every life.

Become more lofty than all height, and lower than all depth. Collect into thyself all senses of [all] creatures—of fire, [and] water, dry and moist. Think that thou art at the same time in every place—in earth, in sea, in sky; not yet begotten, in the womb, young, old, [and] dead, in after-death conditions.

And if thou knowest all these things at once—times, places, doing, qualities, and quantities; thou canst know God.[370]

Therefore, for the initiated, God is to be "understood":

For It doth will to be, and It is both Itself and most of all by reason of Itself. Indeed, all other things beside are just because of It; for the distinctive feature of the Good "that it should be known." Such is the good, O Tat.

TAT. Thou hast, O father, filled us so full of this so good and fairest Sight, that thereby my mind's eye hath now become for me almost a thing to worship.

For that the Vision of the Good doth not, like the sun's beam, fire-like blaze on the eyes and make them close; nay, on the contrary, it shineth forth and maketh to increase the seeing of the eye, as far as e'er a man hath the capacity to hold the inflow of the radiance that the mind alone can see.

Not only does it come more swiftly down to us, but it does us no harm, and is instinct with all immortal life.[371]

God Is in Each Atom

God is for all time, even for the non-initiated, visible by His/Her creation!

First of all, God can be seen in the awe-inspiring cosmos, in magnificent Nature, in the human body, and in animals, plants, and minerals.

But if what is within thee even is unmanifest to thee, how, then, shall He Himself who is within thy self be manifest for thee by means of [outer] eyes?[372]

Her. Is God unseen?

Mind. Hush! Who is more manifest than He? For this one reason hath He made all things, that through them all thou mayest see Him.

This is the Good of God, this [is] His Virtue—that He may be made manifest through all.

For naught's unseen, even of things that are without a body. Mind sees itself in thinking, God in making.[373]

But if thou wouldst Him also contemplate, behold the ordering of the Cosmos, and [see] the orderly behaviour of its ordering; behold thou the Necessity of things made manifest, and [see] the Providence of things become and things becoming; behold how Matter is all-full of Life; [behold] this so great God in movement, with all the good and noble [ones]—gods, daimones and men!

Tat. But these are purely energies, O father mine!

Her. If, then, they're purely energies, my son—by whom, then, are they energised except by God?

Or art thou ignorant, that just as Heaven, Earth, Water, Air, are parts of Cosmos, in just the selfsame way God's parts are Life and Immortality, [and] Energy, and Spirit, and Necessity, and Providence, and Nature, Soul, and Mind, and the Duration of all these that is called Good?

And there is naught of things that have become, or are becoming, in which God is not.

TAT. Is he in Matter, father, then?

HER. Matter, my son, is separate from God, in order that thou may'st attribute unto it the quality of space. But what thing else than mass think'st thou it is, if it's not energised? Whereas if it be energised, by whom is it made so? For energies, we said, are parts of God.

By whom are, then, all lives enlivened? By whom are things immortal made immortal? By whom changed things made changeable?

And whether thou dost speak of Matter, or Body, or of Essence, know that these too are energies of God; and that materiality is Matter's energy, that corporality is Bodies' energy, and that essentiality doth constitute the energy of Essence; and this is God—the All.[374]

THE MANIFOLD COSMOS

We saw in the first discourse of the *Corpus Hermeticum* how Hermes came into contact with the highest consciousness in the shape of *Poimandres*. In the eleventh book of the same collection, another meeting occurs between the Thrice-Great Hermes and the highest consciousness, called simply "Spirit." Here again, Hermes' consciousness flows with the All Consciousness (in the form and name of "Spirit"), thereby gaining deep knowledge and insight. What concerns the cosmos, Hermes is told, is an image of Eternity; and this is the image of God. And this reveals a wonderful unfolding of profound esoteric knowledge. I will again let the text speak for itself—first, because it is incredibly beautiful, and second, because I want to prevent a cut-and-dried explanation. May the wisdom unfold itself in your own consciousness, as was customary in the hermetic circles.

MIND. Hear [then], My son, how standeth God and All.

God; Æon; Cosmos; Time; Becoming.

God maketh Æon; Æon, Cosmos; Cosmos, Time; and Time, Becoming.

The Good—the Beautiful, Wisdom, Blessedness—is essence, as it were, of God; of Æon, Sameness; of Cosmos, Order; of Time, Change; and of Becoming, Life and Death.

The energies of God are Mind and Soul; of Æon, lastingness and deathlessness; of Cosmos, restoration and the opposite thereof; of Time, increase and decrease; and of Becoming, quality.

Æon is, then, in God; Cosmos, in Æon; in Cosmos, Time; in Time, Becoming.

Æon stands firm round God; Cosmos is moved in Æon; Time hath its limits in the Cosmos; Becoming doth become in Time.

Æon, moreover, is God's image; Cosmos [is] Æon's; the Sun, of Cosmos; and Man, [the image] of the Sun.

The people call change death, because the body is dissolved, and life, when it's dissolved, withdraws to the unmanifest. But in this sermon (logos), Hermes, my beloved, as thou dost hear, I say the Cosmos also suffers change—for that a part of it each day is made to be in the unmanifest—yet it is ne'er dissolved.

These are the passions of the Cosmos—revolvings and concealments; revolving is conversion and concealment renovation.

The Cosmos is all-formed—not having forms external to itself, but changing them itself within itself. Since, then, Cosmos is made to be all-formed, what may its maker be? For that, on the one hand, He should not be void of all form; and, on the tother hand, if He's all-formed, He will be like the Cosmos. Whereas, again, has He a single form He will thereby be less than Cosmos.

What, then say we He is? —that we may not bring round our sermon (logos) into doubt; for naught that mind conceives of God is doubtful.

He, then, hath one idea, which is His own alone, which doth not fall beneath the sight, being bodiless, and [yet] by means of bodies manifesteth all [ideas]. And marvel not that there's a bodiless idea.[375]

Where Heaven Fell in Love with Earth

Everything originates in God, the Supreme Good, thus God is by definition good. This means that the Creation, starting off with the cosmos, is in reality "okay." "Nothing exists where God does not live," says the *Hermetic Definitions*.[376] Thus, there is a remarkable difference between this and certain Gnostic movements that consider the cosmos (and everything derived from it—Earth, humanity, etc.) as bad. According to this opinion, these things have not been created by God, but by a demi-god—a sort of shadowy God, a demiurge.

During the 2nd century, in classical Gnosticism, the rift between the Creator and Creation expanded greatly due to the emergence of numerous intermediary stages or levels of existence called *aeons*. The spiritual world is filled with *aeons*, emanations of God (usually called "Spirit" in classical Gnosticism)—as many as 356. The last and least powerful emanation is responsible for the creation of the cosmos and the previously ruling demi-god. In this dark shadowy world, numerous powers exist that are ultimately responsible for the material creation of humanity and all that lives on Earth. In such a scheme, the highest Being, Spirit (or God) is definitely very far separated from humanity. We do not have the space here to delve into the more intrinsic meanings behind these teachings.[377] But I can say this: some are more negative than is suggested here; others are less so. It is a different way of thinking and describing the universe. Even in the *Hermetica*, we encounter passages where humanity is described as being "bad,"[378] and it appears that only ascetics can assure an escape from the great poverty of matter.[379] In contrast, there are writings that show nothing but elaborate praise for humanity.[380]

Nevertheless, what I outlined above is not applicable to all ancient gnosis. Outside the *Hermetica*, there are also positive Gnostic statements about body and soul,[381] while inside the *Hermetica*, we find writings that contain quite negative descriptions of Earth and the human body.[382] The philosophy of those days reflects the same differences. So the sober *stoa* clearly had a more negative outlook than, for example, the Neoplatonists. Just like the hermeticists, the Neoplatonic philosopher Plotinus recognizes the One, from which all emanates.[383] And if the One is good, it follows that Creation is also good. In *Poimandres*, the first book of the *Corpus Hermeticum*, heavenly humanity even falls in love with Nature. Heaven and Earth become lovers!

> But All-Father Mind, being Life and Light, did bring forth Man co-equal to Himself, with whom He fell in love, as being His own child; for he was beautiful beyond compare, the Image of his Sire. In very truth, God fell in love with His own Form; and on him did bestow all of His own formations.
>
> And when he gazed upon what the Enformer had created in the Father, [Man] too wished to enform; and [so] assent was given him by the Father.
>
> Changing his state to the formative sphere, in that he was to have his whole authority, he gazed upon his Brother's creatures. They fell in love with him, and gave him each a share of his own ordering.
>
> And after that he had well learned their essence and had become a sharer in their nature, he had a mind to break right through the Boundary of their spheres, and to subdue the might of that which pressed upon the Fire.
>
> So he who hath the whole authority o'er [all] the mortals in the cosmos and o'er its lives irrational, bent his face downwards through the Harmony, breaking right through its strength, and showed to downward Nature God's fair Form.
>
> And when she saw that Form of beauty which can never satiate, and him who [now] possessed withing himself each single energy of [all seven] Rulers as well as God's [own] Form, she smiled with love; for 'twas as though she'd seen the image of Man's fairest form upon her Water, his shadow on her Earth.
>
> He in his turn beholding the form like to himself, existing in her, in her Water, loved it and willed to live in it; and with the will came act, and [so] he vivified the form devoid or reason.
>
> And Nature took the object of her love and wound herself completely round him, and they were intermingled, for they were lovers.[384]

The more matter, in a systematic build-up, is separated from God, the more points of friction appear. In concrete language, this means that, in the material world, several forces are battling to get the upper hand. The "mortal" aspect and the "immortal" aspect of the human consciousness are in disharmony with each other. Gnosis creates an awareness of this disharmony that allows it to be resolved. We will speak about this now while discussing the human "part."

God's Grandchild

> God, Cosmos and Man are grades of being. Each is a sun, as it were, in their operations, or powers or rays. God's rays are His energies or self-realising operations; those of Cosmos are the natures of things, those of Man are the arts and science.[385]

In the preceding chapter, we discussed Hermes calling humanity "a great wonder." To be human is to be mortal in body and immortal in spirit. But to be human is not a static state. Humanity changes. It can lean toward matter[386] or reach out for God. The material body has been formed by matter, but the spirit has been breathed in by higher powers. This pure Gnostic postulate is found unabridged in the *Hermetica*, presented in a less dualistic manner than in Christian Gnosticism. It seems, just as in ancient Gnosticism, as if there are two creators when Hermes teaches Tat:

> For the one created with the first essence, which is bodiless, the other created itself with bodily essence, which is self-propagating.[387]

Everything, however, does return to the One.

Isis tells Horus how human attributes have been infused:

> "Then sending for me," Hermes says, "He spake: 'Soul of My Soul, and holy mind of My own Mind, up to what point, the nature of the things beneath, shall it be seen in gloom? How long shall what has up to now been made remain inactive and be destitute of praise? Bring hither to Me now, My son, all of the Gods in Heaven.' said God'—as Hermes saith."
>
> And when they came obedient to His command—"Look down," said He, "upon the Earth, and all beneath." And they forthwith both looked and understood the Sovereign's will. And

when He spake to them on human kind's behalf, they [all] agreed to furnish those who were to be, with whatsoever thing they each could best provide.

Sun said: "I'll shine unto my full."

Moon promised to pour light upon the after-the-sun course, and said she had already given birth to Fear, and Silence, and also Sleep, and Memory—a thing that would turn out to be most useful for them.

Cronus announced himself already sire of Justice and Necessity.

Zeus said: "So that the race which is to be may not for ever fight, already for them have I made Fortune, and Hope, and Peace."

Ares declared he had become already sire of Struggle, Wrath, and Strife.

Nor yet did Aphrodite hesitate; she also said: "I'll join to them Desire, my Lord, and Bliss, and Laughter [too], so that our kindred souls, in working out their very grievous condemnation, may not exhaust their punishment unto the full."

Full pleased were all, my son, at Aphrodite's words.

"And for my part," said Hermes, "I will make men's nature well endowed; I will devote to them Prudence and Wisdom, Persuasiveness and Truth, and never will I cease from congress with Invention, but ever will I benefit the mortal life of men born underneath my types of life. For that the types our Father and Creator hath set apart for me, are types of wisdom and intelligence, and more than ever [is this so] what time the motion of the Stars set over them doth have the natural power of each consonant with itself."

And God, the Master of the universe, rejoiced on hearing this, and ordered that the race of men should be.[388]

God's grandchild was born![389]

Consciousness versus Godlessness

Humanity differs from the animals and plants because our souls hold self-consciousness capable of slowly unrolling itself like a serpent.

> For where is Soul, there too is Mind; just as where Life, there is there also Soul.
>
> But in irrational lives their soul is life devoid of mind; for Mind is the in-worker of the souls of men for good—He works on them for their own good.
>
> In lives irrational He doth co-operate with each one's nature; but in the souls of men He counteracteth them.
>
> For every soul, when it becomes embodied, is instantly depraved by pleasure and by pain. For in a compound body, just like juices, pain and pleasure seethe, and into them the soul, on entering in, is plunged.
>
> O'er whatsoever souls the Mind doth, then, preside, to these it showeth its own light, by acting counter to their prepossessions, just as a good physician doth upon the body prepossessed by sickness, pain inflict, burning or lancing it for sake of health.
>
> In just the selfsame way the Mind inflicteth pain upon the soul, to rescue it from pleasure, whence comes its every ill. The great ill of the soul is godlessness; then followeth fancy for all evil things and nothing good.
>
> So, then, Mind counteracting it doth work good on the soul, as the physician health upon the body.[390]

If reason does not rule self-consciousness, it will become irrational.

> But whatsoever human souls have not the Mind as pilot, they share in the same fate as souls of lives irrational.
>
> For [Mind] becomes co-worker with them, giving full play to the desires towards which [such souls] are borne—[desires] that from the rush of lust strain after the irrational; [so that such human souls,] just like irrational animals, cease not irrationaly to rage and lust, nor ever are they satiate of ills.[391]

It is interesting to read, in a letter from Asclepius to King Ammon, that a connection is made between the godless humanity and natural disasters:

> Morever, as His Light's continuous, so is His Power of giving Life to lives continuous, and not to be brought to an end in space or in abundance.
>
> For there are many choirs of daimons round Him, like unto hosts of very various kinds; who though they dwell with mortals, yet are not far from the immortals; but having as their lot from here unto the spaces of the Gods, they watch o'er the affairs of men, and work out things appointed by the Gods—by means of storms, whirlwinds and hurricanes, by transmutations wrought by fire and shakings of the earth, with famines also and with wars requiting [man's] impiety—for this is in man's case the greatest ill against the Gods.
>
> And under Him is ranged the choir of daimons—or, rather, choirs; for these are multitudinous and very varied, ranked underneath the groups of Stars, in equal number with each one of them.
>
> So, marshalled in their ranks, they are the ministers of each one of the Stars, being in their natures good, and bad, that is, in their activities (for that a daimon's essence is activity); while some of them are [of] mixed [natures], good and bad.
>
> To all of these has been allotted the authority o'er things upon the Earth; and it is they who bring about the multifold confusion of the turmoils on the Earth—for states and nations generally, and for each individul separately.
>
> For they do shape our souls like to themselves, and set them moving with them—obsessing nerves, and marrow, veins and arteries, the brain itself, down to the very heart.[392]

How humanity can keep itself aloft in this enormous energy field—yes, even gaining control of it—we will discuss in the following chapter. There seems to be only one true way out of this dilemma. Hermes teaches Tat that all prayers are fruitless if they are not applied practically:

> There is just one service of worshipping God: To be a good human.[393]

Chapter 12
Hermetic Instructions

During the many conversations Hermes holds with his disciples Asclepius and Tat—and sometimes with others—on just about all kinds of topics, he comes to consider the profound how and why of existence. In this chapter, we will discuss some of these issues with the help of selected citations.

Why Evil?

Religion, philosophy, and psychology have kept themselves, each in its own way, busy with evil. What purpose does evil serve? If, as religion teaches, God is good and almighty, why does something described as evil even exist? Why does He allow evil to exist in the world? This is indeed the same question that Asclepius poses to Hermes: "Is God not capable of cutting and removing evil away from this reality?"[394] Hermes' answer is amazingly simple:

> They say that God ought to have freed the World from bad in every way; for so much is it in the World, that it doth seem to be as though it were one of its limbs.
>
> This was foreseen by Highest God and [due] provision made, as much as ever could have been in reason made, then when He thought it proper to endow the minds of men with sense, and science and intelligence.[395]

Evil therefore has a purpose in the world. Diversion from evil stimulates gnosis. This is one of the first steps on "the Way of Hermes," the path to self-realization. Or, as expressed so concisely in the *Hermetic Definitions*: "Evil is the absence of good!"[396] So, whoever performs good work shies away from evil. Humanity itself chooses between good and evil:

> ...for 'tis not God, 'tis we who are the cause of evil things, preferring them to good.[397]

Evil is not directly created by God, for "God has only one passion, the Good."[398] It does appear, however, as Hermes tells Asclepius, during the course of evolution:

> And do not thou be chary of things made because of their variety, from fear of attribution of a low estate and lack of glory unto God.
>
> For that His Glory's one—to make all things; and this is as it were God's Body—the making [of them].
>
> But by the Maker's self naught is there thought or bad or base.
>
> These things are passions which accompany the making process, as rust doth brass and filth doth body; but neither doth the brass-smith make the rust, nor the begetters of the body filth, nor God [make] evil.

Fortasse Licebit, Hermes chases away Evil, in the shape of the Devil.

It is continuance in the state of being made that makes them lose, as though it were, their bloom; and 'tis because of this God hath made change, as though it were the making clean of genesis.[399]

The Liberating Insight

To turn evil into good, humanity must first become aware of good and evil. We have to eat from the tree of knowledge, gnosis. We have to awaken from our sleep and drunken state of being. Hermes calls out: "And I began to preach to men the Beauty of Devotion and of Gnosis: O ye people, earth-born folk, ye who have given yourselves to drunkenness and sleep and ignorance of God, be sober now, cease from your surfeit, cease to be glamoured by irrational sleep!"[400]

Do not think the path of gnosis is free of pain. Humanity, Hermes tells Tat, is prone to suffer due to its nature.

> All things incorporal when in a body are subject unto passion, and in the proper sense they are [themselves] all passions.
>
> For every thing that moves [another] is incorporal; while every thing that's moved is body.
>
> Incorporals are further moved by Mind, and movement's passion.
>
> Both, then, are subject unto passion—both mover and the moved, the former being ruler and the latter ruled.
>
> But when a man hath freed himself from his body, then is he also freed from passion.
>
> But, more precisely, son, naught is impassible, but all are passible.
>
> Yet passion differeth from passibility; for that the one is active, while the other's passive.
>
> Incorporals moreover act upon themselves, for either they are motionless or they are moved; but whichsoe'er it be, it's passion.
>
> But bodies are invariably acted on, and therefore are they passible.
>
> Do not, then, let terms trouble thee; action and passion are both the selfsame thing. To use the fairer sounding term, however, does no harm.[401]

In *Asclepius*, Hermes teaches the same escape from suffering:

> But when unknowingness and ignorance persist, all vicious things wax strong, and plague the soul with wounds incurable; so that, infected with them, and invitiated, it swells up, as though it were with poisons—except for those who know the Discipline of souls and highest Cure of intellect.
>
> So, then, although it may do good to few alone, 'tis proper to develop and explain this thesis: wherefore Divinity hath deigned to share His science and intelligence with men alone. Give ear, accordingly![402]

A Cauldron Filled with Consciousness

Liberating insight, gnosis, has been given by God to humanity. Sometimes the question is raised when studying Gnostic writings whether they are applicable to everyone, or if only a select group is eligible to come into contact with gnosis. I must say, the *Hermetica* makes a more positive statement about a general salvation than the authors of some Nag Hammadi manuscripts. Indeed, a certain exclusivity is apparent here and there in the *Hermetica*, but after taking a closer look, we discover in almost all cases that the general welfare is the main goal. However, this is a state that has to be earned. Gnosis does not fall from the sky. You have to become conscious of it. Only then can it be born in yourself. This is the general principle of the hermetic writings and it is described very graphically in the fourth discourse of the *Corpus Hermeticum*, entitled "The Cauldron":

> He filled amighty Cup with it, and sent it down, joining a Herald [to it], to whom He gave command to make this proclamation to the hearts of men:
>
> Baptise thyself with this Cup's baptism, what heart can do so, thou that hast faith thou canst ascend to Him that hath send down the Cup, thou that dost know for what thou didst come into being!
>
> As many then as understood the Herald's tidings and doused themselves in Mind, became partakers in the Gnosis; and when they had "received the Mind" they were made "perfect men."

> But they who do not understand the tidings, these, since they possess the aid of Reason [only] and not Mind, are ignorant wherefore they have come into being and whereby.[403]

Listen to your inner voice; pay close attention to the call. This is almost exactly the same kind of hermetic axiom as "as above, so below" and "who knows himself knows the All." And it is definitely the most active of the three. You have to bring yourself into action. The hermetic Theosophy points to a living experience, not to the dead letter. This also explains what, at first glance, seems to be an apparent paradox that we encounter in specific texts (sometimes in one and the same treatise). The words serve as a metaphor for a more profound reality, which is only known (made conscious) by experiencing it. This is exactly what we see in the hermetic circles—the reading of books to open the soul, then the *General Teachings* to ripen the soul, and, only after this, the actual rising of the soul. More about this later.

Death Does Not Exist

Whoever possesses gnosis does not have to fear death anymore. In the conversation in the temple, Hermes educates his disciples about physical death:

> The expectation and the fear of death torture the multitude, who do not know True Reason.
>
> Now death is brought about by dissolution of the body, wearied out with toil, and of the number, when complete, by which the body's members are arranged into a single engine for the purposes of life. The body dies, when it no longer can support the life-powers of a single man.
>
> This, then, is death—the body's dissolution, and the disappearance of corporeal sense.
>
> As to this death anxiety is needless. But there's another [death] which no man can escape, but which the ignorance and unbelief of man think little of.[404]

What Hermes actually says is that death does not exist at all:

> For there's no death for aught of things [that are]; the thought [this] word conveys, is either void of fact, or [simply] by the knocking off a syllable what is call "death," doth stand for "deathless."
>
> For death is of destruction, and nothing in the Cosmos is destroyed. For if Cosmos is second God, a life that cannot die, it cannot be that any part of this immortal life should die. All things in Cosmos are parts of Cosmos, and most of all is man, the rational animal.[405]

Life is the making-one of Mind and Soul; accordingly Death is not the destruction of those that are at-oned, but the dissolving of their union.[406]

Since:

> Naught is there in it throughout the whole of Æon, the Father's [everlasting] Re-establishment—nor of the whole, nor of its parts—which doth not live.
>
> For not a single thing that's dead, hath been, or is, or shall be in [this] Cosmos.
>
> For that the Father willed it should have Life as long as it should be. Wherefore it needs must be a God.[407]

Dead matter does not exist! And this calls for our respect.

The Immeasurable All-Consciousness

The word "soul" has been used many times so far in this study. In the *Hermetica,* a lot is said about the soul. It is the "middle part," the link between body and spirit. The term "spirit" has caused many misunderstandings, as we have noticed.[408] Many of its usages are confusing. By spirit, we sometimes mean God; at other times, we use it to mean the (All)-Consciousness. The term God is theological. But ancient Gnosticism speaks more of spirit than of God as being the highest principle to avoid confusion between "Spirit" and the theological "personified God."

The *Hermetica*, which is neither a religion nor a theology, speaks freely about God, using many other terms with the same meaning, like "the One."

In the hermetic philosophy, everything streams forth from the One and carries something of the One within itself—consciously or unconsciously. In classical Gnosticism, this is usually called *pneuma*, the breath of spirit (spirit is also *pneuma* in Greek). Thus the breath of Spirit forms a soul and this soul incarnates in an Earthly body.

Now, the division into body, soul, and spirit is definitely not uniquely hermetic. We discover it, for example, in the New Testament of the Christian Bible, as well as in Plato and Aristotle, who go even further and divide the soul into three parts: a rational soul as the highest part, a vegetative soul as the lowest, and the "animal" or perceptive soul in between. This applies, in other terminology, to the disciples of Ammonius Saccas, the Neoplatonist Plotinus, and the Christian Father Origines as well.[409] I come back to this in the next chapter, since these observations, of course, are also found in the *Hermetica.*

The *Hermetica* knows that the first principle—God, the One, or however it may be called—contains within itself *Nous*. The Greek word *Nous* is translated by most scientists as "spirit" or "consciousness," depending on the context.[410] Remember, the *Hermetica* did not flow from the pen of one single writer.

In our texts, *Nous* almost always means "consciousness"—the consciousness of Spirit, total Consciousness, or more exactly put, All-Consciousness. The One is All-Consciousness. The All-Consciousness is found in all that flows from God, who is, by definition, All. All things, therefore, carry something of the All-Consciousness in themselves, but never in the pure unfiltered form, as is present in the One. In essence, a "compression" takes place depending on how great the distance of separation is from the One. The cosmos is already "compressed"—obscured, as it were—and humanity is even less transparent. The Light of the All-Consciousness is too strong to be carried unveiled in the passive body:

It is, son, in a body made of earth that this arrangement of the vestures comes to pass. For in a body made of earth it is impossible the mind should take its seat itself by its own self in nakedness.

For neither is it possible on the one hand the earthy body should contain such immortality, nor on the other that so great a virtue should endure a body passible in such close contact with it. It taketh, then, the soul for as it were an envelope.

And soul itself, being too a thing divine, doth use the spirit as its envelope, while spirit doth pervade the living creature.

When then the mind doth free itself from the earth-body, it straightway putteth on its proper robe of fire, with which it could not dwell in an earth-body.

For earth doth not bear fire; for it is all sen in a blaze even by a small spark. And for this cause is water poured round earth, to be a guard and wall, to keep the blazing of the fire away.

But mind, the swiftest thing of all divinge outthinkings, and swifter than all elements, hath for its body fire.

For mind being builder doth use the fire as tool for the construction of all things—the Mind of all [for the construction] of all things, but that of man only for things on earth.

Stript of its fire the mind on earth cannot make things divine, for it is human in its dispensation.[411]

The astral body is partially identified, in modern esotericism, as what we understand as the *aura*. It is also called the subtle body, which is wrapped around the gross material body. It is also the principle of vitality (*prana)* that, as it were, nourishes the human body.

Thus, it appears to be necessary that the soul functions as a filter for the spirit. And a soul without the presence of spirit (or consciousness) is diminished; it is a divine law: "The soul enters by necessity the body, but Consciousness (*Nous*) enters the soul by judgement."[412]

By the way, consciousness is reserved strictly for human souls.

But in irrational lives Mind is their nature.[413]

But whatsoever human souls have not the Mind as pilot, they share in the same fate as souls of lives irrational.

> For [Mind] becomes co-worker with them, giving full play to the desires towards which [such souls] are borne—[desires] that from the rush of lust strain after the irrational [so that such human souls], just like irrational animals, cease not irrationality to rage and lust, nor ever are they satiate of ills.[414]

> For Darkness will be set before the Light, and Death will be thought preferable to Life. No one will raise his eyes to Heaven; the pious man will be considered mad, the impious a sage; the frenzied held as strong, the worst as best.[415]

The Bottomless Reservoir of the All-Soul

However strange it may sound, the soul existed even prior to the appearance of humanity. Soul was first called "human." Only at a later date were bodies formed in which the soul could be found:

> ...When God had created the Cosmos first, the one and only, he observed how beautiful it was, filled with good things, He admired it and loved it as his own child. Therefore, He decided, with his Almightiness and Goodness, another being should arrive, born out of Him, to observe the Cosmos (and to admire it and love it). At once, He created Human, who could contemplate God's thoughts and take over His care for the world. I said "at once" because He immediately accomplishes what He wills, when He decides, it happens instantaneously. He made him "spiritual," meaning to say: As a soul, and He noticed human could not take care of everything if He did not clothe him in a material covering: This is why He covered the soul of the first human with a body as it's habitation.[416]

In the propedeuse of the hermetic circles, the disciple is made to understand that all individual souls, as well as those of the animals, originate in the soul of one All-Soul. With separation from the All-Soul and the individualization of the soul, the differences become visible:

HER. For it is possible, my son, that a man's soul should be made like to God, e'en while it still is in a body, if it doth contemplate the Beauty of Good.

TAT. Made like to God! What dost thou, father, mean?

HER. Of every soul apart are transformations, son

TAT. What meanest thou? Apart!

HER. Didst thou not, in the General Sermons, hear that from One Soul—the All-Soul—come all these souls which are made to revolve in all the cosmos, as though divided off?

Of these souls, then, it is that there are many changes, some to a happier lot and some to [just] the contrary of this.[417]

In actuality, what you read here is that there are not only individual souls, but also an All-Soul—a great reservoir of souls, as it were—out of which soul substance is being individualized into a temporary state of separateness. Like the ocean and each drop of water. The individualized parts of the All-Soul all want to return to their origin, the reservoir. The wailing of the soul is shown very graphically in the *Korè Kosmou, Virgin of the World*, when it is asked to reincarnate:

Listen, my son Horus, for you will hear now a secret scene, given by Hermes to the patriarch Kamephis...

I watched a scene of souls about to be locked into bodies. Some of them wailed and complained. Others resisted their fate, like noble animals, caught by clever hunters and dragged from their familiar habitat. One soul screamed and called out, looking from above to below: "O' Heaven, fountain-source of Existence, brightly shiny stars and eternal Sun and Moon, Light and Life-Breath of the One, all of you who partake of this home of ours—how cruelly we are torn away from such heavenly splendour! We are being chased away from this holy atmosphere and away from this blissful life we are leading here to be enclosed in a minimal and distressing place. What strenuous demands await us? What kind of dreadful actions shall we have to undertake to be able to supply the needs of a body which will soon disintegrate?"[418]

Forgetfulness

When a soul individuates, it arrives in a kind of forgetfulness. It becomes unaware of its origin. This scene is reproduced very beautifully, but also poignantly, in the *Discourse of the Soul*[419] found near Nag Hammadi, in which the soul becomes more and more forlorn until the moment it remembers the "home of the Father"—the beginning of the path to liberation. As Hermes teaches Tat, the soul, which originated in the All-Soul, carries consciousness and gnosis in itself; but when it descends into the Earthly body, a great forgetfulness comes over it—not directly with conception or at birth, but in the first life phase:

> Her. Behold an infant's soul, my son, that is not yet cut off, because its body is still small and not as yet come unto its full bulk.
>
> Tat. How?
>
> Her. A thing of beauty altogether is (such a soul) o see, not yet befouled by body's passions, still all but hanging from the Cosmic Soul!
>
> But when the body grows in bulk and draweth down the soul into its mass, then the soul cut off itself and bring upon itself forgetfulness, and no more shareth in the Beautiful and Good. And this forgetfulness becomes vice.[420]

Therefore, not all the powers of the soul enter at conception or at birth:

> The powers which accompany the soul do not enter all at once. Some enter the soul at birth and influence the irrational parts of the soul. The purest forces enter only at adolescence and co-operate with the mental part of the soul.[421]

There is always talk of development. This development can be active in the motion toward gaining more consciousness. The veils then grow thinner and thinner. The development can also be passive, unconscious. The soul is then vegetative and the forgetfulness becomes strong.

> The soul, which is incorporeal, has its own veils, which are immaterial. These veils are the veils of the soul's own "breath of life." When they wear thin and transparent, the soul is intelligent. When they are thick and muddy, as the air during stormy weather, the soul can not see far and is only conscious of what is about it.[422]

During the "transition"—what people call death—the Earthly body binds itself again to matter. The soul flies away. Where? This depends on the acquisition of consciousness during its life. In most cases, says Hermes, it will be toward another human body. We will talk about this in the next chapter.

Chapter 13

A Secret Doctrine

George Robert Stowe Mead was a scholar. Born on March 22, 1863 in Nuneaton in England, the young Mead studied at the Rochester Cathedral School and later at St. John's College at Cambridge, where he changed his original study of mathematics to classical languages. When he completed his studies at Cambridge, he read the *Esoteric Buddhism* of A. P. Sinnett,[423] an English magazine publisher in India. This book made a deep impression on him. He immersed himself in Eastern philosophy and, besides holding a job in education, he began a study of philosophy at Oxford.[424]

George Mead met Helena Petrovna von Hahn, better known as Madame Blavatsky, for the first time in May 1887. Two years later, he entered full-time employment as her secretary. This turned out to be of short duration, because H. P. B., as insiders called her lovingly, died on May 8, 1891.

Nevertheless, Mead remained active in the Theosophical circle that had formed around Madame Blavatsky. He was an early editor of the *Theosophical Review* together with Annie Besant, became president of the Theosophical Society, and later assumed sole editorship the *Review*. He was also responsible, along with the same Annie Besant, for the publication of the remaining notes and writings of Blavatsky, a part of which were published under the title *The Secret Doctrine III*. Mead was also chairman of the Blavatsky Lodge in London and later of the British and even European section of the Theosophical Society.[425] One year after the death of Blavatsky, Mead published his first essay (about Simon the Magician) and many more publications followed.

Mead's 1896 translation of the *Pistis Sophia* is remarkable; his *Fragments of a Faith Forgotten* concerning ancient Gnosticism was extremely influential; and in 1906, he produced a translation (plus commentary) of the *Corpus Hermeticum*, *Asclepius*, and the hermetic *Fragments of Stobaeus* and other ancient writers.[426] Mead is universally praised for his beautiful translations, and numbers Roelof van den Broek and Gilles Quispel among his admirers. Mead knew his subject. He was a Classicist and Theosophist in the broadest sense of the words. A beautiful combination.

Reincarnation and Karma

We will meet George Mead again in the second part of this book. I introduce him at this point for a special reason. With his commentary and translation of the Hermetic writings, his thoughts, in all probability, must have dwelled on the book that brought him into contact with the Theosophy of the day—*Esoteric Buddhism* by A. P. Sinnett. In it, Sinnett discusses subjects that were totally unknown to the West. Today, you can go into any bookstore and find popular books about reincarnation, despite the opposition to these ideas from religion and science. Do not forget that, after the Age of Enlightment, the ideas of reincarnation and karma were almost unknown in Western Europe and the United States until Sinnett, and specifically Blavatsky, reintroduced them to the West. It was, in those days, *bon ton* in better circles to ask with a laugh: "How is your karma today?"[427]

We also encounter karma and reincarnation in the *Hermetica*. Hermes teaches about those who live without God or holy commandment:

> Tris. [To those], however, who have lived in other fashion impiously—[to them] both is return to Heaven denied, and there's appointed them migration into other bodies unworthy of a holy soul and base; so that, as this discourse of ours will show, souls in their life on earth run risk of losing hope of future immortality.[428]
>
> Thou see'st, son. how many are the bodies through which we have to pass, how many are the daimones, how vast the system of the star-courses [through which our Path doth lie], to hasten to the One and Only God.[429]

We have to reincarnate as many times as is needed until we meet up with our true destiny. This is a long process. In the tenth discourse of the *Corpus Hermeticum*, entitled "The Key," Hermes teaches Tat about reincarnation:

> The soul in man, however—not every soul, but one that pious is—is a daimonic something and divine.
>
> And such a soul when from the body freed, if it have fought the fight of piety—the fight of piety is to know God and to do wrong to no man—such soul becomes entirely mind.
>
> Whereas the impious soul remains in its own essence, chatised by its own self, and seeking for an earthy body where to enter, if only it be human.
>
> For that no other body can contain a human soul; nor is it right that any human soul should fall into the body of a thing that doth possess no reason. For that the law of God is this: to guard the human soul from such tremendous outrage.[430]
>
> Wherefore, my son, thou shouldst give praise to God and pray that thou mayst have thy mind Good [Mind]. It is then, to a better state the soul does pass; it cannot to a worse.[431]

Purification

Humanity has been gifted with self-consciousness and can break up the spiral of birth, death, and repeated reembodiment.[432] In the East, this is called the path of purification, the discarding of *karma*. In popular esotericism, it is often stated you have to work off your (wrong) actions in the next life. This is indeed the same warning Hermes gives to humanity, and the same that Isis gave to Horus:

> Be aware you will now get the retribution of what you did before, primarily through incarnation.[433]

Christian doctrine states that wrong-doings will be punished in the hereafter. We also find the doctrine of a *kama-loka*, a place of purification, in more serious esoteric literature. You can also read about it in *Esoteric Buddhism* (and the works of Blavatsky), which is why Mead would not have been so surprised when he read in *Asclepius*:

> [And as to the punishments] they're all the more severe, if in their life [their misdeeds] chance to have been hidden, till their death. For [then] they will be made full conscious off all things by the divinity, just as they are, according to the shades of punishment allotted to their crimes.[434]

According to Hermes, God has appointed a sort of ruling judge over souls, who examines, together with each deceased, his or her past Earthly life. If it has been a pious life and the newly arrived soul has fulfilled its destiny as a person, then the soul will occupy the place "belonging to her."[435] In the reverse case, the sould will go to a place of purification where it will suffer at the hands of punishing angels.[436] This is an old archetypal image we encounter in many writings, and also in Gnostic texts.[437]

This theme has been magnificently and extraordinary paraphrased in one of the *Hermetic Definitions*:

> Similar to a body appearing full-grown from the mother's womb, so a soul will only escape the body (after the series of reincarnation) when it is has been perfected. And just as the body, which comes out immature, is imperfect and needs a new body. The knowledge of Beingness perfects the soul. Just as you treat your soul during your life's span, so the soul will treat you after your death.[438]

A more lucid and shorter description of karma and reincarnation can hardly be found anywhere.

Reincarnation should not be confused with spiritual rebirth. Spiritual rebirth stops reincarnation. This is why world teachers like Jesus did not speak outright about reincarnation, only about spiritual rebirth, which is the ultimate goal of humanity. Spiritual rebirth is the state of being completely self-realized—a state in which the person becomes a God. Hermes speaks of spiritual rebirth thus: "This is, my son, Rebirth—no more to look on things from body's view-point (a thing three ways in space extended)."[439] He asks Tat, after having completely initiated him: "Dost thou not know thou hast been born a God, Son of the One, even as myself?"[440]

A Well-Kept Secret

During our discussion about the soul, we read that Plato and Aristotle, and later also Plotinus and Origines, agreed on the three-fold composition of the soul.[441] In the *Hermetica*, in some instances, there is also talk about several "parts of the soul," as is stated in *Asclepius*.[442] Also in the fourth excerpt of Stobaeus we find talk of a three-fold soul—a divine (spiritual) soul; a human (embodied) soul, and an irrational (animal) soul.[443] And Asclepius teaches Ammon that daemons penetrate "the *emotional* and *passionate part* of the soul," but that "the *spiritual part*" cannot be controlled by them.

> For on each one of us being born and made alive, the daimones take hold on us—those [daimones] who are in service at that moment [of the wheel] of Genesis, who are ranged under each of the Stars.
>
> For that these chage at every moment; they do not stay the same, but circle back again.
>
> These, then, descending through the body to the two parts of the soul, set it awhirling, each one towards its own activity.
>
> But the soul's rational part is set above the lordship of the daimons—designed to be receptacle of God.[444]

This is not unimportant, for it means a three-fold character is given to the soul in accordance with the philosophical and religious tenets of the day.

But there is more. Agathodaimon, father and teacher of Hermes, must have said once: "The soul is situated in the body, the spiritual Consciousness (*Nous*) in the soul and the *Logos* in the spiritual Consciousness.

> Her. Soul is in Body, Mind in Soul; but Reason (Logos) is in Mind, and Mind in God; and God is Father of [all] these."[445]

Hermes then explains this to Tat:

> The Reason, then, is the Mind's image, and the Mind God's [image]; while Body is [the image] of the Form; and Form [the image] of the Soul.
>
> The subtlest part of Matter is, then, Air; of Air, Soul; of Soul, Mind; and of Mind, God.[446]

Logos is the principle that reveals the consciousness (*Nous*) of God. So when we acquire consciousness (*Nous*), we address the highest part of our being. We then carry consciously within ourselves the "image of God." Outside *Nous* and *Logos*, there is mention of the soul, air, and matter (the material body). Arranged from the bottom up, you then get:

a. Body and air
b. Soul
c. Logos
d. Nous

Earlier we saw that the soul is three-fold. But there are actually seven principles. The answer to this lies within the book called "The Key," where we read:

> Now then principles of man are this-wise vehicled: mind in the reason (logos), the reason in the soul, soul in the spirit, [and] spirit in the body.
>
> Spirit pervading [body] by means of veins and arteries and blood, bestows upon the living creature motion, and as it were doth bear it in a way.[447]

We see here the same division: *Nous*, *Logos*, soul, and body, but air has also been added. This is here called "(life) breath." And this breath is nothing other than the astral body mentioned in many hermetic treatises[448] that nourishes the material body.[449] In the East, they have a special name for it: *prana*.

As said, we find the crucial passage in "The Key," a key that rightfully locked away a centuries-old secret. The hermeticists knew seven principles, a seven-fold composition of humanity:

1. Material body
2. Astral body (life breath, *prana*)
3. Animalistic (passionate) soul
4. Emotional (human) soul
5. Mental and spiritual (highest) soul
6. Logos
7. Nous

As a young man, George Mead became fascinated by the *Esoteric Buddhism* of A. P. Sinnett. He read in it, among other things, about reincarnation and karma. But he also read something else—something that was worked out later in a masterful way by the woman whom he served as secretary for several years. He read that humanity possessed a seven-fold constitution—not the five of Plato, Aristotle, and Origenes (body, three-fold soul, spirit), but seven. Since Sinnett was an editor in India, he used Sanskrit as well as English words to denote the seven principles: *rupa, prana, linga sharira, kama rupa, manas, buddhi,* and *Atma.*[450] In later theosophical works, other names are used (primarily translations), but the seven-fold scheme, based on the old Eastern principles, was always kept.

About 1500 years prior to Sinnet's *Esoteric Buddhism* and Blavatsky's *Secret Doctrine,* Hermes taught a seven-fold constitution of humanity.

Truly a well-kept secret.

CHAPTER 14

THE MYSTERY OF THE SELF

As we saw before, the hermeticists considered the cosmos to be a living organic system. The stars, planets, and zodiacal signs—yes, even the "divine" decanates and degrees—were seen as the outer faces of divine energy fields. Each disciple within the hermetic circles must have been exposed to this knowledge. The writings in the previous chapters on astrology, healing arts, magic, and alchemy would certainly not have been absent in the library of the lodge.

The divine energy fields—let's call them that for the sake of convenience—were energies corresponding to the force fields in and around humanity itself. Someone, for instance, might have been born with a strong Mars influence, meaning the person was born in the period when the Sun stood in Mars, sign of Aries, or had Aries as an Ascendant, or had Mars placed in a prominent place in the horoscope (in the First House, for instance). This person would have characteristics connected with the Mars energy. In principle, each person possesses all characteristics, but certain particulars can be more pronounced than others.

Each person, in the Theosophy of the *Hermetica,* has to deal with the "bad" influences of all these various deities (heavenly bodies), starting with the most pronounced. Some negative traits belonging to Mars energy, for instance, are temper, anger, hotheadedness; some of the positive energies are courage and resilience. A Mars person should, in the first place, reckon with the negative aspects of this energy by learning how to control the passions, transfer hotheadedness into friendliness, and stimulate courage and resilience. Immediately following, the influence of the other heavenly bodies will be worked out.

The Ascension after Death

In the *Hermetica*, as well as in ancient gnosis, we see that the confrontations between these named energies are visible on two fronts: in everyone's daily lives, and when our time has arrived and we are approaching death. Hermes asks Poimandres how this comes about:

> Well hast thou taught me all, as I desired, O Mind. And now, pray, tell me further of the nature of the Way Above as now it is [for me].
>
> To this Man-Shepherd said: When thy material body is to be dissolved, first thou surrenderest the body by itself unto the work of change, and thus the form thou hadst doth vanish, and thou surrendeest thy way of life, void of its energy, unto the Daimon. The body's senses next pass back into their sources, becoming separate, and resurrect as energies; and passion and desire withdraw unto that nature which is void of reason.
>
> And thus it is that man doth speed his way thereafter upwards through the Harmony.
>
> To the first zone he gives the Energy of Growth and Waning; unto the second [zone], Device of Evils [now] de-energised; unto the third, the Guile of the Desires de-energised; unto the fourth, his Domineering Arrogance, [also] de-energised; unto the fifth, unholy Daring and the Rashness of Audacity, de-energised; unto the sixth, Striving for Wealth by evil means, deprived of its aggrandisement; and to the seventh zone, Ensnaring Falsehood, de-energised.
>
> And then, with all the energisings of the Harmony stript from him, clothed in his proper Power, he cometh to that Nature which belongs unto the Eighth, and there with those-that-are hymneth the Father.
>
> They who are there welcome his coming there with joy; and he, made like to them that sojourn there, doth further hear the Powers who are above the Nature that belongs unto the Eighth, singing their songs of praise to God in language of their own.
>
> And then they, in a band, go to the Father home; of their own selves they make surrender of themselves to Powers, and [thus] becoming Powers they are in God. This the good end for those who have gained Gnosis—to be made one with God.[451]

This last I add because it illustrates, with this revelation, everything you need to know about what has been told; it is time to become a guide yourself!

It is not only the planetary deities whose powers have to be subdued that influence us; the twelve signs of the zodiac also have their own energized radiation.

> HER. Torment the first is this Not-knowing, son; the second one is Grief; the third, Intemperance; the fourth, Concupiscence; the fifth, Unrighteousness; the sixth is Avarice; the seventh, Error; the eighth is Envy; the ninth, Guile; the tenth is Anger; eleventh, Rashness; the twelfth is Malice.
>
> These are in number twelve; but under them are many more, my son; and creeping through the prison of the body they force the man that's placed within to suffer in his senses. But they depart (although not all at once) from him who hath been taken pity on by God; and this it is which constitutes the manner of Rebirth. And.... the Reason (Logos).[452]

Spiritual rebirth takes place when God's grace is experienced by humanity. This is truly not a passive, but an active, process. To go the "way of Hermes" means *transformation.*

It sounds quite pleasant, with no strings attached, to speak about transformation in such a way. To change *überhaupt* ("regardless of anything") something within ourselves is the most essential condition to acknowledging that specific part of ourselves. This is why *gnooti seauton*, know yourself, is the absolute maxim in classical antiquity. It decorated the front of the most important temple of Apollo in Delphi and Socrates uttered these classic words as well.[453] Recall the hermetic saying: "Who knows himself, knows the All."[454] We already pointed to the strong resemblance of the logion about self-knowledge from the *Gospel of Thomas*.[455] In another Nag Hammadi script, *Lessons of Sylvanus*, we read:

> For no one, though he desires to do so fervently, will ever be able to know God as He really is, nor Christ, nor the Spirit, nor hosts of

> angels and the Thrones of spiritual Beings nor the sublime dominions and the Great Consciousness. If you do not know your self, you will not be able to know all of this. Open the door of your self, to know the One-who-is. Knock at your own door, so the Logos will open up for you.[456]

In the same era (probably the second half of the 2nd century A.D.), someone wrote down the words Jesus may have said to Thomas: "He who does not know himself, knows nothing. But he who knows himself, has also obtained knowledge regarding the depth of the All."[457] In the Judeo-Christian tradition, we find this delivery: "God wants mercy, no sacrifices; Self-knowledge no fire-offerings."[458] And Poimandres reveals to Hermes: "And he who thus hath learned to know himself, hath reached that Good which doth transcend abundance...,"[459] since "he who learns himself comes to Him." Hermes endorses this completely: "Right was thy thought, O thou! But how doth 'he who knows himself, go unto Him,' as God's Word (Logos) hath declared?"[460]

But—between self and Self there is an essential difference.

The Two Selves

In psychology as well as in esotericism, it is common to speak about the lower self and the higher Self. The lower self is the "psychological" self; it encompasses our psychic tendencies, and characteristics like cunning, deceit, desire, vanity, greed, over-confidence, impulsiveness, irrational lunacy, untruthfulness, unconsciousness, lack of self-control, injustice, jealousy, trust in evil, wrath, hotheadedness, and anger.[461]

This lower, or still unconscious, self has to be known. In the texts, this is sometimes called "hating" the body, or placing it as a second priority.[462] So Hermes teaches Tat:

> Her. Unless thou first shalt hate thy Body, son, thou canst not love thy Self. But if thou lov'st thy Self thou shalt have Mind, and having Mind thou shalt share in the Gnosis.[463]

You can only love what you know. You cannot love the unknown. Getting to know your (lower) self should lead to loving your Self, according to Hermes. This is a path to self-realization. It is this path that was taught in the *General Teachings*. The higher Self only becomes visible if the lower self (the ego) has been thoroughly learned and conquered. At this moment, the disciple is ripe for initiation under the capable guiding hand of a teacher who has also experienced it—witnessed in the heavens above the seven "psychic" spheres. In hermetic literature, this area is named the "Eighth and Ninth Heavenly Sphere." During this initiation, the disciple comes face to face, as it were, with his or her own Self, the "True Human."[464]

Hermes teaches that, "For that man is a thing-of-life divine; man is not measured with the rest of lives of things upon the Earth, but with the lives above in heaven, who are called gods."[465]

Initiation

We are fortunate to have the recently discovered *Treatise of the Eighth and Ninth Heavenly Sphere*—a unique hermetic initiation text found near Nag Hammadi. It is rare, since the highest steps of initiation in the old mysteries were never written down. Although there were many mystery religions in antiquity, discourses about actual initiations that gave detailed descriptions are extremely rare. Just as K. H. E de Jong, in 1943, indicates: "What it actually concerns, we can only find very short references or similarities, written in purposely obscure language by authors who were disciples of these secret religions which are only comprehensible by the initiated themselves."[466] This is absolutely not the case with the *Treatise of the Eighth and Ninth Heavenly Sphere*.

In the text, a dialog enfolds between the initiator, Hermes, and his disciple, usually called in manuscripts of this time "son." Let us follow their conversation, which leads up to the holy event:

> Tat. O' my father, yesterday you promised me you would lead my consciousness to the Eighth followed with an introduction

to the Ninth. You indicated this being the sequence according to tradition.[467]

In "The Secret Revelation on the mountain," Tat asks Hermes about his experiences during the ascension to the eighth heavenly sphere:

Magical formula in the *Treatise of the Eighth and Ninth Heavenly Sphere.* The photo inset shows the location of discovery of the Nag Hammadi writings, which included text at right.

> TAT. I would, O father, hear the Praise-giving with hymn which thou didst say thou heardest then when thou wert at the Eight [the Ogdoad] of Powers.[468]

Yesterday does not have to be taken literally here, although we have every reason to believe that, during initiation into the highest degree, disciples often stayed temporarily "interned." This certainly points to a strict established procedure.

The dialog continues as follows:

> HER. O', my son, indeed this is the sequence… When I had received the spirit by the power, I entrusted to you the working of it. Certainly now understanding is in you (is it) or the power is rising in me. While I became pregnant of the fountain-source welling up in me, I brought (continuously) forth…
>
> TAT. O', my father, from you I want to receive the power of the discourse, which you will pass on to me as we were both told. Let us pray, O' my father.
>
> HER. O', my son, it is fitting to pray to God with all our consciousness, with all our heart and soul, and beg him to forward us the gifts of the Eighth and all can receive what is his. To you, it is to understand, to me to pass on the discourse, thanks to the well overflowing within me.
>
> TAT. Let us pray, O' my father.

"I hail thee,
thou who rules the kingdom of the energy;
whose word gives light birth
and whose speech is immortal, eternal and unchangeable;
it is his will who creates life in forms, everywhere;
his nature gives form to the substance;
by him the souls and the powers and the angels are set into motion;
since it is through him the word expands to all which exists;
his providence extends to everyone here;
she brings forth all;
he divided the aeon among the spirits;

he created all;
he is the one who contains himself
and in his wholeness takes care of all;
the invisible God whom all address silently;
his image moves in the giving to
and gives to the motion.
O', energy of the power,
who is exalted above the majestic,
who is more magnificent than the honoured,

Zoxathazo
a
òò
ee
òòò
èèè
òòòò
èè
òòòòòò
ooooo
òòòòòò
uuuuuu
òòòòòòòòòòòòòòò
Zozazoth.

Lord, grant us wisdom from your energy, engulfing us, so we may witness for ourselves the Eighth and Ninth (Heavenly Sphere).

We have reached the seventh sphere, because we are pious, behaving according to your law and will at all times.

For we have walked your path and have left the evil behind us to arrive at the observation.

Lord, grant us truth in the image;

make us see, through the spiritual energy the form of the image, of which there is no lacking.

Accept from us, by our song of praise, the imprint of the pleroma and recognize the spirit working in us.

For through thee, the All received soul.

For from thee, the unawakened, the awakened has come.

The birth of the self-awakened has been assisted by you, awakener of all awakened beings who exist.

Accept from us, the spiritual gifts we offer up to you with all our heart and soul and all our energy.

Save what is inside of us and grant us immortal wisdom."[469]

Ecstatic Experience

"We have already reached the seventh sphere," says the prayer—and indeed, "because we are pious." The pupil has already passed through the "psychic" heavenly spheres and has dealt with the capacities of the spheres that were attached to the soul. They have been transformed. This is why the initiate is now capable of observing the spheres above the seven heavens. By pronouncing the magical names of God, which we discussed in the chapter about magic, the initiator and the initiated arrive in the higher vibrational frequency of the harmony of the spheres and are ready to step over to observation of it.

> "Let us kiss each other lovingly, O' my son. Rejoice about it. Now the energy comes to us, which is light."
>
> "I see, yes, I see inexpressible depths."
>
> "How shall I say it to you, O' my son... How shall I tell you about the All? I am consciousness."[470]

For the higher initiate, the experience of the observation is shocking when experienced for the first time. Images of immeasurable depth unfold and the candidate reaches an ecstatic state of mind. Hermes, to the contrary, remains calm and practically unmoving and says, "He is consciousness." Moreover, in the revelation on the mountain, he clearly gives Tat an explanation:

> HER. What may I say, my son? I can but tell thee this. Whene'er I see within myself the Simple Vision brought to birth out of God's mercy, I have passd through myself into a Body that can never die. And now I am not what I was before; but I am born in Mind.
>
> The way to do this is not taught, and it cannot be seen by the compounded element by means of which thou seest.
>
> Yea, I have had my former composed form dismembered for me. I am no longer touched, yet have I touch; I have dimension too; and [yet] am I a stranger to them now.
>
> Thou seest me with eyes, my son; but what I am thou dost not understand [even] with fullest strain of body and of sight.[471]

During this same revelation, Tat arrives at the same state of consciousness:

> In heaven am I, in earth, in water, air; I am in animals, in plants; I'm in the womb, before the womb, after the womb; I'm everywhere![472]

This true state of being is the complete self-realized human, when the lower self has been completely dissolved and the higher Self is one with the All. On the outside, nothing changes; on the inside, everything changes. For the spiritual viewer, the initiated, this is clearly visible.

The initiated in our discourse has not progressed very far yet, and is still totally mesmerized by the images appearing in front of him, and in turn is brought to joy and to fear. Tat begins the dialog with Hermes:

> "I see also another consciousness which moves the soul.
> I see him who moves me through a holy ecstasy.
> You give me energy!
> I see myself!
> I want to speak!
> Fear halts me.

I found the source of the power, which is above all other powers, and does not have a source itself.

I see the source overflowing with life."

"I told you, O' my son, I am consciousness."

"I have observed. It is impossible to bring this into words."

"Fully the Eighth, O' my son, filled with souls, angels singing songs of praise in silence. And I, consciousness, encompasses it."

"How do they then sing, father?"

"Now you have come so far, no one can speak with you."

"I am already silent, O' my father, I want to praise you in silence with a song."

"Yes, do such, I am after all consciousness."

"I know, Hermes, the consciousness cannot be explained since it is enclosed within itself. I rejoice, O' my father, I see you smiling; the All rejoices. This is why not one being is seperated from your life, for you are the Lord of all citizens in each place. Your providence protects. I call on to you, Father, aeon of the aeons, great divine Spirit. For through the Spirit he showers rainwater on all of us. What can you tell me about such, O' my father, Hermes?"

"I cannot speak about such, O' my son, since it is especially for God we should keep silent about such which is hidden."

"O', Trismegistus, let not my soul be deprived of the divine observation. You after all have power over everything, as master of the Universe."

"Return to your songs of praise, O' my son, express yourself in silence and ask what you want in silence."[473]

The initiate sees himself, his true (higher) Self. In the *Poimandres*, we also saw that the ascending soul was still "in possession of the true Self." All superficial attributes had disappeared. As said before, Hermes remains his usual peaceful self. He bids the boy to be silent, to keep still. This we see also in the revelation on the mountain:

> And now, my son, be still and solemn silence keep! Thus shall the mercy that flows on us from God not cease.
>
> Henceforth rejoice, O son, for by the Powers of God thou art being purified for the articulation of the Reason (Logos).

> Gnosis of God hath come to us, and when this comes, my son, Not-knowing is cast out.
>
> Gnosis of Joy hath come to us, and on its coming, son, Sorrow will flee away to them who give it room. The Power that follows Joy do I invoke, they Self-control. O Power most sweet! Let us most gladly bid it welcome, son! How with its coming doth it chase Intemperance away!
>
> Now fourth, on Continence I call, the Power against Desire.
>
> .... This step, my son, is Righteousness' firm seat. For without judgment see how she hath chased Unrighteousness away. We are made righteous, son, by the departure of Unrighteousness.
>
> Power sixth I call to us—that against Avarice, Sharing-with-all.
>
> And now that Avarice is gone, I call on Truth. And Error flees, and Truth is with us.
>
> See how [the measure of] the Good is full, my son, upon Truth's coming. For Envy hath gone from us; and unto Truth is joined the Good as well, with Life and Light.
>
> And now no more doth any torment of the Darkness venture nigh, but vanquished [all] have fled with whirring wings.[474]

The disciple, captured by the beauty of the revelation, asks Hermes if he can assure that his soul continues with the observation. He, however, does not have to worry about that. To his son, Tat, Hermes has explained that, once he has gone this far, he will be completely occupied by a totally other way of seeing, hearing, feeling, and living. "For the observation has a characteristic quality: It completely occupies those who have already observed and draws them towards it, as one says, like a magnet attracting iron."[475]

In the meantime, the mystical ascension in our discourse is coming to an end.

> When he ended his songs of praise he called out: "Father Trismegistus, what shall I say? We have received this light and I see the same observation within the inside of you. And I see the eight-fold with the souls there and the angels praising the ninth sphere and her

power. And I see him who has power over them all and who creates with his spirit."

"It is good from now on we keep silent. Do not speak hastily about the observation. From now on we have to sing songs of praise to the Father until the day we leave our body."

"What you just said, O' my father, I want to also say. I sing a song of praise from the bottom of my heart."

"Now you have come to a point of rest, be active in the songs of praise. For you have found what you were looking for."

"But is it fit, O' my father, from songs of praise my heart is overfilled?"

"It is good to send your songs of praise towards God, so it may be written down in his unforgettable book...

Write then an oath on the book, so those who read the book do not misuse the name or use her contrary to the workings of destiny. They can better submit to the law of God without trespassing it, to ask nothing and God in purity for wisdom and Gnosis. For those not brought up with this from the beginning, remain only the general, exoteric teachings. He will not be in state to read what has been written in this book, though his conscience is pure, not having committed anything scandalous, nor agrees to it. Only by passing through each cycle of development will he come to the path of immortality and as such will come to understanding of the eight-fold which reveals the Ninth Heavenly Sphere..."[476]

The Secret Words

Secrecy is the duty of each initiate. "For it is not possible for the non-initiated to grasp such divine secrets," Hermes teaches Asclepius.[477] Keeping silent is, in the beginning, very difficult, for what the heart is filled with overflows in the mouth. Tat, having seen his higher Self and the All in the revelation on the mountain, is enthusiastic as well. Hermes answers again in a calm manner:

> Her. This is, my son, Rebirth—no more to look on things from body's view-point (a thing three ways in space extended), ... though this Sermon (Logos) on Rebirth, on which I did not comment—in

> order that we may not be calumniators of the All unto the multitude, to whom indeed the God Himself doth will we should not.[478]

Secrecy is not an affair for the elite to be maintained among themselves. It is, in fact, considered a sin to confide the intimacies of the path to ignorant and unaware beings. They are not able to understand and would turn against the revealers. This secrecy is not uniquely hermetic; we see it, for example, in early Christianity as well.[479] It is a matter of self-preservation not to waste energies on beings who are not sufficiently attuned to resonate with them.

In Alexandria, at the beginning of our calendar, several movements ran parallel. They influenced each other, but never merged. Many thought, for a long time, that Neoplatonism was the most magnificent legacy from this metropolis, with Christian Gnosticism, despite it short-lived history, running a close second. However it was the *Hermetica* that, over time, has left the most lasting traces on human consciousness, as we shall see in the rest of this book.[480]

> But what is time?
> An illusion?
> Hermes says: Time is measurement.[481]
>
> The past is gone and no longer more
> and the future does not exist as yet, since she is still to come.
> Even the present is not permanent. She does not last.
> Time does not keep a second still.[482]

Interlog:
The Fame of Hermes

I am the Lord of all wonders,
who piled up the seven spheres,
who has become Master of the brilliant Sun
and of the shining Moon
and who the tree
of illuminating wisdom
has planted.
Whoever eats of her fruit,
will never hunger,
and without meat or drink will be sustained.
He will become spiritual and divine,
his wisdom will never be subdued
and his good works
will never end.[483]

Chapter 15
Hermes and the Philosopher's Stone

The influence of Hermes Trismegistus on later generations is difficult to overestimate. It is enormous and stretches over more than 4000 years. But, alas, no longer in the land where it all began—Egypt.

One of the last great Alexandrians who was still strongly influenced by Hermes was the alchemist Zosimus. He was one of the first in a long line of thinkers inspired by the theosophical approaches of the Thrice-Great Hermes.

Zosimus, the Great Alchemist

Zosimus of Panopolis was born at the end of the 3rd century B.C. in Panopolis, currently Akhmin, in Upper Egypt. Later he departed for Alexandria, where he wrote his most important works and had contact with many hermeticists. We do not know if Zosimus came into contact there with the *Corpus Hermeticum*. The fact is that he knew this book very well and often referred to it.[484]

It is plausible that Zosimus was schooled by temple priests in alchemy. As we saw in the first part of this book, the Egyptian temples were the cradle of science. Temple priests had more than a religious function. In fact, you could say that science and religion were completely permeated by each other. Throughout his life, Zosimus maintained a close relationship with a priestess named Theosobia, who was an extremely knowledgeable alchemist.[485] He dedicated his most important work to her and bequeathed her his autobiographic memoirs, *Ultimate Freedom*. He called her his "sister." But he also criticized his *soror mystica*—mystical sister.[486] Unlike her, he found it objectionable to safeguard alchemical knowledge for initiates alone.[487]

Zosimus' education by temple priests runs through his dreams and visions:

> I fell asleep and saw a priest in front of me making a sacrifice on top of a shell-shaped altar. Fifteen steps led to the altar's top. The priest stood up and I heard a voice from above speaking to me: "I have accomplished the descent of fifteen steps of darkness and I have completed the fifteen steps of light and the one who has sacrificed revitalizes me, thus removing all bodily impurities; and a priest consecrated by necessity I became a spirit." When I heard the voice of the one who standing on the shell-shaped altar, I posed a question to get to know who he was. He answered me in a weak voice: "I am Ion, the sanctuary's priest and I have survived incredible violence. Since someone entered passionately this morning, split me open with a sword, tore me completely to pieces based on the law of composition. He scalped me with his hand-held sword; he mixed my bones with my flesh and burnt them in the fire of the process. This is how I learned by transformation of the body to become a Spirit."[488]

This horrifying dream was described and analyzed in the 20th century by the "rediscoverer" of alchemy, Carl Gustav Jung.[489] The transforming element in the dream is very clear. The transformation process is painful and purifying. Transforming from body to spirit is also described in the *Corpus Hermeticum* in the fascinating treatise of the divine mixing bowl filled with spirit that God sent down to Earth:

> But they who have received some portion of God's gift, these, Tat, if we judge by their deeds, have from Death's bonds won thier release; for they embrace in their own Mind all things, things on the earth, things in the heaven, and things above the heaven -if there be aught. And having raised themselves so far they sight the Good; and having sighted It, they look upon their sojourn here as a mischance; and in disdain of all, both things in body and the bodiless, they speed their way unto that One and Only One.

This is, O Tat, the Gnosis of the Mind, Vision of things Divine; God-knowledge is it, for the cup is God's.

TAT. Father, I, too, would be baptised.

HER. Unless thou first shalt hate thy Body, son, thou canst not love thy Self. But if thou lov'st thy Self thou shalt have Mind, and having Mind thou shalt share in the Gnosis.[490]

A Mixing Bowl and a Stone

The *kratèr*, mixing bowl, appears in a rather flexible way in another dream of Zosimus', in which he sees the same priest in the shape of a copper man supervising an altar plate filled with bubbling water in which a group of humans are being boiled alive. The priest confesses to him that the copper man can become silver—and yes, even after some time, gold.[491]

We see here the typical alchemical symbology: spiritual transformation is described in symbols of material chemistry. But, as we saw before, the investigation of spirit and matter goes hand in hand. According to the hermetic principle "as above, so below," the research into the transmutation of metals goes hand in hand with spiritual transformation. With Zosimus, this parallel is quite clearly evident. His knowledge of chemistry, moreover, becomes the foundation for his alchemical experiments. Helen de Jong indicates that this was not the case in Byzantine alchemy at a later date.[492] Later in history, we read about alchemists from whose work the spiritual aspect had totally disappeared. In the service of greedy kings, they tried to transmute inferior metals into gold. The search for the Philosopher's Stone has an interesting history.

For Zosimus, the quest for the *lapis philosophorum*, the Philosopher's Stone, was central. To find it, he knew that the heart first had to come to rest. He points out in his treatise *Regarding apparatus and ovens*, that sages like Hermes were superior because they avoided distress and joy.[493] He warns his "mystical" sister, Theosobia, of the low conniving of bad demons who "hunger for the human soul." He gives her advice "as a woman" to learn to control herself and to subdue her passions:

> By doing this you will acquire the true and natural (tinctures) which are applicable at certain times. Do these things until your soul is perfected. When you have realized your perfection and have obtained the natural (tinctures), spit on the matter while hastening yourself towards Poimandres and receive the baptism in the mixing bowl and hasten yourself towards your own kind.[494]

These are very obvious references to the first and fourth treatises of the *Corpus Hermeticum*. Zosimus had read Hermes very thoroughly. Furthermore, he considered him, as did so many after him, to be the founder of the sacred science of (al)chemistry. As a seeker for the Philosopher's Stone, Zosimus found the answer in Hermes. He discovered that it was an inner search. According to Zosimus, the Philosopher's Stone is a many-formed something that truly has no form, something precious without a price—"a stone, not being a stone, an unknown something, known to everyone."[495]

The Letter Omega

The most well-known and quoted work of Zosimus is *Regarding apparatus and ovens; authentic commentaries on the letter* Omega. It is part of a much longer discourse[496] entitled *Alchemistical Subjects* and is dedicated to "sister" Theosobia. Omega is the last letter of the Greek alphabet and corresponds with Cronos (Saturn). It also stands for lead, the principle of all fluidity.[497]

The first part of the work does not deal very much with apparatus and ovens. It is a theosophical treatment of humanity's liberation. Zosimus quotes from a book of Hermes not known to us anymore—*On the Inner Life*—in which Hermes writes that spiritual humanity, having arrived at the point of knowing itself, does not need magic anymore, and is no longer dependant on fate, since fate rules matter and the body, but not humanity's divine essence. Hermes says that, when humanity has learned in this manner to get to know God, he will face God's Son, "who for the sake of the holy souls became all things in order to free them from the grasp of Fate and to guide them towards the spiritual... Since, because he allows all, he can be anything he desires to be, and he listens to the Father, while he enters fully each body and enlightens the spirit of each soul..."[498]

This mention of the Son of God is remarkable. Even more remarkable is the fact that, a bit further in the text, he names Jesus Christ—a surprising reference from the hand of a hermetic philosopher and alchemist. Christ accompanies Adam and leads him to the place "where the so-called light-beings formerly dwelled."[499] Preceding this, another story is told, in which Adam, in addition to his bodily form (which can suffer), possesses a spiritual form, *phos*, or "Light." It is this form that is carried away by Jesus Christ. But "powerless" humanity sees only its material form, even though the spiritual Adam is always present in its (sub)consciousness and stands by it.

In paragraph twelve, the manuscript changes rather suddenly to the technical part of the "hermetical Alchemy"—in this case to tinctures (solutions) of treated metals[500]— and turns directly to a philosophical divergence: Not everyone, says Zosimus, reaches his goal in the same way, since people have different characters and are subject to the ever-changing constellations of the stars. This must be considered in the art of alchemy, just as it is in the science of healing. So here again, we find a connection between philosophy, astrology, alchemy, and the art of healing.

After these reflections, Zosimus delves deeper into the technique of alchemy. He makes a sketch of a retort, very similar to an antique distillation tube. Then, in the midst of a series of alchemical formulas, he includes a number of wonderful signs as a sort of magical formula.[501] It is ironic that the same person who chastized his mystical sister for the secrecy of her art cannot himself avoid dabbling in magical formulas. And not an unimportant formula, it seems. For the words written around it imply that "who comprehends this formula is rich."[502]

In the closing paragraphs of the discourse, Zosimus refers to Agathodaimon. It is, in conclusion, a work inspired by Hermes.

It Is Completed

> When I woke up again, I said to myself: I have understood it correctly; it is all about the liquids in the art of metals. The one who carried the sword said: "You have completed the ascension of the seven degrees." The other continued, at the same time he dissolved lead through all the fluids: "The work is completed."[503]

The material lead had been transmuted into spiritual gold. In one of his numerous visions, Zosimus saw that he had climbed the "seven steps" after many earlier efforts had failed. The task was completed.

Zosimus was one of the last great Alexandrians. It is significant that the last heir of the Egyptian alchemists, Stephanus of Alexandria, left Egypt in the 7th century A.D. for Constantinople, where Hermes himself had found shelter. The repression had started centuries earlier. In 292 A.D., Emperor Diocletian had issued a proclamation beginning the persecution of alchemists.[504] When texts were found, they were burnt.

Alexandria was no longer an intellectual metropolis of the ancient world. Where once hemeticists had taught wisdom, where illustrious teachers like Philo, Basilides, and Valentinus had accomplished high intellectual and religious achievements, dogma and ignorance now crept in. After the era of the profound *Logos* doctrine of Origines and the mystical reflections of the Neoplatonist Plotinus came the century of Athanasius, the orthodox fighter against the refined philosopher and Church Father Arius. Athanasius decided once and for all what Christians—and those who were not Christian had better convert quickly for fear of their lives—were allowed to read and what they were forbidden to read.[505] This was also the century when Christians ransacked and burned the *Serapeion*, leaving the most famous library of all time in ashes and losing forever a collection of rare material that had taken centuries to assemble.[506] Is this what Hermes' lamentation was about?

> Dost thou not know, Asclepius, that Egypt is the image of the Heaven; or, what is truer still, the transference, or the descent, of

all that are in governance or exercise in Heaven? And if more truly [still] it must be said -this land of ours is Shrine of all the World.

Further, in that 'tis fitting that the prudent should know all before, it is not right ye should be ignorant of this.

The time will come when Egypt will appear to have in vain served the Divinity with pious mind and constant worship; and all its holy cult will fall to nothingness and be in vain.

For that Divinity is now about to hasten back from Earth to Heaven, and Egypt shall be left; and Earth, which was the seat of pious cults, shall be bereft and widowed of the presence of the Gods.

And foreigners shall fill this region and this land; and there shall be not only the neglect of pious cults, but—what is still more painful—as though enacted by the laws, a penalty shall be decreed against the practice of [our] pious cults and worship of the Gods—[entire] proscription of them.

Then shall this holiest land, seat of [our] shrines and temples, be choked with tombs and corpses.

O Egypt, Egypt, of thy pious cult's tales only will remain, as far beyond belief for thy own sons [as for the rest of men]; words only will be left cut on thy stones, thy pious deeds rcounting!

And Egypt will be made the home of Scyth or Indian, or some one like to them—that is a foreign neighbour.

Ay, for the Godly company shall mount again to Heaven, and their forsaken worshippers shall all die out; and Egypt, thus bereft of God and man, shall be abandoned.

And now I speak to thee, O River, holiest [Stream]! I tell thee what will be. With bloody torrents shalt thou overflow thy banks. Not only shall thy streams divine be stained with blood; but they shall all flow over [with the same].

The tale of tombs shall far exceed [the number of the] quick; and the surviving remnant shall be Egyptians in their tongue alone, but in their actions foreigners.[507]

CHAPTER 16
HERMES IN THE ORIENT

In the summer of 1999, the eighteenth World Congress of *The International Association for the History of Religions* took place in Durban, South Africa. Among the speakers was the Dutch researcher Dr. Annine van der Meer, who spoke about the influence of Hermes in Harran.[508]

The inhabitants of Harran, a city in northern Mesopotamia under Arab rule,[509] had "converted to Hermes" *en masse*. Was it possible that Hermes had pitched his tent permanently in the East? Had Hermes become an Arab? It wasn't until the late Middle Ages that Hermes was rediscovered in the West. Meanwhile, much was lost. It is thanks to the Arabs, who cherished an immense interest in Hermes, that the West regained contact with the richness of hermetic thought. Arab Hermeticism—we'll call it that for the moment—is infinitely complicated. Much is obscure and still unpublished. Who better than Annine van der Meer to help me with my own research into Hermes? I have woven much of her accumulated research into this chapter, for which I thank her.

TERRA INCOGNITA

It is commonly known that, during the 9th and 10th centuries B.C., Arab Muslims were extremely interested in ancient philosophy, medicine, and the exact sciences.[510] They searched widely for Greek writings to study and assimilated the knowledge contained therein. Less known, however, is the fact that the Muslims were extremely interested in the *Hermetica* and have left us an imposing amount of Arab hermetic texts.[511] It wasn't until the 20th century that Western science made a serious effort to catalog this great body of work.[512]

The Arabs seem to have had a preference for the somewhat more "technical" *Hermetica.*[513] We encounter magical works about good-luck charms; texts about astrology, including books about the relationship of the astral world to climates, plants, colors, and stars; and a great many books about alchemy. Of Arab alchemy alone there are more than 2000 writings accredited to Hermes of which we know.[514] And this is not all. Beside these, we encounter, in many other Arab writings, numerous citations from hermetic texts, and references to Hermes and his hermetic writings are bountiful. This research, after an initial cataloguing, is still in its infancy. Many of the Arab texts have not yet been translated and remain, for Western science, a true *terra incognita.*[515] The history of the Arab *Hermetica* has yet to be written.

The Arabs passed down to us profound texts of great beauty. Take, for example, the alchemical text *The large letter about the spheres of Hermes of Dendera.* This letter was found in a subterranean tunnel in the Egyptian temple at Dendera, under a statue of Artemis. Hermes reveals herein his creative labor:

> He who has long served the highest light, for him things go as wished. I am the Lord of all wonders, who piled up the seven spheres, who has become Master of the brilliant Sun and of the shining Moon and who the tree of illuminating wisdom has planted.
>
> Whoever eats of her fruit, will never hunger, and without meat or drink will be sustained. He will become spiritual and divine, his wisdom will never be subdued and his good works will never end.[516]

Thrice-Great Hermes and Super-Hermes

In Islam, the God Thoth-Hermes undergoes a transformation from God to *hero,* an exceptional man who has performed extraordinary feats for the sake of humanity's desire for wisdom. There are, in fact, areas where the cultic worship of Hermes as a God flourished for a long time.[517] The mystic Hermes, the wise philosopher, in fact appears in Islam in three forms—the first, second, and third Hermes, or Thrice-Great Hermes. This is not really new, since we saw in Part

I of this book that this tradition is very old and was handed down by writers like Manetho.[518]

Abu ma'Shar is one of the first Arab authors to write about more than one Hermes (around 845 A.D., or 232 of the Islamic calendar).[519] His works, which became a source of information for many writers after him, move Hermes' place of origin, perhaps understandably, from Egypt to the Middle East. The first Arab Hermes is even a grandchild of the biblical Adam, from the land between the Euphrates and the Tigress rivers.[520] This is the same Hermes who gave the world medicine and built temples and pyramids on whose walls he engraved all sciences, techniques, and crafts for fear that they would be lost to humanity. It was also this same Hermes who first predicted the deluge.

It is significant that Abu ma'Shar—who probably borrowed his information from the letter of Manetho—identifies Hermes as Henoch in the Old Testament.[521] This Henoch was called Indris by the Arabs. Thus Hermes, in the 9th century A.D., was clothed in both Old Testament and Koranic garments. It is this first Hermes who played an important role in the Arab literature.

The "second" Hermes, in Arabic *Al-Babili*, also lived in Babylonia after the deluge. He possessed outstanding knowledge of medical science, philosophy, and algebra. Pythagoras seems to have been one of his pupils.[522] He brought the study of the sciences back to life. It was this Hermes who immigrated to Egypt.[523]

The "third" Hermes lived in Egypt—also, of course, after the deluge. He excelled in most forms of science and crafts. He was an alchemist, physician, and philosopher.[524] It is this third and last Hermes who passed on the knowledge to his pupil Asclepius, who put it in the *Corpus Hermeticum*.

Through all of this runs another tradition. There is another story dedicated to Hermes that tells about all poisonous animals, the so-called *Snake Book*. In this manuscript, we hear of the existence of a Hermes who is all-powerful among all the Hermes (*Hirmis al-Haramisa*).[525] This patriarch Hermes is described as the ancient grandfather of the third Hermes, the writer, who tells us that he distinguished himself with three characteristics: strength, wisdom, and royal dignity.[526]

The Arab Hermes

In the years 987 and 988 A.D., the Muslim Ibn an-Nadim wrote the first Arabic encyclopedia, the *Kitab al-Fihrist*,[527] in which he gives extensive coverage to the Arab philosopher Al-Kindi. Hermes appears in the work as a welcome and frequent guest. Here, as in many other Arab sources, Hermes is seen primarily as a great philosopher.[528] But Hermes is also represented in the encyclopedia as an astronomer and is apparently perceived by the Arabs as a healer as well, functioning as a type of archetypal physician. In this role, he is succeeded by the famous Roman physician Galenus, and by eight other great physicians, among them Aesculapius, Paramedus, Plato, and Hippocrates.[529] Furthermore, Hermes is a great magician.[530] And most certainly, as we observed earlier, Hermes is the alchemist par excellence.

> People who are interested in the science of Alchemy—meaning the transmutation of metals into gold and silver—propose the first human being speaking about this art, was Hermes, the wise man and Babylonian, who moved to Egypt when people scattered away from Babylon. He was King of Egypt, a wise man and Philosopher, who gave the Art (of Alchemy) its status and wrote many books on the subject. He observed the specific and spiritual characteristics of phenomena and augmented his knowledge about the Art of Alchemy by research and observations. He also knew how to make amulets and wrote many books about this...[531]

Silver Water and Starry Earth

Returning from the hermetical exhibition in Venice (discussed in Part II of this book), I studied the elaborate catalog very thoroughly[532] and discovered, in an article on the *Tabula Smaragdina*, a footnote referring to "the sayings of Hermes." I was able to obtain a photocopy of this particular article in the magazine *Ambix* with the assistance of the Bibliotheca Philisophica Hermetica. When I read it, a world of wonders opened up before me.[533]

I am quite familiar with the "sayings," the *logia*, of Jesus, having written a book about them not long ago.[534] The enunciations of Jesus were of great importance for his followers. Some researchers recognize, in the science of the *Hermetica*, a sort of prototype for these in the sayings of Hermes—like those, for example, that we rediscovered in the previous century in the *Hermetic Definitions*.[535] This, in fact, is how the well-thought-out article in *Ambix* viewed the sayings of Hermes.

Of quite another character is an alchemical compilation probably dating back to around the 10th century, but certainly based on an older source going back at least to the 3rd century A.D.[536] The compiler is a certain Ibn Umail, an Arab scholar wrote an alchemical work, *Key to the great Wisdom*, and a poetic ode with the intriguing title *Letter of the Sun to the new Moon*, with the commentary, *Mã'Al-Waraqi*, which means "Silver water and starry Earth."[537] In this last work, many citations of Hermes have been added, along with citations from great alchemists like Maria the Jewess and Democritus. Sometimes the citations consist of only one sentence, like this one:

> Hermes said: "Something corresponds with what is closest."[538]

Sometimes they are complete discourses, like the one below pertaining to the embryo. It has an alchemical character in the truest sense of the word—that is to say, it declares the connection of matter with spirit. An illustration:

> Hermes said: "Everything fine is part of the gross." He points with this explanation at the entry of Water on Earth. The spiritual ascension takes place and the body receives after its death, eternal life.[539]

The language used to address non-alchemists, as we have often seen, is rather obscure. What do we, for example, make of this?

> Hermes said: O' my son, work gold in pure silver Earth. Hermes calls "pure Water" here "gold," since the colourful soul is hidden

in her Water as spirit above her, due to her colour and purity, and begins to rule. He calls her pure body, pure silvery Earth.[540]

Sometimes it is quite recognizable:

> As Hermes, the outstanding Sage, who is an Ocean of wisdom, said: "Rule the Highest and the Lowest. It will lead to wonders— these opposities— because both will turn black and white, and also red..."[541]

Black stands for *nigredo*, lead; white for *albedo*, silver; red for *rubedo*, gold. Besides material elements, these colors symbolize psychic aspects as well (nigredo, confrontation with darkness; albedo, reflection, a rather unbalanced equilibrium toward integration; rubedo, strength, energy, unity).[542]

From Womb to Retort

The most intriguing text cited in the *Ambix* article is the discourse on the embryo. Hermes declares that water is the primordial matter from which all is formed, including the human child:

> Hermes said: "Know the secret and the life of everything is Water." Water is susceptible to be handled by human... In Water hides a great secret. For it is in Water what makes wheat ferment, wine in the grapevine, oil in the olive, resin in the turpentine-bark, oil in the sesame seed, different fruit in the trees.
>
> The start of the child begins in Water for the womb closes itself seven days after a man's sperm descends into the woman's womb. The seed having entered the womb becomes rarefied water. It stays seven days in the womb until it emerges into all the limbs of a woman because of her fluidity and fineness. After such, it covers the flesh and becomes flesh, it covers the bones and becomes bones, it covers the hair and sinews and becomes also such; and forth onto all parts of the limbs. On the eighth day, it hardens and coagulates. Then, on the sixteenth day, it turns red, manifests itself and one can determine its limbs just as one can observe individual

> hairs. Then, on the thirty-second day, it assumes a fixed shape and becomes a human being... On the fourtieth day, the soul manifests itself and appears in it (body). From the fourtieth day on, blood starts streaming through the navel into the embryo. The soul, then, becomes visible due to the presence of blood, entwining itself with the body and little by little it begins to grow and become stronger. Know, Water serves the embryo in the womb for the first three months, afterwards Air for the following three months, then Fire the next three months. It (Fire) creates a boiling state and completes it. When the nine months are completed, the blood having been used as food for it (embryo) via the navel, stops, rises up to the breasts of the woman and becomes as snow. It is (then) transformed into food for it (child).[543]

The text continues with Hermes' explanation regarding the symbolic representation of the alchemical process—the womb being the alchemical bowl, the retort:

> ...Know this marriage and conception takes place by decomposition in the lower part of the bowl (the retort). The birth of this child... takes place in the air at the top of the bowl...[544]

Hermes was well-known to the Arabs.[545] He reveals himself in the Middle East in various forms. He appears as the inventor of almost all arts and sciences,[546] the one who laid down the foundation for the doctrine of the stars and numerology.[547] He instructed the people in how to fabricate clothing.[548] We can also trace the art of chemistry and glass-blowing back to him.[549] At the same time, he is the inventor of medicine. Hermes also deeply influenced the mystical branch of Islam, the Sufi tradition.[550] Moreover, the Arabs gave him a role we have not seen him in before—they called him a prophet. This tradition is associated with Harran. Hermes was apparently one of the prophets of the inhabitants of Harran.

Enoch

Hermes becomes Enoch, the Arab Indris, as we saw before. This transformation is illustrated in a mystical story called *Light thrown on the life of Hermes of all Hermesses, for whoever desires it.*[551] In it, Hermes discovers a trove of scientific treasures hidden away in a cave in Ceylon. From this science,[552] he derives his teachings. This legend is based on the existence of the three Hermes, of whom the first is associated with Enoch. It is this treatise that was the first to be translated into Latin in Europe.

We also encounter the beloved theme of the cave in a fascinating story in *Picatrix*,[553] in which the "spirit of perfected nature" reveals itself to Hermes.[554] When Hermes, inspired by this, investigates the secrets of the earth and finds a subterranean cave, he sees nothing and cannot ignite a light due to strong winds blowing within the cave. Then, in a dream, a beautiful figure appears advising him to enter the cave with a windbreaker and search for the talisman buried there. He is told to look in the four corners and promised that, after he finds the talisman, the winds will cease and he will discover the secret of Creation. Upon hearing this, Hermes questions the beautiful figure to learn its identity. The apparition answers him:

> I am your perfected nature. If you wish to see me, call me by my name.[555]

This mythical representation, however, does not explain exactly why Hermes is transformed from God to prophet—to Enoch, alias Indris. Prior to the arrival of the Arabs, there were many places where Hermes (as Mercury) was honored as a God. This tradition was maintained for a long time, thus we read in al-Nadim's encyclopedia, the *Fihrist*, this announcement:

> On the twenty-eighth day, they leave a village called Sabta situated close to one of the gates of Harran... There they sacrificed a large bull to Hermes, the God, and they also slaughtered nine lambs in honour of the seven divinities...[556]

The Sabians, about whom we speak here, worshipped Hermes as founder of their cult, as one of their Gods,[557] as the fountain of wisdom, and later as their prophet as well. They linked the Greek Hermes, who was well known to them, with the Roman Mercurius and the Egyptian Thoth.[558] But when and why did Hermes become Indris?

We know exactly when Hermes became a prophet. Under Harun al-Rashid's reign (786–809 A.D.), Hermes was not yet known as a prophet.[559] The earliest evidence we find of his transformation is in 845 A.D.[560] Around this time, Abu ma'Shar writes that "Hermes the wise, from Harran, was the grandson of the Hebrew Adam, being the biblical (H)Enoch (Uhnuh, Hanuh) and Indris out of the Koran."[561] After this, the combined name Hermes-Indris appears many times.[562] But why?

The New Alexandria

To understand the development of Hermes from God to *heros* to prophet, we have to go to Harran. This city, now located in southeastern Turkey, was, during the Middle Ages, an important metropolis. Once the dwelling place of the patriarch Abraham and situated at an intersection of caravan routes, it developed under the Muslims into a center for science and culture. Under the dynasty of the Umayaden, Harran was already an important political and military center.[563] Under Caliph Umar II (682–720 A.D.), schools for medicine and philosophy, and later the Neoplatonic Academy, moved from Alexandria to Harran.[564] Harran became the center of the learned Islamic world. Later, this center moved to Baghdad.[565]

The Muslims esteemed ancient philosophy very highly, as we saw. Sometimes we forget that many Greek philosophical writings would have been lost forever if they had not been preserved in translation by the Arabs and later given back to the West. Christianity did not necessarily preserve much of what they considered heathen (that is, non-Christian) literature. On the other hand, the Muslims maintained their love and respect for ancient wisdom, despite their belief in only one God. Thus in Harran, Allah always remained central no matter how learned their philosophers became, and no God besides Allah was allowed. This meant, of course, that Hermes could no longer be worshipped as a God.

An Arab keeper of chronicles describes to us how, in 832 A.D., the attention of Caliph Al-Manun was attracted by deviations in the clothing and hairstyle of Harran's inhabitants. This did not please the Caliph. He asked them to which conquered race they belonged. They answered that they were Harranians. The ruler asked then if they were Christians, or Jews, or perhaps magi—and if they were none of these, whether they possessed a Book or a Prophet. When the Harranians refused to answer, he ordered that they be wiped out. The inhabitants of Harran reacted by saying they would gladly pay land taxes. The Caliph replied that land taxes were only acceptable from people who were members of the non-Islamic sects mentioned in the Book by Allah—the groups of people who possess a Book:

> Since you do not belong to either one of those groups, you may choose one of two alternatives: Accept Islam's religion or one of the religions Allah decrees in his Book. If not, I will wipe you out to the last man...[566]

The Harranians faced a dilemma. In the past, they had had to endure a lot from conquerors. In the year 386 A.D., their famous temple dedicated to the Moon Goddess Sin—according to eye-witnesses more beautiful than the Serapeion temple—was destroyed at the command of the Christian Emperor Theodosius.[567] Out of pure survival instinct, many of them converted to Islam and Christianity and changed their clothing and hairstyle. But a small group maintained their ethnic identity. They called themselves Sabians.[568]

What exactly did this manoeuvre accomplish? The word "Sabian" is used three times in the Koran[569] to describe a small group that, like Jews and Christians, formed a protected religion. Under the umbrella of this group, Harran's inhabitants were forthwith protected.[570]

The Hermetic Beliefs of the Sabians

Styling themselves Sabians was not the only tactic the Harranians used to mask their continued worship of Hermes. Their intelligentia did their utmost to bend "the old religion," adapting it in such a way as to avoid suspicion in the eyes of the Muslims. But they still had to be cautious not to arouse suspicion again. Learned Sabians tried to convince Muslim authorities that Islam had developed in a natural way from Sabianism.[571] In their writings, they called upon shared memories of the past. Abraham had also lived in Harran, and had turned from a star-worshipper to a monotheist. So they used Abraham to reinforce their case. Another figure from the Old Testament, Enoch (the Islamic Indris) had, as we have seen, also been associated with Hermes.[572] And, in the Koran, Indris is a prophet.[573]

So now we know why Hermes was identified with Indris. Indris was co-opted by the Sabians so that they did not have to convert to Islam. Hermes became a true prophet, with an ascension and all the trappings. Since Indris is described in the Koran thus, "...And we have exalted him to a venerated place,"[574] Hermes in his guise as a legitimate Islamic prophet needed to ascend to Heaven as well.[575]

According to the Arab author as-Sahrastani (1076–1154),[576] there were several groups of Sabians—idol-worshippers and philosophers who idolized fate. According to them, the highest God could not be known and could only be communicated with through intermediaries, divine beings. The divine beings, sometimes called angels whose home is among the stars, intervened via the seven known planets.[577] The Sabians investigated these constellations, their conjunctions and oppositions, and the classification of days, nights, hours, symbols, and climates. Based on this investigation, they made rings on which they inserted their seals and also other amulets.[578] In *Picatrix*—actually called *Gayat al-Hakim*, or "the Great Book of Magic"—we also find instructions for rituals and prayers to the seven planets worshipped by the Harrans. The author of this work made use of an old Nabatian source[579] that gives colorful information about the heathenism of Harran. Some researchers believe this source to be truly "hermetic."[580] The content of this Book of Magic reveals a surprising similarity to the Greek *Kyranides*, discussed in Part I of this book.[581]

Prophets and a Holy Book

The first teachers who would have taught this wisdom were Agathodaimon and Hermes[582]—the prophets of the Sabians.[583] Hermes is inserted into a long list of prophets who were forerunners of Mohammed. According to Arab author Masudi, Agathodaimon, Hermes, Umirus (Homerus), and Aratus are the prophets of the Sabians.[584] Another Arab author, Biruni, posits another sequence.[585] And according to yet another author, Ibn Hazm, the Sabians did not accept the prophecies of Mohammed:

> The followers of these religions agree with us (the Muslims) about the Oneness of God, they also acknowledge the prophetic missions, the wonders of the prophets and the sending of God's written Revelation to Earth; but they are in disagreement with us on the point they acknowledge only the authenticity of some prophets. The Magi… refuse to recognize Moses or Jesus or any prophets of the Israelians nor Mohammed and do not believe any of these were a prophet. The Sabians are divided in various sects. Some of them accept Abraham as a prophet, but others deny it. However, all Sabians recognize as prophets… Hermes, his son Tat, Agathadaimon, Arani, the Eldest, Arani the Younger and Asclepius; but about the other prophets they are in disagreement.[586]

Any true prophet must have a holy book, a revelation, so one was supplied. We read in several chronicles:

> Al-Kindi says he saw a book which these people [the inhabitants of the city Harran] recognized [as their holy book].[587] It was The Explanations of Hermes on the Oneness, which he wrote for his son. It was the best of the best about the subject of the Oneness. Any Philosopher taking himself seriously could not do without these books and had to be in total agreement with the content.[588]

Hermes was a prophet in Harran, but also elsewhere as well. And his holy book, his "bible," was *The Explanations of Hermes on the Oneness*. Arab authors have given us priceless information about the religion of the Sabians that was at one time prominent in the Arab world. And in this religion, Hermes played a leading role.

Many of the Greek texts we are familiar with about or by Hermes have been delivered to us by the Arabs; otherwise we would not have known any of them. Western students followed courses on *Hermetica* at Arab universities, like those in Toledo, Spain, and Sicily. There they came into contact with their own heritage. In the following chapter, we will discuss the Western face of Hermes.

CHAPTER 17
HERMES ON THE CHRISTIAN WITNESS STAND

Hermes was often called upon in the late Middle Ages to act as witness to the Christian faith—as witness to the immanent arrival of Christ; as witness to the Trinity. This very honorable old Egyptian was considered to have pointed to Christ and revealed the Christian truth, together with Jewish prophets and Greco-Roman sibyllines. Michelangelo painted prophets and sibyllines on the ceiling of the Sistine Chapel of the Vatican Palace. And an unknown artist painted 1500 sibyllines and two Hermes on the dome of the Zutphen Walburgis Church.[589]

HERMES IN ZUTPHEN

In the beginning of the 20th century, two Hermes reappeared from under the whitewash of the Saint Walburgis church at Zutphen. They now look down at the congregation from high up in the arched roof.

Actually only one of the figures is Hermes, since the second one is a mistake. Here's what happened.

Above one of the Hermes figures, which bears the humble description *phs* (philosopher... the rest of the name has disappeared), a winding banderole is seen with the words *monos monodem genuit et in seipsum reflexit ardorem* (Oneness brings forth oneness and Love's glowing power reflects upon itself).[590] This is on the north side of the dome. On the south side, we find another Hermes figure with the label: Mercurius Hermes. A beautifully furled banderole reads: *O Sol, iterum me vidibis, Christus nascetur ex virgine, in quem credo* (O' Sun, you will see me again, Christ will be born of a Virgin, in which I believe).

The last saying is not by Hermes. It is actually anonymous, but was later attributed to Plato. So it was not Hermes but Plato who was supposed to be depicted here—a mistake by the painter.[591]

The first Hermes is correctly placed, but the saying enhancing his image is not actually a citation from any known hermetic writing; it is a saying from *Liber XXIV Philosophorum* (The Book of the Twenty-four Sages). We read there: *Deus est monas monadem gignens, in se unum reflectens ardorem* (God is Oneness, who brings forth oneness and reflects a glow upon himself). In some of the twenty-two known fragments of the *Liber XXIV Philosophorum*, these sayings are attributed to Hermes Trismegistus.[592]

This does not entirely agree with the story in the introduction. For we find out that, prior to the completion of this work, a debate took place between twenty-four sages, with the final question being posed as to who and what God actually is. This is the same interpretation passed down in a hermetic fragment of Stobaeus.[593] After long contemplation, each philosopher gives his own definition. One claims that "God is in all what is of Him," while another declares: "God is always moving, unmoving."[594] There is another saying that has been cited through all time:

> God is an infinite sphere, whose center is everywhere and whose circumference is nowhere.

This profound definition is cited for the first time by Alain van Rijssel, whom we shall discuss later. But, for example, Meister Eckhart and Marsilio Ficino also used this quotation frequently. It is this definition that decorates another portrait of Hermes in a manuscript in Milan called the *Ambrosiana*.[595]

Hermes, Christ, and the Logos

The West was not entirely impoverished after the "relocation" of Hermes to the East. Writings of the Church Fathers[596] and sages[597] often referred to Hermes, and the hermetic text *Asclepius* was known in the West during the Middle Ages.

Furthermore, some magical and astrological writings attributed to Hermes were in circulation. Certainly, the great revival of hermetic thought took place during the Renaissance,[598] specifically due to the translation of the rediscovered *Corpus Hermeticum*. Prior to this, however, in certain circles, as we saw in Zutphen, there was knowledge of and interest in the Thrice-Great Egyptian. Let us now bring a little order into these observations.

In Part I of this book, we saw that Clemens of Alexandria wrote about the forty-two books of Hermes. Elsewhere in his *Vlechtwerken* (also known as *Stromata)*, he also mentions Trismegistus: "Hermes of Thebe and Asclepius who lived among the Egyptians elevated to Gods by the people."[599] But three quarters of a century prior, Justinus the Martyr had also mentioned Hermes in his works. Very remarkably, he had tied Jesus to Hermes, with the *Logos* as the link:

> We continue by saying the Logos, the first which was brought forth by God, without conception was created, namely Jesus Christ our teacher... then we come with something quite startling if one compares it to stories about the so-called sons of Zeus... such as Hermes, the interpreting Logos and teacher of all; further Asclepius who was a physician...[600]

Justin traveled around as a philosopher before he became a Christian. He knew the concept of the *Logos* from the Greeks and interpreted it—just as the evangelist John would do—as being "embodied" in Christ. In his defense of the Christian faith in front of the Roman authorities, he made an interesting comparison between Christ and Hermes:

> If we truly say, He was born in a deviating way, different from a normal birth, as the Logos of God is born out of God... then one can see such which we have in common with you, which Hermes being God's messenger calls the appearing Logos.[601]

Magister Omnium Physicorum

It is, however, primarily in North Africa that the Christian Church Fathers quote Hermes. Bishop Cyprianus writes that Hermes Trismegistus, just as the Christians, talks about the One God and teaches He is for us "unfathomable and incomprehensible."[602]

Another North African, Tertullianus, calls Hermes *magister omnium physicorum*[603] and identifies him as Plato's mentor.[604] According to Tertullianus, the doctrine of reincarnation can be traced to Hermes: "Some say it was the opinion of Pythagoras, while Albinus[605] considers it to be a divine enunciation, probably by the Egyptian Mercurius (Hermes Trismegistus)."[606]

Here, Tertullianus quotes Hermes from an unknown hermetic manuscript, in which he reputedly said: "The soul after her separation of the body does not flow back into the World-Soul, but keeps her own individuality, and is therefore able to accept responsibility to the Father for all the deeds which she has committed while in the body."[607]

Arnobius also calls Hermes the teacher of Plato and Pythagoras,[608] a speculation eagerly adopted during the Renaissance.[609] Only one work by Arnobius survives—*Adversus nationes*, "Against the heathens," an optimistic title for someone who was considered a heathen himself by orthodox Christians. Nonetheless, Arnobius recognizes that, besides the highest God, there are also several other Gods—for instance, the Demiurge, the Creator, who creates the human soul. This soul is mixed in character—corporeal yet divine, transitory yet immortal.[610] It is the mediator, a term we also come across in *Asclepius*.[611]

Whether Arnobius himself ever saw authentic hermetic texts is not known, but seems probable. His much more famous pupil, Lactantius, certainly did. In *Divinae Institutiones* (Divine Teachings), he gives us many citations from known and unknown hermetic documents. Therefore, it is interesting that he delivers citations from *Asclepius* in Greek (from the original *Logos teleios*).[612] Still another North African—a certain Quodvultdeus, Bishop of Carthagena from 437 to 439 A.D.—translated Greek fragments into Latin that appeared in a small printing of a limited "alternative" *Asclepius*.[613] More about this version later.

Going back to Lactantius, he writes about Hermes Trismegistus in full admiration. He sees him as a true prophet of Christ: "How he did it, I do not know, but Trismegistus has investigated almost all of the complete Truth."[614] He tells us that Hermes wrote many books containing knowledge pertaining to things divine and the majesty of the One God, naming him Lord and Father. This God is nameless, as Lactantius quotes from Hermes: "God is One and He who is One does not need a name..."[615] God has no father or mother, for he who brought forth everything was created by no one.[616] Hermes calls God his Father and Mother simultaneously.[617] On the nature of humanity, Lactantius lets Hermes speak: "From the two natures, mortal and immortal, He (God) made one Nature, human partially mortal and partially immortal. Thus, He brought forth divine immortal nature next to the changeable mortal nature, in order that He, as the observer of all things, would admire everything."[618]

The Fall of Rome

In the year 410 A.D., a shock went through Latin Europe. On the fourteenth day of the month dedicated to Emperor Augustus, Rome was conquered by the West Gothic King Alarik. The eternal city was plundered for three days. Rome was not Rome anymore. Of course, for a long time prior to this, Rome had not been the Rome of Caesar or Augustus. The pivotal points of the Empire had been moved to Milan, Ravenna, and especially Constantinople. But Rome still possessed the magical sound and aura that is difficult to put into words; Rome was a myth. The conquering of the city was experienced as the collapse of the Old World—which, in reality, is what happened piece by piece.

Soon after, accusations were heard that the fall of Rome was the Christians' doing. The old Roman Gods had become angry because humanity had stopped worshipping them. Despite opposition, primarily from the Roman intelligentia, the Christian Emperor Theodosius had proclaimed that Christianity would be the sole state religion in the Empire. Centuries-old temples were devastated,[619] statues of Gods were destroyed, and the world-famous library of Alexandria, the Serapeion, went up in flames.[620] Was the plundering of Rome justified punishment in the eyes of the Christians?

The North African Church Father Augustine of Hippo felt compelled to write a kind of defense against the allegations brought against Christians for the fall of Rome. He spent thirteen years working on this defense, *The City of God*. The Dutch translation contains about 1200 pages,[621] of which several are dedicated to Hermes.

The City of God

Augustine knew Hermes from his time studying with the Manicheans, who considered Hermes one of their many prophets.[622] According to Faustus, the Manichean teacher to whom Augustine dedicated a controversial work,[623] Hermes was a prophet who foretold the coming of Christ. Ephraim the Syrian also wrote, in 365 A.D. in his city of Edessa: "For they (the Manicheans) proclaimed Hermes in Egypt and Plato with the Greeks and Jesus from Judea were 'Messengers of the One Good to the world.'"[624]

In the work of his youth, *Confessions of Faith*, in which he confesses his Manichean past, Augustine does not touch on the subject at all. But in *The City of God*, he does. There, he places Hermes in the direct line of sages.

> For what indeed concerns Philosophy, which promises to teach something which can make humans happy: The emphasis of this kind of knowing... only became famous during the time of Mercurius, whom they called Trismegistus. This was indeed a long time prior to the Sages and Greek philosophers, yet after Abraham, Isaac, Jacob and Joseph, yes, even after Moses. In the time Moses was born, the great astronomer Atlas lived, brother of Prometheus. It was him who was the maternal grandfather of the elder Mercurius, of whom Mercurius Trismegistus was the grandson.[625]

Augustine here maintains the tradition of the existence of multiple Hermes, as we came across with the pseudo-Manetho, the Roman author Cicero, and the Arabs. It is the grandson, Hermes Trismegistus, whom Augustine mentions elaborately in a long discourse about demons and images of Gods. He starts off with the statement that Hermes had other ideas about this than Apuleius, the "Platonist":[626]

> Hermes says, however, the visible and touchable images, so to speak, are the bodies of Gods and within them certain spirits did enter by invitation, spirits who have a certain power to either hurt or fulfill certain wishes of people who gave divine tributes and paid homage by worshipping them.[627]

There then follow several long citations from *Asclepius*.[628] Referring to a remark from Hermes—"There will come a time which will prove the Egyptians occupied themselves in vain so devoutly to their Religion"—Augustine reacts cheerfully:

> Hermes… gives the impression herein he can predict the present, now the Christian religion… throws over all these deceptive fabrications…[629]

But instead of being happy, he concludes, Hermes seems to complain about it:

> The Egyptian Hermes knew the time would arrive when the untrue, deceptive, corrupted and sacriligious rituals would be discontinued, and he was sad about such. This sadness was however just as unashamed as his knowledge foolish.[630]

This is unmistakeably quite sharp criticism from this Church Father, who at the same time states that Hermes says many things about the one God, the Creator of the world—"many things which coincide with the truth."[631]

In the twenty-fourth chapter of *The City of God*, Augustine quotes again from *Asclepius*.[632] In this chapter, Hermes teaches Asclepius about humanity's divine nature—this despite the erring ways of the forefathers who did not believe in Gods:

> Since, then, our earliest progenitors were in great error—seeing they had no rational faith about the Gods, and that they paid no heed unto their cult and holy worship—they chanced upon an art whereby they made Gods [for themselves].[633]

It is primarily this sentence that Augustine highlights. Hans van Oort counts this quotation at least twelve times.[634] Augustine uses Hermes "to counteract his heathen opponents."[635] He compliments him on the one hand—he is more sensible than Apuleius[636]—but accuses him, on the other hand, of having a kind of nostalgia:

> But nay, the same man who considers human's art of creating Gods as the most wonderful in humanity, is... saddened the time will come when the introduced fabrications of Gods by humanity will also be removed by the laws...[637] The real reason for his sadness seems to be... the chapels of our martyrs will replace their temples and sanctuaries.[638]

Then Augustine continues strongly:

> What happens now to the so-called lamentation about the Egyptian land of sanctuaries and temples, which will end up as a nation full of graves and dead? The untruthful spirit, which drove Hermes to utter this lamentation, probably saw himself compromised, admitted by the same Hermes, Egypt was already a land full of graves and dead, whom they worshipped as Gods. What he spoke through his mouth, was rather the sorrow of demons, who bewailed the punishments awaiting them at the memorial chapels of the martyrs. At many of these locations they are actually being tortured, making their confession and are being exorcized out of the bodies of possessed men.[639]

We see that Augustine writes less positively about Hermes than, for example, Lactantius, but there is no radical denial of Hermes. In his fascinating article "Hermes and Augustinus," Hans van Oort notices that "it is therefore very understandable, later generations through independent investigation of the *Hermetica* and for example via Lancantius, arrived sometimes at other conclusions."[640] I think Van Oort is correct in this. Hermes Trismegistus had an overwhelmingly positive attraction for philosophers from the late Middle Ages and was enthusiastically embraced during the Italian Renaissance. More about this in Part II.

Hermes and Mysticism

The fact that there was considerable appreciation of Hermes, despite the criticism of the mighty Church Father Augustine, derives from still another factor. According to Carlos Gilly, archivist of the Bibliotheca Philosophica Hermetica in Amsterdam, modern scientific research shows that the "alternative" version of *Asclepius* by Quodvultdeus had a great influence on thinkers of the medieval West.[641] The *Asclepius* citations were included in an antithesis against the Aryans, *Adversus quinque haereses* (Against the five heresies), which was for a long time attributed to Augustine. Thus the criticism of Hermes by Augustine in *The City of God* was rather softened.

Nevertheless, after Augustine, it was another 600 years before Hermes was quoted again from *Asclepius* by the Bishop of Utrecht named Adabolt II (we will return to him later).[642] After Adabolt, many followed. More than a century later, Alain van Rijssel quotes several times from *Asclepius* in his book *Against the Heretics* (Cathars).[643] His contemporaries, Thomas of York and Thierry de Chartres, do so as well.[644] Where the latter is more cautious, the followers of his school were more outspoken. Bernardus Silvester incorporated many hermetic thought patterns into his influential *Cosmographia*.[645] Even the great Peter Abelard used *Asclepius* in his theological work just a century later.[646]

During the same period, we encounter both approval and disapproval of Hermes. William of Auvergnie, Bishop of Paris, had been an avid admirer of *Asclepius* in his youth, but severely criticized the manuscript later on. Thomas Aquinus turned out to be quite neutral, rarely quoting Hermes; he knew Hermes strictly from Augustine's book *The City of God*. On the other hand, his mentor, Albertus Magnus (the Great), spoke about Hermes more than 100 times.[647] He called Hermes a philosopher, physicist, and alchemist, and identifies him as an astronomer/astrologer and a magi. Only in the last capacity does he condemn Hermes.

Carlos Gilly shows us an interesting link between Albertus Magnus and German mysticism (Meister Eckhart) via his Dominican brothers and disciples. It was probably the hermetic passages in Quodvultdeus' *Contra five heresies* (the "alternative" Asclepius) that caused this part of Eckhart's teachings to be condemned as heresy during the events that took place in Cologne and in the papal bull of Pope John XXII.[648]

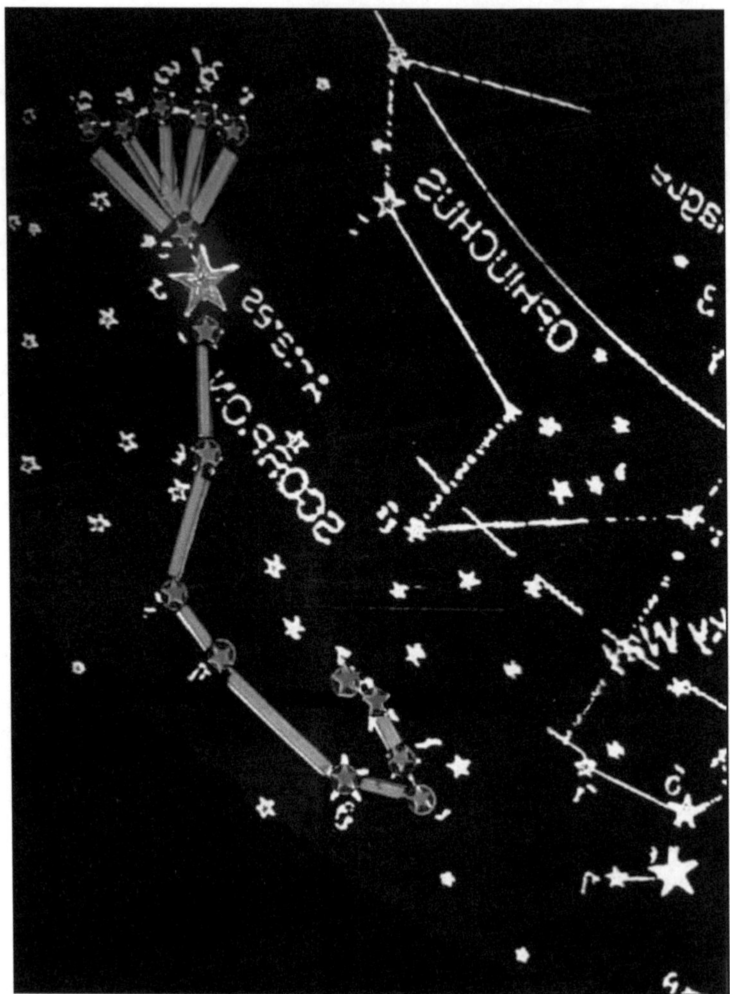

Plate A: Hermes to Asclepius, Asclepius 24: "Or don't you know, Asclepius, that Egypt is the counter-image of the Heavens?" (© W.H.Zitman)

Eckhart is not the only mystic who was most likely influenced by Hermes. Gilly names Tauler, Seuse, and Ruusbroec.[649] I maintain that Hildegard von Bingen was also inspired by Hermes. In my book *Mystiek en Spiritualiteit* (Mysticism and Spirituality), I have shown the close relationship between passages from the *Asclepius* and Hildegard's own discourse, *Causae et Curae*.[650]

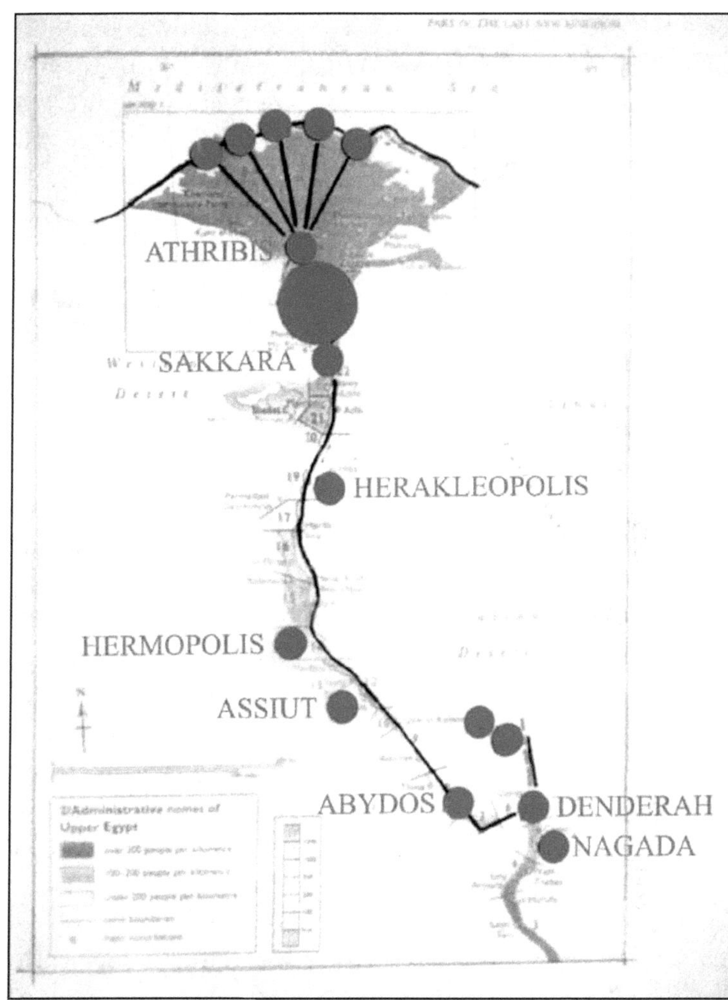

Plate B: Wim Zitman showed that the constellation of Osiris (Scorpio) is right above the holy places along the Nile (© W.H.Zitman)

It is Nicolaüs Cusanus, or Klaus Krebs from Kues on the German Moselle, who ends the lineage of medieval Western pilosophers who were interested in Hermes. The Cardinal not only quotes open-heartedly from *Asclepius*, he even possessed an authorized copy of it—the oldest we know of, dating back to the 9th century A.D. Gilly calls it an irony in the history of philosophy that the man who owned the oldest manuscript of *Asclepius* was totally ignorant of the *Corpus Hermeticum*, which was available during his lifetime in as many as two Greek versions published in his country of birth.[651] And with Cusanus, we are poised on the edge of the Renaissance, which led literally to a rebirth of Hermes.

Hermes and the Grail

We see in the Middle Ages that the Arab alchemists often used the image of the *kratèr*, the mixing bowl (the cup or monad), from the *Corpus Hermeticum*.[652] There is talk about a cauldron filled with consciousness that was sent to Earth by God. In alchemy, in which the goal is to transform "Earthly" matter into the "gold of spirit," the *kratèr* is the vessel, or mixing bowl, in which the transformation takes place. Modern research shows a connection between the Saracene God Tervagant, identified with Hermes, and *Trevizent*, meaning three-fold knowledge. Trevizent symbolizes the All-Wise in the medieval legend of the Grail. When Percival, the seeker, is overcome by doubt and allows his horse to find its own path, he arrives at the hut of Trevizent. He stays fourteen days in this hermit dwelling, where he is cured of his ignorance because Trevizent tells him of the Grail—the Grail, the Greek *kratèr*, the bowl of Hermes.[653] (See Frontispiece)

Today, there are some scientists who want to expunge the "romantic" idea of the existence of a "Hermetic tradition."[654] They seem to be correct if you focus strictly on the philosophical *Hermetica*—and even then, only in the West. For indeed, there is a gap of at least 600 years in that tradition. But previous chapters here have shown that this was not true for the hermetic-alchemical tradition.[655] Alchemy is truly also philosophy and these matters were not seen as separate in medieval times. Mercurius (the Latin Hermes) was a common figure in the Middle Ages—not only as a person, but especially as a characteristic. "The spirit of Mercurius" is literally and figuratively the "winged word." Mercurius is the *alpha* and *omega* of the transformation process. He is the process himself!

PART II
HERMES UNVEILED

Still through Egypt's desert places
Flows the lordly Nile,
From its banks the great stone faces
Gaze with patient smile.
Still the pyramids imperious
Pierce the cloudless skies,
And the Sphinx stares with mysterious,
Solemn, stony eyes.

But where are the old Egyptian
Demi-Gods and kings?
Nothing left but an inscription
Graven on stones and rings.
Where are Helios and Hephaestus,
Gods of eldest eld?
Where is Hermes Trismegistus,
Who their secrets held?

Where are now the many hundred
Thousand books he wrote?
By the Thaumaturgists plundered,
Lost in lands remote;
In oblivion sunk forever,
As when o'er the land
Blows a storm-wind, in the river
Sinks the scattered sand.

Trismegistus! Three times greatest!
How thy name sublime
Has descended to this latest
Progeny of time!
Happy they whose written pages
Perish with their lives,
If amid the crumbling ages
Still their name survives!

Thine, O' priest of Egypt, lately
Found I in the vast,
Weed-encumbered sombre, stately,
Grave-yard of the Past;
And a presence moved before me
On that gloomy shore,
As a waft of wind, that o'er me
Breathed, and was no more.[656]

CHAPTER 18
HERMES IN ITALY

On Palm Sunday, April 11, 1484, during the pontificate of Sixtus VI, a man named Giovanni Mercurio da Correggio aged thirty-three, rode through the streets of the papal city seated on a black horse. He was dressed in a black toga secured by a golden belt wearing purple-colored shoes. Being preceded by two servants dressed alike in symbolic garments, he rode in the direction of the Vatican, and next he dismounted by the river and continued further by foot across the green bank. Only then one noticed his hair, styled as a Nazarene, was crowned by a bloodied crown of thorns, and his chest was adorned with a silver shield in the shape of a waxing Moon engraved with an enunciation of the Holy Ghost: "This is my Son Pimander (Poimandres) whom I have chosen. From early youth on he has grown to sublime heights and I have instilled upon him all my benevolence to chase away the demons and establish Truth and Justice among the people. Do not oppose him! Listen to him and obey him with fear and respect. The Word of the Lord God and Father of the holy of the holiest on this earth, Jesus Christ."

Next, Giovanni Mercurio proclaims the Message and proceeds to throw handfuls of leaves around from his travelling bag. The gathered crowd runs towards him: Some think he is mad, others think he lives up to his promise; the majority announce him as a Prophet. He mounts his horse again, going in the direction of the Campo dei Fiori, crosses the St. Peters square, where the papal guards, as if inspired by a divine deviation, open a path for him. He enters the Basilica and further speaks out his Message. During the following days he answers the questions of people who thirst for wisdom. Afterwards he returns to Bologna, where wife and children are awaiting him.

The Inquisition picks up his trail and arrests him at 2 A.M. in the morning. The police hand him over to the Papal Court of Justice

> who condemns him to the pillory showing him to the people. There is also threatened with the burning staple. Finally, he is released after a good thrashing and he places himself in 1486 under the protection of the King of France.[657]

Giovanni da Correggio was under the impression that he was the reincarnation of Poimandres and added Mercurio (Hermes) to his name.[658] Although we do not hear much more from him,[659] this story is truly illustrative of the enormous popularity of Hermes during the Italian Renaissance. And this interest existed several decennia prior to the extravagant behavior of Giovanni Mercurio da Correggio.

Hermes Arrives in Florence

We find the trail again. According to numerous sources, Cosimo de' Medici, a Florentine gentleman, acquired an extremely special manuscript in the year 1460. It seemed to have been written by a certain Hermes Trismegistus and came from the East, brought by a monk on his return from Macedonia. It was (at least part of it) the *Corpus Hermeticum*, most certainly originating in Byzantium. In this part of the eastern Roman Empire during the 14th and 15th centuries, Hermes Trismegistus was extremely popular,[660] appearing in many published writings and manuscript sources of the most diverse kind. (See Color Plate 2)

It is possible that, during the 11th century, the Byzantine scholar Michaël Psellus gathered diverse hermetic treatises together and composed from them the *Corpus Hermeticum*. In any case, he provided the discourses with a commentary.[661] In contrast to the West, where only the *Asclepius* was read, the East had unbroken access to the *Corpus Hermeticum* in a variety of forms. And not only the *Corpus*. There was a lively interest in the other "hermetic sciences" as well, and they were all studied in relation to their underlying connections. So, in 1320, a certain Johan Katrones from Thessalonica wrote a work about astrology, the *Hermippus*,[662] in which he used various treatises from the *Corpus*.[663]

Moreover, it wasn't only scholars who occupied themselves with hermetic discourses. Hermes also stood in high esteem with the clergy, in particular the medical, astrological, and theosophical writings attributed to him—although, with regard to the magical texts, there was a much greater reserve. In 1370, this even led to an extensive court case against various scholars who possessed or even composed magical writings. The accused called very cleverly upon giants like Hippocrates and Galenus, who had apparently written the same things[664] and they were accordingly acquitted.

The Downfall of a Culture

There are several events in the history of the world that have left an inirradicable impression on the collective memory of humanity. Some of these were dramatic conquests like the fall of Jerusalem in 70 A.D., so unusually and suspensefully described by the admirable Jew in Roman service, Flavius Josephus.[665] A still bigger shockwave went through the ancient world with the fall and ransacking of the "Eternal City," Rome in the year 410 A.D. We read previously that this catastrophe was the direct cause of the magnum opus of Augustine, *The City of God.* And then in 1453, an event took place that is engraved in the memory of more people than any of these other events. In the spring of that year, a powerless and divided Europe (there is nothing new under the Sun) had to watch as the Ottoman Turks surrounded the ancient Imperial city of Constantinople. Sir Steven Runciman describes in a dramatic way the besieging and final conquest of the world city:

> Easter is the big celebration of the Orthodox Church, during which each Christian is overjoyed with the knowledge of the Ascension of Christ. But little joy existed in the hearts of the population of Constantinople on Easter Sunday in 1453. Easter fell on April 1, after a stormy winter spring arrived in the Bosporus. In the whole city fruit-trees were blooming. The nightingales had returned to sing in the thicket and storks were building their nests on the rooftops. In the sky, huge colonies of migrating birds appeared after their return from the North. In Thracia one could truly hear the sound of a large army advancing of men, horse and oxen pulling creaking wagons.[666]

Two months later, the city fell—the last stronghold and symbol of magnificent Greek antiquity. Runciman continues:

> The fall of the city meant for the Greeks much more. For them it was indeed the final word of a chapter. The magnificent Byzantine culture had played its role in the cultural process of the world and now it died with the dying city. Still she was not yet dead. The shrunken population of Constantinople at the threshold of its fall, withheld many of the greatest minds of the time, men who had been educated by a supreme civilized tradition, going back to ancient Greece and Rome.[667]

It is almost certain that, prior to this time, manuscripts had found their way to the West. Joost Ritman, founder of the famous Bibliotheca Philosophica Hermetica in Amsterdam, describes in a touching way how, in 1439, the representatives of two economic and religious world powers that bordered on the Mediterranean Sea met each other.[668] They uttered a warning against the downfall of Christian culture in the old Byzantine Empire. But it did not help. Fourteen years later, it happened. Where religion and politics failed, science tried to save as much as could be saved. Ritman describes "the most important salvation action of Western historical culture, namely the salvation of thousands of handwritings of pre-Christian Platonic, early-Christian and hermetical thoughts which had been translated in Greek."[669]

Much has surely been lost. But fortunately, part of it was saved for coming generations. Anyone who studies the imposing inventories of the most outstanding European libraries (as far as they have been categorized) has to be impressed by our cultural heritage. The Italian Renaissance in particular has contributed to the unveiling of this cultural legacy. The Renaissance was the time of the rebirth of Plato, the Neoplatonists, and, above all, Hermes Trismegistus—the latter primarily by means of the publication and translation of the *Corpus Hermeticum*, which, as we saw above, arrived in Florence in 1460. Let's have a look at how this came about.

Pimander

At the extraordinary international religious Council that took place in Florence in 1439 (see above), a notable Byzantine scholar, Georgius Gemistos (nicknamed Plethon), was present. He spoke with such candor about Plato that Cosimo de' Medici, also present at the Council, decided to found a new *Academia*—a renewal of the old Platonic Academy that had been closed in 529 A.D. by Emperor Justianus. That idea was forgotten, but, nevertheless, Plato was studied extensively in Florence—something that had not happened for almost 1000 years in the West. Plato was hardly known in the Middle Ages—Aristotle was the order of the day in medieval philosophy.

Plethon left several very talented pupils in Florence, among them a monk called Johannnus who named himself after his idol, the Egyptian recluse Bessarion. He had left Byzantium to attend the Council in Florence and, thanks to the advancing Turkish armies, decided to stay there. In the same year, he became a Cardinal, which did not stop him in the least from carrying on his scientific studies. In 1469, he published an epoch-making epistle[670] in which he pleaded for the amalgamation of Platonism and Christianity, something absolutely unheard of at that time. Until that time, Plato and the Neoplatonists had been considered the "enemies" of Christianity in the West. Bessarion took the first step toward reinstating the popularity of Plato in Florence—and far beyond.

In the meantime, around 1462, a new *Academia* was finally established in Florence. In the middle of all this philosophical fervor, we find the young[671] Marsilio Ficino, who had been commissioned by Cosimo de' Medici to begin a translation of the *Corpus Hermeticum* in the fall of 1462. This translation took only five months to complete, but it led to a true explosion of consciousness. Just six months after Ficino's translation of the *Corpus Hermeticum* into Latin, an Italian version appeared by his friend Tomasso Benci. Within the next few years, Ficino's Latin translation appeared in more than forty manuscripts.[672] In 1471, the work was published for the first time[673] and many editions followed. These contained the fourteen treatises of the *Corpus* purchased by Cosimo and translated by Ficino entitled *Pimander*. In actuality, Ficino used the first treatise's title for the entire work, and the title remained *en vogue* for a long time.

A World Discovery

How did Ficino come to translate Hermes? The answer is simple. He was commissioned by Cosimo de' Medici. Earlier, the young Ficino had been approached by the doge to unveil Plato for future generations. Having just begun to carry out that commission, he was requested to translate Hermes. Now there are two legendary versions of how this came to be—both of which are only partially true. The first, more romantic, version has Cosimo, an ardent admirer of Plato, storming into Ficino's work room in an exalted state and summarily commanding that he immediately stop the translation of Plato. In his hands he was holding the manuscript of the monk from Macedonia—an authentic manuscript of the Thrice-Great Hermes, mentor of the god-like Plato.[674] How much of this is true?

It is true that Hermes was seen as the mentor of Pythagoras, who was in turn the mentor of Plato. I will come back to this later. It is not true that the manuscript was, as it were, still warm from its journey from the Balkans to Florence. Cosimo had it, according to almost all sources, in 1460, two years before his commission of the translation. It remains unclear why he waited so long to authorize the translation, given that he was so vitally interested in this text. Of course, there is another possibility. In my article "Ficino and Hermes," I suggest that the year 1460 may not be correct. The urgency with which Cosmio demanded the translation may suggest that is was acquired in 1462 rather than two years before.[675] This would also explain the gift of thanks Ficino received for his translation, in the form of a villa in the hills of Florence—in Careggi, to be precise.[676] So we may conclude that, either the date 1460 is incorrect, or that the commission was less urgently given than is suggested in contemporary literature.

The second version of how Ficino came to translate the *Corpus* has only very recently been dismissed as a fable. This story claims that the copy of the *Corpus Hermeticum* that was acquired by Cosimo in 1460 (or 1462) was the first and only one to make its appear-

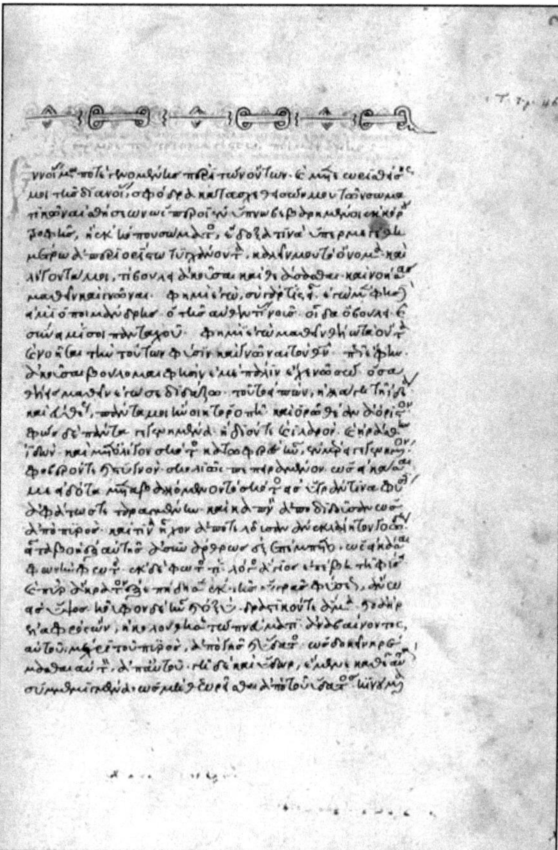

The *Corpus Hermeticum* is probably the oldest handwritten Greek manuscript (from the collection of Cardinal Bessarion).

ance in the West. This appears now not to be true. The previously mentioned Joost Ritman discovered that another copy was known in Florence prior to 1460. Even more remarkable, this turns out to be a handwritten manuscript entirely in Greek that includes the treatises missing from the Ficino document. This manuscript had been bought in June 1458 by Cardinal Bessarion.[677]

Joost Ritman rediscovered this magnificent manuscript in Venice at the library of San Marco, the *Bibliotheca Marciana.*[678] It had arrived there as part of Bessarion's donation of his extensive personal library of more than 100 manuscripts to the library,[679] which even included a third copy of the *Corpus Hermeticum.*[680] Moreover, the Cardinal possessed other hermetic writings, such as the *Asclepius,* the *Tabula Smaragdina*, some astrological works, and even a part of the *Kyranides*.[681] Thus magic, astrology, alchemy, medicine, philosophy, and theology were still intimately connected with each other in the Renaissance—and even acknowledged to be so by a number of highly placed men of the Church!

Multicolored Links

Hermes reappeared in Florence, but prior to that he was known elsewhere. In fact, he never went away. We have tracked several links in the chain to the East, to Byzantium, and to the Western medieval world. And we also know that the discovery of Joost Ritman in Venice is a perfect example of the persistence of this tradition, and that (much) more will be unveiled in the future. From antiquity onward, humanity has been inspired by Hermes, whoever he may have been in their eyes. I call it the hermetic tradition. As we saw, one of the arguments against such a tradition is the apparent gap of more than 600 years in its written traditions. At the end of the Interlog, I counteracted this by pointing at the unbroken tradition of hermetic magical, alchemical, astrological, and iatrological writings.[682] Another argument made against the existence of a continuous hermetic tradition is based in the fact that it was not only Hermes who was revived during the Renaissance, but also the ancient Greek philosophical tradition spearheaded by Plato. This is entirely true, although you could reasonably argue that Plato became as popular as he did because he was a student of a student of Hermes.[683]

These things are very hard to distinguish. Studies of the Classics have proven that many issues influence each other. When cultures encounter each other, influence occurs. In the time after Alexander the Great, the Hellenic period, a mantel of Greek culture was thrown over the other regional cultures. These cultures—for example, the Egyptian and Jewish cultures (to mention the extremes)—did not disappear and continued to hold their own characteristics, although on some points they adjusted. It is also true that ancient cultures often served as foundations for newer ones. This is very clearly seen in the Roman culture, which was built on Etruscan and Greek foundations, just as Christianity was, for the most part, built on elements of the lost Roman Empire.[684]

Hermes continued to live in philosophy and theology, astronomy and astrology, and in magic, alchemy, and medicine—sometimes under his own name, often in combination with other learned men, and sometimes completely anonymously, as in the just-mentioned *Hermippus*. This broad unknown philosophical territory, experienced as a conceptual unity by contemporaries, is exactly what makes the history of the *Hermetica* so fascinating. If we use the materialistic scientific method[685]—by which things are torn apart, as it were—this unity mostly falls apart and what usually remains is misunderstanding (as, for example, with Festugière and Cumont).[686] On the one hand, scholars are extremely fascinated by these phenomena; on the other hand, they are not able to make the connections necessary to come to an understanding of the experiential world of the disciples of Hermes. The materialistic scientific model does not allow enough philosophical space to comprehend "Hermes" in his full spectrum.[687]

During the Renaissance, specifically in Florence, not only Hermes but also Plato and the Neoplatonists were revived. The Italian Humanists[688] saw the ancient wisdom teachings as being composed of an unbroken chain in which both Pythagoras and Plato were links, as well as Zoroaster (Zarathustra), Moses and, of course, Hermes.[689] Even Christianity was part of this ancient wisdom; Christian revelation and "heathen" philosophy were both based on a common source. The fascinating thing about this cultural era is that they looked first to the similarity and unity of all, and not to the lacerating differences.[690]

When Plato was revived in the Renaissance, it was as a product of Chaldean-Egyptian thinking. Plato was seen as one of the later links in the centuries-old chain of wisdom—a tradition that, as Ficino said, originated with the Thrice-Great Hermes. Later, Hermes was replaced by Zoroaster, who became the progenitor of knowledge and heir to hermetic wisdom. Let's have a look at how this all fits together.

The *Prisca Theologia*

Ficino received his commission to translate the *Corpus Hermeticum* from his superior, Cosimo de' Medici. He had to stop his work on Plato, which he had just begun. Cosimo was known to be a great lover of Plato. Hermes must have been very important in his eyes for him to give priority to Hermes over the "divine Plato." How did Cosimo know of Hermes? We do not know for sure. However, there are clues. One, of course, points to Plethon and the Council held in Florence in 1439 that we discussed earlier. A student of Plethon, Agyropoulos, taught Greek philosophy at the University of Florence. His lectures were attended by Lorenzo de' Medici, the inquisitive grandson of Cosimo. Cosimo himself was often a guest at the Sunday-morning sessions held at the home of Agyropoulos, where lecture material was studied in depth.[691]

Another trail leads to a learned humanist named Niccollò Niccolli, whose passion for collecting classical manuscripts brought him to the edge of bankruptcy. From Cosimo, he received *carte blanche* to purchase them, not for himself, but for the library of the Medici. This inspired collector was also a copyist. Thus, a manuscript in his hand of the *Divinae Institutiones* (Divine Instructions) from Lactantius survives,[692] and this was certainly not the only writing from Lactantius in Tuscany at this time. The Medici library in Florence, the *Bibliotheca Medicea*, contains, among many other works, a medieval translation of passages from the works of Lactantius pertaining specifically to Hermes Trismegistus.[693] Cosimo was undoubtedly familiar with *The City of God* of Augustine and with other works attributed to Augustine in which Hermes was praised.[694] Cosimo had read about Hermes and he was so enthusiastic about Trismegistus that he placed him above his beloved Plato. Plato, after all, appeared to have been a student of Pythagoras, who in turn had been a student of Hermes. With Hermes, Cosimo had the source in hands.

We find this observation in Ficino's *Argumentum*, the introduction to his translation of the *Corpus*, where he writes that Thoth is named by the Egyptians as the Thrice-Great (Trismegistus) because he is the greatest among philosophers, greatest among priests, and greatest among kings.

> Among the philosophers he was the first turning his back on Physics and Mathematics, studying divine matters instead. He was the first who deeply understood God's Majesty, the hierarchies of heavenly Beings and the changing over of the souls. He is therefore called the first theological writer. After him came Orpheus occupying the second place in the antiquarian world. In the divine Teachings of Orpheus, Aglaophemus was initiated followed by Pythagoras. His follower was Philolaus, the mentor of the divine Plato. Therefore, there is only one divine ancient Philosophy whose source is Mercurius and its zenith in the divine Plato.[695]

Ficino describes, therefore, a direct lineage: Hermes, Orpheus, Aglaophemus, Pythagoras, Philolaus, and Plato. How does he arrive at this hereditary succession? From Pythagoras it is clear: Philolaus was a student of Pythagoras and a mentor of Plato. Chronologically, this may be correct; but factually, it is not. Pythagoras lived for the most part during the 6th century B.C.; Philolaus lived in the 5th; Plato lived mainly in the 4th.

According to an old tradition, Philolaus of Tarentum wrote a book about the doctrine of Pythagoras, from which Plato learned the philosophy of Pythagoras. The fact that we have to be figurative is proven by the fact that Ficino replaced Philolaus with Zoroaster in the lineage, who, in his turn, took over the first place assigned to Hermes.[696] The transfer from Hermes to Orpheus and thence, via Aglaophemus, to Pythagoras has to be interpreted in a symbolic sense. There is mention of a "secret doctrine" by which each one was initiated—an esoteric tradition that was handed down through the ages. From Hermes to Plato. Ficino called this the *prisca theologia*.[697] This concept of an ancient tradition, a revelation that was transferred from one initiate to the next, was not invented by the Italian Humanists. We find this in antiquity, especially with Clemens of Alexandria and Augustine.[698]

There were probably six sages in the lineage for numerological reasons.[699] More interesting is the choice of the six in the group. Why not Parmenides, or Empedokles, or Herakleitos, or Socrates? Why the lesser-known Aglaophemus and Philolaus? We do not know. What we do know is that the Neoplatonist Proclus introduced the chain of *prisca theologia* during the 5th century A.D.[700] and that Ficino was aware it.[701] The lineage introduced by Proclus did not include Hermes, but was exclusively Greek: Orpheus, Aglaophemus, Pythagoras, Philolaus, and Plato. How did Proclus arrive at this mythical succession?

An Egyptian, a Greek, and a Jew

According to the Neoplatonist Iamblichus, whose work Ficino also translated, Pythagoras adopted the "doctrine"[702] from Orpheus.[703] These teachings were called "holy" by Pythagoras, since they belonged to the most secret circle around Orpheus:

> This is the doctrine about the Gods... which I learned after my Initiation in the Tracinian Libretha. There the Initiator Aglaophemus revealed to me Orpheus... stated the ever-lasting essence of the number forms the all-providing source of Heaven and Earth and Nature in between, including the foundation of the continuation of divine humans, Gods and demons.[704]

We now have a picture of Orpheus, his pupil Aglaophemus, and, in turn, his pupil Pythagoras. Which leaves Philolaus and Plato. Once again, it is Iamblichus who hands us the key:

> Philolaus was the first who revealed the three famous books who by Dio of Syracuse on advice of Plato... seemingly purchased from him...[705]

The lineage from Orpheus to Plato is now visible. But how did Hermes end up at the top of the chain? We know this because, in addition to Iamblichus, his contemporaries Porphyrius and Diogenes Laertius also wrote a *Life of Pythagoras*. Porphyrius mentions that Pythagoras had the ability to remember his past lives:

> He recalled his earlier lives and said he first had been Euphorus, secondly Aethalides, thirdly Hermotimus, fourth Pyrrhus and now he was Pythagoras.[706]

This extraordinary story was confirmed by Diogenes Laertius, who writes that, according to rumor,[707] Pythagoras seems to have said of himself that he had lived earlier as Aethalides, among others.[708] And who was this Aethalides? A son of Hermes. Aethalides had been given permission by his father to wish for anything he desired, except immortality. He chose eternal recollection of everything that happened in this life, as well as the life beyond the grave and on into new incarnations. This gave him precise memories of all previous lifetimes—and this included the life of Pythagoras, the reincarnated Aethalides, as well.

For Ficino, the circle was complete. Pythagoras, the mentor of the mentor of Plato, had been initiated by Aglaophemus in the secret doctrine of Orpheus. And in a previous life, he was a real son of Hermes, who had bestowed upon him recollection beyond death.

There is yet another aspect to the *prisca theologia*: Hermes was Egyptian and, according to Iamblichus, Pythagoras and Plato had deciphered the stelae (pillars and plates) of Hermes with the help of the Egyptian priests during their stay in Egypt.[709] The Egyptian Hermes stood, therefore, as the fountain and source of Grecian philosophy. And not only that: The 4th-century Church Father Eusebius even indicated that a certain Artapanus, a Jew, had equated Hermes with Moses,[710] and this Moses/Hermes was allegedly the teacher of Orpheus. In this fashion, not two but three traditions were linked together. Later, there would be a fourth—the Chaldean tradition under Zoroaster.

A World Bestseller

In 1488, Giovanni di Stefano finished his beautiful floor mosaics in the cathedral of Siena. Among the emblems of sibyls, heralds of Christianity, appears a picture of Hermes.[711] To the right side of the venerable sage are two smaller figures. One is, without a doubt, Plato; the other is rather obscure. In the image, Hermes stands next to Plato holding an open book where we can read: *suscipite o licteras et leges egiptii* ("O', Egyptians hereby accept the Letters and the Laws"). The other hand of Hermes rests on a marble stone supported by two sphinxes that bears a carved text referring to *Asclepius*. The image carries the sub-title: *Hermis Mercurius Trismegistus contemporaneous Moysi* ("Hermes Mercurius Trismegistus, contemporary of Moses").[712]

The latter is rather ambiguous. Augustine records, in *The City of God*, that Hermes came after Moses, precisely five centuries later.[713] Ficino continues in the footsteps of Augustine in his *Argumentum*, even quoting him. Although Di Stefano, the mosaic artisan of the dome in Siena, cannot have gained his information from this, there are other well-known ancient writers in the Renaissance who placed Hermes in an epoch prior to Moses.[714] Following in their footsteps, Lodovico Lazarelli criticized the chronology given by Ficino in his *Crater Hermetis* and expressed the opinion that Hermes did not live after Moses, but long before him.[715] That di Stefano was aware of this comment, as Mahé claims,[716] is highly dubious.[717] The fact is that, by placing Hermes as a contemporary of Moses, the link to Greek philosophy was complemented by another link to Judaism and, flowing out from that, Christianity. The marriage between faith and reason had been consummated.

Ficino's translation of the *Corpus Hermeticum* was largely responsible for the popularity of Hermes in Italy. As said before, prior to the first edition, more than forty handwritten copies circulated in Latin. The Italian version by Ficino's friend Tomasso Benci in 1463 counted only twenty copies.[718]

Moreover, there were no fewer than twenty-four editions published in the middle of the 16th century, not only in Italy, but also in other European countries.[719] The first edition of Ficino's Latin translation in France appeared in 1494, written by Jacques Lefèvre d'Etaples, a Christian Humanist. In 1505, a new authoritative edition followed, with the *Asclepius* and the *Crater Hermetis*. The *Crater Hermetis* (Mixing Bowl of Hermes), by the hand of the previously mentioned enthusiastic hermeticist Lodovico Lazzarelli, was, for the most part, based on the fourth treatise of the *Corpus Hermeticum* and the passage in *Asclepius* containing the ensoulment of godly statues for which Augustine later severely criticized Hermes.[720] In the meantime, Lazzarelli also added to the fourteen treatises an original fifteenth, the *Definitiones Asclepii*,[721] published in 1507 by Symphorien Champier.[722] Besides the Italian versions, diverse versions in other languages eventually appeared—in French, Dutch, and Spanish. In short, this was a world bestseller![723]

We do not hear much more of Lazzarelli. He had, after all, a rather single-minded point of view about Hermes. The Thrice-Great would have only half understood Poimandres, his divine instructor, as appears to be the case from the *Asclepius* fragment about the ensoulment of godly statues. Only after an incarnation of Poimandres, in the person of Jesus Christ, could the hermeticist arrive at a complete insight.[724] And who could better bring this insight to fruition than his own mentor, Giovanni Mercurio da Correggio, the alleged reincarnation of Poimandres?

So we come once again to the point at which this chapter started: Easter Sunday 1484. Hermes was born again in the Renaissance; but at the same time, his image was being chiseled away. We must therefore be on our guard when we come face to face with the many instances in history where the hermetic link surfaces in the centuries hereafter.

CHAPTER 19

NOT MERELY THE CORPUS ALONE

In the 10th century, there lived a great wise sage named Krates who bequeathed to us an Arabic book entitled *The Sun and the Moon*. In this book, he writes that he was meditating when he found himself suddenly swept up into the air, following the same path as the Sun and the Moon. To his amazement, during this vision, he was holding a roll of papyrus in his hand whose very meaningful title was: *What repels the Darkness and makes the Light shine*. On this parchment were figures drawn to represent the seven heavens, each ringed by a shining starry view. Along with the Sun and the Moon were five wandering planets.

Suddenly, Krates saw a venerable old man dressed in beautiful white attire. It is Hermes. He sat behind a desk on which is placed an open book that contains the secrets of Hermes. These had been hidden from humanity, but now the time had come to reveal them to the initiated. Krates was therefore summoned to memorize all that he read, heard, and saw and pass it on to others.[725] This meditation of an Arab sage is remarkable in that it parallels the legend about the discovery of Hermes and the *Tabula Smaragdina* that was described in the first part of this book.

HERMES COMES TO LIFE

In the *Poimandres*, translated by Ficino, there is also talk of meditation, but it is Hermes who receives the divine revelations of the coming into being of all things and has the power to propagate the revealed knowledge:

> Why shouldst thou then delay? Must it not be, since thou hast all received, that thou shouldst to the worthy point the way, in order

that through thee the race of mortal kind may by [thy] God be saved?[726]

The ancient wisdom needs to be passed on to those who "have ears to hear." And they now "hear" a fascinating story of Creation. For in the *Poimandres*, we read a new story of Creation to place beside that told by Moses—a new *Genesis*. This was a victory for the Humanists, who had diligently searched for a link in the wisdom revelations between philosophy and faith. The Renaissance man drank in, so to speak, "the doctrine," and Hermes is unveiled and inspires scholars like Ficino, statesmen like the Medici, Church Fathers like Bessarion, and artists like Botticelli.[727] Hermes lives!

Divine Magic

Hermes is brought to life again in the Renaissance—but not due exclusively to the rediscovery of the *Corpus Hermeticum*, as is widely believed. It was due just as much to the influence of the magical-astrological manuscripts arriving in Italy from Byzantium. Through manuscripts like the *Kyranides*, magic *per sé* gained a much higher reputation in the Renaissance than it had received in the Middle Ages.[728] During the Renaissance, the ancient "magical" way of life seems to have been given a new lease on life. In the first part of this book, we read about the high-placed position of magic in humanity's life during antiquity. Strict attention was paid to the position of the stars prior to undertaking anything. Talismans were meant to give protection against malevolent planetary influences. In magic, the divine is linked with the terrestrial (and vice versa). There is a constant striving toward harmony between "above" and "below." The founder of magic, Hermes Trismegistus, is the great mentor, although he stays more in the background than in the philosophical writings attributed to him.

This is very clear, for example, in the *Picatrix*. This "book of Magic" is not ascribed to Hermes, but he is mentioned in it many times with great respect. In the Italian Renaissance, the Latin version of it was read frequently. Pico della Mirandola had a copy of it in his library and Lazarelli was also familiar with it. Whether

Ficino had knowledge of the *Picatrix* is not certain, but he did know Petrus of Albamo's commentaries on it.[729] In the *Picatrix*, three of the most important spheres—*intellectus*, *spiritus*, and *material*—are mentioned. We can compare *intellectus* to the Greek *Nous*, the All-Consciousness. The *spiritus* floats, so to speak, between consciousness and matter. It finds its origin in *intellectus*, but dwells in an enclosed space—matter. This looks very much like the Gnostic scheme found in the texts at Nag Hammadi, in which the soul is captured within the body. The same thing is described in the *Corpus Hermeticum*:

> Be then not carried off by the fierce flood, but using the shore-current, ye who can, make for Salvation's port, and, harbouring there, seek ye for one to take you by the hand an lead you unto Gnosis' gates.
>
> Where shines clear Light, of every darkness clean; where not a single soul is drunk, but sober all they gaze with their hearts' eyes on Him who willeth to be seen.
>
> No ear can hear Him, nor can eye see Him, nor tongue speak of Him, but [only] mind and heart.[730]

In *Picatrix*, it is not the soul that is imprisoned, but Light. And it is through striving to catch this Light (*spiritus)* in matter that the path of searching humanity is enlightened and comes into harmony with the cosmos. The *Picatrix* gives practical methods to achieve this, like using talismans that contain powers from on high. Indeed, these powers must be known, thus the planets, zodiacal signs, and divine decanates are brought into the picture, as we saw, for example, in the *Liber Hermetis*.[731] So, for example, Saturn is depicted as a man with a crow's face, sitting on a throne with a spear in his right hand and an arrow in his left. These kinds of archetypes made a profound impression on the consciousness of people in the Renaissance, and they also played an important role in the iconography of Renaissance artists. Dürer drew Saturn as *Melancholia*[732] and Ficino relates that he struggled with this planet throughout his life.[733] Moreover, it is very meaningful that Ficino's images of planets and talismans look identical to those in *Picatrix*.[734]

Tarot card of Mantegna showing Hermes Mercurius in hunting garb with caduceus.

Venus is shown as a loosely dressed woman in white with flowing hair, riding a deer, holding an apple in her right hand and flowers in her left. Mercurius is seen as a man on a throne holding a cock in his hand that has feet like those of an eagle; he holds fire in the palm of his left hand and has a magical symbol under his feet.[735] As I mentioned before in the description of the decanates in the ancient *Liber Hermetis*, these descriptions recall tarot cards. In fact, Hermes Mercurius is pictured on the card shown above from the famous Tarot of Mantegna (ca. 1460).[736]

Hermes' rebirth during the Renaissance was also seen in the reappearance of divine magic.

Ficino—A Magician

Marsilio Ficino, translator of Hermes via Plato and the Neoplatonists, wrote an impressive discourse called *De vita colitis comparanda* (About life influenced by the stars), the third book of his *De vita libra tres* (Three books about life). The work binds magic, astrology, and the healing arts with Theosophy in a way that is fully in accord with the old (hermetic) wisdom tradition.[737] I quote it here since it is illustrative of the all-encompassing way of thinking about Hermes that prevailed in the Renaissance. The *Vita* was so extraordinarily popular that it was published about thirty times in a very short period.[738] Thus in the eyes of the Renaissance, there was just as much interest in the astrological, magical, alchemical, and medicinal elements of the archaic wisdom tradition—the *prisca theologia* in which Hermes played such a leading role— as there was for the philosophical.

The well-known psychologist Thomas Moore gives a succinct description of Ficino's theory:

> In short, the theory is as follows: Each of the planets contains an extraordinary spiritual quality descending on Earth's situation in the form of rays. This planetary radiation can be seen as food for the soul; she is important in her variety and her peculiarity. In other words, each of us as an individual and environment needs a complete spectrum of all these rays, rays originating from Mercurius, Saturn and Venus etc. In our daily life we have two ways to attract, receive and assimilate these radiations. First of all, we can find in Nature objects attracting such life-entities or energies. We can use them when we need their special energy. Secondly, we can with utmost care, make things in such a way, by their affinity, they would attract specific rays, which the soul is in need of. For Ficino, items or art-works prepared according to traditional methods, are a means of attraction or bait. They attract specific spiritual characteristics to them, which following penetrate deep into their substance. In many religions one is familiar with this thought. One views a holy statue or a holy icon as the embodiment of a divinity or spirit. In Literature, it is sometimes made clear, if the image is

highly crafted, the spirit cannot escape it or cannot resist being drawn into it.[739]

Inclination from the Stars

Just like the ancients, Ficino considers astrology to be associated primarily with the healing arts. This sounds strange to our ears, but in Ficino's time, at least a quarter of the studies in medicine at renowned universities like the one at Bologna were focussed on astrological teachings. Knowledge of astrology, says Ficino, could lead to a happier and more purposeful life. He was convinced that people, through astrology, could become better acquainted with the Divine Consciousness. So he writes in a letter to Lorenzo de' Medici, grandson of Cosimo:

> The Moon stands for the constant movement of our spirits and our body
>
> Mars stands for speed and power
>
> Saturn shows our inertion
>
> The Sun stands for God in us
>
> Jupiter brings connection between divine and human laws
>
> Mercurius means advice, ratio, knowledge and insight
>
> Venus is our human nature, whose soul and spirit are love and relationship.[740]

Ficino followed in the steps of the ancient hermeticists who saw a direct relation between the outer and inner worlds, between the macrocosmos and the inner person. He writes, in the same letter:

> These celestial bodies should not be searched for in any other place; for the Heavens are entirely within us; in us lives the light of life and the source of Heaven.[741]

In his *De vita colitis comparanda* as well, Ficino emphasizes that the "attributes of the Heavens" are within us. "Our human passions are heavenly impulses implanted in us."[742]

Humanity should live in harmony with the heavens, but is not dependent on it. Humanity enjoys free will, Ficino repeatedly emphasizes. Stars "incline"; they do not force. He also criticizes the practices of some astrologers[743] who purport to be able to make personal predictions about the future of individuals.

Each star rules a series of matters like specific animals, plants, metals, and precious stones. The higher draws the lower toward itself. So, for example, a magnetic stone or metal will turn toward the Pole Star and flowers will turn toward the Sun. Those who want to reverse this attraction and receive a particular influence from above must use the proper medicines—medicines that contain herbs linked to specific planets. Moreover, when these medicines are acquired at the correct point in time, the desired heavenly influences are more easily absorbed.[744] Someone who, for example, wishes to receive the energies of the Sun should search for solar metals, stones, plants, and minerals; for gold, myrrh and incense; for plants that turn toward the Sun; and for cinnamon.[745] At the same time, they should nurture sunny thoughts and associate with sunny people. This will all work even better if they do these things when the Sun stands in a good aspect.[746] It also helps to inhale lovely fragrances, consume the proper food, and listen to appropriate songs.[747] They must do all this so that the harmonies of the spheres will reverberate in their being.

A Happy-Go-Lucky Duke

Six years after the translation of the *Corpus Hermeticum*, Ficino degraded Hermes from leader of the *prisca theologia* to second place in the series.[748] In first position, he placed Zoroaster, the Babylonian sage.[749] Was Hermes made to step down because of the prime role Zoroaster played for Ficino? Not at all. Still, it appears that Ficino's original enthusiasm had cooled somewhat. In his first discourse from 1457, *De voluptate* (On Sensuality), Ficino still quoted from *Asclepius* with enthusiasm. And a year later, he agreed wholeheartedly with Hermes in a discussion about God in relation to the soul: "God is a limitless sphere whose centre is everywhere and its circumference nowhere."[750] Later, Ficino used this profound statement several times,[751] but, remarkably, does not attribute it to Hermes.[752] As he grew older, Ficino became more and more fascinated by the Neoplatonists, primarily Plotinus and Proclus. Although he did not abandon Hermes, he clearly does not occupy the same prominent place he once had in Ficino's earlier writings[753]—at least not in the form of citations and praise. We must say, however, that the commentaries of Ficino are saturated with hermetic thoughts that influenced many generations of avid searchers for truth.

Among these was one of the most ingenious men in the history of the Renaissance, Duke Pico della Mirandola. It is doubtful if Pico, in possession of some hermetic works himself,[754] ever intensely studied the *Hermetica*.[755] His most important source was Ficino.

Pico was born the year in which Ficino finished the *Corpus Hermeticum*. He studied in Ferrara, Bologna, and Padua. The difficulties he regularly experienced with women—or, better said, with the men of the families of these women—often required that he depart rather hastily. In Florence, the young Pico befriended Ficino. After a period of time, having been part of the philosophical circle around Lorenzo de' Medici, the restless young man left for Paris to study theology. In 1486, he returned to Florence for a short while, on his way to Rome to pursue a grandiose plan of publishing a comprehensive collection of the ancient wisdom. He also experienced some setbacks on this journey, however. After an attempt to kidnap a lady who was in love with him, he injured himself and spent some time in jail. He repented and decided to continue life as a kind of monk. This did not quite succeed. Venus appeared at times too strong.

An Extraordinary Accomplishment

On December 7, 1486, Pico's ambitious plan was completed. He published no fewer than 900 *conclusiones* (propositions) about theology, philosophy, logic, magic, and other subjects, including the Kabala, in which he was well versed. Since, as expressed in one of his propositions, "No other sciences prove the divinity of Christ in a better way than the Kabala and Magic,"[756] Pico declared himself ready to support his *Conclusiones* in a public debate. Some of these propositions were, mildly put, quite radical and seem to be meant as challenges to certain ecclesiastical teachings. Preceding his public debate, Pico wrote an *oratio* about his propositions that belongs among the most beautiful the world's literature ever produced. It is better known under the title *De dignitate hominis* (On the Nobility of Man).

This speech was never delivered. The Church declared thirteen of Pico's propositions heretical and forbade him to hold a public debate. The young Duke bravely started to write an Apologia, a defense of the challenged propositons. This Apologia was clandestinely distributed, which caused great annoyance among the religious prelates. Pico was banned from Florence and fled to France. Through the conciliatory efforts of Lorenzo de' Medici, he was able to return to Florence, where he lived until his early death at thirty-one.[757]

Pico had not thoroughly studied the *Hermetica*, but he knew what it was all about! It is highly probable that Pico, known for his photographic memory, had only quickly glanced at Ficino's Latin translation. He knew this work well, for nine of the 900 propositions are borrowed from it.[758] The opening sentence of his unparalleled *On the Nobility of Man* points directly to the sixth chapter of the *Asclepius*:

> I read in Arabic writings, honorable Fathers, the Saracean Abdalla, when asked what seemed to him on this stage of the world the most admirable, he responded: "Nothing more admirable than human." With this pronouncement corresponds the well-known saying of Mercurius: "A great miracle, O' Asclepius, is human."[759]

Elsewhere in his masterful work, Pico writes that humanity—possessed of both body and spirit—was created in the image of God, yet occupies a middle position in the heavenly scheme. He can wander in this world and understand it. He can make this world his own through refined religious magic—whether hermetic or Christian—and he can remember his divine origins. This leads him back to the divine state that ultimately belongs to him.

Since humanity is, in origin, related to the "seven Rulers," it can communicate with these seven planetary rulers of the world. Yes, it can even elevate itself above them and, by means of Kabalistic secrets, converse with the angels, thereby participating in all three worlds—the supra-heavenly, the heavenly, and the terrestrial.[760]

Kabala

In her masterwork, *Giordano Bruno and the Hermetic Tradition*, Frances Yates proposes that Pico's magic is not *magia naturalis*, the natural magic of Ficino. It is rather what she calls "spiritual magic," in the sense that it implements the higher spiritual forces of the cosmos (through the use of natural magic). With Pico, this magic is embodied in the Kabala.[761] To the hermetic philosophy of Ficino, he added touches of his popularized and revised Kabala. Both these types of cosmic mysticism have much in common and blend easily in the hermetic-Kabalistic tradition that, after Pico, became such an important movement in the Renaissance.[762] Christian Kabala had, prior to this, already attained a literary form, but Pico definitely put it on the map.[763] This marriage between Hermeticism and Kabala had far-reaching effects, as we will see later in this book.[764]

At this point, you may critically ask yourself: Are we still dealing with a hermetic tradition? In the strictest sense, as far as the *Corpus Hermeticum* and *Asclepius* are concerned, not entirely; in a wider sense, most definitely, in hermetic magic, alchemy, astrology, and medicine. Hermes stands, throughout the ages, as a symbol of ancient wisdom in which all things not only have their proper place but are in reality bound together. In this wisdom tradition, Renaissance scholars claimed, there were philosophers like Pythagoras, Plato, Plotinus, Porphyrius, and Proclus (to mention a few). And in this wisdom tradition, there also stood Christian thinkers and Jewish prophets.

Christian mysticism endeavoured to show how to know God and how to obtain divine powers—powers that were extremely visible to the hermeticist. These powers were captured, as it were, in the "seven Rulers," the planets, as well as in the signs of the zodiac and the divine decanates. Here again, we have a case of the contemplative knowing of the One so majestically expressed in the *Treatise of the Eighth and Ninth Heavenly Sphere*.[765] To each of the seven lower heavens or spheres are attributed psychological functions.[766] Through the psyche, we can know God, as well as our deepest core nature. This ultimate characteristic of Being from the old wisdom religion we find unmasked again in Ficino's contemplations. Through Ficino, we also see it in the amazing Pico della Mirandola. And after him, we will see it in many, many others.

The hermetic stream of the Middle Ages runs into the Renaissance like a waterfall throwing itself downward with thundering sound. Arriving below, the stream is fed by many side currents. Together with these side currents, the crystal-clear hermetic stream develops into a broad running river. In the scope of this book, it is impossible to describe every side current or fork in this stream. A comprehensive telling of the tale is impossible. Many works with many parts would be needed to accomplish that. We must be satisfied to drift along with the current and describe highlights that arise out of the river. And these are many. They encompass those parts of the hermetic link that are still alive and still changing the way we see our world.

Chapter 20
Hermes in Germany

From Roman times on, the German Moselle region has produced fine and delicious wines—and also, great sons. In the 15th century, one of these, Klaus Krebs from Kues (alias Nicolas de Cusa, or Nicolaüs Cusanus), earned a reputation as a learned scholar of the *Asclepius* and became a cardinal.[767] In 1462, another hermeticist, Johann Heidelberg (d. 1516) was born the son of a winegrower on the beautiful Moselle River in the small picturesque town of Trittenheim. Taking the name of his birth site, he carried that name down into history.

Now, it often happens in history that mentors disappear into oblivion after inspiring their famous pupils, who receive all the attention. I think, for example, of the legendary Ammonius Saccas from Alexandria who schooled talents as the brilliant Church Father Origines and the great master of Neoplatonism, Plotinus. These disciples became more famous than their teacher, who is now unknown and almost forgotten. Such was the case with Trithemius, two of whose pupils would play a great role on the world stage and have widespread influence on many following generations. We'll get to them later. Let us first see who Trithemius was and what place he occupied in the hermetic landscape.

A Multi-Talented Abbot

Johann was an extremely inquisitive boy. As the son of a simple winegrower, he was able to get admitted to the university in the old imperial city of Trier, also situated on the Moselle River. He also studied at the prestigious University of Heidelberg. On one of his travels, when he was twenty years old, having already obtained a solid reputation as a scholar, he stayed overnight at a monastery at Sponheim. It must have been the night of his life. The following day, he decided to stay. He took monastic vows and remained in the small abbey for almost a quarter of a century. After a time, he became its abbot. He served as abbot until 1506, when he had to withdraw due to difficulties. Within the year, however, he once again became an abbot, this time of an abbey in Würzburg where he died ten years later.

Although Trithemius may have led a rather secluded spiritual life, his activities can be called very active. He dedicated himself heart and soul to the restoration and improvement of "his" abbey, gathering the necessary money, some angry tongues testified, from successful alchemical experiments. In addition, he developed an ingenious angelic magic[768] that he described in his large work *Stenographia.* This book was published in 1506, although various fragments had been circulated much earlier in several handwritten manuscripts. This had already led to scandals by 1499.[769] An abbot who installed an alchemical laboratory in his monastery, claimed to have contact with angels, and occupied himself with secret codes was, even for the most liberal Church Fathers, more or less suspicious.

Secret services in all centuries around the world have used Trithemius' invention— cryptography, or the coding of text into secret symbols—without knowing it. This invention flowed from Trithemius' need to record his so-called telepathic communications. The abbot believed in something we now call "telepathy" and was convinced that learned men, initiated in the hermetic sciences, were able to transfer their thoughts over great distances to equally tuned-in minds.[770] Trithemius was considered in his time to be a great savant. I would add that he occupied an important place in the rich tradition of Hermes. As a play on the epithet "Thrice-Great," he described himself a Christian for worshipping Christ, a monk for abstaining from worldly affairs, and a philosopher for elevating himself above human passions.[771] The prior of Sponheim set up an extensive library of about 2000 books that was known all over the educated world. Emperor Maximillian offered him an excellent position at his court—a position that would have guaranteed him a lifelong income. But Trithemius preferred the silence and peace of the secluded life that he had found in the two monasteries where he spent most of his active life in the role of abbot.

Agrippa

As mentioned earlier, mentors are often less well known than their pupils. Thus one of Trimethius' pupils was Heinrich Cornelius Agrippa von Nettesheim, born close to Cologne in 1486. Heinrich studied theology, medicine, and law. At the age of twenty-five, he had already given lectures at the Pavia colleges, including some on the *Corpus Hermeticum*. During the same time, he wrote an extensive work based entirely on the Renaissance tradition in which Neoplatonism and Hermeticism were linked with magic and alchemy. As a result of his alchemical research, he published a discourse about an antidote to epidemics. He also occupied himself with Kabala.

Like his contemporary Paracelsus, Heinrich was a tireless traveler. He was a soldier of Maximillian, a clerk in Metz, and a physician in Freiburg. As a physician, astrologer, and alchemist, he worked at the court of Louise of Savoy (mother of King François I) in Lyon. He also worked as a physician in the Netherlands.[772]

In 1533, only two years prior to his death, Agrippa, as he came to be known, published his three volumes *De occulta philosophia* (The Occult Philosophy). In this work, which has had a great influence on philosophers, theologians, and occultists ever since, Agrippa divided reality in three inter-connected realms: the elementary, the heavenly, and the intellectual—in other words, the realms of "natural magic," "heavenly magic," and "ceremonial or religious magic."[773]

It is clear that magic as well as astrology were important parts of Agrippa's work. We find in his writings much of Ficino's philosophy, but also thoughts from the *Picatrix*, which Agrippa certainly knew. It is therefore difficult to call *De occulta philosophia* a "hermetic" work. Agrippa was certainly influenced by Hermes; he even gave lectures about his work. But there is in his work, just as we observed in Pico della Mirandola's interest in Kabala, a mixture of many other diverse influences—something that makes the humanistic Renaissance so extremely interesting.

Agrippa was a controversial figure who stood as prototype for Goethe's *Faust*. This is not so strange when we see that he literally played "devil's advocate" by publishing, some years prior to *De occulta philosophia*, a work that diametrically opposed it. In his 1530

De vanita scientiarum (The Vanity of Science), he attacks the ground of alchemy, Hermeticism, and the Kabala—in short, all the sciences of the time. Some commentators consider this a manouevre of genius, since, by means of this publication, he was able to divert the attention of ecclesiastical authorities and the Inquisition away from his *De occulta philosophia,* which had been circulating as a manuscript for a long time, but was only published shortly after *De vanita scientiarum.*

Agrippa's influence on later generations has been unusually strong. But as Francis Yates so poetically puts it, "Ficino's gentle, artistic, subjective, psychological Magic, Pico's intense, pious and contemplative, cabbalistic Magic are innocent in comparison to the terrible power which Agrippa implies with his Magic."[774]

Paracelsus

Another pupil of Trithemius who outshone his mentor was Paracelsus, whom we met earlier. Actually, he was called Philippus Theophrastus Paracelsus Bombastus von Hohenheim, which he understandably shortened to Paracelsus.[775] After his death, a disloyal pupil, Oporinus, named him posthumously Aureolus,[776] which is why in the literature we often see the name Philippus Aureolus Theophrastus Paracelsus Bombastus von Hohenheim. From now on, we will call him simply Paracelsus.

Paracelsus was born in 1493 in Einsiedeln (Switzerland) as the only son of a physician. The family moved to Tyrol when Paracelsus was nine years old. At this time, he was initiated into the art of astrology and alchemy by the illustrious abbot of Sponheim, Trithemius.[777] In the years 1517–1526, he studied, during and in between his many travels, in Vienna, Cologne, Paris, and Montpellier. He obtained his medical certification in Ferrara in 1519 and, in turbulent years that followed, became an army medical officer in the Netherlands.

In 1526, Paracelsus became Basel's city physician. He owed this position primarily to the Basilian humanist Frobenius, who had received a diagnosis from doctors saying that his leg, which had been painful for many years, had to be amputated. Paracelsus healed him

Portrait of Paracelsus.

in a short time, avoiding that extreme treatment. A friend of Frobenius, Erasmus of Rotterdam, was also cured by Paracelsus.

Paracelsus did not make himself particularily popular in Basel. At the university, it suited him to give lectures in German rather than the usual Latin. Even more shocking was the fact that he broke from the medical doctrine of the legendary Roman physician Galenus, whose statements about the vital bodily fluids were still the norm in medical science. His symbolic burning of the *Canon Medicinae* of Avicenna (from the Galean school) was so provocative that he had to flee the town hastily. After his two rather peaceful years in Basel, he returned to his old job as a traveling physician. Many journeys followed. After an intense life, Paracelsus died in 1541 in Salzburg at the age of only forty-eight.

Paracelsus is best known as a revolutionary physician. But he was, according to the tradition of those days, also an astronomer, magician, alchemist, philosopher, theologian, and even (*avant la lettre*) a psychologist—the latter title was, in any case, given to him by Carl Gustav Jung.[778] In short, he was a Renaissance man, a *uomo universale.*

A Magical Physician

Paracelsus was a master of healing in the true sense of the word. The place for a physician, he said, was at the sickbed, not in the study room. At the bedside, the physician could not only make the correct diagnose, but could also, by his presence, greatly speed up the curing process. This was not the empty boasting of the man who once stated that, for every ten sick people, only one was cured by a physician—three regained health by themselves; the rest simply did not make it. Paracelsus was one of the first who believed in the psychosomatic causes of illness, and he acted consequently as a healing therapist.

As a holistic healer, Paracelsus was convinced of the necessity to treat the human being as a whole and not only the symptoms. Medicine was, in his eyes, a form of alchemical magic with a micro-macrocosmic connection.

> Nature itself is a magician... she creates for herself messengers such as comets and other heavenly signs. The magician can be compared with a physician. The doctor knows the hidden healing force of herbs, but the magician knows the hidden potentials of the stars... Just as the physician applies the healing force of herbs to the patient, thereby curing the disease, so the magician brings the heavenly virtues into human...[779]

Sickness was the material manifestation of astral and ethereal processes. Each sickness was, according to Paracelsus, the result of disharmony—an interruption of the *archeus*, the life vitality (or spirit of life). Through disharmony, a disease-causing *agens* developed, resulting in illness. Paracelsus distinguished five *entia*, which he called respectively *ens naturale*, *ens venale*, *ens astrale*, *ens spiritual*, and *ens dei*. He defined these *entia* as various "active principles or influences which rule and harm our bodies."[780] For each of these causes of bodily disturbances and diseases, there is a specific treatment. In the case of the *ens natural*, for instance, natural healing methods like herbs and baths were prescribed as effective remedies; for the *ens venale*, the application of an "antidote" was required:

"Allein die Dosis macht dass ein Ding kein Gift ist." ("The applied dosage of the medication may not be a poison.")[781]

The teaching of the *entia* points to the hermetic observation that each person possesses many "bodies." Next to the corporeal body, according to Paracelsus, a person also possesses a *sidereal* (or astral) body. This body is the carrier of psychic functions—a kind of "soul body." Moreover, each person is spiritualized by an immortal spiritual body whose nucleus is found in the heart. This "image of God," called by Paracelsus *Athem Gottes*, unites itself after the Earthly death with the "spiritual sphere."

Paracelsus was a hermeticist. It is not surprising, then, that, in his time, he was called *Trismegistus Germanus* and *Hermes Secundus*.[782]

Four Pillars

In his 1531 medical handbook, *Paragranum*, Paracelsus proposes that there are four pillars whereupon the medicinal knowledge of the physician should rest: philosophy, astronomy, alchemy, and virtue.

As far as philosophy is concerned, Paracelsus posited an *eternal light* as divine inspiration and as a possibility to get to know God. The outpouring of this is the *natural light* that gives humanity insight into "natural affairs." Everything is from God and, as such, is inextricably bound together. The knowledge of divine energy fields as they manifest in the cosmos can give people insight into their own true nature. What we see here is a posthumous teaching of the Thrice-Great Hermes.

Intimately connected to this, as a second pillar, are the astrological observations of Paracelsus. Entirely in the tradition of legendary physicians like Hippocrates, he moves out from this hypothesis to learn the reading of the "the stars of the heavens" that will teach the healer to heal:

> First see which star causes the sickness; then, which bodily part is affected by the disease and whether it is located in the weak parts of the body, in the blood or in the skeleton; next check which planet rules the diseased bodily part… One can halt the ailment with

> herbs opposed to the planet causing it... One can also heal through the sympathetic, for every planet cures her own disease...[783]

The last statement is conspicuous—no prescribing of an antidote, just "more of the same." In actuality, this turns out to be the foundation of the later teachings of Hahnemann's homeopathy. Paracelsus was also a pioneer in this field. Entirely in accordance with the hermetic observations (as one can read in the first part of this book), Paracelsus considers the terrestrial person to be a reflection of the "cosmic person." Practically speaking, the head is ruled by Aries, the neck by Taurus, the arms by Gemini, the chest and lungs by Cancer, the heart and back by Leo, the abdomen by Virgo, the kidneys and bladder by Libra, the genitals by Scorpio, the lower legs by Aquarius, and the feet by Pisces.[784] Moreover, the planets also have a place in this spectrum, since "Sun, Moon, Saturn, Mars, Mercury, Venus and all those signs are present in human himself..."[785]

As the third pillar, there is alchemy. Next to his function as a physician, Paracelsus is remembered foremost as an alchemist, although it was primarily a very practical chemistry with which he occupied himself.[786] As the first physician-alchemist, he recognized that chemical reactions in the human body can create an imbalance that can be readjusted by chemical medicines. With this premise, and based on alchemical discoveries and applied medicines, he introduced *iatric-chemistry*, which was further worked out by scholars like the Dutchman Jan Baptista van Helmont (1579–1644).[787] Paracelsus is thus the pioneer of the modern pharmacology.[788] In his laboratory, he refined natural substances into medicine.

> The physician will not use poison but arcana, in all good matters lies also a poison. This poison needs to be removed... this happens by separation...
>
> Through the fire, the poison is removed. All matters are transmuted by fire to return into another form, applicable to human.[789]

Next to the four basic elements (water, earth, fire, and air), Paracelsus distinguished as complementary the *tria prima*: phosphorus, mercury (Mercurius!), and salt—or in other words, the flammable, the evaporative, and the consolidated.[790] The elements form the foundation of the physical body. But Paracelsus recognized a fifth basic element—the *quinta essentia*, the ensoulment of things—that stood above all other elements and penetrated them with the "breath of life."[791] Few things come close to his *archeus* teachings. By *archeus*, Paracelsus meant the spirit of life wherein the core of all life is hidden. It is the "breath of life" that permeates everything. In the macrocosmos, *archeus* regulates "the orbits of planets"; in the microcosmos of the human body, *archeus* manifests as *spiritus vitae*, nurturer and coordinator of the individual organs.[792]

From this, it appears that chemistry, to Paracelsus, meant primarily a spiritual alchemy as well. The physician-alchemist-apothecary separated the fine from the gross in his laboratory, thereby releasing the forces enclosed within the *prima materia*, which are trapped in primordial matter. This was also a spiritual process, since the greatest alchemist of all time, in the eyes of Paracelsus, is God. God's Creation, which came into being when chaos underwent a process of "hardening" or coagulation, developed by distillation and sublimation. In the process, things were sometimes either wrecked or transmuted, as is the case in chemical reactions. This alchemy contains, according to Paracelsus, the code to unravel the universe. The alchemist can, by expanding these reactions in the laboratory, penetrate the secrets of Creation. The person, as the microcosmos, is composed of the same substance as the macrocosmos. As above, so below. It would be nearly impossible to be more hermetic.

Regarding the fourth pillar, virtue, Paracelsus had many vices. He was often very obnoxious and rude to his fellows. Distinguished and prominent men were his primary victims. He called the learned apothecaries from the university town of Montpellier dirty meddlers who prepared their recipes from dung and who had forgotten their respectability as well as their profession. But for many poor stricken and "borderline figures," Paracelsus was truly a very patient healer with high ethical standards and a sense of professional duty.

> Indifference, laziness and rigidity exclude one's servitude on Truth's altar and only frankness and tireless diligence will enhance the practice of true Medicine. The Healer, in this spirit, links himself

directly with the Divinity, Creator of the World, for whose people he helps treat and whose approval makes his heart thrice-great happy.[793]

The German Hermes

Admirers later gave Paracelsus the honorific titles *Trismegistus Germanus* and *Hermes Secundus*—and correctly so, for Paracelsus was a hermeticist. While the Paracelsus specialist Walter Page speaks about the Neoplatonism of Paracelsus, the erudite researcher Will-Erich Peukert states clearly: "The Neoplatonism of Paracelsus is a *hermetical* Neoplatonism."[794] With Paracelsus, in the tradition of Hermes, "the human knows the small world (microcosmos), not so much in his form and bodily substance, but more so in all the powers and virtues which the large world (macrocosmos) knows."[795]

Paracelsus refers at various times to the *Tabula Smaragdina*, especially in his magnificent work *The Dawn of Philosophers*.[796] Hermes is, in this manuscript, called "Father of all philosophers," and acknowledged as the writer of, among other things, the *Book of seven discourses*, which Paracelsus must have known.[797] In another more alchemical work named *The Book about the tincture of philosophers*, Hermes immediately shines forth in the introduction of this unusual text:

> I, Phillippus Theophrastus Paracelsus Bombast, say there has been sought with divine grace in many ways for the tincture of the philosophers, eventually all leading to the same scale and the same goal. Hermes Trismegistus, the Egyptian, approached this task in his own way...[798]

In Paracelsus—in good hermetic tradition originating in the king-priest culture of ancient Egypt—all branches of the "sacred" science (medicine, astronomy, magic, alchemy, and philosophy) coincide and are inextricably linked. With full agreement, he quotes Hermes in his treatise *On the nature of things* when he writes: "Hermes has truly said the seven metals are made and composed of the three substances... spirit, soul and body."[799] When, in the follow-

In the Basilica Chymica famous alchemists from various nations are pictured starting off with Hermes Trismegistus (Upper Left) and ending with Paracelsus (Bottom right).

ing quote, he speaks of the transmutation of iron via silver into gold, it is not the outer appearance that is meant, but the inner one.[800] Also remarkable is the religious context in which Paracelsus (and practically all his contemporaries) placed their observations:

> Prior to everything, having evoked the name of Lord Jesus Christ, our Saviour, we commence our work, wherein we not only explain how lesser metals are transmuted into higher ones—such as iron into copper, copper into silver and silver into gold—but also how we are able to cure diseases—which proud and presumptuous physicians claim to be impossible—and even more so: it (could) guide people to a long, healthy and complete old age. This Art is bestowed by the Lord, our God, the Almightiest Creator...[801]

The above citation forms the introduction of Paracelsus' discourse *On the spirits of the planets*. Further on in the same discourse, Paracelsus writes: "Mercurius Hermes Trismegistus says he who is fully accomplished in this Art, creates a new world."[802]

The "art," we saw, is bestowed by "The Lord Our God." But whoever, like Hermes, is fully accomplished in this art creates a new universe. With Paracelsus, Hermes is not considered a Creator God, but the instrument that gives Creation form.

Hermes is the *Logos* of God.

And Paracelsus his executor.

CHAPTER 21

HERMES IN ENGLAND

The two pupils of the learned abbot of Sponheim, Paracelsus and Agrippa, have had an enormous influence on the way philosophers, theologians, physicians, alchemists, and magis thought and acted after them—not only in Germany, but across the Western world. With them, Hermes went European. The central flame of hermetic Theosophy moved out from Italy, where Hermes was rediscovered, and into the northern regions. In Italy, the forces against Hermeticism became extraordinarily strong when the Catholic Church reformed itself during the Counter-Reformation. It seems as if, suddenly, the curtain came down!

Still, in 1591, a very special work appeared in Ferrara, the *Nova de universes Philosophia* (The New Universal Philosophy) written by Francesco Patrizi. Not only is much of the "universal" philosophy in this book traceable to Hermes, but the "twenty complete books and the fragments of Hermes Trismegistus" are enclosed within it.[803] The physician and philosopher Patrizi dedicated it to his old friend, Pope Gregorius XIV, and urged him that these teachings should be included in the curriculum of all universities, monasteries, and seminaries!

In 1592, another old friend of Patrizi, Pope Clemens VIII, summoned him to Rome to teach hermetic philosophy at the papal university. But the Index Congregation deemed the life work of Patrizi heretical and placed it on the Index.

The Church could not accept that the hermetic teachings represented the most divine knowledge on Earth and stopped Patrizi's reformation before it had even started—just as they tried to stop the revolutions of Bruno and Galileo some years later, as Cees Leijenhorst rightfully tells us.[804] Under the same Pope Clemens, in the year 1600 in Rome, the chair of Platonism was removed from the university.[805] And in the same memorable year in the same city, the hermeticist Giordano Bruno was sentenced to the stake. On the way to the funeral pyre, Bruno's mouth was cruelly sewn shut. Iron pins were horizontally and vertically hammered through his jaw.[806] Hermes was silenced in Italy.

An Englishman in Prague

In 1586, Giordano Bruno (more about him later) stayed a while at the court of Emperor Rudolf II in Prague. This monarch cherished a great interest in the hermetic arts—philosophy, astrology, alchemy, magic, Kabala, and the natural sciences—and he gathered around him people like Giordano Bruno, Michael Maier (more about him later as well), Tycho Brahe, Johannes Kepler, Edward Kelly, and John Dee. The Englishman John Dee (1527–1608) appeared at the same time as Bruno at the court of Rudolf II, but did not stay very long. In 1586, the *apostolic nuncio* was ordered by Rome to deliver a complaint to Emperor Rudolf demanding the extradition of Dee, who was accused of witchcraft. The Emperor was able to secure a temporary safe passage for Dee and Kelly (who shared the same fate), until, after much political backroom dealing, the order for arrest was withdrawn.

At this time, John Dee had already built up a brilliant carrier. He had studied Greek at Cambridge and the natural sciences at Leuven. In 1555, he had been imprisoned for a short while for alleged treason toward Queen Mary. A better recommendation was hardly imaginable for Mary's great rival, Elizabeth, so Dee was invited as a reputable astrologer to calculate the most favorable astrological date for the coronation of Elizabeth as Queen of England.[807] Afterward, Dee became leader of the so-called Elizabethan Renaissance, in which the occult sciences were at the head of the curriculum.[808]

Carlos Gilly calls Dee a humanist, hermeticist, scientist, wise magus, and historian.[809] During his life, Dee built up an immense library, definitely including the *Corpus Hermeticum* translated by Ficino and the last four editions of *Asclepius*, but also containing the *Iatromathematica*[810] and a quantity of hermetic-astrological, magical, and alchemical texts, including—it cannot not be otherwise—the

Tabula Smaragdina.[811] According to Frances Yates, Dee's collection—the largest scientific library in England in those day—embraced the "entire Renaissance."[812]

Dee was not only a great admirer of Trithemius, Agrippa, and Paracelsus, but had also been strongly influenced by them.[813] The first inspired him to propound an elaborate magic of angels. Dee assumed each human was accompanied by his "own" angel. The art was in knowing how to come into contact with this angel. This was possible, according to Dee, by means of magic formulas and mathematical symbols like squares, circles, and diagrams.

Magic

We can hardly imagine now the influence that, even in those times, magic had on daily life. A somewhat older manuscript—the *Summa Magica* of Berengario Ganell—for instance, contained thousands of names of angels, demons, and spirits, and was extremely popular with Dee as well as others.[814] To obtain a good insight into what (pure) magic entails, the writer first of all defines it:

> Magic is an Art in which one learns how to bind (compel) evil and good spirits with the name of God, with their own names and with the names of worldly things. From such follows, Magic is a Science of words, each name being a word, each entity uttered by the tongue is a word which can be written down in letters... Magic occupies itself with wonderful beautiful words which spring forth from a steadfast faith: The Magus needs to believe in the real God and in his Art and in his Master and in his Religion which it stems from.[815]

It appears rather strange to us in the secular 20th century to see the religious connection that writers make between the occult sciences and God. We signaled this earlier in the work of Ficino and Paracelsus.

Another very popular book in this genre during this time was *The Key of Solomon.* This is a collection of magical formulas for incantations dating from the 13th century meant to neutralize negative

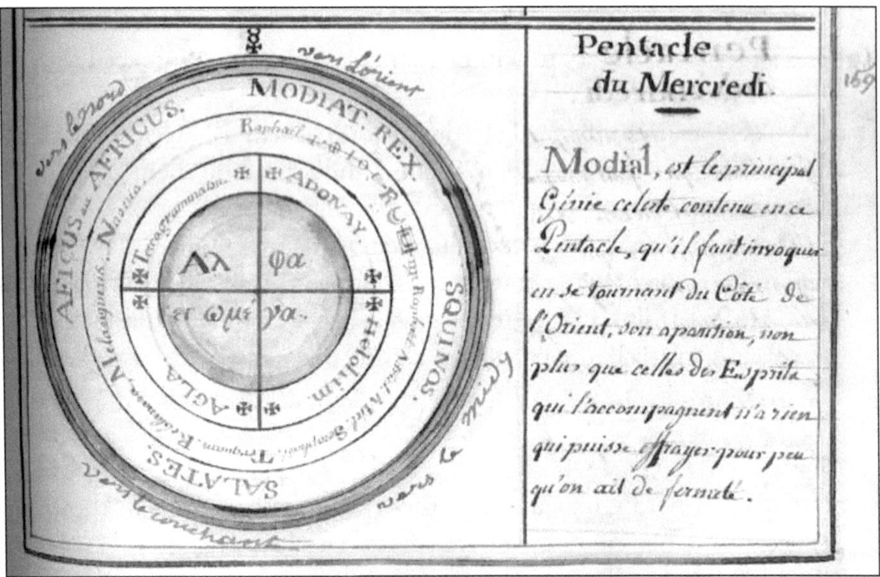

Drawing of a Magical Circle for Wednesday from The Key of Solomon.

forces and create positive situations. Next to drawings of pentacles, amulets, diagrams, and tablets of angels, we also find instructions for the correct attitude during the experiments:

> For an absolute undivided concentration necessary to practise the Greatest Art, the first requirement is a sound insulated and isolated space separated from the confusion of the outside world, since spirit apparitions and intelligences, who due to their spirituality are part of the Divine Nature, will show themselves more readily and will communicate more willingly in silence, peacefulness and solitude.
>
> A small upper chamber or a hidden cabinet not accessible to anyone, specifically not to women or girls, who will contaminate the purity of the atmosphere by their menstruation, would answer extremely well for the assigned purpose.
>
> The chosen space for the application of the Art should be furnished as simple as possible without luxurious or unnecessary decorations which could distract the spirit.

After having cleansed the space thoroughly with "holy" water and by the burning of incense (more about such later) removing evil influences, one should be dressed in impeccable white linen. After such, the spirits should be banned by speaking out loud the following words:

Eterne Deas Sapiens, fortis potens ens entium becator mundy veni in hunc locum et tua presentia majestate sanctifica hunc locum ut in eo sit puritas lastitas et plenitudo logis ut sicut fumus encensistius ad te ascendit sit in hunc locum descendat virtus tue ei benedictio tuo et vos omnes angeli et Spiritus omnes hunc consecrationi adestate presente per Deum verum vivum et eternam qui vos sicut nos uno momento destrere potest et per sapientiam ejus. Amen.[816]

Keep the incense burning and be careful no-one else enters the space other than those who are associated with the performance of specific necessary actions, while there needs to be paid attention to during a period of forty days there is an uninterrupted lamp left burning.

The recommended content in the room to be placed is only a table, a couple of chairs and a cupboard, wherein all the necessities for practicing of the Art can be stored. Completely new furniture is the most suitable, but if it is not possible the furniture should be thoroughly cleansed, fumed with incense and sprinkled with "holy" water, which will be discussed later.

Also be alert there are no pots or buckets for bodily or other waste products present, considering the atmosphere of the space should stay pure and clean. The best time for the experiments to be undertaken is at sunrise, since it is then the spirit is the most peaceful, the tendency for distraction is minimal, and is not yet saturated with outside impressions which could disturb the necessary complete concentration. If truly the condition and the position of the planets, which has to be taken into consideration from the start, make it necessary the experiment should take place in the middle of the day or later, then the day should be spent in a calm contemplative mood so all the necessary preparations can be checked and prepared, so the experiment can precisely as possible,

LIBER NATVRAE APERTVS

IN QVO VTRIVSQVE MVNDI, CVM INTELLECTVALIS, TVM ELEMENTARIS VIRTVTES NVMERO SEPTENARIO COMPREHENSAE, SPECTANDAE PROPONVNTVR, HINC ut mirabilis Superiorum et Inferiorum consensus eo facilius cognosci possit. Studio et opera G H R

In Regno SPIRITALI spectanda veniunt | In Regno ASTRALI | MINERALI | ANIMALI | VEGETABILI

Liber Natvrae Apertus. The seven holy pillars. Classical representation of the connection among others are Gods, angels, demons, planets, days of the week, minerals, bodily parts, animals, and plants.

> without time loss, be executed in the most favourable moment of the planet or the planetary constellations, which have the greatest influence, the strongest force, on the actions.
>
> To prevent mistakes, a summation of the seven planets follows with their compatible metals:
>
> The Sun rules Gold, Mercurius Mercury,
> What for Venus is Bronze, is Lead for Saturn,
> The Moon as a planet points the way to Silver.
> Tin belongs to Jupiter, Mars is married with Iron.
>
> From this follows, Gold belongs to the Sun for actions to be performed on Sunday, Silver to the Moon for actions on Monday, Iron to Mars for actions on Tuesday, Mercury to Mercurius for actions on Wednesday, Tin to Jupiter for actions on Thursday, Bronze to Venus for actions on Friday and finally Lead to Saturn for actions on Saturday. If one therefore desires to create a cabalistic figure or amulet then it should be done on a small plaque of metal ruled by the specific planet. The plates themselves can be round, oval, square or whatever form, such matters very little, as long as the inscription made on it is geometrically symmetrical.
>
> In case one rather uses treated skin instead of metal, it should not be bought from charlatans who claim to possess good treated skin, then one should preferably make it oneself, and as follows...[817]

I quote here rather at length as illustration of the "magical life-experience" that still existed so strongly in those days. But not all experiments were equally innocent, despite the notation of the name of God. In the 19th century, for instance, dangerous experimentation was done during so-called spiritualistic séances, and, even in the 16th century, there were rituals to awaken spirits. This happened quite often by drawing a chalk circle on the ground and uttering magical incantations while using magical tools like holy water, candles, scepters, swords, magical wands, and metal disks. Dee warned repeatedly about these summoned evil forces.[818]

A Hermetic Seal

In 1564, Dee published his most well-known work, *Monas Hieroglyphica*, a classic that cannot be removed from the cultural history of the late Renaissance. He dedicated his work to no less than the Emperor Maximillian. In eighty *theorema* (propositions), Dee explains a hieroglyph of the One—the *Monad*. Dee calls this symbol (*monas hieroglyphica*) a "Hermetic Seal."[819]

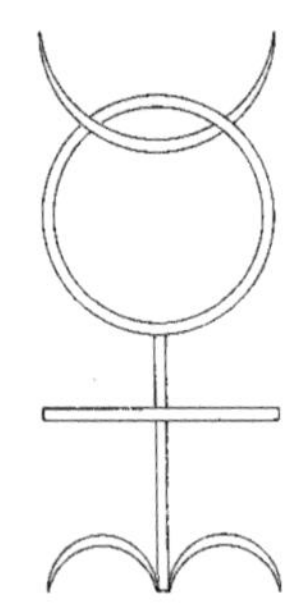

Monas hieroglyphica.

The base of the hieroglyph is indeed shaped by the astrological symbol for Mercurius. Helen de Jong states in her book about the alchemist Michael Maier that, "The meaning of Mercury in Alchemy stretches itself from quick-silver (Mercurius, *argentum vivum*), as the base element from which metals are formed, to the primordial water of Creation (due to Mercury's permanent viscosity) and even to the waters of Doom wherein the soul descends and to the Life Elixir. With this last association lies the meaning of Mercury-Christos."[820] However, Mercury is also, above all, Hermes!

☉	☽	☿	♀	♂	♃	♄
Sun	*Moon*	*Mercury*	*Venus*	*Mars*	*Jupiter*	*Saturn*

Mercury forms the base theme of the hieroglyph, but the Sun and Moon are also represented. Dee himself comments about this in his fourteenth proposition:

> With such it is confirmed the total power of transmutation is dependant on the Sun and Moon. The Thrice-Greatest Hermes assured us repeatedly the Sun is his Father and the Moon his Mother: We truly know the red earth (terra lemnia) is nurtured by the rays of the Moon and the Sun which practice a special influence on it.[821]

It is no surprise that he copied this text directly from the hermetic *Tabula Smaragdina*.

Moreover, we find once again in the *Monas* symbol the signs for Saturn, Jupiter, Mars, and Venus. Anthanasius Kircher (more about him soon) determined the origin of the symbol to be the *ankh*, the famous Egyptian symbol for life—and as we know, Hermes was one of the most illustrious Egyptians.[822]

The cross in the hieroglyph resonates with the four elements, the basic principles of every philosopher-alchemist in those days, but also with the Christian triad of birth, crucifixion, and resurrection. "This hieroglyph represents the complete existence, the macro- as well as the microcosmos," a later admirer would claim.[823]

In his introduction to the translation of Dee's famous book from Latin, C. H. Josten writes:

> The Platonist Dee discovered the power of the Cosmic symbol. He believed this power would make the work of the astronomers unnecessary. This point of view is shown in a passage of the accompanying letter to Emperor Maximillian to whom he dedicated his writings. Therein he states he retraced the signs of the planets and those of the Zodiac back to their actual form, as they actually existed in the past, or at least as our forefathers would have liked to see them. He is therefore not sure whether he is a restorer of the old or the father of a new Science. He claims, in other words, he discovered in himself the actual past by means of finding in himself his own recollection. And he had reached a level of introspection whereby it was possible to bring to development the thought patterns of his spiritual ancestors, the age-old wise men.[824]

John Dee and the Rosicrucians

In front of me lies a book that I bought twelve years ago at an extremely reduced price in a so-called New Age bookstore. Although at the time I had no immediate need for it, I was fascinated by the title: *The Rosie Crucian Secrets. Their Excellent Method of Making Medicines of Metals also their Laws and Mysteries*.[825] Dr. John Dee was named as author. The work of this master of magic consists of three volumes: the first is purely medical-alchemical, the second consists of a sort of alchemical lexicon, the third occupies itself with the six "laws" of the Order of the Brothers of the Rosicrucians. One of these "laws," for example, is the duty to supply medical assistance without asking for a fee.

I put the book aside as an example of anachronism. John Dee died in 1608 and the first Rosicrucian manifest did not appear until 1614. As I was researching and revising my own first book, *De geheime woorden* (The Secret Words), however, I came upon the work once again.[826] I looked critically at the information about the Rosicrucians and consulted actual literature. Therein two facts stood out. The *monas* hieroglyph also appeared in the Rosicrucian writings. Moreover, the *Alchemystical Marriage* had definitely been circulated as a manuscript during the early years of the 17th century[827]—a practice that was common in those times, as we saw with the manuscripts of Trithemius and Agrippa.

Although no less than the well-known theosophist Arthur Waite had, in 1893, strongly challenged the authenticity of the manuscript, which had been distributed by a former member of the famous (or infamous) *Hermetic Order of the Golden Dawn*, I gave the benefit of the doubt to Langford Garstin, its new publisher. Frances Yates definitely played a role in refocusing attention on the work with her book *The Rosicrucian Enlightment*,[828] in which she rather inspirationally writes about the enormous influence that John Dee had on the Rosicrucian movement.

A couple of years and several publications later, I concluded—along with the illustrious librarian of the Ritman Llibrary in Amsterdam, Carlos Gilly—that Dee's influence on the Rosicrucian movement was noticeably less than we had thought, and was definitely not as great, for example, as that of Paracelsus. The *monas* symbol, actually the *Mercurius Hieroglyphicus*, was obtained by Johan Valentin Andreae[829] from a later alchemical writing[830] and probably not from John Dee's book.

John Dee rests in peace after a highly active life. We will cover the Rosicrucians extensively at a later point.

Chapter 22

A Comet Rages over Europe[831]

On the crest of the hills surrounding Utrecht, near Bilthoven in the middle of the woods, lies a magnificent conference center that belongs to one of the Rosicrucian communities, the Dutch *Lectorium Rosicrucianum*. On May 4, 2002, the central hall was filled with several hundred people assembled for a symposium on Giordano Bruno—a welcome initiative. Bruno is one of the independent thinkers who nudged the evolution of Western philosophy a step forward—although this is totally unknown to many.

Wouter Hanegraaff writes, in his publication *The New Age Movement and the Esoteric Tradition*, that the Hermeticism of the Renaissance, certainly in New Age circles, is completely unknown to many: few "recognize the names of Ficino, Bruno or Jacob Böhme, while many others have heard of the *Gospel of Thomas* or about the Catharen."[832] These gaps in our knowledge are, however, being filled by symposia like those mentioned by Hanegraaff and by several interesting publications that appeared in rapid succession.[833]

At the symposium about Giordano Bruno, many speakers gave speeches. A fascinating summary of the program appeared a short while ago in print.[834]

A Flamboyant Personality

Giordano Bruno was born in 1558 as Giovanni in Nola, a small town under the shadow of Vesuvius. His later name, Giordano, he assumed in the Dominican monastery where he was educated. Here, his obstinate opinions caused a confrontation with the clergy—and this would certainly not be the last time this happened in his life. Not long after the argument with the clergy of the monastery, he broke away from the Church and was, for the rest of his life, pursued by the *dominici canes*, the "hounds of the Lord." Finally, in Venice in 1592, he was arrested by the Inquisition and delivered to Rome. After an imprisonment of eight years with endless interrogations and the usual accompanying tortures, he was burned alive at the stake on February 17, 1600 at the Campo dei Fiori.

Giordano Bruno was a contemporary of John Dee, although the two men never met. This is quite remarkable, since Bruno spent three flamboyant years in London, where John Dee also worked at the same time. Later, they both frequented the court of Rudolf II in Prague. Whether they would have become friends if they had known each other is doubtful, as the differences between their two personalities were great. They were both hermeticists, but they applied their knowledge in totally different ways. Dee was a magus; Giordano was a visionary. His ideas regarding the composition of the universe were truly spectacular for the time and far surpassed in audacity those of other contemporaries like Copernicus and Galileo. During the above-mentioned symposium, Frans Smit held the audience spellbound with these observations:

> Without exaggeration one can say Bruno was 400 years ahead of his time. And I do not think immediately of what is presently called holistic Science, which primarily attracts attention only in the measure of its floating with the waves of continuously new and fashionable trends. No, it is about revolutionary scientists from reputable institutions such as Princeton and Stanford, who by means of the "zero-point-field" theory, have come to accept as a temporary axioma, there exists no such thing as empty space. A substructure of electromagnetic fields exist as a fundamental base of the Universe. This energy field is capable of recording everything and to allow everything to communicate with each other, thus also at the level of Consciousness, in fact one large field of resonance. The writer of an article about this, which recently appeared in the magazine Ode, summarizes the findings as follows: "The notion of individuality is replaced by one of eternal interconnectivity." Thereby it is confirmed what ancient Theosophical doctrines in India knew for centuries: the human individuality is in its essence

completely One with the All, with the All-Being, and each separateness is based on illusion.[835]

Limitless

The cosmological viewpoint of Giordano Bruno can be found throughout his entire work. In his exciting dialog *Ash Wednesday Meal*,[836] dating from 1584, he shows himself to be an insightful reader of the "Asclepicist" Cusanus[837] with his idea about the infinite universe. However, Bruno goes even further. He argues enthusiastically for the existence of countless worlds and star systems. In the dialog *On the Cause, the Beginning, and the One*, from the same year 1584, he writes:

> The Universe is therefore One, infinite and immobile... One (is) the Being. One, the greatest and the best, which is not meant to be comprehended and is therefore indefinable and limitless, and therefore infinite and limitless, and as resulting immobile.[838]
>
> ...All things in the Universe are in correspondence with one another. It is not matter, for it has no form and cannot obtain it, it has neither limit nor can it be limited. It has no form, for it does not form or shape anything else, since it is everything, the largest is, One is, the Universe is. It is not measurable and is no measurement. It does not surround itself for it is not larger than itself. It is not surrounded by itself since it is not smaller than itself. It does not coincide with itself since it is not one or the other: It is One and the same.[839]

Here, it seems as if we are reading the very ancient Gnostic script, the *Secret Book of John*, where we find this:

> He is the invisible Spirit. One may not present Him as the Gods or something similar for He is greater than the Gods, since there is no one above Him. No one is Lord over Him, and He is not subordinate to anyone, since there is no one who is not in Him.

> He alone is eternal and does not need Life, for he cannot be Perfected.
>
> He is not missing anything which can make Him Perfect, for he is continuously Perfect.
>
> He is the Light.
>
> He is limitless, for no one preceded Him who can limit Him
>
> He is indefinable, for there is no one who preceded Him who can define Him.
>
> He is immeasurable, for there is no one who can measure Him.
>
> He is invisible, for no one has seen Him.
>
> He is eternal, He exists in Eternity.
>
> He is indescribable, for no one has succeeded in describing Him.
>
> He is unnamable, for no one has preceded Him to be able to give Him a name.[840]

This passage from the *Secret Book of John* speaks, not so much about the universe, as about the ordained power within it. This is exactly what Bruno believed: in the universe, there is an order, an efficient cause. "This universal Intellect is the only eminent principle of the organized complexity of the Universe: Spirit, God, the Being, Truth, Fate, Ratio, Order."[841]

Bruno's Spectacular Cosmology

Bruno was an admirer of Copernicus, who discovered that it is not the Earth that stands central in the Milky Way, but the Sun. His perspective that the Earth revolves around the Sun, and not the Sun around the Earth, was rather "revolutionary" for his time.[842]

Copernicus, however, still adhered to the idea that the fixed stars were the outer limit of the universe. By contrast, Bruno's universe was infinite and without limits. The space in this universe, according to him, was characterized by a homogeneous and endless continuity. Thus, the infinite universe does not need an external engine to keep it moving. It is, unto itself, immobile, since there is nothing that can cause it to move; yet everything within the universe is in motion.[843] This is quite similar to what Bruno had read in the *Asclepius*:

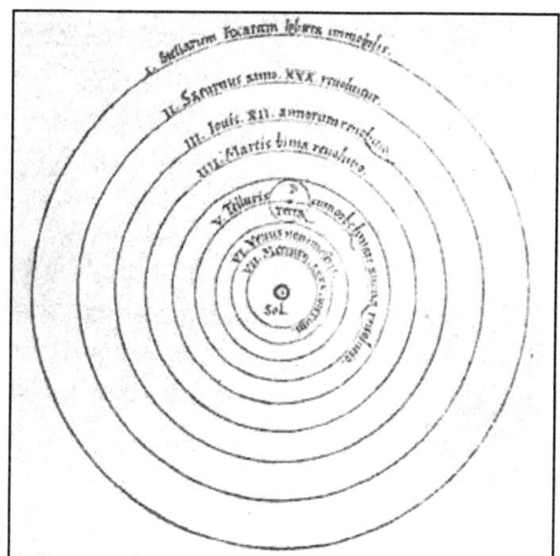

A cosmic scheme in Copernicus' *De Revolutionibus Orbium Coelestium.*

> Seen as such everything is bound by such a Law, nothing exists which is fixed or certain and there is nothing motionless in existence, neither in Heaven nor on Earth.
>
> Only God is immobile. Such speaks for itself. For only He is to Himself, from Himself and in Himself whole, complete and perfected. He stands immovable and cannot by any external force be moved. This is because everything is within Him (outside of Him there is nothing) though it is true He is within All.[844]

Bruno also subscribed to the hermetic principle that God is present within all things—indeed, this stands central in his work: *natura est deus in rebus* (Nature is the divinity in all things).[845] From the infinite universe in all time is born new abundance. This is the Gnostic-Hermetic principle that all things come from the One.

> He, then, alone who is not made, 'tis clear, is both beyond all power of thinking-manifest, and is unmanifest.
>
> And as He thinketh all things manifest, He manifests through all things and in all, and most of all in whatsoever things He wills to manifest.[846]

According to Bruno, all heavenly bodies are thus made from identical elements with the same homogeneity, consistency, and structure. The universal matter consists, according to him, of space, ether, atoms, and light. In the infinite universe neither Sun nor Earth have cosmological privileges over the other heavenly bodies; there is no essential difference between the terrestrial world and the heavenly world.[847] As above, so below.

According to Bruno, motion in the universe is indeed universal, but all heavenly bodies move differently and none of these movements are perfectly regular. Also according to him, there is no absolute time. In the universe, the quantity of time corresponds to the quantity of heavenly bodies. The universe itself has no beginning in time; it will also have no end; it is eternal. Or, as Bruno read in the *Asclepius*:

> For this [Re-]birth of Cosmos is the making new of all good things, and the most holy and most pious bringing-back again of Nature's self, by means of a set course of time—of Nature, which was without beginning, and which is without an end. For that God's Will hath no beginning; and, in that 'tis the same an as it is, it is without an end.[848]

There are, says Bruno, no absolute empty spaces or complete vacuum states in the universe or outside of it; the universe is one single whole. Also, the planets do not exist in a vacuum, but in a medium that Bruno calls *ether*.[849] It is interesting to see how Bruno's definitions of emptiness, which does not exist, are parallel to Hermes' revelations in the *Asclepius*:

> Now on the subject of a "Void"—which seems to almost all a thing of vast importance—I hold the following view.
>
> Naught is, naught could have been, naught ever will be void.
>
> For all the members of the Cosmos are competely full; so that Cosmos itself is full and [quite] complete with bodies, diverse in quality and form, possessing each its proper kind and size.
>
> And of these bodies—one's greater than another, or another's less than is another, by difference of strength and size.

Of course, the stronger of them are more easily perceived, just as the larger [are]. The lesser ones, however, or the more minute, can scarcely be perceived, or not at all—those which we know are things [at all] by sense of touch alone.

Whence many come to think they are not bodies, and that there are void spaces—which is impossible.

So also [for the Space] which is called Extra-cosmic—if there be any (which I do not believe)—[then] is it filled by Him with things Intelligible, that is things of like nature with His own Divinity; just as this Cosmos which is called the Sensible, is fully filled with bodies and with animals, consonant with its proper nature and its quality; [bodies] the proper shape of which we do not all behold, but [see] some large beyond their proper measure, some very small; either because of the great space which lies between [them and ourselves], or else because our sight is dull; so that they seem to us to be minute, or by the multitude are thought not to exist at all, because of their too great tenuity.

I mean the daimones, who, I believe, have their abode with us, and heroes, who abide between the purest part of air above us and the earth—where it is ever cloudless, and no [movement from the] motion of a single star [disturbs the peace].

Because of this, Asclepius, thou shalt call nothing void; unless thou wilt declare of what that's void, which thou dost say is void; for instance, void of fire, of water, or things like to these.

For if it should fall out, that it should seem that anything is able to be void of things like these—though that which seemeth void be little or be big, its still cannot be void of spirit and air.[850]

Innumerable Worlds

About 100 years ago, scientists all over the world were absolutely certain of this: There is only one Milky Way and it is ours. Then in 1925, Edwin Hubble observed nebula with his telescope, then the largest in the world, and identified them as far-distant star systems.

The visionary Giordano Bruno, however, had come to the same conclusion about three centuries earlier—and without a telescope, which had not yet been invented. Against the enormous pressures of his culture and the Inquisition, he claimed that there are innumerable suns and planets in the universe. The Sun is a star in the infinite universe and other stars are suns within their own star systems. Those innumerable suns and planets are inherently finite.[851] They move freely in space. The Sun moves, just as all heavenly bodies; it turns around its own center. The long-held opinion which persisted even after Bruno that the fixed stars, located at equal distance from the Earth, formed the boundaries of the firmament Bruno called an illusion. With this, he dismissed Copernicus, whom he so greatly admired. Science agreed with him—although posthumously.

Just as remarkable is Bruno's claim that, next to the visible planets, there are also invisible planets that travel around the Sun, although we cannot see them due to their distance from Earth and their relatively small size.[852] Without a telescope, Bruno knew that there must be other planets beyond Saturn—and, in fact, scientists discovered Uranus in 1781, Neptune in 1846, and Pluto in 1930.

How was all this possible? At the above-mentioned symposium in Bilthoven, Erich Kaniok gave a most intriguing theory:

> In the Pre-Asian department of the Pergamon Museum, the municipal museum of Berlin, lies under catalog number VA1243 probably the oldest Star Chart of humanity. This chart is 5000 years old and therefore dates back to the third millennium B.C. It is a clay tablet belonging to the Akkadi, once situated in Mesopotamia between the Euphrates and Tigris, in the present Iraq. On this map, our galaxy is shown correctly and to scale: In the middle, the Sun. Around such, in correct sequence, is the small Mercury, Venus and the Earth (almost the same size), the Moon. Then Mars, the two larger planets Jupiter and Saturn and following Uranus, Neptune and the dwarf planet Pluto. There is even another planet shown, still unknown today, although some astronomers suspect its existence.
>
> Nicaulus Copernicus published in the year 1543 his "About the circular movement of the Heavenly bodies," five years prior to Giordano Bruno's birth, wherein he writes down the very dangerous claim, the planets move around the Sun. But 4000 years prior to Copernicus it was already known! This knowledge was lost in

> the labyrinth of time, like what was once known disappears or is kept hidden within various groups or circles of different cultures, then to reappear at some point in time, and to emerge on an even greater scale into the consciousness of Humanity.[853]

Renovatio Mundi

Giordano Bruno was a hermeticist. During an extremely productive year (1584), he wrote another fascinating work with a similarily intriguing title: *Spaccia della bestia trionfante*r (The Driving Away of the Triumphant Beast). This is one of his many dialogs in which Sophia, Isis, and Momus take part. Frances Yates holds it as possible that this dialog was inspired by the *Korè Kosmou* (Virgin of the World),[854] one of the hermetic texts handed down by Stobaeus.[855] And it is indeed remarkable that Momus, whom we encounter in the *Korè Kosmou*, also plays a part in Bruno's work.[856]

The Driving Away of the Triumphant Beast is a satirical and extremely profound manuscript about a new, more virtuous embodiment of the planets. In it, although the planets reflect the world of the Gods, a change—a contamination—took place over a span of time. This draws on the thoughts of Bruno himself, who felt that he was living in a kind of end-time. The scholar who introduced the Dutch translation of *Spaccio della bestia trionfante* writes:

> According to Bruno the world during his time had reached an all-time low not comparable to anything else. Europe is bent under the violence of religious wars and the "pedantic" hold the power: Scholars who play on words and lose grip on reality… and reformers who create a larger distance between human and God, resulting in an unsurpassable chasm and schismatics with each their own catechism. Bruno strives towards a "renovatio mundi" by recovering the natural order and the actualization of old values, whereby justice and truth can return.[857]

Was Bruno's hope for a *renovatio mundi*—a renewal of the world, a moral hierarchy of the planetary forces—based on Hermes' revelation to Asclepius? For in the *Asclepius*, we read:

> This, when it comes, shall be the World's old age, impiety—irregularity, and lack of rationality in all good things.
>
> And when these things all come to pass, Asclepius—then He, [our] Lord and Sire, God First in power, and Ruler of the One God [Visible], in check of crime, and calling error back from the corruption of all things unto good manners and to deeds spontaneous with His Will (that is to say God's Goodness)—ending all ill, by either washing it away with water-flood, or burning it away with fire, or by the means of pestilent diseases, spread throughout all hostile lands—God will recall the Cosmos to its ancient form; so that the World itself shall seem meet to be worshipped and admired; and God, the Maker and Restorer of so vast a work, be sung by the humanity who shall be then, with ceaseless heraldings of praise and [hymns of] blessing.
>
> For this [Re-]birth of Cosmos the making new of all good things, and the most holy and most pious bringing-back again of Nature's self, by means of a set course of time—of Nature, which was without beginning, and which is without and end. For that God's Will hath no beginning; and, in that 'tis the same and as it is, it is without an end.[858]

In the Egyptian world of the Thrice-Great Hermes, there was still a great purity. But this, according to Bruno, was destroyed by the Christians.[859] In *The Driving Away of the Triumphant Beast,* he quotes extensively from the lamentation of Hermes about the decline of the Egyptian religion.[860] It is time, he claimed, for a moral purification. The old natural hermetic order had to be reinstated; justice and truth, together with a host of other good virtues, would form the new Heaven of Bruno.

In his *Spaccio della bestia trionfante*, Bruno openly glorifies the religion of the Egyptians[861] at the expense of Jews and Christians. He lets the high God, Jupiter, call out:

> But do not let him conclude the purpose of Greek Magic comes from and is derived from the Jewish Kabala, for it has been proven the Jews are the lowliest of Egypt, and no one has ever with any

> certainty proven the Egyptians have adopted any worthy or unworthy principle from them.[862]

The Egyptians existed prior to the Greeks and the Hebrews (and naturally the Christians), Bruno points out, and possessed the best religion, the best magic, and the best laws.[863] It was for these points of views, as well as for his cosmological observations, that the Inquisition stepped in to bring Bruno, as an atheist, to justice.

The Soul of the Universe

Outside of the *Asclepius*, Bruno was familiar with the sixteenth treatise of the *Corpus Hermeticum*,[864] "A letter from Asclepius to King Ammon," which deals with the *sympathy* of all things—a principle that is so strongly present in Bruno's own viewpoint.

> Thus, then, will I begin the sermon by invocation unto God, the universals' Lord and Maker, [their] Sire, and [their] Encompasser; who though being All is One, and though being One is All; for that the Fullness of all things is One, and [is] in One, this latter One not coming as a second [One], but both being One.
>
> And this is the idea that I would have thee keep, through the whole study of our sermon, Sire!
>
> For should one try to separate what seems to be both All and One and Same from One—he will be found to take his epithet of "All" from [the idea of] multitude, and not from [that of] fullness—which is impossible; for if he part All from the One, he will destroy the All.
>
> For all things must be One—if they indeed are One. Yea, they are One; and they shall never cease being One—in order that the Fullness may not be destroyed.
>
> See then in Earth a host of founts of Water and of Fire forthspirting in its midmost pats; in one and the same [space all] the three natures visible—of Fire, and Water, and of Earth, depending from one Root.

Whence, too, it is believed to be the Treasurey of every matter. It sendeth forth of its abundance, and in the place [of what it sendeth forth] receiveth the subsistence from above.

For thus the Demiurge—I mean the Sun—eternally doth order Heaven and Earth, pouring down Essence, and taking Matter up, drawing both round Himself and to Himself all things, and from Himself giving all things to all.

For He it is whose goodly energies extend not only through the Heaven and the Air, but also on to Earth, right down unto the lowest Depth and the Abyss.

The World Intelligible, then, depends from God; the Sensible from the Intelligible [World].

The Sun through the Intelligible and the Sensible Cosmos, pours forth abundantly the stream from God of Good—that is, the demiurgic operation.

And round the Sun are the Eight Spheres, dependant from Him—the [Sphere] of the Non-wandering Ones, the Six [Spheres] of the Wanderers, and one Circumterrene.

And from the Spheres depend the daimones; and from these, men.

And thus all things and all [of them] depend from God.[865]

This discourse must have made an impression on Bruno. He talks at various times about *l'anima de l'universo*, the soul of the universe that is the principle of the movement of the heavenly bodies—the immanent motor. Just as the human soul holds all parts of the body together and connects them, so the soul of the universe does the same for its "members." We should imagine the soul of the universe, according to Bruno, as the principle and the Being of the universe, although its true nature is extremely difficult to grasp.

The universal soul is found in everything, and there is no tiny body, however minimal, that is not ensouled by it. The universal soul is capable of bringing forth everything out of nothing.[866]

Statue of Giordano Bruno at the Campo dei Fiori in Rome.

We are not sure if Giordano Bruno knew about the penetrating revelation of which Hermes himself was a part. The similarities are noticeable:

> Further, the Æon's soul is God; the Cosmos' soul is Æon; the Earth's soul, Heaven.
>
> And God's in Mind; and Mind, in Soul; and Soul, in Matter; and all of them through Æon.
>
> But all this Body, in which are all the bodies, is full of Soul; and Soul is full of Mind, and [Mind] of God.
>
> It fills it from within, and from without encircles it, making the All to live.[867]

Bruno was a hermeticist in the truest sense of the word. His cosmological observations agree perfectly with the philosophical *Hermetica*. But above all, his spirit must have traveled through the infinite spaces.

Once, Hermes had told his son, Tat:

> Would it were possible for thee to get thee wings, and soar into the air, and, poised midway 'tween earth and heaven, behold the earth's solidity, the sea's fluidity (the flowings of its streams), the spaciousness of air, fire's swiftness, [and] the coursing of the stars, the swiftness of heaven's circuit round them [all]!
>
> Most blessed sight were it, my son, to see all these beneath one sway—the motionless in motion, and the unmanifest made manifest; whereby is made this order of the cosmos and the cosmos which we see of order.[868]

This experience must have become a part of Bruno—an experience he had to pay for his with death.

Fortunately, however, his death was not in vain.

CHAPTER 23

THE END OF A TRADITION?

In the early morning of a cold day in March in the year 1580, three men left the synagogue in the Emperor's city, Prague. They sped in the darkness to the banks of the Vlatava just outside Prague. There, they formed, out of clay from the river, a human figure and brought it to life with several magical rituals. The *golem* was born.[869]

THE CREATION OF A HOMUNCULUS

One of the three participants in this miraculous creation was Jitzchak ben Sjimsjon Katz, who wrote a gruesome description of the event that came to light in the last century through a publication by a certain Rosenberg who had bought the manuscript from someone who had smuggled it out of the library in Metz. Stories about the creation of an artificial human are not now, and were not then, new. Already in the 3rd century A.D., the hermetic alchemist Zosimus had written about a small copper figure that floated out of a phial, changing alternately into a small silver and a golden human being. In the same era, the concept of a *golem*, an artificial human created out of clay, appeared in Jewish legends. In the 13th century, Arnaldus of Villanova reports the alchemical creation of a *homunculus* (literally, small human). And, angry tongues claimed, no one less than Paracelsus could have created such a creature.[870]

The best-known story about the creation of a golem, however, is that of Jitzchak Katz, which takes place in the extremely tolerant city of Prague during the reign of the Hapsburg Emperor Rudolf II, who succeeded his father, Maximilian, in 1576. In the history books, Rudolf II is usually described as mentally disabled, an eccentric who kept to himself, occupied with his horse breeding, curiosity collection, and occult affairs. His brothers and nephews accused

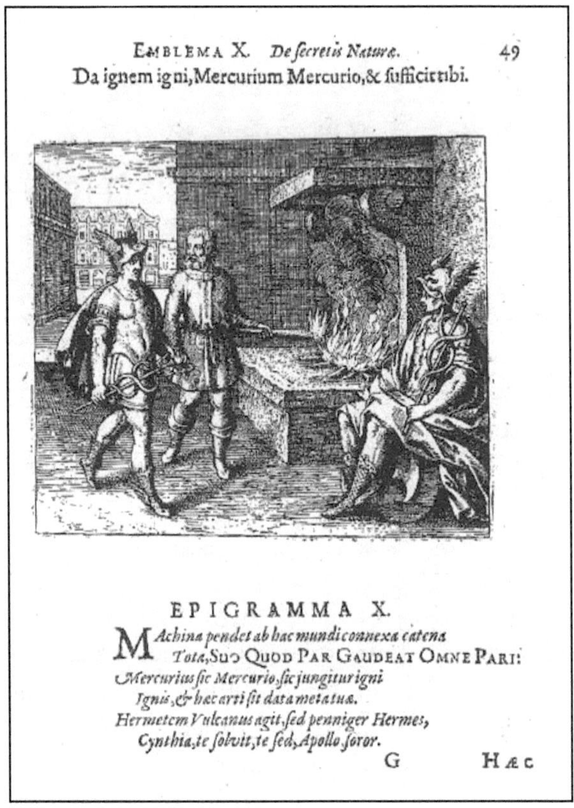

EMBLEMA X. *De secretis Naturæ.* 49

Da ignem igni, Mercurium Mercurio, & sufficit tibi.

EPIGRAMMA X.

Machina pendet ab hac mundi connexa catena
Tota, SUO QUOD PAR GAUDEAT OMNE PARI:
Mercurius sic Mercurio, sic jungitur igni
Ignis, & hæc arti sit data meta tuæ.
Hermetem Vulcanus agit, sed penniger Hermes,
Cynthia, te solvit, te sed, Apollo soror.

G HÆC

Page from Michael Maier's *Atalanta Fugiens*. On the illustration one sees a double Hermes-Trismegistus and above it the motto: "Give fire to fire, Mercury to Mercury, and that will be enough" for you to know. In the epigram underneath one can read among other things that Mercury is linked with Mercury and fire with fire, for like attracts like: "Vulcanus brings Hermes in motion." See opposite page.

him of being increasingly unable to reign and pulled more and more power to themselves. In 1609, Rudolf II proclaimed freedom of religion within his empire, a remarkable act for a Catholic emporer. He surrounded himself with revolutionary scientists of diverse disciplines, among whom were the mage John Dee and the philosopher Giordano Bruno, as well as Michael Maier, the alchemist, who, from 1608, served as the personal physician of the monarch.

28

FUGA X. in 2. infrà.

Gib Fewer zum Fewer/Mercurium zum Mercurio, vnd es ist dir genug.

Atalanta Fugiens.

Machina pendet ab hac mun di connе xa catena To-

ta su o quod par gau deat omne pari, pari.

Hippomen. Sequens.

Machi na pendet ab hac mun di conne xa catena

To ta su o quod par gau deat omne pari.

Pomum Morans.

Machina pendet ab hac mundi connexa catena

Tota, suo quod par gaudeat omne pari.

X. Epigrammatis Latini versio Germanica.

DAs gantz Gebäw an dieser Ketten hänget der gantzen Welt/
Daß ein jedes zu dem/das jhm gleicht/sich gesellt:
Mercurius wirt so zu seiner Art gefügt/ vnd das Fewr
Zum Fewr/diß laß dir seyn ein Ziel dieser Kunst so thewr:
Vulcanus treibt den Hermetem, der Hermes wider entbindt
Cynthiam, so sich rächet an dich/ Apollo, geschwindt.

EMBLE-

Here are the words of Epigram X put to music in the shape of a fuga.

Illustrated Books

Michael Maier was born in 1568 in Rendsburg (Holstein). In 1597, he obtained his doctorate in Rostock. From 1608 until Rudolf II's death in 1612, he was his personal physician. Thereafter, he traveled via Amsterdam to England, where he came into contact with the world of thought of Robert Fludd (see further on). In 1616, he returned to Germany, where he, among others, was personal physician to Maurits of Hessen. Maier died in 1622 in Maagdenburg.[871]

Maier wrote diverse works in which his interest in alchemy is expressed without disguise. He compiled a discourse about the important influence of gold in the world.[872] Herein, he showed a correspondence "between the human heart as centre of the human

Hermes Trismegistus, ruler of the four elements, carries (with feet on the Earth) the kosmos (in the Air). With his left hand he points to the coniunctio of Sun and Moon (Fire and Water). Illustration from Michael Maier's *Symbola aureae.*

body, gold as the perfect centre among metals and the Sun as centre of the planets."[873] In the same year, 1616, he published a manuscript showing the significance of Mercury in alchemy. A year later, he exposed the errors and fraudulence of the "pseudo-chemists." Alchemy is not a business for dumb gold makers, he declared, but should be founded on the *artes liberales*, the liberal arts—grammar, rhetoric, dialectic, mathematics, geometry, astronomy, and physics (which included music). But Maier's most important work is definitely the *Atalanta Fugiens* (The Fleeting Atalanta), which appeared in Oppenheim in 1617. This is a so-called "emblem book," and indeed one the most beautiful of its kind. The illustrations are copper engravings by Matthaeus Merian, a famous engraver of the time, who also supplied the engravings for the fascinating *Museum Hermeticum* (1625).[874] As remarkable as the images in the *Atalanta*, however, are the textual the references to the Thrice-Great Hermes,

Museum Hermeticum.

specifically in the "constitution" of the alchemists, the *Tabula Smaragdina*.

Maier lived in a time when the great alchemical anthologies—the *Theatrum Chemicum* and the *Rosarium Philosopher*—were published, with magnificent illustrations full of alchemical symbology. One of the most beautiful books in this field was published in 1609 by the hermeticist Heinrich Kunrath, the *Amphitheatrum Sapientiae Aeternae* (Amphibious Theatre of the Eternal Wisdom). Kunrath was a Paracelsian physician who also worked for some time at the court of Rudolf II in Prague.[875]

Kunrath's roots were in the Renaissance. He acknowledged several "true sciences"—*theosofia*, *physica*, *physicomedicina*, *physicochemica*, *mageia*, *physicomageia*, *hyperphysicomageia* and *kabbala*[876]—and referred to Hermes Trismegistus when he wrote that these true sciences can only be learned at the "University of God."[877]

Music was undoubtedly part of the true sciences. In a breathtaking perspective drawing, we see a large space to the left with a private altar where an alchemist is deeply sunk in prayer. On a table in center front lie several musical instruments. Engraved in the table is the joyful message: Music not only drives away sorrow, but also evil spirits (see figure page 291).

Marsilio Ficino had already written that music formed the link between the human and divine and was, therefore, of universal and vital importance.[878] The influential Renaissance architect Alberti had even called architecture "frozen music."[879] Music is thus not a theoretical observation, but a magical practice. And this is how Michael Maier presents music in his famous emblem book *Atalanta Fugiens*.[880] Each illustration contains an epigram with a *fuga* for three voices.[881] Maier's friend Robert Fludd had also occupied himself with music.[882] Who was this Fludd?

A Shifting of the World's View

Robert Fludd (1574–1637) studied medicine at Oxford. We have already seen, however, that physicians played a very important role in the hermetic spectrum. We could even say that medicine, in the broadest sense of the word, formed the heart of the hermetic "art." Frances Yates called Fludd "one of the most famous hermetical philosophers" who stood in the middle of the hermetic-Kabalistic Renaissance tradition that had started more than a century before with Ficino and Pico della Mirandola.[883] But Fludd was also strongly influenced by Agrippa, Paracelsus, and his compatriot John Dee, and was befriended by Michael Maier.[884] With Fludd, several lines therefore converge—especially if we consider his appreciation for the Rosicrucians and his involvement in the controversy surrounding astronomer John Kepler (more on this later).

Next to his physician's practice in London, Robert Fludd ran an alchemical laboratory where he also prepared medicines for his patients. Still, Fludd was more of a "spiritual" than a practical alchemist. The Philosopher's Stone was, in his eyes, nothing less than the "cornerstone," Christ, and "Christ, the noble cornerstone, is in us."[885] Beyond his work in alchemy, Fludd published many books about Kabala, the natural sciences, astrology, philosophy, and music. According to Yates, he became "saturated with the *Corpus Hermeticum*... and with the *Asclepius*, and it is hardly exaggerated to find on almost each and every page citations from the texts of Hermes Trismegistus."[886] For Fludd, Trismegistus was "the most divine of all philosophers."[887]

Above, I said that Fludd was known for his enthusiasm about the Rosicrucian movement and his part in the controversy surrounding Kepler. As a student in Tübinger, Kepler was well acquainted with Johann Valentin Andreae, author of the Rosicrucian manifestos. The years he spent at the court of Emperor Rudolf II as assistant to Tycho Brahe must have been extremely educational as well. In his *Mysterium cosmographicum* (1596), Kepler reasons from the hermetic precept that a World Soul causes the movement of the planets. However, in a reprint of his cosmological discourse in 1606, he replaced the World Soul with the more neutral concept of "force." Fludd objected, and a strong controversy developed between the two men. However, as suggested, it was not a battle between a hermetic mystic and a materialistic scientist. Kepler was as ardent a student of the *Corpus Hermeticum* as Fludd was.[888] The difference between the two was more in their approach. Fludd held to the hermetic analogy between macro- and microcosmos. Kepler, by contrast, studied the heavenly phenomena themselves, separate from this analogy. Somewhat teasingly, he suggested that Fludd illustrated his cosmological ideas with "hieroglyphs" and "pictures," whereas he, Kepler, supported them with mathematical diagrams.[889]

An Attack on Hermes

Fludd was one of the last individual hermeticists. After him, hermetic ideas were presented more by groups than by prominent individuals. Another factor also played a role here. In 1614, a certain Isaac Casaubon published an extremely erudite discourse called *De rebus sacris et ecclesiasticis exercitationes XVI*. Although you may forget the name of this discourse immediately, this text was rather important for the history of the hermetic tradition. Based on precise textual analysis, Casaubon came to the conclusion that the *Corpus Hermeticum* did not date back to ancient Egypt at all, but must have been composed in the 2nd century A.D. by Christians.[890] With this assertion, the previously undisputed authority of Hermes Trismegistus came under serious pressure. Hermes not an ancient Egyptian sage, but a product of Christian Plato-loving philosophers? As we saw in the first part of this book, Casaubon was undeniably correct regarding the dating of the writings. However, this does not exclude the possibility that older material was used in these later manuscripts or prove that they do not reveal any Egyptian influence. Modern research at the end of the 20th century points undeniably to an Egyptian origin of the revelatory thoughts of the *Corpus*.[891]

Although the discovery of Casaubon was, in a certain sense, disillusioning for most hermeticists, Fludd was absolutely not deterred. He ignored the dating with the greatest ease and continued to regard the *Hermetica* as the wisdom teachings of the old Egyptian sage himself.[892] He did not even enter the ensuing debate. Ralph Culworth, a learned Platonist from Cambridge, however, did. He pointed out that Casaubon dismissed the entire *Corpus* based on only three treatises.[893] Further, he indicated subtly, after extensive research, that there was definitely an Egyptian sage who was known by the name Thoth, Theut, or Taut, and this figure was known as Hermes by the Greeks and as Mercurius by the Romans. Literary arguments that indicate a Christian falsification contradict Culworth by showing that the translation from Egyptian to Greek was rather lacking, just as Iamblichus had noticed many centuries prior.[894]

Thomas Hofmeier, in the celebrated Venetian catalog, wrote a captivating article about the Casaubon-Cudworth controversy, ending his contribution with: "In him (Cudworth), Casaubon found his master and in Hermes, a great apologist."[895] Furthermore, it is notable that the very extensive alchemical, magical, astrological, botanical, and iatrochemical hermetic literature is not affected by Casaubon's timeline, nor by that of his opponent Cudworth.

Casaubon died shortly after his research. Cudworth, who was yet to be born, wrote his anti-thesis in 1678. Strangely enough, no one

The famed Rosarium image is featured on the cover of Jacob Slavenburg's book about the becoming one of female and male, "...and the two shall be one." Original coniunctio-illustration from the *Rosarium Philosophorum* (1550).

listened to Cudworth. Hermes seemed to have disappeared from the (public) scene.

Was It a Decline?

Let's put things in sequence: Giordano Bruno's mouth had been literally and figuratively shut; Europe was at the beginning of a destructive religious war; the existence of Hermes had been fought against and suspicion was cast on "his" writings. Inquisition; Counter-Reformation; end of the Renaissance. A decline?

Bruno was reflecting these events when he quoted the lamentation of Hermes about the decline of the Egyptian king-priest culture that, for centuries, had been credited with passing on knowledge and wisdom:

> Your Gods will become a myth out of forgotten times. Your divine liturgies, your deeply impressive ceremonies and holy revelations, will be for the descendant incomprehensible hieroglyphs, which are chiselled out of stone, and admired by tourists. And you, O' river, there will come a day when you will inundate of blood instead of water and bodies will be piled up against the dikes. There will be no mourning of the dead any longer, but more for the living.[896]

Had the hermetic tradition come to an end? Had the stream dried up?

In 1604, a spiritual alchemist from distant Moravia, Michael Sendivogius—forget the name, but remember the message—published his *Novum lumen chymicum* (The New Alchemistical Light).[897] It was a call to "all true seekers of the great chemical Art, the sons of Hermes." In the rich symbolic language of the alchemists—searching for the *coniunctio*, the union, often shown so wonderfully in the beautiful coitus of king and queen, of Sun and Moon—Sendivogius raves about the unveiled Diana who opens the gates of Nature in order to enter her innermost sanctuary:

> The times are nearing, the many secrets of nature will be revealed to human.
>
> The fourth or northern monarchy stands at the point of being established;
>
> the mother of knowledge will come quickly...
> Mercy and Truth will meet each other;
> Peace and Justice will look down from the heavens...
> and knowledge will be common property of all.[898]

Consoled, we can continue our search for Hermes. In this chapter, we saw that the Thrice-Great was a source of inspiration for Robert Fludd and Michael Maier. But both hermeticists had also fallen under the spell of another expression of spirituality—the Rosicrucians. And here, Hermes played a role as well. More about this in the next chapter.

Chapter 24
Hermes and the Rosicrucians

It is already well past midnight. I am still engrossed in the Rosicrucian literature. Fourteen years ago, I had already done research into the Rosicrucian movements,[899] some of which flow like a ribbon through the history of the New Age. And now, I bump into them again while doing research on Hermes. I find this in a publication that appeared as a result of the exhibition of the Rosicrucian movement in the Koninklijke Bibliotheek (Royal Library) in The Hague (winter of 1998–1999): "The founders of the Rosicrucian Manifestos, respectively the *Fama Fraternitatis oder Brüderschaft der hochlöblichen Ordens des Rosenkreutzes*, the *Confessio Fraternitates R.C. ad eruditos Europae* and the *Chymische Hochzeit Christiani Rosencreutz* from 1614, 1615 and 1616, who have also contributed from the wisdom teachings which are attributed to Hermes Trismegistus."[900]

My research of the last couple of days does not make this immediately clear. In the manuscripts mentioned, the name of Hermes appears only once. Now, a cultural historian has to be able to read between the lines and, yes—Hermes becomes more visible. My eyes are getting heavy from lack of sleep. I shall stop for now.

The Healing Effects of a Dream

Just after going to bed, I had a lucid dream. I saw myself on the way to Epidaurus. The vision is unusually clear and bright. The mountain range of Peloponnesos is beautiful and several prospects out over the ever-blue Aegean are breathtaking. Suddenly, I am there. The holy site of Asclepius is hidden between the green hills. I see the impressive ruins. And, as if by magic, the statues of Asclepius appear one after another in front of my spiritual eye. During my many travels throughout the Mediterranean, I have encountered countless statues of Asclepius. In almost every ruin of every Greek city, from Spain to Turkey, there is still a (copy of a) statue of Asclepius. The originals decorate many musea and are immediately recognizable: a noble figure with long curly hair, full beard, and gentle—yes, even loving—eyes. With those eyes, Asclepius looks at me. I am thinking of the mystical experience of Doctor Thessalos, who beheld Asclepius, as described in the first part of this book. It moves me. And I know: there must be links between Hermes, Asclepius, and the Rosicrucians.

The holy site at Epidaurus is not the only *askleieion*, but it is indeed the most famous.[901] From near and far, sick people streamed to this holy site. In the temple, the followers of Asclepius lay asleep, the divinity appearing as they knew him from his images in their dreams. He often acted in the dreams like a practicing physician—for example, "laying on hands" and prescribing treatments that we now call "natural healing methods," like the use of herbal remedies and taking beneficial baths.

Originally, Asclepius himself, son of Apollo, walked with nobility between the rows of the sick, accompanied by two serpents that licked the ailing parts of the patients. Later, the patients would dream about this treatment.[902] This collective method of healing—common in antiquity until Hippocrates stepped over to a more personal type of treatment—must have delivered tremendous results, as can be seen by the many chiseled stone descriptions of miracle cures that I observed in the local museum and of which I now dream.

The next morning, I was once again awake early. The dream still lingered in my mind, which yesterday had been weighed down so heavily by too much information. Now I could see several links. Besides the self-evident connections found in literature, I saw a "'happy" agreement. Earlier, I had noticed how important medicine was in antiquity—the consecration and healing in the king-priest culture of Egypt; the divine healer Imhotep, spiritual ancestor of Asclepius,[903] sometimes coupled with Thoth; the *asklepieia* in the ancient Greece; the subterranean healing caves of which Peter Kingsley writes so breathtakingly; the interweaving of astrology, botany, magic, and alchemy. A row of illustrious names passed before me: Ficino, Agrippa, Paracelsus, Patrizi, Maier, Khunrath, Fludd—all the heirs of Asclepius. The serpents of Asclepius (Latin, Aesculapis) now appear on physicians' cars—as well as on the *caduceus*, the staff of Hermes.

Thoth, Hermes Trismegistus, Imhotep, Asclepius. Hermes and his pupil Asclepius; it all binds together nicely. But where do the Rosicrucians come in?

The Rosicrucian Manifestos

In the year 1614, an extraordinary manuscript appeared: The *Fama Fraternitatis, des Löblichen Ordens des Rosenkreutzes*, also called *The Call of the Brotherhood of the Noble Order of the Rosicrucians*. The *Call* was aimed at the heads of state, governments, and scholars of Europe. The manuscript unveiled the existence of a wise sage—"Father Brother C. R., a German, head and founder of the Fraternity."[904] In the bloom of his youth, this C. R. took a journey to the East. He changed his original plan to visit Jerusalem and traveled instead to Damcar (now Damascus) in Arabia, where sages were supposed to live "to whom the entire Nature is revealed." In Damcar, he was admitted to the circle of Wise Men. "There he also learned the Arabian language, so in the beginning of the following year he translated the book M. into good Latin and took it with him. In this city, he equally acquired knowledge of Physics and Mathematics, over which the world could truly rejoice, in case the love would be greater than the jealousy."[905]

Via Egypt, C. R. journeyed to Fez in Morocco and, after a stay of approximately two years, he returned via Spain to Germany. After futile efforts to share his acquired treasures of wisdom with scholars and political leaders, he founded a fraternity with several spiritual equals. They built a home, called *Sanctus Spiritus*, and agreed to the following:

> None of them were allowed any other profession except of the healing of the sick and even completely free of charge.
>
> None of them would be forced by the Brotherhood to wear specific garments but each had to blend in with the national customs.

> Each Brother would gather each year, on day C, at (the House of) the *Sanctus Spiritus* (the Holy Spirit) or give the reason of their absence.
>
> Each Brother would look for a person who could at some time follow in his footsteps.
>
> The word R.C. would be their seal, password and sign.
>
> The Brotherhood would be kept secret for a hundred years.[906]

In the *Confessio Fraternitatis* (Confession of the Brotherhood), which appeared one year later, the secret initials C. R. were replaced by the complete name: Christian Rosencreutz. In the *Confessio*, the message of the *Fama* is repeated.

What is immediately apparent in the Constitution of the Rosicrucians (the *Fama*) is the first article regarding altruistic healing. It seems that the Rosicrucians also followed this centuries-old tradition.

Nor is this, by far, the only connection with Hermes. In the *Fama Fraternitatis*, we find an intriguing story about the grave of Christian Rosencreutz. After 120 years, the Brothers of the Rosicrucians discovered a secret door on which they read: "After one hundred and twenty years, I will open."[907] Behind the door was a small altar with four figurines. On one of them were the words *nequaquam vacuum*, "there is no empty space."[908] This citation from Asclepius was used to convey that, practically, there must be more:

> Still we had not found the dead body of our caring and wise Father. Therefore, we moved the altar aside and were able to lift a heavy yellow-copper plate of brass. Thereunder was found a beautiful and noble body, completely intact without a trace of decomposition… in full ornament with all his qualities. In his hand, he held a small book, called T., written in golden letters on parchment, which, after the Bible, is our greatest treasure now and understandably must not to be lightly delivered to the judgement of the world.[909]

This bears a striking resemblance to stories about the discovery of the still-intact body of Hermes Trismegistus holding in his hand the *Tabula Smaragdina* (The Emerald Table).[910] Long after their deaths, the graves of both Hermes Trismegistus and Christian Rozencreutz are discovered with them holding in their hands a text that would change the world. It all looks like a metaphor for new knowledge that blossoms when the time is right. The learned son of Pharaoh Ramses II, Setne Chamus, had to return the Book of Thoth to the grave after many problems arose because the time did not appear to be right for the full revelation of the knowledge of Thoth.[911]

The grave of Imhotep, on the other hand, has yet to be discovered.[912] Are we (still) not ready for a radical alternative way of healing? Is this why the grave of Jesus has not yet been discovered, because we are still far removed from being able to shape a world according to his principle of Love?

Each opening of a grave is a symbol for renewal. And this was precisely what the writers of the Rosicrucian Manifestos so eagerly desired.

A Sacred Marriage

Two years after the *Fama* and one year after the *Confessio*, a third Rosicrucian Manifesto appeared: The *Chymische Hochzeit Christiani Rozencreutz* (The (Al)Chemical Marriage of Christian Rozencreutz). The text begins with an invitation to Christian Rozencreutz to attend a royal marriage. The invitation is sealed and decorated with the *monas* symbol, the "Hermetic Seal."[913] The royal marriage happens on "dies I," day one of the seven-day Path of Initiation[914] of the then eighty-one-year-old Nestor.[915] Rozencreutz goes traveling and, after the necessary hardship, reaches the gate of the palace where the marriage will be consummated. Above the gate hangs a board with the text: *procul hinc, procul ire prophani*, "Away, away from here, O' uninitiated"—a clear sign that the story entails more than just an exciting fairy tale. On arriving at the palace, the marriage guests are subjected to several tests and exercises that are symbolic of the Path of Initiation. One by one, these are described in detail.[916] Finally, after all the tests, Christian Rozenkreutz and several other guests remain to celebrate the marriage of the royal couple.

Indeed, the manifesto is rightly called *Chymische Hockzeit*. It is filled to the brim with alchemical symbology—indeed, the leading lady of the marriage guests is named *Alchemeia*. And on the fifth day, the guests sail across a lake[917] to the "tower of Olympus," where a large laboratory is situated. On the sixth day, the alchemical labor is completed, each day on a floor higher up. The tower actually symbolizes a retort: the higher you go in the "bottle," the more transparent the process becomes, and the finer the matter. Finally, the royal couple is regenerated out of the decapitated[918] bodies of the old kings. In their splendid nudeness, bride and groom lay together, the alchemical symbol of the *coniunctio*, the unification. What began in the spirit receives form in the flesh. On the seventh day, the marriage takes place. The guests are placed as "knights of the golden stone." They have guided the alchemical process up to the Philosopher's Stone. In the chapel where Christian Rozencreutz is knighted, he leaves the following words behind: "*Summa scientica nihil scire*"—"the highest knowledge is knowing nothing."[919]

Thus the *coniunctio*—the marriage—goes beyond the limit of rational thinking. Just as the disciple of Hermes in the *The Treatise of the Eighth and Ninth Heavenly Sphere* walks through the "Seven Heavens" and comes to the perception of the true Self, so Christian Rozencreutz, symbol of a person searching for enlightment, reaches his true Self in seven days. He has, also according to the last word in the manuscript, literally "come home."[920]

For the Brothers of the Rosicrucians, it was all about spiritual alchemy, the spiritual inheritance of Hermes Trismegistus. They stayed aloof from the materialistic alchemy that was frequently practiced in those days. So we read in the *Fama*:

> As far as what the ungodly and cursed producing of gold concerns, this has gained in our time the upper hand, which primarily many villains... herewith conduct large villainous acts.[921]

Hermes Is the Fountain-Source

On "dies IV," the fourth day, the guests are guided to a well, above which is a text:

Hermes is the primordial fountain-source.
After to the human species

many injuries have been inflicted,
indeed I ... here unto,
bring the healing arts.
Whoever can, drink of me.
Whoever desires, cleanse yourself in me.
Whoever dares, bring me in turmoil,
Drink, brothers, and live![922]

The fountain-source is Hermes. This is made apparent—not only by the announcement in the initiation text of the mystical marriage, or by the striking agreements in the "manifestation legends" concerning the discoveries of the still-intact bodies of Hermes and Christian Rozencreutz, or by the just-mentioned emphasis on medical science—but by many more references as well. Indeed, the compiler of the Rosicrucian Manifestos, Johann Valentin Andreae himself, and the circle surrounding him left very little doubt about the issue. According to a French researcher, the young Andreae knew the *Corpus Hermeticum* quite well.[923] Another member of the circle, Christoph Besold, was certain that the foundation of the philosophy of the Rosicrucians could be traced to Hermes Trismegistus, and indeed to the *Pimander* (the *Corpus Hermeticum*) and the *Asclepius*.[924] Also, in what is sometimes called the fourth Rosicrucian Manifesto,[925] the author links the *parergon*, the Rosicrucian insight, directly to the doctrine of Hermes Trismegistus.[926] The manifestos indeed breathe out a universal sphere. In the *Confessio*, we read that the Brotherhood does not acknowledge any other philosophy "than one in which all sciences, arts and faculties are united together, also Theology and Medicine..."[927] This clearly points to a hermetic source.

Modern researchers all emphasize the Christian-Hermetic foundations of the movement,[928] which was, at the same time, a reaction to the Counter-Reformation that tried to restore the doctrine of Aristotle at the expense of Plato and Hermes. On this, the historian Van Wissen says:

> When one reads the manuscripts thoroughly, one gets the impression of a religious movement which thrives for the deepening of

the evangelical piety. The Alchemy is used for such to come to a more intense religious experience. Next to such, they thrived for a reformation of Science by developing scientific methods not based on the Philosophy of Aristotle but on hermetical principles.[929]

A Circle of Friends

The honored English art historian Frances Yates starts her book about the Rosicrucians (*The Rosicrucian Enlightenment*) with a description of a magnificent royal marriage between the English Princess Elizabeth and the German Elector Friedrich V. This fairy-tale marriage takes place in England in the year 1613. The marriage has a great political value. "The Rhine is united with the Thames; Germany goes together with England." So writes a member of a modern Rosicrucian Order and rightfully so.[930] Is it possible in this way to avoid a horrendous religious war? There is universal hope for a stable, peaceful, and affluent society.

Tobias Hess, writing in Tübingen in southern Germany, was also convinced that the time was ripe for big changes.[931] In 1604, the same year that Michael Sendivogius published his *Novem lumen chymicum*, a super nova appeared between the star clusters Serpentarius and Cygnus. In 1607, Hess brought together a circle of friends that Johann Valentin Andreae joined one year later, followed by Christoph Besold two years later. It was in this context and environment that the Rosicrucian Manifestos appeared. *The Call of the Rosicrucians* paints the richness of the sources of inspiration that were present in the libraries of Hess, Andreae, and Besold. Besold possessed about 6000 publications and manuscripts, Andreae (prior to the fire) about 3000.[932] According to the most recent research by Carlos Gilly and Martin Brecht among others, it is certain that Johann Valentin Andreae was the author of all three manifestos.[933] He seems to have written the *Fama* and *Confessio* in 1608 and 1609 as a member of the "Tübinger Circle." It is pretty much certain that Hess, and later Besold, helped him with it.

Andreae had written the *Chymische Hochzeit* earlier. This is the only work he fully admitted to having compiled. In his autobiography, *Vita ab Ipso Conscripta,* he claims that he had already written the *Chymische Hochzeit* in 1605.[934]

The manuscripts circulated at first in a close circle, but that didn't remain so for long. They were copied clandestinely and spread out over Germany. This we know because a certain Adam Haslmayr—a musician, philosopher, alchemist, and theosophist from Tyrol—printed a reaction to the *Fama* two years prior to its publication. This is, by the way, the first printed edition in which the name Rosicrucian is used.[935] When the *Fama* was published in 1614 without the knowledge and approval of the circle of friends, the dam was opened. Soon Europe was flooded with writings for and against the Rosicrucians. The reactions, at least 400 in the first ten years after its publication, were strong.[936]

Among the passionate defenders of the Rosicrucian ideas, as already mentioned, were the hermeticists Robert Fludd and Michael Maier. In 1616, Fludd published his *Apologia Compendiara Fraternitatem de Rosae Cruce suspicionis et infamiae maculus aspersam, veritatis quasi Fluctibus abluens et abstergens* (A short outline of the defense of the Brotherhood of the Rosicrucians, having been pulled through the mud by suspicion, now being cleansed by the waters of truth). The defense may be short, but the title definitely isn't. By the way, *Fluctibus* is a play on Fludd's own name. One year later, his second apologia appeared: "Defense Treatise for the Integrity of the Rosicrucian Society."[937] Maier also wrote two apologies for the Brotherhood—*Symbola Aurea Mensae* in 1617 and *Themis Aurea* (The Golden Laws) one year later.[938]

The Turn Around

According to Edighoffer, the end of the 16th century and the beginning of the 17th were, in fact, the Golden Age of religious Hermeticism.[939] I think he is mostly correct, although it is a Christian-colored Hermeticism. The hermetic science flourished during this time—in England in the so-called Elizabethan Renaissance, and in Germany with the driving force being the court of Rudolf II, nicknamed the "German Hermes." In Italy, by contrast, we see counter pressure growing (witness the execration of Patrizi and Bruno). Although the Counter-Reformation moved forward (backward?), there was still, in the early 17th century, full hope for better days, however overshadowed it was by the dark clouds in the background. It was in this era that the Rosicrucian Manifestos appeared—documents that would have a great influence on the history of Western esotericism. Thus, it is not really so important who exactly was the author of these manifestos; and it is even less important whether Christian Rozencreutz was a real person or a symbolic figure.[940] The manifestos are real and have achieved a far-reaching influence. They were composed in the language of the time. Frances Yates comments rightly:

> The observant reader of the manifestos is touched by the contrast between the serious tone of their religious and philosophical message and the fantastical character of the framework in which the message is presented.[941]

Unfortunately, the dark clouds converged into a pitch-black sky. Frederick V, Duke of Paltz, in whom "progressive" Europe had put their hope, ruled only one season as King of Bohemia. Then this "King of Winter," as he was called, was devestatingly defeated at the battle of the White Mountain in Bohemia in 1619. The liberal, artistic, and tolerant Prague of Rudolph II was burned down, literally and figuratively. Officers of Emperor Ferdinand of Hapsburg criss-crossed the city with a "black list" that contained the name of Amos Komensky, who was able to flee the city just in time. We encounter him again under the name by which he became known: Comenius. He would propagate the Rosicrucian thought pattern, bringing it, among other places, to the Netherlands.

In Germany, an ear-deafening silence surrounded the Brothers of the Rosicrucians. Yet their influence in spreading the hermetic body of thought and teachings can hardly be overestimated.

CHAPTER 25
HERMES IN THE LODGE

Venice is a most enjoyable city. So much beauty all together—the illustrious palaces seen from the Grand Canal; the extraordinary light that inspired artists to incredible masterpieces; the ever-presence of water enclosed within narrow canals or even flowing widely in the largest lagoon; narrow streets and alleys with countless small bridges and surprising vistas. The exposition about Hermes, which was held in Venice, was a wonderful excuse to wander endlessly once again through the city. A person still has to have an excuse for his work.

The entrance to the exhibition about Hermes Trismegistus and the hermetic tradition on the square at Saint Marco was especially not to be missed. It was being held in the former *Bibliotheca Nazionale Marciana*, a beautiful Renaissance palace. It is always a revelation to come face-to-face with cultural treasures from bygone times—treasures that have inspired humanity to reflect upon the purpose of life. But something else caught my attention as well—something that stood at the entrance to the exhibition that, for some reason, we were not able to enter. In fact, the staircase to the actual reception hall was "hermetically" sealed.

There, in that hall, they had built a strange structure—a puppet theater with closed mini-curtains. In the half-light, you could just barely see a painted placard with these intriguing words:

Se avete un vero desiderio
se avete un vero corragio ed intelligenza
tirate questa tenda

Or:

If you have a true wish
and you have the real courage and intelligence
pull the curtain open.

Several visitors were standing around the structure giggling. But no one dared to pull the curtains open. There was just something scary about it.

I am a happy person and therefore have only one wish. So, not too abruptly, I pulled the curtains aside. And…I saw myself. In a mirror. At the edge of the mirror there was written, in many different languages, the ancient Greek saying: *Gnooti seauton*, Know thyself. An exhibition sign indicated that it belonged to a former Freemason Lodge. In the 18th century, it had been seized by the Inquisition and, in 1985, it was rediscovered.

Know thyself! Indeed, the motto of Freemasons all around the world. This is not just a hermetic injunction, but also a universal Gnostic motto. Often, life is too short to come to true self-knowledge—to reach knowledge of our true Selves. Did not Hermes tell us that we have to learn to look deeply into ourselves for that? Must you not already have to know the "imprints" of the "Seven Heavens" and have transformed them before you are able to observe your true Self? Indeed, in earlier times, this was called "going the way of Hermes."

We have seen, throughout all times, that there have been people who had the courage and resilience to follow such a path, often at risk to their own lives. For in a world focussed on the outer, there is usually ignorance about—or resistance to—the inner world. Living a life of inner knowledge and awareness frees us, and that is not always in the best interests of the people or institutions who are bent on power. They want to manipulate us with other goals, often masked with pretty words. They want to keep the curtain shut so that the mirror image remains hidden and we are led to identify ourselves with surrogate images that have been put in its place—images that we tend to adopt, to desire, to pursue, and that then hold us in a state of dependency. These were, among other things, my deep contemplations after my mirror experience. I have not had to invent these thoughts for myself. There have been many wise men who taught this and brought it into practice—Krishna, Buddha, Christ, and, of course, Hermes. His words are crystalized in the *Hermetica;* the living experience is up to us.

Spiritual Craftsmen

On June 24, 1717 in London, four Freemason lodges united into one Grand Lodge. This event is marked, in general, as the founding date of Freemasonry. The fact that four lodges combined, of course shows that Freemasonry existed prior to this date, so we are not faced with the dilemma we encountered at the end of the previous chapter where we had to account for a gap of about a century in the Rosicrusian tradition. In fact, the hermetic tradition does not contain any abrupt gaps, only smooth transitions. And Freemasonry is one of the many unmistakable links.

Freemasonry is a spiritual movement born of an inner desire that reveals itself in a constant striving toward development of all the qualities of spirit and courage that raise humanity to a higher spiritual and moral level. We read this in the *Constitution of the Order of Freemasons of the Great-Eastern Section of the Netherlands.*[942]

Opinions differ about the origins of Freemasonry. Pater Michel Dierikx, not a Freemason himself but fascinated by the phenonema, sketches in his book *De vrijmetselarij* (Freemasonry) the medieval guild structures that were the foundation of the present movement. In this, he concurs with the most generally accepted scholarship, according to which blueprints for the construction of cathedrals in Great Britain seem to have been made in the lodge, the building hut, following age-old geometric principles based on sacred mathematical measurements. The word "lodge" soon obtained a wider meaning, however, derived from the Freemasons organization, the *loge.* The sharing of this "secret" age-old knowledge resulted, especially in the 17th century, in an increase of laymen joining the Freemason guilds. In London, the increase was so large that the London Company of Freemasons founded a Company of Masons in 1656 that was only accessible to people of the trade itself.

Not every researcher is in agreement with this reading of history. According to some researchers, there were no Freemason guilds in medieval England.[943] The movement, they claim, derived from the Order of the Knights Templar.[944] At first, this may seem reasonable if you look for a link with the construction of the Temple of Solomon where, according to legend, the actual origin of Freemasonry lies. We'll return to these legends shortly in great detail. An enormous amount of romanticizing about the secretive Templars and other mysterious orders has recently appeared, as in a book by two shameless journalists who captivated the world with unproven theories about the secret genealogy of Jesus as forefather of the French kings. Such speculation is always fodder for another world bestseller that touts these fantasies on its front cover![945]

Even more popular is the opinion that Freemasonry derived from the Rosicrucian movement.[946] And indeed, striking similarities cannot be denied. We come once again to Robert Fludd, about whom some claim that "both streams come together, when he speaks of the right-angled cornerstone in *Summum Bonum* (The Highest Good)..."[947]

In fact, there was a Freemason lodge close to Fludd's house that makes a link more believable. But there are also other great men who claim a link between Rosicrucianism and Freemasonry. The researcher Hans Schick Johan Amos Comenius refers to "the bridge between Rosicrucians and Freemasonry."[948] Comenius, as we saw before, had to leave Prague precipitously and went on to found the College Lucis in Amsterdam in 1667, an illustrious group inspired by the Brotherhood of the Rosicrucians.[949] In life, Comenius was the embodiment of the *homo humanis*, a person who answers, first and foremost, to his (divine) fate—a principle that was stimulated by the Rosicrucian tradition and by early Freemasonry as well.[950] Moreover, both these traditions owe partial tribute to the age-old wise Hermes. Comenius even suggested a societal structure that would answer to this ideal:

> ...There must come three ruling bodies. The High Ruler of each of these bodies will be Hermes Trismegistus (the Thrice-Greatest interpreter of God's will for human, the High Prophet, the High Priest and the High King), meaning to say Christ, who as the only one has the power to rule all.[951]

The links between the Rosicrucians and early Freemasonry are also illustrated by a verse that appeared in Edinburgh as early as 1638: "For we be brethren of the Rosie Crosse, we have the Mason's word and second sight."[952]

Later, in the 18th century, the history of Freemasonry and the Rosicrucians appears as an inseparable conglomeration of societies, organizations, and brotherhoods that are allied with each other at numerous levels. The eighteenth degree of the Scottish rites of the Freemasons is the *Knight of the Rosicrucians*.[953] To be admitted to the first of the nine degrees of the German *Orden der Goud-und Rosenkreutzer*, initiates had to pass the first three degrees of Orthodox Freemasonry.[954]

Let's return to the beginning. Two facts are indisputably true: On the May 20, 1641, the Scotsman Robert Morey was admitted to the Freemason Lodge of Edinburgh and, according to his own dairy, the learned Elias Ashmole joined a Masonic lodge on October 16, 1646.[955] If the exact origin of Freemasonry is clouded in veils of golden legend, then these facts are remarkable, since they indicate the existence of Freemason lodges that link up seamlessly with the late blossoming of the first generation of Rosicrucians.

The Temple of Solomon

> The legendary Temple of Solomon was for the Templars, as well as for the later Freemasons, the most beautiful fruit and the best example of all sacred Geometry. It was not only an extreme delight to the eyes of everyone who viewed it or who fulfilled their religious duties inside, it also arose far above the five senses. It was considered to be in an unique and transcendental way resonant with the divine harmony of Heaven itself; its length and width, height and depth were entirely in unison with the measurements which the Universe most desired. The Temple of Solomon was, if you wish, the Soul of God carved in stone.[956]

This citation is taken from one of the many modern books that promise, once and for all, to reveal all the numerous plots that have suppressed a mysterious hidden religion that connects John the Baptist, Mary Magdalene, Jesus, the Grail, the Templars, Leonardo da Vinci, Freemasonry, and many other unexpected elements.[957] One persistent historical link in the Freemason tradition is the one that ties the legendary Temple of Solomon to the origin of Freemasonry. It is highly probable that the story of the building of the Temple of Solomon by Master Builder Hiram had circulated in the lodges long before the foundation of the order, and most likely had been part of the formulation of its rules and laws. But it is not until 1762 that the legend about Hiram was published.[958] According to this legend, Hiram was murdered by three evil villains (Jubila, Jubilo, and Jubilum) who tried to steal his "password"—presumably, the key to the secrets of architecture that were truly passed on from generation to generation.

Another legend points out the difference between King Hiram of Phoenicia, the deliverer of the expensive Libanese wood for the temple, and Hiram Abif, the Master Builder. In fact, modern research shows that the Temple of Solomon spoken of in legend is not the only magnificent large-scale structure we know of from this time. The temple, in fact, seems to have been of a typical Phoenician style[959] that was, in turn, based on the Egyptian style.[960] According to researchers, the measurements and blueprints represent almost an exact copy of a Sumerian temple to the God Ninurta that was built 1000 years prior. The legendary Jewish temple must have been a small structure, not much larger than a village church and probably not half the size of the Palace of Solomon. Indeed, the home of Solomon's harem must have been twice as large as the temple to his God.[961] Some historians even claim that the temple was no more than a private chapel attached to the royal palace.[962]

Grand or not, the Temple of Solomon has always appealed to the imagination. It has truly become an icon, as did Solomon himself. In the late Middle Ages, many magical writings surfaced that were attributed to an author named Solomon, some of which certainly date back to Hellenistic Alexandria, a cultural melting pot in which many Jews lived. In Syria, in the 2nd century A.D., the influential *Odes to Solomon* [963] were composed.

Solomon was seen in certain circles as a wise magus. The Solomon-Hiram legend that is depicted in the discourses of the rules and laws of Freemasonry is thus a mystical story from a later time period, with a truly historical background.[964]

The Legendary Pillars of the Temple

I am not a Freemason myself, but I am frequently invited to speak at Freemason lodges. Often this takes place in the "temple" of the lodge. In these spaces, several things keep catching my attention: the "Know Thyself" motto above the entrance, the zodiacal signs on the ceiling, and the two pillars, one decorated with the letter B, the other with the letter J. These pillars are copies of those decorating the earlier Temple of Solomon and have a great significance in the Freemasonry. They also appear in the "constitution" of Freemasonry—the *Constitution* of Anderson—that gives a history of Freemasonry dating back to 4000 B.C.[965]

After the founding of the Great Lodge, Scottish Pastor James Anderson was given the task of designing a fitting constitution for the order. This was completed in 1723. Therein, Anderson referred to previous statutes of Freemason orders and also used articles that he found in older manuscripts. In the statutes, there are guidelines for the handiwork and, above all, the ethical duties of the members, like the duty to be good, honest, and just and to establish true friendships among people. The three stages of Apprentice, Journeyman, and Master take initiates through practical and "spiritual" degrees of initiation. New members give an oath and swear to absolute secrecy. Initiation to a higher degree is accompanied by a precisely composed ritual.

One of the manuscripts to which Anderson referred was the so-called Cooke manuscript from 1450. This document describes seven fundamental sciences that correspond to the *artes liberales*. The most interesting part of this document, whose origins must go back to 1400, is its historical content. The manuscript states that, prior to the deluge, there lived a certain Lamech who was of the seventh generation after Adam. Lamech had two wives, Adah and Zillah. With his first wife, Adah, he had two sons, Jabal and Jubal (note the partial resemblance of these names to those in the legend of Hiram).

Jabal was the first to discover the geometry of the art of masonry and he built houses.

Lemach's sons knew truly that God would take revenge on humanity for its sins. They decided to engrave all knowledge into two types of stone: marble, which cannot burn, and a material called "lacerus," that possessed the quality of being unsinkable. From these materials, Jabal made two pillars on which all wisdom was chiseled. After the great deluge, these two pillars were rediscovered—one by Pythagoras, the other by Hermes "the Philosopher."[966]

Another manuscript, attributed to the famous English architect Inigo Jones, is called *The Old Duties*. Herein, the Cooke story is told again, this time more elaborately:

> One of the pillars was made of marble, for it does not burn in fire. And the other stone was made of "lacernes," for it does not drown in water. Our intention is to tell you the truth how and in which way these stones were found upon which this knowledge was written.
>
> The Great Hermes, called Trismegistus because he is also King, Priest and Philosopher, found one of them... Some claim him to be the grandchild of Cush, who in turn was a grandchild of Noah. He was the first to learn something about Astronomy so as to be able to admire the other wonders of Nature. He proved there was only one God, Creator of everything. He divided the day into twelve hours: He is also held as the first to divide the Zodiac into twelve signs. He was minister of Osiris, King of Egypt. And he discovered the ordinary script and the hieroglyphs, the first laws of the Egyptians and various sciences and he taught them to other people.[967]

The pillars also have names: Boaz and Jachin. Knight and Lomas, two Freemasons who brought a lively study to light, claim that these symbolize "power" and "foundation," which together generate stability.[968] Others specify that the meanings of the names are "In Him is Power" and "He affirms." In any case, both theories point to a Hebrew origin, for, according to the legend, the two pillars stood in front of the eastern entrance of the Temple of Solomon.[969] Jachin was allegedly, according to one tradition, the first high priest of this temple. He represents the priestly pillar. Boaz, the great-grandfather of David, represents the royal pillar.

Knight and Lomas go from the assumption that the two pillars find their origin in the Egyptian pillars that represented the two Kingdoms before they became one some 5000 years ago—the Pillars of the Two Lands.[970] These pillars were then called the Pillars of Hermes.[971] This does not seem likely to me. It is somewhat doubtful to presume that the two previously separate Egyptian lands had one specific pillar as their symbol. One, or multiple, obelisks seem to be more likely. This does not completely rule out an Egyptian origin, however. The pillars of the Temple of Solomon are of the free-standing type. They were, therefore, not meant to support a roof. This type of pillar was common around 1000 B.C. in Syria and Phoenicia, and on Cyprus.[972] On the other hand, the Egyptian *djedd* pillar, consecrated to Osiris, was also widespread in Phoenicia, as well as in Palestine.[973] The Egyptian word *djedd* means "stability" or "duration." Free-standing pillars, as an essential part of the cosmological character of the Egyptian temples, appeared in Sakkara at the previously mentioned step-pyramid, as well as in other places.[974] In fact, two such pillars stood at the Thoth temple in Hermopolis.[975]

The pillars, as symbolic reservoirs of archaic wisdom, represented the foundations of an esoteric doctrine that was truly lost from later Jewish tradition.[976] The great Jewish scholar Gershom Scholem sees the pillars as representatives of the two heavenly guardians who, in the *Merkawa* tradition, protect the heavenly palaces (*heikaloth*).[977] Once again, we are dealing with an initiation mystery.

Loss of Potency

Hermes is clearly present in the lodge. In addition, in later branches of Freemasonry, the Thrice-Great sage surfaces regularly, as in the Order of the Magi of Memphis, of which one of the degrees is the "Exalted Philosopher Hermes."[978] According to Antoine Faivre, this is the only ritual where Hermes Trismegistus is made one with the architect Hiram.[979] During the admittance ritual, the candidate says that Hermes, priest and king of Egypt, has taught the secret science about the deepest secrets of Nature. In this role, the candidate calls out at the conclusion: "Live well! Remember me! My real name to the Egyptians is Mercury, to the Phoenicians it is Thoth, to the Greek it is Hermes Trismegistus and over the whole world it is Hiram"...[980]

It is not possible, within the scope of this book, to mention all the movements that have backgrounds linked to Rosicrucianism or Freemasonry. There were, in Western Europe alone, several hundred. In his enormous three-volume work, Karl Frick, the Austrian researcher of a number of "secret societies," covers almost three centuries of history of "secret occult movements."[981] Of the more than 1500 pages in this work, almost seventy deal with Hermes Trismegistus, while there are countless mentions of the term "hermetic." But alas, not all of these movements were permeated with the true hermetic principles. In my book, *De geheime woorden* (The Secret Words), I have described the less attractive side of some "sect leaders."[982] The hermetic river is, for about one and a half centuries, somewhat murky and a little opaque in some places, although it also carried in its stream genuine pearls and beauty.

For the loss of potency of Hermeticism, the works of Kriegsman and Kircher are illustrative. Kriegsman saw Hermes as the patriarch of the German people. He freely associated Thoth with Theut, and further, with the word "Teutonic," and thus "German."[983] Kircher (1602–1680) was a Jesuit. He saw the Egyptian religion as the original religion and the *Corpus Hermeticum* as original knowledge and linked them both to Egyptian hieroglyphs, establishing himself as one of the greatest linguists of all time—a reputation that came under strong pressure when Jean François Champollion deciphered the hieroglyphs with the help of the Rosetta Stone.

Of Kircher, there remains nothing. In the land of the blind, the one-eyed man is king. Kircher used the *Hermetica* to confirm his controversial theories about the superiority of Catholic doctrine. He placed Hermes at the front of his religious argument and made him into a museum piece. Joscelyn Godwin, fascinated by Kircher's pretty etchings, subtitled his book *A Renaissance Man and The Quest For Lost Knowledge*.[984] Carlos Gilly's reaction was not so soft:

> Kircher… had no affinity with the Renaissance or with Humanism; he was a Baroque-figure; and the so-called lost knowledge which he went in search of, was not at all lost, as he was trying to make his readers believe… the reason Kircher went in search of this so-called lost knowledge: To stop it.[985]

On page eight of Gilly's book about Kircher, an illustration has been added from the front page of his work *Ars Magna Sciendi* (The Great Art of Knowledge). At the top of the illustration an intriguing symbol has been engraved: An eye within a shining triangle. The so-called *Eye of Horus*! I looked at it fascinated, since I had seen it before. And then the light dawned—the American dollar is decorated with this same symbol.[986] (No, we will not move on to a whole chapter about Hermes in America!)

A Mechanical World View

At the time of Kirchner's birth, René Descartes was six years old; when Kircher died, Isaac Newton was thirty-eight. Factually, he was therefore a contemporary of both. Newton is seen as the creator of the mechanical world view. This is not entirely correct. From Newton on, the world view became strongly influenced by discoveries in the field of mechanics. But Newton himself still had an eye for the metaphysical. He was also especially interested in alchemy. It is true that, through Newton's research, a mechanical point of view of the world started to emerge in which it is assumed that all phenomena can be explained by the laws of mechanics. In this view, everything becomes predictable. Magic, alchemy, astrology, and worship of God are no longer needed. According to French mathematician and astronomer Pierre Simon de Laplace (1749–1827), scientific research would lead to a "world mind" capable of detecting the position and speed of each particle at any moment and calculating its future and past behavior at all times. Thus nothing can occur that is new or unexpected. God became the remote mover; once everything is set in motion (in this dualistic paradigm, God was obviously portrayed as male), he can rest on his laurels for the rest of time.

Title page of *Ars Magna Sciendi* of Kircher. At the top is the "Eye of Horus," still to be seen on the American dollar.

But it was actually René Descartes who stands as the first propounder of the mechanical world view. On November 10, 1619, Descartes experienced a vision "of The Angel of True Reality" that revealed a machine-like world ruled by mathematical laws without any inherent spontaneity or freedom whatsoever. This became the nucleus of mechanistic natural science.[987] Descartes' theories of natural science were truly quite quickly rejected (by Newton, among others), but his proposition that Nature has no soul became a common assumption in the Enlightenment and is still true for most scientists. "The Philosophy of Descartes pulled the Soul out of the totality of the natural world; the whole Nature was lifeless, soulless and sooner dead than alive," noted the ground-breaking British scientist Robert Sheldrake.[988]

Sheldrake observes that, three and a half centuries later, mechanical biologists still dream about Descartes when they propose that a mature organism can be calculated on the basis of its genetic information. "In reality, one has never found to this date a similar mechanical explanation for the development of even one simple plant or animal form, yet the conviction such an interpretation is in principle possible, is still one of the most elementary articles of belief of the mechanical conviction."[989] Hermes is dismissed. Or perhaps not, after all?

It was against the unveiling of the cosmic unity as seperate isolated particles without souls that the English mystic and artist William Blake protested. On Plate 22 of the poem in his majestical work *Jerusalem*—wherein he refers to the *Tabula Smaragdina*—Blake asks science, here personified as Newton:

Why wilt thou number every little fibre of my Soul
Spreading them out before the Sun like stalks of flax to dry?
The Infant Joy is beautiful, but its anatomy
Horrible ghast & deadly! nought shalt thou find in it
But dark despair & everlasting brooding melancholy![990]

William Blake's drawing of Newton as the Creator of a mechanical world-view.

The visionary Blake was familiar with the *Hermetica.* In his works, he refers many times to Hermes.[991] Blake is one of the genuine pearls of beauty in the sometimes muddy stream of which I spoke earlier.

Another pearl is the hermetic manifesto, *The Secret Figures of the Rosicrucians*, from the years 1785–1788. This is a most revealing text for young students of the "School of the Holy Spirit" that is decorated with magnificent jewels of illustrations.[992] It is the last manifesto of international Hermeticism from the epoch between the Renaissance and the Age of Revolution.[993]

Humanity Reaches Godhood

We started this chapter with Freemasonry. One of the most illustrious Freemasons was Wolfgang Amadeus Mozart.[994] He was one year older than William Blake, although their lives ran completely different courses. In a recent interesting study, Tjeu van den Berk showed that there is a wealth of symbolic language from Rosicrucianism, Freemasonry, alchemy, and Hermeticism in Mozart's *Die Zauberflöte* (The Magic Flute).[995] In his chapter "Hermes in Vienna at the End of the Eighteenth Century," van den Berk shows how, in those days, Rosicrucianism and Freemasonry were intermingled, as though entangled in a loving embrace.

At that time, innumerable lodges were intensively involved with alchemy. Depending on the whims of monarchs, sometimes Freemasons themselves, the lodges either worked in relative openness or were driven underground. Yet their world view wavered. In the new mechanical view, a materialistic scientific model emerged that tried to explain old and new phenomena from matter or substance. Spirit disappeared from the scene. "Spirit" was nothing more than "mind." But if spirit is ignored, the soul is as well, and the connections between spirit and Nature can no longer be understood and souless humanity ends up in a fatal divided state—separate from the cosmos and separate from God. Rosicrucianism and spiritual Freemasonry tried, where possible, to turn this tide. The quest for the true Self—the Self in the mirror—continued. Almost desperately, they continued to search for the alchemical principle of the *coniunctio*, the becoming one, the Unity. This can not be expressed more dramatically then in the words of Freemason Johann Emanuel Schikaneder[996] who wrote the libretto for the *Magic Flute* for which his "brother" Mozart provided with heavenly music:

> Mann und Weib und Weib und Mann
> Reichen an die Gottheit an.
> ("Man and Woman touch Divinity")[997]

CHAPTER 26

HERMES ACROSS THE OCEAN

> Our work is a plea for the recognition of the Hermetic Philosophy, the ancient universal wisdom Religion, as the only possible key to the absolute in Science and Theology.[998]

On November 17, 1875 in New York, a small group of people established a society. At face value, this was not earth-shaking news. Every day there are clubs founded somewhere in the world. In this case, it was a spiritual society, but again, this was not particularily extraordinary. The 18th and 19th centuries had seen numerous small groups and groupings who occupied themselves with many forms of occultism and spirituality. Although the term "occultism" has, in our "enlightened" time, taken on a dark connotation, it is, in fact, nothing more than the doctrine of the "occult," that which is what is hidden or silent. Like esotericism, occultism is focussed on the hidden reality behind the visible façades that are usually interpreted as reality.

Back to New York in 1875. In fact, a worldwide movement was born from this seemingly unexceptional event—one that has had a great influence on Western thought and given direction to the spiritual yearnings of aspiring humanity. On this day in November, the Theosophical Society was founded, with Colonel Henry Steel Olcott as its chairman, William Quan Judge as its legal counselor, and Helena Petrovna Blavatsky as its secretary. Blavatsky was ultimately the one of these three to become most famous beyond the circles of the Theosophical Movement through her two extremely voluminous books: *Isis Unveiled* and *The Secret Doctrine*.[999]

AN EXTRAORDINARY WOMAN

Who was Helena Petrovna Blavatsky? Lovingly called HPB by her followers, she was born Helena Petrovna von Hahn on August

12, 1831 in Russian Ekaterinoslov (the present Djnepropetrovsky). During my research for a small book I once wrote about Madame Blavatsky and Theosophy,[1000] I came across an unexpected wealth of biographical material on this remarkable woman.[1001] Her life history only becomes really interesting for our research, however, when she set foot in the United Sates in July 1873. There, at a spiritualistic gathering in Vermont, she met ex-Colonel Henry Steel Olcott, who was attending the séance in his professional role as a journalist, which he occasionally pursued in addition to his law practice.

Back in New York, Henry and Helena met again. On one of these occasions, Olcott introduced Blavatsky to William Quan Judge, another young lawyer. In 1875, they formed the core of the Theosophical Society, whose goal is

> To form a core of the Universal Brotherhood of Humanity, without distinction of race, belief, sex, caste or color.
>
> To encourage the study of comparative Religion, Philosophy, and Science.
>
> To investigate the unexplained laws of nature and the latent powers in human.[1002]

At first, the movement barely grew. Only after Blavatsky published *Isis Unveiled* did interested parties come streaming in. After that, another lodge was established in London. In1878, Olcott and Blavatsky left for India, where they set up temporary headquarters for the Theosophical Society in Bombay. Thus a part of the ideal of "Universal Brotherhood" that was so contrary to the existing spirit of the time was made visible. Hindus, Buddhists, Jews, Muslims, and Christians—white, yellow, brown, or black, regardless of distinction or caste—participated together in the many gatherings of the society and, in this way, began to understand each other better. In 1879, Helena met the previously mentioned Alfred Sinnett, head editor of the influential Indian newspaper *The Pioneer*, who would play an extremely important role in the development of the Theosophical Movement—not least through his involvement with the heavily challenged so-called *Mahatma Letters*.

Sinnet, along with others, allegedly received so-called "letters of the Masters" that contained teachings and counsels.[1003] For Sinnett, this formed the groundwork for his popular works *The Occult World* (1881) and *Esoteric Buddhism* (1883). Great literary giants like William Butler Yeats, George A. E. Russell, and George R. S. Mead were so inspired by these works that their later membership in the Theosophical Society may, to a large degree, be attributed to them. But the letters also had another, less positive, impact. After Olcott and Blavatsky traveled to Europe in 1884 to attend to some difficulties occurring in the London lodge (more about this shortly), they were accused, from India, of fraud in relation to the Mahatma Letters. Returning to India, Blavatsky tried to straighten things out, but her position there was never the same. Disappointed, she resigned all her functions in the society and left India—this time, for good.

The period of purification that followed was apparently fruitful for her, for, in 1888, she delivered her greatest work—*The Secret Doctrine*. In this voluminous, two-part book, Blavatsky tried to create a synthesis between science, religion, and philosophy, with a heavy emphasis on Eastern wisdom.

Three years later, this extraordinary woman passed away and left behind a flourishing society with more than 100,000 members all around the world.

The Secret Doctrine of Hermes

In her books *Isis Unveiled* and *The Secret Doctrine*, Blavatsky refers to Hermes on at least sixty pages. In fact, Hermes occupies a prominent position in all the early Theosophical teachings. We already saw, in the opening citation of this chapter, that the hermetic philosophy is proposed as the only key to knowledge of the inner essence of things. During and after her stay in India, Blavatsky linked this "Universal Wisdom Religion" to the manifestation of the ancient wisdom religions in the East. They flow from the same original source, she proposed in her magnum opus *The Secret Doctrine*. The secret doctrine described is, according to the master writer, a collection of wisdom from all ages.

> The fundamental law about the central point where everything is born out of, is the one homogenous divine principle of substance. The Universe is the periodical manifestation of this unknown essence... Everything in such a Universe is conscious, provided therefore with its own consciousness at different planes of consciousness. Also in stones there is consciousness. Dead matter does in no way exist. The Universe is directed and guided from within to without. "As above, so below, as it is in Heaven, so it is on Earth; and the human—the microcosmos and the smaller image of the macrocosmos- is the living proof of this universal law."[1004]

As one of the premises of this doctrine, Blavatsky sees "an omnipresent, eternal, limitless and unchangeable principle, which goes beyond all reflection, which transcends the power of human conception and can only be tainted by human expression or comparison...." This is true "because it is beyond the scope and the range of the human thought." It is, in short, "an absolute reality which precedes all the limited manifestations."[1005]

This connects seamlessly to Hermes' teaching to Tat in the first Stobaeus fragment:

> It is impossible to speak of God. For the corporeal cannot express the incorporeal. The unperfected cannot comprehend the perfected.[1006]

The archaic wisdom primarily presented by Blavatsky—that everything contains consciousness and there is therefore no "dead" matter—was a cry in the materialistic wilderness in those days. With broad agreement, Blavatsky quotes Hermes in another fragment from Stobaeus:

> So Hermes says, the Thrice-Greatest Trismegistus: "O' my son, matter becomes; earlier she was; for matter is the vehicle of the becoming. Becoming is the activity of the not yet created Deity. After the matter has been endowed with the germ of becoming, she is born, for the creative force models her according to the ideal

> forms. Matter not yet brought forth has no form; she becomes, when she is put into motion."[1007]

The *Poimandres*, the first treatise of the *Corpus Hermeticum*, made an especially deep impression on Blavatsky, and she refers to it many times:

> In the "Book of Hermes" Poimandres appears to Hermes, the oldest and the most spiritual of the Logoi of the western continent, in the shape of a fiery Dragon of "Light, Fire, and Flame." Poimandres, the personified "Divine Thought," says: "The Light is me, I am the Nous, I am thy God, and I am far older than the human principle which escapes from the shadow..."[1008]
>
> It is clear... the original universal divine thought is neither the unknown unmanifested One, since it is present to a large degree in both sexes (is man and woman) and is also not the Christian Father, since the latter is male and not androgynous.[1009]

Blavatsky compares the Gnostic "Creation Myth" in *Poimandres* to the stories of Creation in Genesis that are most well-known in the West:

> In Genesis, on which no metaphysical energy has been spent, but only an acuteness and ingenuity to veil the esoteric truth, the "Creation" begins at the third stage of manifestation. "God" or the Elohim are the "Seven Rulers" of Poimandres... which means in so many words, they separated the higher manifested (angelic) heaven or plane of consciousness from the lower or material plane; the (to us) eternal and unchangeable aeons from those eras which are in space, time and duration; for the uninitiated the Heaven from Earth, the unknown from the known. Such is the meaning of the sentence in Poimandres, which says: "THOUGHT, the divine, which is LIGHT and LIFE, brought through its WORD or first aspect, the other brought THOUGHT into motion, which as the God of Spirit and Fire formed Seven Rulers, who within their circle enclosed the world of senses, called 'Fate.'" This latter pertains to Karma: The "seven circles" are the seven planets and planes, and

> also the seven invisible spirits in the spheres of the angels, of which the seven visible symbols are the seven planets, the seven rishi's of the Great Bear and other signs.[1010]
>
> ...In Poimandres, the seven original humans, created by Nature from the "Heavenly Human," all part of the qualities of the "Seven Rulers" or Rulers, who humans—their own reflection and synthesis—loved.[1011]

With extraordinary acuteness, Blavatsky noticed that, in the hermetic writings, there is an essential germ of the Trinity: "In the 'Book of Hermes'... the whole dogma of the Trinity as accepted by Christians is explained in distinct and unequivocal sentences." She refers to *Poimandres*, where we already read:

> "The Light," he said, "am I, the Spirit, thy God, who existed prior to the moist substance which appeared from out of the darkness. The shining Word, which came from the Spirit, is the Son of God."[1012]

> What then? say I. Know that what sees in thee and hears is the Lord's Word (Logos); but Mind is Father-God. Not separate are they the one fom other; just in their union [rather] is it Life consists.[1013]

Synthesis between East and West

The Books of Hermes, according to Blavatsky, have not gone unchallenged through time. We no longer have the original texts and the contradictions in the underlying hermetic treatises prove that "a quantity of generations of mystics of all kind wrote under the general pseudonym of Hermes."[1014]

> The writings compiled to the books of Thoth have been destroyed and burned in Egypt by the command of Diocletianus during the third century of our era. All the others, including "Pymander"[1015] are in the present form mostly memories, more or less rather vague and incorrect, from various Greek or even Latin authors, who often

did not hesitate to put their own interpretations on pure hermetical fragments.[1016]

...The "Pymander"... is an abridgment of one of the Books of Thoth, by a Platonist from Alexandria.[1017] However truly esoteric and in accordance with the Secret Doctrine "Pymander, the divine thought" is of Hermes, can only be inferred from the original and first translations of such in Latin and Greek only.[1018]

To underline this, Blavatsky quotes this profound revelation from the second discourse of the *Corpus Hermeticum*:

God is not an ability of the mind, but the cause of the existence the ability of the mind; not a spirit, but the cause of the existence of the Spirit; not light, but the cause of the existence of the Light.

And she continues:

The above shows clearly the "Divine Pymander," however much this is also turned around in some parts by Christian "smoothing," is nonetheless written by a Philosopher, while most of the so-called "hermetical fragments"[1019] are from sectarian pagans who had a preference for the conception of an anthropomorphic Supreme Being. Yet both form the echo of the esoterical Philosophy and the Hindu Purânas.[1020]

Here Blavatsky refers to the Hindu Purânas. And so we return to the East. The archaic "wisdom of the East" was barely known in Europe before the 19th century. Even in the East, moreover, their awareness of their own ancient wisdom tradition had been greatly reduced. It is one of the greatest accomplishments of the Theosophical Movement that they introduced, as it were, this wisdom to the West and made it more accessible in the East as well. Indeed, we see a striking similarity in both wisdom sytems, as Blavatsky herself proposed:

> So it can be shown all the fundamental truths of nature were in antiquity extended and the basic ideas about spirit, matter and the universe, or about God, substance and human were the same. If one takes the two most ancient religious systems of the world, the Hinduism and the Hermeticism, from the scriptures of India and Egypt, then the accordance between the two is easy to see.[1021]
>
> ...Because the precepts of the Eastern doctrine have always been kept secret and because the reader can hardly hope the original texts will be shown, unless he becomes an accepted disciple, then the learned in Greek and Latin best turn to the original texts of hermetical Literature. Let him, for example, carefully read the first pages of the Poimandres of Hermes Trismegistus; he will see our teachings incorporated in it, however veiled the text of such also is. There he will also find the evolution of the Universe, of our Earth (in Poimandres called "Nature") and of everything else, from the "moist principle"—or the great Deep, FATHER-MOTHER—the first differentiation in the manifested Kosmos. First the "universal ability of the mind," which, which was in the oldest Christian translations transformed into God...[1022]

According to Blavatsky, Alexandrian Ammonius Saccas, mentor of Plotinus and Origen in the 3rd century A.D., had already linked Hermes to the Vedas:

> It was Ammonius who first taught every religion is based on one and the same underlying truth; the wisdom is such which is found in the Books of Thoth (Hermes Trismegistus), from which books Pythagoras and Plato had learned all their Philosophy. And he claimed the teachings of the first part were the same as the earliest teachings of the Brahmans, which are embodied in the oldest Vedas.[1023]

Through the fire that destroyed the library at Alexandria, Eastern writings were lost to the West for quite a long time, along with the most original hermetic writings, the "Books of Thoth."[1024]

Thanks to new translations that appeared years before the publication of *The Secret Doctrine*, Blavatsky includes in her discussion, not only *Poimandres*, but also *Asclepius*[1025] and the *Fragments of Stobaeus*.[1026] This strengthens her position that the hermetic philosophy, together with the Vedic philosophy, forms the foundation of all esoteric knowledge.[1027] The marriage between East and West is no longer secret; it has become public.

A Hermetic Lodge

When Blavatsky and Olcott departed for Europe in 1884 to attend to difficulties in the London lodge of the Theosophical Society, the chairman of that lodge was the learned physician Anna Kingsford.[1028] However, the same lodge included among its members Alfred P. Sinnett, who had just returned from India. Kingsford and Sinnett did not get along very well. Sinnett enjoyed a great standing in the movement since he had apparently received letters from the so-called "Masters."[1029] Kingsford doubted the existence of the Masters.[1030] Moreover, the teachings reputedly contained in the letters—which had recently appeared in Sinnett's book *Esoteric Buddhism*—were, according to Kingsford, more Buddhist than esoteric. In return, Sinnett was rather critical of some of Kingsford's earlier work in his discussion of her collected lectures in *The Perfect Way or the Finding of Christ*.

Anna Kingsford worked very closely with Edward Maitland, vice-chairman of the lodge. They cleary both valued Gnostic Christianity and the hermetic philosophy more than the Eastern teachings to which Sinnett and a number of other lodge members were strongly attached.[1031] You can surmise from this that, within the lodge, a battle raged between East and West.

In December 1883, Sinnett received a letter from "Master K. H." about this controversy. The Mahatma spoke in defense of Anna Kingsford, because "the Western public" had to understand that the Theosophical Society was "a philosophical school based on the old hermetical foundation."[1032] "The Hermetic Philosophy is universal and is non-sectarian..." and "fits in with each Faith and each Philosophy and is not opposed to any. She is the endless ocean of Truth,

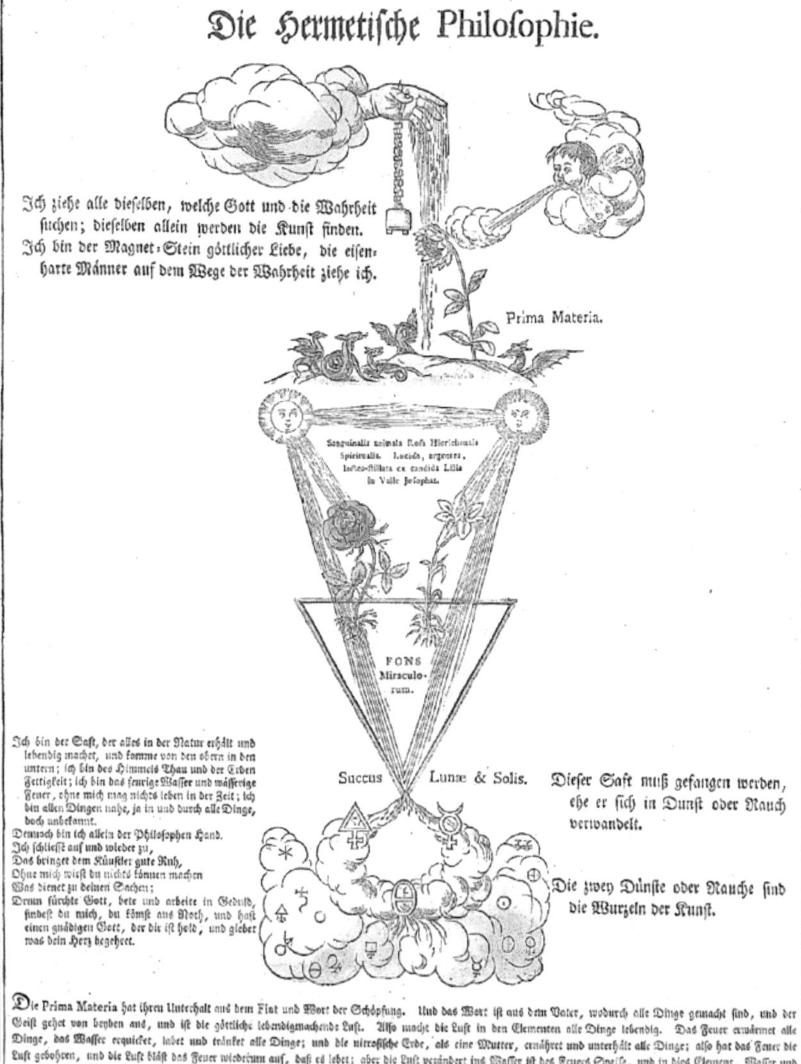

Illustration of *Secret Figures: The Hermetic doctrine.*

the central point where each river and each stream flows towards and comes together -whether the source lies in the East, West, North or South."[1033] In the meantime, the writer concluded, Anna Kingsford was the most suitable "to lead the movement in England with success."[1034] Nonetheless, in 1884 there was a public division in the movement when a sympathizer of Sinnett named Finch was chosen as chairman of the lodge (with Sinnett as vice-chairman).

When HPB involved herself personally in the matter, a solution was found. Anna Kingsford, together with Edward Maitland, was allowed to start her own group, called the Hermetic Lodge.[1035] This quickly became the independant Hermetic Society. The movement was, from the start, a great success.[1036] A year after the division, Kingsford's beautiful translation[1037] of a quantity of hermetic fragments appeared, including those of Stobaeus, and was augmented with a new translation of *Asclepius* and the *Definitions of Asclepius*.[1038] It is from this translation of the learned theosophist that Blavatsky gratefully quotes many times in her book *The Secret Doctrine*.[1039]

Hermetic Orders

Kingsford was not the only one who founded a hermetic organization contemporary with the Theosophical Society. During the same time, rumors spread about the so-called Hermetic Brotherhood of Luxor. In a modest advertisement[1040] in 1884, those with titles were invited to make contact with a certain Theosi, a.k.a. Max Theon.[1041] Although the movement insisted on strict secrecy (apparently some experiments dabbled in the use of hallucinogenic drugs and sexual magic), it developed quite rapidly during the years between 1884 and 1888. According to the historians of the movement, they carried on a fierce competition with the Theosophical Society—a competition so intense that, in 1888, it spawned its own "esoterical section."[1042]

This is far from the truth, however. In a clear article, Dutch researcher Daniël van Egmond shows that the organization, prior to 1888, consisted of three levels of development. The second level became more defined in 1888.[1043] In this "esoteric section," Blavatsky gave instructions about the correspondence between the construc-

In one of the buildings of the Amsterdam's Bibliotheca Philosophica Hermetica, Hermes Mercurius can be seen, standing in the middle of a fountain and under a glass dome with the famous saying: "God is an infinite sphere, whose center is everywhere and whose circumference is nowhere." Through the roof of the glass dome, part of the "Westerntoren" in Amsterdam is visible.

tion of the cosmos and the seven-fold principle of humanity.[1044] In addition to the "esoteric section," there was also an "Inner Group" that came into being in 1890 and enjoyed only a short life due to the death of HPB in 1891.[1045] The "esoteric section," however, remained active after Blavatsky's death.

On a much smaller scale, but of great historical impact, was a hermetic movement that started in the same year, 1888: The Hermetic Order of the Golden Dawn. Even though the movement, at its height, did not count more than 100 members, it gained a reputation greater than any other group in its time (excluding the Theosophists). This was more due to its prominent members than to its content. The most famous member is undoubtedly the great literary giant William Butler Yeats (1865–1939), but the order also counted other illustrious individuals like Israel Regardie, Aleister Crowley, Arthur Edward Waite, Edward Munch, August Strindberg, Bram Stoker, and Violet Mary Firth, who became better known as Dion Fortune.

The movement, which arose from contacts with Freemasonry and the *Societas Rosicruciana in Anglia,* was brought to life by a certain Dr. William Wynn Westcott, a London pathologist. Westcott was in close communication with Dr. William Robert Woodman, a physicist, and Samuel Lidell MacGregor Mathers, who was married to a sister of the French philosopher Henri Bergson.[1046] Like the Luxor Brotherhood, they stood for a more practical approach to occultism rather than a mostly theoretical one like that which the Theosophical Movement maintained.[1047]

Magic rituals formed an integral part of the Golden Dawn practices. We can see this from the inventory of the Westcott Hermetic Library,[1048] which contains many works on alchemy, magic, astrology, Kabala, and Egyptology. Just as in the case of the Luxor Brotherhood, however, we find that Hermes appears as not much more than an ascription. This is somewhat misleading.

In this same period, a bestseller by Edouard Schuré was published with the intriguing title *Les Grands Initiés* (The Great Initiates).[1049] Here, Hermes Trismegistus receives, in the ancient tradition of the *philosophia perenis,* a beautiful chapter. Hermes appears after Rama and Krishna, but prior to Moses, Orpheus, Pythagoras, Plato, and

Jesus. And so it should be. One and a half centuries later, Manly Palmer Hall does something similar. In Hall's description of "Twelve World Teachers,"[1050] Hermes takes second place (after Ahnaton, but before Orpheus, Zoroaster, Buddha, Confucius, Lao-Tse, Plato, Jesus, Mohammed, and several others).

A Restored Image

During the last years of her life, Blavatsky, who had such an enormous influence on opinions about occultism, was flanked by another particularily extraordinay person—George Robert Stowe Mead, who, from 1888 to 1891, was HPB's private secretary. This was no easy task, as I discussed in my contribution to a book on hermetic gnosis, that came into being under the inspiring editorship of Gilles Quispel.[1051]

After the death of HPB, Mead worked with Annie Besant to edit a theosophical magazine and worked on the publication of Blavatsky's remaining writings. However, he also published his own projects, including a translation of *Pistis Sophia*, an essay about Simon the Magus, a book about Apollonius of Tyana, another one about Jesus based on Jewish source material, and a progressive volume about the Gnostics, *Fragments of a Faith Forgotten*. But his most famous work is the absolutely magnificent translation of the *Hermetica: Thrice-Greatest Hermes*, which appeared in 1906.[1052] Even now, despite the many new publications that have seen the light in the last century, this work remains impressive.

As we have seen, there are many myths regarding the discovery of Hermes. They symbolize the reanimation of the image of Hermes that had been stored for centuries in the subconscious of the Western mind. The "psychological" aspect we will discuss in the following chapter when we make acquaintance with the hermetic thoughts of Carl Gustav Jung. Over and over, the "image of Hermes" is, as it were, rediscovered. It resurfaces in our consciousness. The image is blurred by centuries of dust, but has also often been "retouched." Color is added, so the image changes in appearance.

This had already happened in antiquity when the Egyptian original (the symbolic and partially practical Book of Thoth) was placed in a Greek philosophical frame and somewhat restyled. Sometimes—during the Western Middle Ages, for instance—it was completely obscured and could no longer be seen in its totality. Then this clouded image received a Christian varnish. In the Renaissance, it was rediscovered and effectively restored. The Christian varnish stayed partially intact—which, to some extent, may have contributed to the preservation of the image. From then on, the image was regularly provided with new colors, embellishments, and frills. This is evident in the large number of small groups that occupied themselves with Hermeticism (or what they thought was hermeticsm) in the 19th century—for instance, the Luxor Brotherhood and the Order of the Golden Dawn. For them, the term "hermetic" became synonymous with "occult."

In *The Secret Doctrine*, Helena Petrovna Blavatsky pointed this out and suggested how this polluted image could once again be restored. In Blavatsky, the image of Hermes is thoroughly purified of its many Christian, pseudo-magical, and Kabalistic elements, and cleansed of the many other layers that were added to the original over the last centuries. Like that of Giordano Bruno three centuries before, the "image of Hermes" has regained its luster and radiance. This effect was even more enhanced by the eminent work of George Robert Stowe Mead during the early 20th century. There, of course, had to be a reaction.

Color Plate 1. One of two images of Hermes Trismegistus in the Medieval Walburgis' church in Zutphen (the Netherlands) (See Page 222)

ARGVMENTVM MARSILII FICINI FLORENTINI IN MERCVRIVM TRIMEGISTV DE POTESTATE ET SAPIENTIA DEI ABEO TRADVCTVM E GRAECA LINGVA IN LATINAM AD COSMV MEDICEM PATRIAE PATREM

O TEMPORE QVO MOSES NATVS EST floruit Atlas astrologus Promethei physici frater ac maternus auus maioris Mercurij cuius Nepos fuit Mercurius trismegistus. Hoc autem de illo scribit Aurelius Augustin. quamquam Cicero ac Lactantius Mercurios quinque per ordinem fuisse uolunt quintumque fuisse illum qui ab aegyptijs Them a Graecis autem Trismegistus apellatus est. Hunc asserunt occidisse Argum. Aegyptijs praefuisse eisque leges ac litteras tradidisse. litterarum uero caracteres in animalium arborumque figuris instituisse. Hic in tanta hominum ueneratione fuit ut in deorum numerum relatus sit. Templa illius numini constructa quamplurima. Nomen eius proprium ob reuerentiam quandam pronumptiare uulgo ac temere non licebat. Primus Anni mensis apud egyptios nomine eius cognominatus. Oppidum ab eo conditum quod etiam nunc graece nominatur Hermopolis id est Mercurij ciuitas. Trismegistum uero id est ter maximum nuncuparunt. quoniam philosophus maximus. Sacerdos maximus. Rex maximus extitit. Mos .n. erat Aegyptijs ut scribit Plato ex philoso

Color Plate 2.
Above: Ficino's Introduction (Argumentum) to the Corpus Hermeticum, in which there is handwriting of Lorenzo de Medici.

At right: View of Florence from the villa of de' Medici.

(See page 226)

Color Plate 3. Hermes in conversation with other philosophers.
See page 255

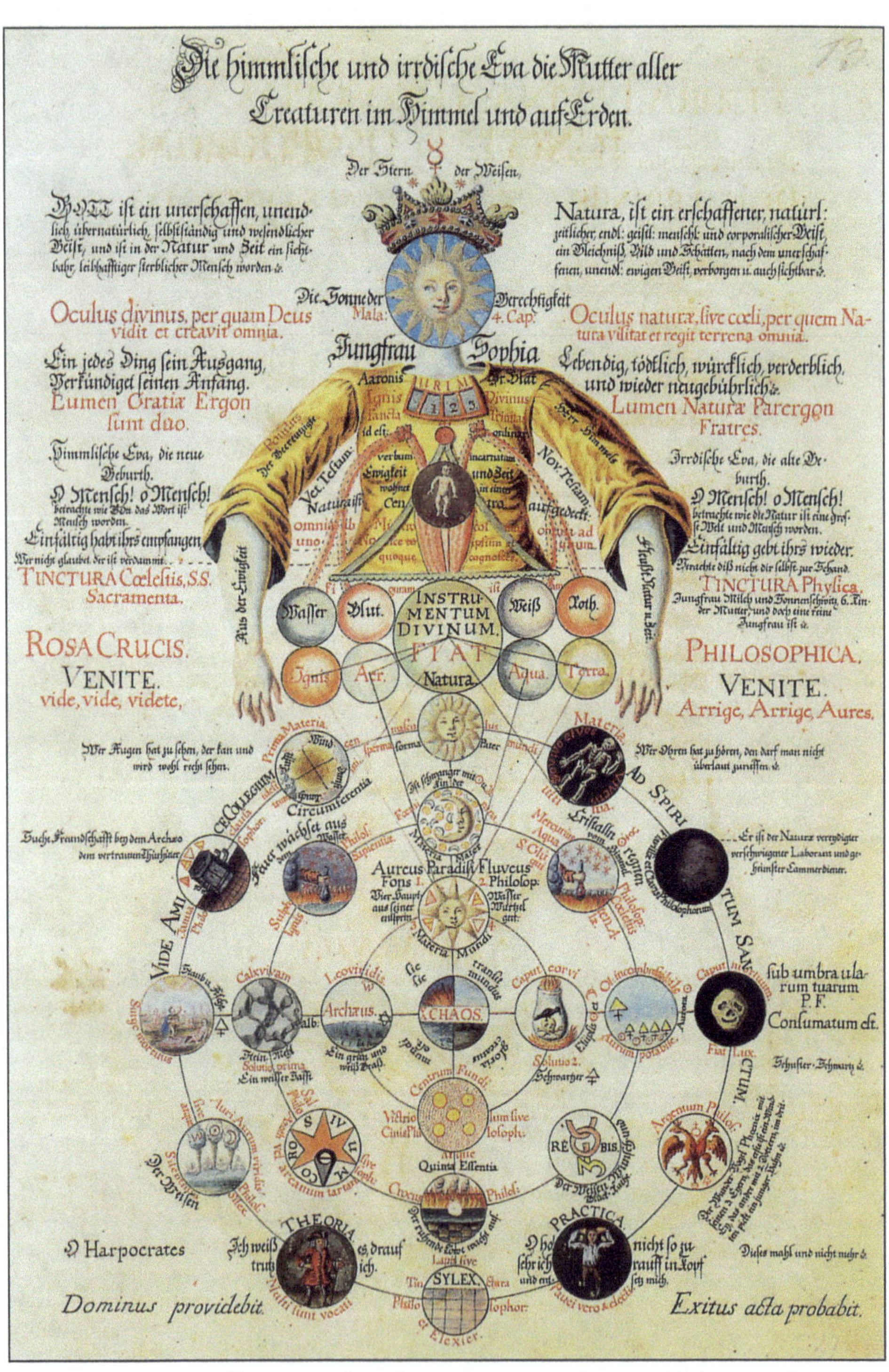

Color Plate 4. Illustration from Secret Figures with a personification of Sophia, wisdom. (See page 294)

CHAPTER 27
HERMES ON THE THRESHOLD OF A MILLENNIUM

The 20th century began, as we saw,[1053] with a strong advance from what was, almost a half century before, so carefully nurtured—the view that Hermes was the carrier of ancient wisdom. Casaubon wrote that the *Corpus Hermeticum* that originated in the 2nd century B.C. was of no value. Madame Blavatsky proved that the origin of these texts could be traced to much older times—back to ancient Egypt. This opinion was fiercely attacked by the then-trend-setting French scholar André-Jean Festugière, but is confirmed by modern research on the *Hermetica*. More about that shortly. First, we go back to the early 20th century.

SEVEN HERMETIC PRINCIPLES

Apparently out of nowhere, in the year 1912, an intriguing document appeared: the *Kybalion*.[1054] It was written by three anonymous "Initiates." According to these writers, the secret hermetic doctrine had been handed down orally from teacher to disciple. Or, as the *Kybalion* says: "When the ears of the disciple are ready to hear, then the lips will fill them with wisdom."[1055]

This wisdom, reprinted many times, is compressed into the seven "principles of the truth"—spirit, coincidence, vibration, polarity, rhythm, cause and effect, and gender. These hermetic principles are discussed at great length in the *Kybalion*, which resembles Blavatsky's *Secret Doctrine*. Blavatsky started each chapter of her two-volume work with a motto, a "stanza[1056] upon which she then expanded. Likewise, the authors of the *Kybalion* placed a "motto of Truth" above each chapter and followed up with commentaries and explanations.

The seven principles of *The Kybalion* are as follows:

I. THE PRINCIPLE OF MENTALISM.

THE ALL is MIND; The Universe is Mental.

II. THE PRINCIPLE OF CORRESPONDENCE.

As above, so below; as below so above.

III. THE PRINCIPLE OF VIBRATION.

Nothing rests; everything moves; everything vibrates.

IV. THE PRINCIPLE OF POLARITY.

Everything is Dual; everything has poles; everything has its pair of opposites; like and unlike are the same; opposites are identical in nature, but different in degree; extremes meet; all truths are but half-truths; all paradoxes may be reconciled.

V. THE PRINCIPLE OF RHYTHM.

Everything flows, out and in; everything has its tides; all things rise and fall; the pendulum-swing manifests in everything; the measure of the swing to the right is the measure of the swing to the left; rhythm compensates.

VI. THE PRINCIPLE OF CAUSE AND EFFECT.

Every Cause has its Effect; every Effect has its Cause; everything happens according to Law; Chance is but a name for Law not recognized; there are many planes of causation, but nothing escapes the Law.

VII. THE PRINCIPLE OF GENDER.

Gender is in everything; everything has its Masculine and Feminine Principles Gender; manifests on all planes.[1057]

Concerning the latter, Anna Kingsford writes, in her *The Perfect Way or the Finding of Christ*:

...To express the Divine in words, they contain and represent both genders; though when only one gender is indicated does not necessarily mean that the other is missing but only veiled. That is why the individual should possess male and female characteristics within oneself, in order to become God's image as seen from a spiritual point of view, both male and female. Human is only perfect when the whole of humanity is revealed within one and that happens only when the totality of humanity's Spirit, which is God, is revealed by Him... That is the doctrine of all hermetical writings...[1058]

The "initiated" listened well to Hermes. But they also gave attention to the Eastern sages[1059]—not so strange after Blavatsky's effort to create a synthesis between East and West. In that sense, the remarkable manuscript is more theosophical than purely hermetic. The Thrice-Great Hermes would certainly have recognized himself in it.

Jung's Gnosis

At a Jung symposium on the *School for Universal Wisdom* in Nijmegen (Netherlands), I engaged in an animated conversation with a grandson of Carl Gustav Jung. Both of us had delivered a lecture on Jung. His had been dotted by sketches and memories of his famous grandfather; mine had been about Jung and gnosis. He told me how thrilled his grandfather had been by the discovery of the Nag Hammadi codices. They affirmed, in principal, Jung's conclusions about the soul's spiritual center in each person.

In disagreement with accepted Christian doctrine, Jung had developed an early interest in gnosis. He writes about this in his biography:

From approximately 1918 to 1926, I delved into the Gnostics, because also they too had encountered archetypal world of the Unconscious. They had occupied themselves with its content and images entangled, as it were, with the world of passions. It is difficult for us to say in what manner they saw these images, due to

> rather scarce information, which furthermore we have to mostly thank their opponents, the Church Fathers... For my formulations the Gnostics were too far in the past to be able to connect to them.[1060]

Only after a quarter of a century did gnosis reappear in Jung's work. In the meantime, the Nag Hammadi codices had been discovered. Its first codex was even named after Jung.[1061]

In 1928, Jung began an energetic study of alchemy, which appeared to him to be the link between Gnosticism and the modern psychology of the unconscious. His exploration began with a manuscript that he had received from the German sinologist Richard Wilhelm, *The Secret of the Golden Flower*.[1062] Jung was fascinated with the manuscript and noticed immediately that Chinese alchemists used symbology for mental composition and conditions that were very familiar to him in his psychiatric practice. In Western alchemy he found the same symbology. As a collector of rare alchemical works and folios, he had gathered together quite a nice library of some 200 volumes by the time of his death. He published various influential papers in this field, among which *Psychologie und Alchemie* became the most famous.[1063]

In Jung's last years, Aniela Jaffé was his secretary. She writes, looking back at this period:

> Alchemy would not have played such an important role in Jung's research concerning the Unconsciousness and his organized method, and would not have had such an influential impact as a historical base for his investigations, if there had not been such a great affinity between him and the Adepts of the ancient Hermetic Art.[1064]

And so we arrive at our goal—pointed there by Hermes.

Jung's Hermes and the Spirit Mercurius

In Egypt, Hermes was originally known as the God Thoth with the ibis head. Therefore he was considered the bird-symbol of the prin-

> ciple of transcendency. During the Olympic era of Greek Mythology, Hermes was once again given the attributes of a bird's life in addition to his chthonic nature as a serpent. His staff gained wings above the serpents and became the caduceus or the winged staff of Mercurius.[1065]

This citation is typical of Jung in his "practice of Hermes." In 1912, Jung experienced one of his many lucid dreams, in which he sat on a golden Renaissance throne in a magnificent Italian gallery. Before him, he saw a rare beautiful table made of green stone. It looked like an emerald table and it reminded him immediately of the discovery of the *Tabula Smaragdina.*[1066] Jung often makes references to the Hermes of the *Tabula Smaragdina*—the "alchemical" less than the "philosophical" Hermes. In *Psychologie und Alchemie*, Jung draws primarily on several of Hermes' citations from the rich alchemical literature. The "alchemical" Hermes is Mercurius. Certainly there are many correspondences between Mercurius and the Thrice-Great Hermes. However, the resemblance to the Greek God Hermes is many times greater.

At the so-called *Eranos-Tagung* in 1942, Jung gave two lectures on "the Spirit Mercurius."[1067] His intention was to highlight the concept of Mercury in alchemy. Reitzenstein, whom Jung admired,[1068] had shown Jung that this was not just a pure chemical process, but one that had a Gnostic-philosophical content.[1069] In alchemy, the characteristics of the Greek Hermes blend together with the Latin Mercurius, giving the latter a rather complicated nature.[1070] Jung considers Mercurius as the world-creating spirit caught up in matter. Mercurius consists of all conceivable opposites. That is to say, he is dualistic, though he is still called one. He is matter as well as spirit. He is the process by which lower matter is transformed into higher spirit. He is a devil, but at the same time, a liberating guide to souls, a deceiver, and God's reflection in material Nature. He is the reflection of the mystical experience of the alchemist blending opposites with his labor. On the one hand, the spirit Mercurius represents the self; on the other hand, he symbolizes the individualization process.[1071]

Mercurius is the pivotal point in the alchemcal process of liberation. The goal of this process, as we saw before, is the discovery of the *lapis philosophorum*, the Philosopher's Stone—seen from a psychological perspective, the deepest Self. So Jung translates the alchemical symbology into a psychological one. For him, the *materia* in alchemy stands for the (unconscious) self, which needs to be examined carefully. According to Jung, in the alchemical "matter"—and thus in the self—lies the *anima mundi* ("soul of the world"). And this world soul is personified by the spirit Mercurius.[1072]

Hermes without Trismegistus

When Antoine Faivre speaks, in *Eternal Hermes*, about Jung as the rediscoverer of the hermetic heritage,[1073] it is, in my eyes, no more than just a part of the heritage. I think that the greatest contribution Jung made, at least in this area, was to revive an awareness of the rich alchemical symbology. And Hermes Trismegistus, in general, may certainly be seen as the "inventor" of alchemy. He does not really play a role in the process itself. Rather he *is* alchemy, the transformation. And on the path to this transformation, Gods play a role. Thus Hermes/Mercurius is of central importance. But in this case, it is Hermes *without* Trismegistus.

In *Memories, Dreams, and Reflections*, Jung describes in gripping fashion how he, as a four-year-old boy, had a lucid dream about a cave containing a pillar of living flesh with an eye on it.[1074] He hears his mother's voice telling him that this is the man-eater. Jung realized later that this referred to a phallus. This dream is quite often associated—completely incorrectly—with the Thrice-Great Hermes.[1075] The most you can say is that it is an analogy with the Greek archaic Hermes, the God of the hermeticists—stone stellae with erect phalli.[1076]

The Jungian author Jean Shinoda Bolen used the Greek Hermes, along with other Olympian Gods, as a class of human, an archetype.[1077] Again, Hermes *without* Trismegistus. This shows that Jung did indeed leave us a great heritage—the consciousness that we carry all these images and symbols within ourselves.

In this sense we are, in our innermost selves, Hermes himself.

An English Classicist and a French Dominican

During 1945, the first critical edition of the *Corpus Hermeticum* was published—an excellent co-production of the Englishman Arthur Darby Nock (1902–1963) and the Frenchman André-Jean Festugière (1898–1982). In the years that followed came the critical edition of *Asclepius* and hermetic fragments by ancient writers, specifically those from Stobaeus.[1078] Although, as stated, we do not agree any longer with the conclusions of either of these scholars, these editions deserve to be recognized as world-class scholarship.

The classicist Arthur Darby Nock spent twelve years compiling an extremely accurate textual comparison of most extensive Greek editions, as well as twenty-eight other manuscripts.[1079] The learned French Dominican Father André-Jean Festugière translated Nock's philological work and added his own commentaries. Earlier, however, he had started on a much more extensive commentary on other hermetic texts. In 1944, the first volume, *La Révélation d'Hermès Trismégiste*, was published, followed by three more volumes between then and 1954.[1080] This was, literally and figuratively, a monk's work. The first volume, as we have seen here repeatedly,[1081] covered astrological, iatrosophical, magical, and alchemical hermetic treatises. In the other three volumes, we find commentaries on the so-called "philosophical" *Hermetica*. Festugière himself shows a clear difference between the "philosophical" and "technical" hermetic writings.

As we saw, Festugière could discover very little Egyptian content in the *Hermetica*. He perceived them strictly against a pure Greek background and found them, in that sense, pseudo-philosophical—in other words, a weak surrogate of the greatest Hellenic philosophy. He also refused to believe that hermetic communities ever existed.

Despite his exhausting work over many years, Festugière never really warmed up to "the hermetical heritage." This does not take away from the fact, however, that he put down something of incredible value to us. Alongside all the enthusiastic and sometimes very chaotic writings on hermetics, he gave us a majestic critical edition that has served as the foundation for almost all editions and translations thereafter.[1082]

A Hermetic Chair

A scholar who truly made no use of the work of Nock and Festugière was the Dutch Rosicrucian Jan van Rijckenborgh.[1083] In the 1930s, Jan van Leene (his real name) founded a new branch of the Rosy Cross, the Lectorium Rosicrucianum, which became an international movement based on the Rosicrucian Fellowship of Max Heindel. What is remarkable is that this movement re-adopted the legacy of the earliest Rosicrucians—the art of healing.[1084] In the hermetic tradition, the healing of the body is considered part of the total healing of humanity, on both a psychic and a spiritual level.[1085]

Between 1960 and 1965, Van Rijckenborg published his *De Egyptische archaic-Gnosis* (The Egyptian Archaic Gnosis), a translation of the *Tabula Smaragdina* and *Corpus Hermeticum* complemented by extensive commentary.[1086] Here, he placed Hermes, once again, in the center of the spiritual movement—a worthy affirmation of the "alchemistical marriage" between the Rosicrucians and Hermes.

Van Rijckenborgh had a totally different vision of Thrice-Great Hermes Trismegistus than, for example, that of Festugière. Festugière placed everything against a Greek background; van Rijckenborgh clearly did not. The title of his book, *De Egyptische oer-gnosis* (The Egyptian Archaic Gnosis) speaks for itself on this point. Both of these scholars had benefited from the spectacular discovery at Nag Hammadi in 1945. The rediscovered hermetic treatises weren't published until the late 1970s, however.[1087] It is these three manuscripts (two parts of *Asclepius* and *The Treatise of the Eighth and Ninth Heavenly Sphere*) that caused a revolution in the scientific thinking about the *Hermetica*.

As we saw in the first part of this book, a more relaxed attitude toward the Greek and Egyptian background of the hermetic texts developed at the end of the 19th century.[1088] That these texts are no longer studied solely in occult circles is proven by the fact a Chair of History of the Hermetic Philosophy and Related Currents was inaugurated at the University of Amsterdam in 1999. Thus "enlightened" science was also taking an interest in Hermes.

An institute that has been involved with Hermes for much longer is the previously mentioned Bibliotheca Philosophica Hermetica, also in Amsterdam. It possesses an impressive and absolutely unique collection of old manuscripts and early editions in the field of the *Hermetica*, mysticism, alchemy, and Rosicrucianism. In contrast to many other libraries, which take a passive role, the Amsterdam library is extremely active. To facilitate this activism, the Ritman Instituut was created as a study and documention center with the mission to research the field of the *Hermetica*. The Ritman Institute strives to document the history of the *Hermetica* in the West, especially in the Netherlands, in collaboration with national and international libraries and other institutes. Through this work, the library has contributed greatly to the knowledge of Hermes and the hermetic tradition. The catalogs of their spectacular exhibitions are a treasure trove of information[1089] and have become indispensable for every researcher of the hermetic phenomenon. Beyond the beautifully printed catalogs, the institute periodically releases important publications concerning the *Hermetica*. The library commissioned a modern translation of the *Corpus Hermeticum* in Dutch, thereby increasing its accessibility to a larger public.[1090] Several years later, a Dutch translation of *Asclepius*[1091] was published with an erudite commentary by Gilles Quispel. And in the near future, Roelof van den Broek will present his translation and commentary on the *Fragments of Stobaeus* and the *Hermetic Definitions* at the library.

This does not signal the end of the labor "for Hermes"; it only indicates a new beginning. Can the archaic Hermes Trismegistus be of any value to us in the new millennium? We'll explore this in the Epilog.

EPILOG: THE HERMETIC LINK

(And then Isis spoke to her son Horus:)
It is not proper, my son,
that I leave this story unfinished.
I must tell you what Hermes announced
when he hid the books.
He spoke thus:

"Sacred books,
written by my immortal hand,
and embewed with the medicine of immortality,
withstand the decay of ages
and remain invisible and unnoticed
for all transversing the planes of this land,
until the moment when the ancient Heaven
will bring forth Souls worthy of thee."

When he had spoken this prayer
about the labour of his hands,
he was taken into the sanctuary
of the everlasting fields.[1092]

We have come, at the end of our historical search for the legacy of Hermes Trismegistus, to a universal feeling for life. And at the same time, we stand at the beginning—the beginning of the assimilation of this feeling for life within ourselves so that we can experience the completeness of it all once again. That is not a return to error. The path that Hermes has taken through the centuries has not been in vain, although some reductionists feel that it has. Apparently not much changes. Humanity now still experiences wars, epidemics, starvation, cruelty, suppression, and all sorts of disasters. So where is the renewal?

An Apparently Recurring Theme

An image from the musical film *Hair* remains burned in my memory. Soldiers in large columns march into the gaping mouth of a transport plane to be flown to Vietnam. While the airplane engines roar, one of the soldiers, the hippie Berger, sings of a dying nation and of listening for new-told lies. The aircraft takes off. In the next shot, we see the tombstone of Berger, who has perished in Vietnam. From all directions, people now run to this spot. An immense crowd builds. In front of the White House, hundreds of thousand of people gather to sing the song of eternal hope: "Let the Sun shine in…"

Mystical Silence

The silence within us gives answers to our questions, although we can hardly hear the silence anymore. We scream out loud above the silence what we think is important (at this moment) to us.

In the *Perfect Sermon*,[1093] Hermes, Asclepius, Tat, and Ammon gather together in the temple room:

> When Ammon too had come within the holy place, and when the sacred group of four was now complete with piety and with God's goodly presence—to them, sunk in fit silence reverently, their souls and minds pendent on Hermes' lips, thus Love Divine began to speak.[1094]

When Hermes son, Tat, asks the meaning of this, he teaches him that the Divine Love reveals itself in the silence of the heart:

> TAT. [Now] in the General Sermons, father, thou didst speak in riddles most unclear, conversing on Divinity; and when thou saidst no man could e'er be saved before Rebirth, thy meaning thou didst hide...
>
> HERMES. Wisdom that understands in silence [such is the matter and the womb from out which Man is born], and the True Good the seed.
>
> TAT. Who is the sower, father? For I am altogether at a loss.
>
> HER. It is the Will of God, my son.
>
> TAT. And of what kind is he that is begotten, father? For I have no share of that essence in me, which doth transcend the senses. The one that is begot will be another one from God, God's Son?
>
> HER. All in all, out of all powers composed.
>
> TAT. Thou tellest me a riddle, father, and dost not speak as father unto son.
>
> HER. This Race, my son, is never taught; but when He willeth it, its memory is restored by God.[1095]

Spiritual wisdom reveals itself in our consciousness. It is captured as an archetype in humanity's collective memory and becomes known again when we become conscious of it. Hermetic consciousness is a cosmic consciousness.

But what do we still know today of this consciousness?

"And what is that actually, consciousness?" asks journalist W. L. Brugsma in an interview with Wim Kayzer and Frans Waal.

Kayzer answers: "Consciousness is... getting access to an enormous reservoir of memories and being able to reflect it."

Brugsma replies: "All these terms: consciousness, sub-consciousnes... arises from that software nonsense of the 20th century."[1096]

This is typical of so-called "modern thought."

Modern Scientific Thought

Consciousness appears, completely unexpectedly, in another conversation. In 1993, 10,000 people were glued to the TV for seven consecutive Sunday nights—not for a game show or a soap opera, which account for the greatest part of broadcasts nowadays, but to hear six scholars discuss the state of modern science. Daniel C. Dennett[1097] gives an optimistic point of view:

> I believe, our knowledge is increasing considerably fast, thus soon we will be able to say very accurately how it feels to be a bat. We are not as yet so far, but we can tell what it is not, since we know a number of restrictions in the nervous system of the bat. We know it can not be so as many people imagine it to be. That is progress.[1098]

Rupert Sheldrake[1099] does not really agree with his fellow panelist:

> I think this conversation to be rather plebeian (out of context). We except that consciousness is limited to animals on Earth. But how about the consciousness of the Sun? Many traditional points of view indicate that the Sun has a Spirit. If people agree that the activity of Spirit and the functions of the brain consist of changing electromagnetic patterns, we can find legions of those in the Sun. The more research is done regarding the Sun, the more we will discover about her incredible potentiality. How about the possibility that the Sun can think or employ another spiritual activity which is connected to electromagnetic patterns?

Steve Gould[1100] indeed reacts:

> That is close to it, Rupert, but I want to go back to it when you have found a way to speak to the Sun to get to know something about her consciousness. At that time we will start this conversation again. For the time being, no thank you.

Daniel Dennett joins Gould:

> I want to emphasize it even stronger. If you can give us a raison d'être for the consciousness of the Sun... Our consciousness came into being as a result of evolution; we had to care for ourselves... If you, therefore, can come up with a reason why the Sun would benefit of a Spirit, I think we could become serious, about the fact that he has one. Otherwise it looks to me like a nonsensical thought.

This shows the disentangled manner of thinking, which Sheldrake opposes:

> Does a ruling principle exist during the evolution of life on earth? Maybe it is true the Sun has a Spirit, being as it were the brains of the whole galaxy. Not only the Earth. And if we are searching for a ruling principle, I would look first at the Sun and the whole galaxy instead of immediately jumping into the concept of a mechanical God[1101] as according to Paley.[1102]

Taking Spirit out of Matter—the Final Theory

The mechanical point of view of the world and God to which Sheldrake refers is a legacy, as we saw, from the historical Age of Enlightment, which claimed that God, or whatever metaphysical power you posit, is, in the best case, only a sort of simplified Creator God. The philosopher Heidegger identified one of the characteristics of the modern age as *Entgötterung* ("the taking of spirit out of matter").[1103] This appears to be the sacrifice made by modern science.

"The further Science progresses, the more she creates a disenchantment with the world," states Stephen Weinberg.[1104] According to him, we now know how all living beings were created without any plan or guiding hand.[1105]

"Natural Science," says Berger, "starts with counting and measuring and from this draws the conclusion that Reality is strictly based on quantifiable facts. Qualitative and quantitative differences are only translated in quantities... The ideal of Natural Science dreams of a *Theory of Everything*, the final theory."[1106]

Whether this can be discovered from a purely materialistic point of view is highly doubtful. Stephen Hawkings is optimistic. Copernicus, Rutherford,[1107] Niels Bohr,[1108] and Friedman,[1109] have cleared the way for the expanding balloon theory, the black hole theory, the integral path model, string theory, the worm hole model, and the concept of an expanding universe.

Does this make you dizzy? That's because the "final theory" has not yet been discovered, as Stephen Hawking says:

> As soon as we have discovered a complete theory, it will be understandable for everyone, and not only for a handful of scholars. Then philosophers, scholars and simple people can all participate in a discussion about why we and the Universe exist. When we know the answer to that question, it will be the ultimate victory of the human mind—for then we will know the spirit of God.[1110]

The commentator of the popular television series on the Universe of Stephen Hawkings stated: "But that is not to say that we know everything about the Universe. The history of becoming does not give any answer to age old philosophical questions about the reasons for our existence."[1111] Hawking admits to this as well:

> With the rise of Quantum Mechanics the perception has grown in us that we cannot predict events with full certainty, but that there is always a certain measure of uncertainty. If we want to, we can apply this coincidence to God's immersion...[1112]

Thus "God" is coming little by little into the picture.

From a materialistic point of view, evolution is seen as a material process—that is to say, a process in which only part of the total is seen and researched. The letting go of "hermetic" inclusion, wherein the observation of the total has always stood central, leads to cutting and fragmentation that does not make us any happier.

However, evident changes are noticeable. In his book *Mystagogie*, Dutch Professor Tjeu van den Berk makes a strong plea for a renewed development of what he calls "symbolic consciousness."[1113] He quotes natural scientist David Bohm,[1114] who "would have been welcomed as their own son by the old hermeticists" when he proposes:

> We consider the world to be one unbroken unity, and this is in opposition to the classical idea, in which you can analyse the world as totally independently existing parts.[1115]

By "classical idea," Bohm means the scientific ideas since the Age of Enlightenment. Even exceptionally brilliant beta scientists appear to have a short memory. The actual "classical idea" is, after all, the hermetic conception of an ensouled universe. That image is now coming back to life—from a completely unexpected direction.

The Roaring Sixties

The story of the musical film *Hair* takes place during the turbulent years of the Sixties—the hippie years, the era of flower power, large anti-Vietnam War demonstrations, and the May revolts. In those years, however, there was talk of another revolution. Scientists developed the Big-Bang Theory. The universe, they say, started with an original explosion that formed the dynamic world of organic matter. This can no longer be seen, therefore, as coming from mechanical principles.[1116] Thus the consciousness of an ensouled cosmos was reborn—except that now, the organizing principles are called "fields," not souls.[1117]

This is not the first time that we thought we had reached the "boundary of physics." Niels Bohr developed the complementary principle, which, in short, posits that there has to be a totality that is not overseeable by us. This is hindered, Bohr proposes, by the indivisibility or individuality of quantum physical states.[1118] Atomic reality is defined in waves and particles. According to Fritjof Capra, quantum physics describes the unity beyond waves and particles. And that corresponds with the ancient Chinese *Tao* principle.[1119] Beyond illusory duality lies hidden the unity of All. It is as if Hermes has arisen from the grave.

A second shocking result of the research of quantum physics is that atomic phenomena cannot be separated from the observer. They form an inseperable whole in the process of observation.[1120] Thus science becomes a participant; what we search for and how we search for it influences what we find.[1121] The researcher is no longer only an observer, but a participant in this process!

Slowly but surely, more hints can be heard that science wants to expand its horizons. Rupert Sheldrake proposes in *Een schitterend ongeluk* ("A beautiful accident") as a reaction to Darwin's proposal that matter is the source of existence:

> Something existed already: According to a traditional point of view they were natural laws which are immaterial, only after such were energy or energy fields created by the Big-Bang. Matter, in the strictest sense of the word, as something you can hold in your hands, arrives on the scene much later; in a fire of a billion degrees Celsius, matter does not exist, at least not in the normal sense of the word. There are fields, there is energy, there are vibrating structures, but there is no concrete matter.
>
> In my opinion, the traditional point of view is human consciousness is a lower aspect of a higher form of consciousness, and that the whole Universe is permeated by a form of Spirit or Consciousness; in any case, Earth has one. At the very top, one finds the Consciousness or Spirit of God, and below it exists a hierarchy of intelligences: In traditional interpretation called Angels, associated with Stars and Planets. There are, therefore, all kinds of higher forms of organized intelligences. Human intelligence is one of the lower forms. For as far as human consciousness jumps forward, humanity is inspired by higher levels of consciousness, incomprehensible to us, precisely because they go beyond our ability to comprehend them. Mystics and prophets from all cultures speak about it. It is, therefore, a kind of descending from a higher level, and as (Stephen) Gould indicates: "This occurred without a cosmic plan or a conscious Creator, but by pure coincidence," and such is no different than materialistic dogmatism. He knows this no more than anyone else; he simply states his own ideology.[1122]

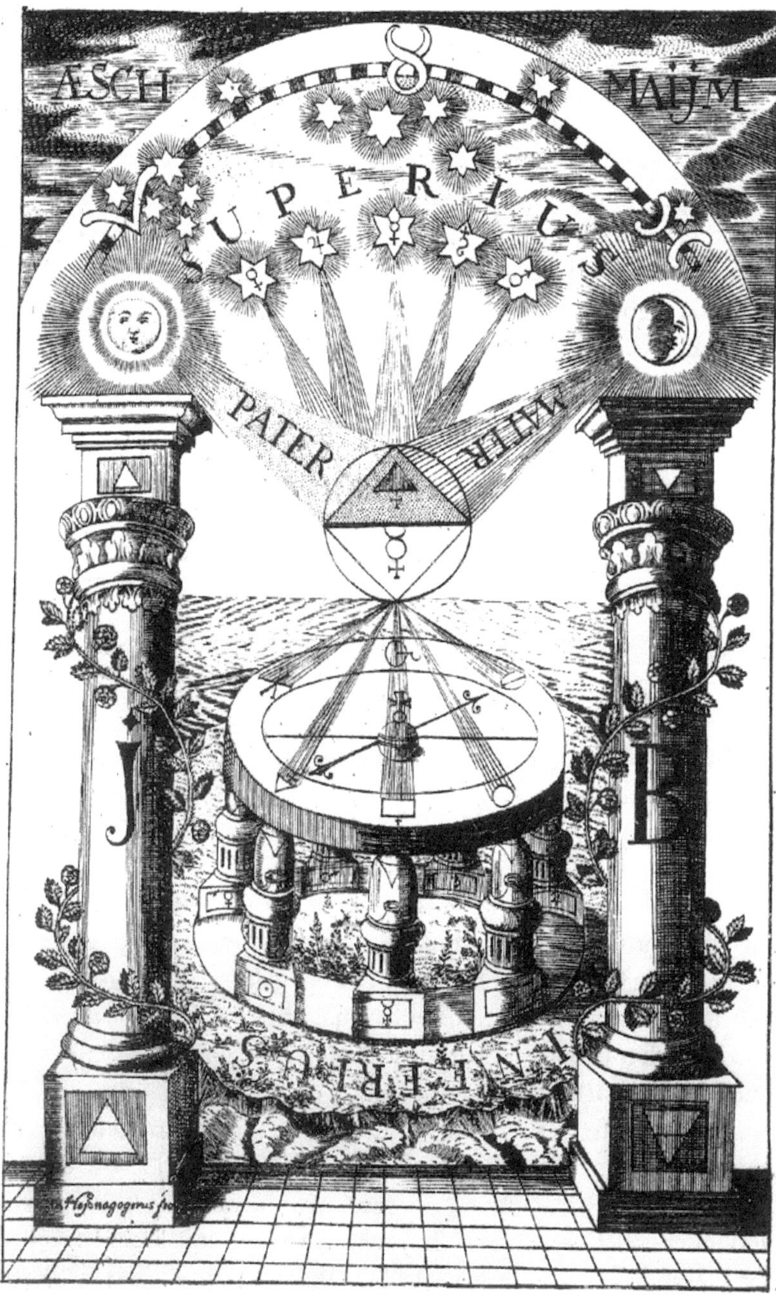

Symbol of a Freemason Lodge with the two pillars: Jachin and Boaz

The Missing Link

We live in an unusually fascinating time. Science fascinates. We all want to know who we are, where we came from, and where we are going. We look with respect at science, which we believe gives us the answers. But for the first time in centuries, we see the limitation of the scientific method. The iron-clad method is showing cracks through which light can shine. "There is a crack in everything, that's how the light gets in...," sang Canadian bard Leonard Cohen[1123] before he became a cook in a Buddhist monastery.

Somewhere
Inside something
There is a rush of greatness
Who knows what stands in front of our lives...
Silence tells me secretly
Everything
Everything.

In this silence, we feel connected with our Selves, with the Earth, with the cosmos, with spirit. This is what Hermes never tired of trying to tell us. Still we cannot, and we do not want to, go back to the era of the Thrice-Great. Consciousness has been transformed from a collective experience to that of an individual pure knowing. Our consciousness has been enlarged by time. From a collective unconscious link with "The High," we have developed ourselves, via matter, to a (more) conscious individual state.[1124] We appear to have become other people. However, still deep within ourselves, the same nucleus lies waiting to be unfolded.

If we can, from this "new" consciousness, come in contact with gnosis, as Hermes predicted, then we and the world will change overnight. More and more, people have become more individual and independent of each other—more aware of the universal feeling for life and consciousness that all is linked with all and everyone with everyone, and that we are part of an ensouled cosmos. This is the renewal entering softly among us all. We live, more people realize, within a unity that cannot be explained by mere reason alone. No actual separateness exists. For each part carries within itself the whole.

More and more books of Hermes and his spiritual brethren are being discovered all the time. They have withstood the teeth of time and remained invisible and unnoticed for many centuries. They contain the missing link in our consciousness. The time appears to have come, as Isis predicted, for the ancient Heaven to bring forth souls worthy of Hermes.

Bibliography

Original Sources

Pre-hermetic texts:

Book of Thoth

Egyptian magical papyri: Citations 5, 71 and 115

Egyptian Book of the Dead

Hermetic treatises:

Aphorisms of Hermes

Alch.Gr. (*Alchemista Graeca*) 115.10

Asclepius

Book of Hermes to Asclepius about the plants of the seven stars

Brontologion

Corpus Hermeticum:

I. Poimandres—The Shepherd of Men

II. The General Sermon

III. The Sacred Sermon

IV. The Cup Or Monad

V. Though Unmanifest God Is Most Manifest

VI. In God Alone Is Good and Elsewhere Nowhere

VII. The Greatest Ill among Men Is Ignorance of God

VIII. That No One of Existing Things Doth Perish, But Men in Error Speak of Their Changes as Destructions and as Deaths

IX. On Thought and Sense

X. The Key

XI. Mind unto Hermes

XII. On the Common Mind

XIII. The Secret Sermon on the Mountain

XIV. A Letter to Asclepius

XVI. The Definitions of Asclepius unto King Ammon

XVII. Of Asclepius to the King

XVIIIa. The Encomium of Kings

Prayer of Thanksgiving

The religious experience of Doctor Thessalos

Secret method of Hermes Trisgemistus on each initiative

Greek magical papyri (*Papyri Graecae Magicae* -PGM):

PGM I *Ritual*

PGM IV *Isis' complaint*

To the waning Moon
Magic spell to do business
PGM V *The ring of Hermes*
Incantation for shy men
Hymn on Hermes
PGM VI *Lamp fortune-telling*
PGM VIII *Love formula of Astrapsoukos*
PGM XII *Dream wish*
PGM XVIIb *Hymn on Hermes*

The Holy Book of Hermes to Asclepius

Hermetic Definitions
Iatromathematika of Hermes Trismegistus to the Egyptian Ammon
Kyranides
Kyranis
Koiranide
Liber Hermetis
On the plant called peony
On the influence of the planets on plants
Peri Seismon
Salmeschoiniaka
Stobaeus, Johannes, *Anthologium*

1. *Fragment of conversation between Hermes and Tat*
3. *Of the same (Hermes)*
4. *Fragments of conversations between Hermes and Tat*
5. *Fragments of conversations between Hermes, Tat and Ammon*
6. *Fragment of conversation between Hermes and Tat*
9. *Fragments of conversations between Hermes and Tat*
10. *Fragment of conversation between Hermes and Tat*
16. *Fragments of conversations between Hermes and Ammon*
23. *Koré Kosmou (Virgin of the World)*
24. *(Isis to Horus)*
28. *Aphorisms*
29. *From Hermes (About the planets)*

Tabula Smaragdina
Therapeutical handbook of Harpokration
Received from the Angels as a gift from the indescribable God, the God Hermes Trismegistus, to be shared with those gifted with understanding
From Hermes Trismegistus about the plants of the twelve signs
Treatise of the Eighth and Ninth Heavenly Sphere
[Hermetic] *Treatise about the Soul*
Abridged medical book by Hermes Trismegistus according to the astrological Science and the natural influence of animals, assigned to his pupil Asclepius

Authentic Book of Sophé
Viennese Fragments

OTHER ORIGINAL SOURCES

The Acts of Thomas
Anonymous
  Alch.Gr. (Alchemista Graeca) 408. 4
Apollodorus, *Bibliotheca*
Arnobius, *Adversus nationes*
Augustinus:
  Confessions
  Contra Faustum
  The City of God
Bolos (Demokritos) of Mendes, *Physika kai Mystika*
Cicero, *De natura deorum*
Clemens of Alexandria:
  Excerpta ex Theodoto
  Stromateis
Cyprianus, *Quod idola dii non sint*
Cyrillus of Alexandria, *Contra Julianum*
Diodorus Siculus, *Diodoi bibliotheca historica*
Diogenes Laertius, *The Life of Pythagoras*
Dydimus, *de Trinitate*
Eusebius:
  Church History
  Preparatio Evangelica
Firmicus Maternus, *Mathesis*
Flavius Josephus, *The Jewish war*
Herodotus, *Histories*
Hesiod, *Opera et dies*
Homer:
  Hymn on Demeter
  Hymn on Hermes
  Odyssey
Iamblichus:
  Life of Pythagoras and his followers
  On the Mysteries
Justinus Martyr, *Apology I*
Cologne Mani Codex
Coptic Magical papyri:
  Maria's Prayer
  Maria's curse of Martha
  Aphorism for a man to obtain a friend
Lactantius, *Divinae Institutiones*

Leiden's Creation of the World
Nag Hammadi codices:
  Book of Thomas, the Camp Fighter
  Gospel of Thomas
  Gospel according to Filipus
  The Holy Book of Johannes
  Holy Book of the Great, Invisible Spirit
  Lessons of Sylvanus
  Revelation of Paulus
Olympiodorus:
  Alch.Gr. (Alchemista Graeca) 83. 4
  Alch.Gr. (Alchemista Graeca) 84. 12
Pausanias, *Graeciae descriptio*
Plato:
  Cratylus
  Phaedo
  Phaedrus
  Philebus
Plotinus, *Enneads*
Plutarch:
  Moralia
  On Isis and Osiris
Proclus, *Theoligia Platonica*
Pseudo-Clementines:
  Homiliae
  Recognitiones
Ptolemaeus, *Tetrabiblios*
Quodvultdeus, *Adversus quinque haereses*
Tertullianus:
  De anima
  Versus the Valentines
Vettius Valens, *Anthologion*
Zosimus:
  About apparatus and ovens; authentic commentaries on the letter Omega
  Final Dispensation
  Thirty-five Chapters by Zosimus to to Eusebia:
  Alch.Gr. (Alchemista Graeca) 175.12
  Alch.Gr. (Alchemista Graeca) 188.7

Medieval Sources

Hermetic treatises:
  Book of the Secret of Creation
  Large letter about the spheres by Hermes of Dendera
  A perspective on the life of Hermes of Hermesses, for those interested

Liber XXIV Philosophorum
Liber Alcidi
Silver water and Starry earth

Other treatises:

Al-Maqdisi, the book on Creation and History
Letter of the Sun to the new Moon
Hermippus
Kitbag al-Fihrist
Picatrix
Key to Great Wisdom
Key of Solomon
Sun and Moon
Hildegard von Bingen, *Causei et Curae*

NEW AGE SOURCES

Agrippa:
De occulta philosophia
De vanitate scientiarum
Bessarion, *In calumniatorem Platonis*
Blake, *Jerusalem*
Bruno, Giordano:
Ash Wednesday meal
De immenso
Regarding the cause, the beginning and the One
Exorcizing the triumphant beast
Casaubon, *De rebus sacris et ecclesiasticis exercitationes XVI*
Chymische Hochzeit Christiani Rosencreutz
Confessio Fraternitates R.C. ad eruditos Europae
Copernicus, *De Revolutionibus Orbium Coelestium*
Corsi, Giovanni, *Vita Marsilii Ficini*
Dee, John, *Monas Hieroglyphica*
Fama Fraternitatis oder Brüderschaft der hochlöblichen Ordens des Rosenkruezes
Ficino:
Argumentum
Commentarium Convivium
Commentarium in Philebum
De christiana religione
De vita coelitus comparanda
Disputatio contra iudicium astrologorum
Theologica Platonica
Fludd, Robert
Apologia Compendiaria Fraternitatem de Rosae Cruce suspicionis et infamiae maculus aspersam, veritatis quasi Fluctibus abluens et abstergens

Lapis Lydius
Medicina Catholica
Tractatus Apologeticus
Utriusque Cosmi, majoris silicet et minoris, metaphysica, atque technica historia
Haslmayr, Adam: *Antwort an die lobwürdige Brüderschaft der Theosophen von RosenCreutz*
Jones, Inigo, *The Ancient Duties*
Kepler, *Mysterium cosmographicum*
Kircher, Athanasius:
Ars Magna Sciendi
Obelisci Aegyptiaci
Kriegsmann, W. Chr., *Conjectaneorum de germanicae gentis originae*
Khunrath, Heinrich, *Amphitheatrum Sapientiae Aeternae*
Lambsprinck, *De Lapide Philosophico Libellus*
Lazzarelli, Lodovico, *Crater Hermetis*
Maier, Michael:
Atalanta Fugiens
De Circulo Physico Quandrato
Symbola Aurea Mensae
Themis Aurea
Mathew Cooke Manuscript
Mögling, Daniel, *Speculum Sophicum Rhodo-Stauroticum*
Museum Hermetucum
Paracelsus:
Book on the tincture of the Philosophers
Aurora of the Philosophers
De Natura Rerum
End of the birth and observation of the Stars
On the Spirits of the planets
On the nature of things
Organography of the Healing Arts
Patrizi, Fransesco, *Nova de universis Philosophia*
Pico della Mirandola:
Apologia
De dignitate hominis
Pseudo-Dee, *The Rosicrucian Secrets*
Rosarium Philosophorum
Schikaneder, *die Zauberflöte*
Sendivogius, Michael, *Novem lumen chymicum*
Theatrum Chemicum
Trithemius, *Stenographia*

Literature

Aalders, C., J.H. Plokker and G. Quispel, *Jung- een mens voor deze tijd* (Jung, a Man of this Age), Rotterdam, 1975.

Albright, William F., *Archeology and the Religion of Israel*, Baltimore 1941.

Alitt, John Stewart, "Music and Marsilio Ficino" in Michael Shepherd (ed.), *Friend to Mankind, Marsilio Ficino* (1433-1499), London 1999, pp. 133–142.

Allen, Michael J.B., *Synpotic Art; Marsilio Ficino on the History of Platonic Interpretation*, Florence 1998.

————, "Marsilio Ficino, Hermes Trismegistus and the *Corpus Hermeticum*," in Michael J.B. Allen, *Plato's Third Eye, Studies in Marsilio Ficino's Metaphysics and its Sources*, Aldershot 1995, XII, pp. 38-47.

Aminrazavi, Medhi, "The Significance of Surhawardi's Persian Sufi Writings in the Philosophy of Illumination" in Leonard Lewisohn (ed.), *The Heritage of Sufism I*, Oxford 1999, pp. 259–285.

Andreae, Johann Valentin, *De Chymische Bruiloft van Christian Rosencreutz anno 1459* (The Chemical Marriage of Christian Rosencreutz, dd. 1459), Zeist 1982.

Arnold, Klaus, *Johann Trithemius (1462–1516)*, Würzburg 1991 (2nd edition).

Arnold, D., *Building in Egypt, pharaonic stone masonry*, New York/Oxford 1991.

Aubel, A.F.L., *De vrijmetselarij. Oorsprong, wezen en doel* (Freemasonry, Origin, Meaning and Goal), The Hague 1933.

Augustinus, Aurelius, *De stad van God* (The City of God), translation and introduction by Gerard Wijdeveld, Amsterdam 2002.

Bachmann, Manuel and Thomas Homelier, *Geheimnisse der Alchemie* (Secrets of Alchemy), Basel 1999.

————, "Hermes-Vater der Alchemie" (Hermes-Father of Alchemy) in *Geheimnisse der Alchemie* (Secrets of Alchemy), Basel 1999, pp. 22–28.

Baigent, Michael and Richard Leigh, *The Temple and the Lodge*, London 1989.

Barker, A. Trevor (ed.), *The Mahatma Letters to A.P. Sinnett*, Pasadena 1997.

Bartelink, G.J.M., *Twee Apologeten uit het vroege christendom: Justinus en Athenagors* (Two Apologists of Early Christianity: Justinus and Athenagoras), Kampen 1986.

Bauval, R and A. Gilbert, *The Orion Mystery*, Houten 1994.

Bayard, Jean-Pierre, *De Rozenkruisers, Historie, traditie en rituelen* (The Rosicrucians, History, Tradition and Rituals), Baarn 1994.

Berger, *Metafysica, een dwarse geschiedenis* (Metaphysics, a Slanted History), Budel 2003.

Berghuys, J.J.W., *Mens en kosmos—een groots verband. Uitweg uit de crisis in rationeel denken* (Man and Cosmos, a great connection. Escape from the crisis of rational thinking), Kampen 1995.

Berk, M.F.M. van den, *Die Zauberflöte, een alchemische allegorie* (Die Zauberflöte, an Alchemical Allegory),Tilburg 1995.

Berk, Tjeu van den, *Mystagogie. Inwijding in het symbolisch bewustzijn* (Mystagogy. Initiation into Symbolic Consciousness), Zoetermeer 1999.

Bernal, Martin, *Black Athena Writes Back*, Durnham/London 2001.

Berthelot, Marcellin and Charles-Émile Ruelle, *Collection des Anciens Alchimistes Grecs* (Collection of Ancient Greek Alchemists), 3 volumes, Paris 1887–1888.

Betz, Dieter (ed.), *The Greek Magical Papyri in Translation (including the Demotic Spells)*, Chicago/London 1986.

Blavatsky, H.P.B., *The Secret Doctrine*, 2 volumes, London 1888.

————, *Isis Unveiled*, New York 1877.

————, *Geheime Leer III; Esoterische opstellen en instructies* (Secret Doctrine III; Esoteric Essays and Instructions), Utrecht/Wassenaar 1980.

————, *Collected Writings*, Vol. I-XV, Boris de Zirkoff (ed.), Wheaton/Madras/London 1950–1991.

Blomhert, Bastiaan, *Mozart in de tempel. Raakvlakken tussen componist en Vrijmetselarij* (Mozart in the Temple. Common Ground between Composer and Freemasonry), Kampen 1991.

Boehme: "Een zeer lichte morgenster is opgegaan" (Boehme: A very soft morning star has arisen), Haarlem 2001.

Boer, Ch., *Marsilio Ficino: The Book of Life*, Dallas 1980.

Bolen, Jean Shinoda, *Goden in elke man* (Gods in Every Man), Rotterdam 1989 (Rainbow Pockets 2002, 2nd edition).

Booz, AdaMah, *Die Siebe heiligen Grundsaulen der Ewigkeit und Zeit*, Leipzig 1783.

Borghouts, J.F., *Egyptische sagen en verhalen* (Egyptian Sagas and Stories), Houten 1988.

————, *Ancient Egyptian Magical Texts*, Leiden 1978.

Bouché-Leclercq, Auguste, *L'astrologie grecque*, Paris 1899.

Boylan, Patrick, *Thoth, The Hermes of Egypt*, London 1922 (unabridged reprint, Chicago 1974).

Brann, Noel. L. *The Abbot Trithemius (1462–1516); The Renaissance of Monastic Humanism*, Leiden 1981.

————, *Trithemius and Magical Theology*, Albany 1999.

Brecht, Martin, "Der Alte Johann Valentin Andrea und sein Werk—eine Anzeige" in *Rozenkreuyz als europäischenes Phänomen im 17. Jahrhundert*, Amsterdam 2002, pp. 75–85.

Broek, Roelof van den, *De taal van de Gnosis. Gnostische teksten uit Nag Hammadi* (The Language of Gnosticism. Gnostic Texts from Nag Hammadi), Baarn 1986.

———, "A Dutch Painting of Mercurius Hermes" in *Ésotérisme, Gnosis & Imaginaire Symbolique*, (Mélanges offerts à Antoine Faivre), Leuven 2001, pp. 3–17.

———, *Bibliotheken en geleerden in de Oudheid*, (Libraries and Scholars in the Antiquity), Utrecht 1984.

———, "Hermes en Christus: 'Heidense' getuigen voor de waarheid van het christendom" (Hermes and Christ: "Heathen" Witnesses to the Truth of Christianity) in F.G.M. Broeyer and E.M.V.M. Honée (ed), *Profetie en godsspraak in de geschiedenis van het christendom; studies over de historische ontwikkeling van een opvallend verschijnsel* (Prophecy and Oracles in the History of Christianity; Studies about the Historical Development of a Remarkable Phenomena), Zoetermeer 1997, pp. 214–238.

———, "Hermes en Christus: 'Heidense' getuigen voor de waarheid van het christendom" (Hermes and Christ: "Heathen" Witnesses to the Truth of Christianity) in G. Quispel (ed.), *De Hermetische Gnosis in de loop der eeuwen*, (Hermetic Gnosticism over the Centuries), pp. 9–27, Baarn 1992.

———, "Religious Practices in the Hermetic 'Lodge': New Light from Nag Hammadi" in Roelof van den Broek and Cis van Heertum (ed), *From Poimandres in Jacob Böhme: Gnosis, Hermetism and the Christian Tradition*, pp. 77-97.

Broek, Roelof van den and Cis van Heertum (ed), *From Poimandres to Jacob Böhme: Gnosis, Hermetism and the Christian Tradition*, Amsterdam 2000.

Broek, Roelof van den, and G. Quispel, *Corpus Hermeticum*, Amsterdam 1990.

Brul, Lex van den, "Jan van Rijckenborgh" in *Moderner Rosenkreuzer und hermetischer Gnostiker* in *Rosenkreux als europäisches Phänomen im 17. Jahrhundert*, Amsterdam 2002, pp. 379–397.

Brunner, Helmut, *Altägyptische Religion*, Darmstadt, 1989.

Bruno, Giordano, *Italiaanse dialogen* (vertaald door Yond Boeke en Patt Krone, toegelicht door Frank van Lamoen) (Italian Dialogs, translated by Yond Boeke and Patty Krone, with commentary by Frank Lamoen), Amsterdam 2000.

Caldwell, Daniel H. and Henk J. Spierenburg, "A Historical Introduction" in Henk J. Spierenburg: *The Inner Group Teachings of H.P. Blavatsky*, San Diego 1995, vii–xxix.

Capra, Fritjof, *De tao van de fysica* (The Tao of Physics), Amsterdam 1982.

Carl, Hans, *Hermetische Heilkunde; Paracelsus und die Alchemie* (Hermetic Healing Arts; Paracelsus and Alchemy), Sersheim 1957.

Churton, Tobias, *Geschiedenis van de Gnosis: De kennis van het hart* (History of Gnosticism: Knowledge of the Heart), Utrecht 1989.

Chwolson, D., *Die Ssabier und der Ssabismus; Die Entwicklung der Begriffe Ssabier und Ssabismus und die Geschichte der harranischen Ssabier oder die syro-*

hellenistischen Heiden im nördlichen Mesopotamien und in Bagdad zur Zeit der Chalifats, I and II, Petersburg 1856 (2nd edition, Amsterdam 1965).

Cimelia Rhodostaurotica, Die Rosenkreuzer im Spiegel der zwischen 1610 und 1660 *entstandenen Handschriften und Drucke* (catalog at the exhibition of the Bibliotheca Philosophica Hermetica in Amsterdam and the Herzog August Library in Wolfenbüttel), Amsterdam 1995.

Clarke, J.R., "A New Look at King Solomon's Temple and its Connection with Masonic Ritual" in *ARS Quatuor Coronatorum*, November 1976.

Clarke, J.R. and R. Engelbach, *Ancient Egyptian masonry: the building craft*, London 1930.

Colpe, Carsten and Jens Holzhausen (eds.), *Das Corpus Hermeticum Deutsch*, 2 volumes, Stuttgart 1997.

Comenius, Johannes Amos, *Via Lucis* (The Path of Light), Amsterdam 1992.

Copenhaver, Brian P., *Hermetica, The Greek* Corpus Hermeticum *and the Latin* Asclepius *in a new English translation, with notes and introduction*, Cambridge 1992.

Corpus Hermeticum; ingeleid and toegelicht door Roelof van den Broek and Prof. G. *Quispel* (Corpus Hermeticum: Introduced and Elucidated by Roelof van den Broek and Prof. G. Quispel), Amsterdam 1990.

Corpus Hermeticum, Texte établi par A.D. Nock et traduit par A.J. Festugière, 4 volumes, Paris 1945–1954.

Coudert, Allison, *Alchemie; de steen der wijzen* (Alchemy; The Philosopher's Stone), Deventer 1984.

Courcelle, Pierre, *Connais-toi toi-même*. De Socrate à St. Bernard, Paris 1974.

Cranston, Sylvia, *HPB: Het bijzondere leven en invloed van Helena Blavatsky* (The Extraordinary Life and Influence of Helena Blavatsky), Pasadena/ Den Haag/ München 1995.

Craven, William G., *Giovanni Pico della Mirandola, Symbol of his Age, Modern Interpretations of a Renaissance Philosopher*, Geneva 1981.

Cumont, Franz, *Astrologie et Religion chez les Grecs et les Romains*, Brussel/Rome 2000.

———, *Astrology and Religion among the Greeks and Romans*, New York 1960 (reprint of 1912).

Damstè, Onno, *Homèros, Ilias & Odyssee*, Utrecht/Antwerpen 1984.

Dierickx, M., *De vrijmetselarij. De grote onbekende 1717–1967*, (Freemasonry. The Great Unknown), Antwerpen/Utrecht 1967.

Dietzfelbinger, Konrad, *Mysteriescholen. Van het oude Egypte via het oerchristendom tot aan de rozenkruisers in deze tijd* (Mystery schools. From Ancient Egypt via Early Christianity up to the Rosicrucians of this Time), Deventer 2000.

Dirkse, P.A., J. Brashler and D.M. Parrott, *Nag Hammadi Codices V, 2–5 and VI with Papyrus Berolinensis 8502, 1 and 4*, NHS 11, Leiden 1979.

Divine Pymander of Hermes Trismegistus in XVII Books, Translated formerly out of the Arabic into Greek, and thence into Latin and Dutch, and now out of the Original into English by the learned divine Doctor Everard, London 1884 (London 1650, 1st edition).

Docters van Leeuwen, Onno and Rob, *De Tarot in de herstelde orde* (The Tarot in the Corrected Order), Utrecht 1995.

Dubbink, J.H., "Nieuw materiaal betreffende de Esoterische School" in *Geheime Leer III; Esoterische opstellen en instructies* (New Material Regarding the Esoteric School in the Secret Doctrine III; Essays and Instructions), Utrecht/Wassenaar 1980, pp. 479–714.

Dumas, F.R., *Histoire de la Magie* (History of Magic), Paris (not dated).

Ebeid, Nabil I, *Egyptian Medicine in the Days of the Pharaohs*, Cairo (not dated).

Edighoffer, Roland, "Hermeticism in Early Rosicrucianism" in Roelof van den Broek and Wouter J. Hanegraaff, *Gnosis and Hermeticism; from Antiquity to Modern Times*, Albany 1998, pp. 197–217.

Egmond, Daniël van, "Western Esoteric Schools in the Late Nineteenth and Early Twentieth Centuries" in Roelof van den Broek and Wouter J. Hanegraaff, *Gnosis and Hermeticism; from Antiquity to Modern Times*, Albany 1998, pp. 311–347.

Egyptische dodenboek, Het (in de vertaling van M.A. Geru) (The Egyptian Book of the Dead in the Translation by M.A. Geru), Deventer 1985.

Eliphas Levi, *Leer en Ritueel der Hogere Magie* (Doctrine and Ritual of Higher Magic), Amsterdam 1987 (original edition Paris 1856).

Erkelens, Herbert van, "Het spanningsveld tussen mystiek en natuurwetenschap" in *Encyclopedie van de mystiek* (The Area of Tension between Mysticism and Natural Science in *Encyclopedia of Mysticism*), Kampen/Tiel 2003, pp. 311–323.

——————, *Het spel van de wijsheid. Pauli, Jung en de menswording van God* (The Game of Wisdom. Pauli, Jung and the humanization of God), Kampen 1995.

——————, "De tempelslaap at Asklepios" (The Temple Sleep of Asklepios) in *Prana* Magazine 99 (Feb/Mar 1997), pp. 40–49.

Faivre, Antoine, *The Eternal Hermes. From Greek God to Alchemical Magus*, Grand Rapids 1995.

——————, "Renaissance Hermeticism and the Concept of Western Esotericism," in Roelof van den Broek and Wouter J. Hanegraaff, *Gnosis and Hermeticism; from Antiquity to Modern Times*, Albany 1998, pp. 109-125.

——————, *Access to Western Esotericism*, Albany 1994.

Fama Fraternitatis, Oudste manifest der Rozenkruisers broederschap bewerkt aan de hand van teruggevonden manuscripten door Pleun van der Kooij (Oldest manifest of the Rosicrucian Brotherhood compiled from rediscovered manuscripts by Pleun van der Kooij), Haarlem 1998.

Fauerbach, U., (ed.), *Ägypten, Die Welt der Pharaonen*, Keulen 1997.

Ferwerda, Rein, "Inleiding" in Plotinus, *Enneaden* (Introduction in Enneads, Plotinus), Baarn/Amsterdam 1984.

Festugière, André-Jean, *La Révélation d'Hermès Trismégiste*, 4 volumes, Paris 1944–1954 (especially Vol. I, L'astrologie et les sciences occultés, Paris 1950).

——————, *Hermétisme et mystique païenne*, Paris 1967.

Ficino, Brug naar de Hermetische Gnosis (Bridge to Hermetic Gnosis), Haarlem 2001.

Fihrist of Al-Nadim: a tenth-century survey of Muslim culture, B. Dodge (ed. and trans.), Vol. I and II, New York/London 1970.

Filkin, David, *Stephen Hawking's universum* (Stephen Hawking's Universe), Warnsveld 1997.

Flavius Josephus, *De joodse oorlog & Uit mijn leven* (The Jewish War and From my Life), Baarn 1992.

Flowers, Stephen Edred (ed.), *Hermetic Magic. The Postmodern Magical Papyrus of Abaris*, York Beach (ME), 1995.

Fludd, Robert, *Medicina Catholica*, Frankfurt 1629.

Fowden, Garth, *The Egyptian Hermes, a historical approach to the late pagan mind*, Cambridge 1986.

Franz, Marie-Louise von, *Alchemie, een inleiding tot haar symboliek en psychologie* (Alchemy, an Introduction to her Symbology and Psychology), Amsterdam 1983.

French, Peter J., *John Dee. The World of an Elizabethan Magus*, London 1972.

Frick, Karl R.H., *Die Erleuchteten. Gnostisch-theosofische und alchemistisch-rozenkreuzerische Geheimgesellschaften bis zum ende des 18.Jahrhunderts —ein Betrag zur Geistesgeschichte der Neuzeit*, Graz, 1973.

——————, *Licht und Finsternis. Gnostisch-theosofische und freimaurerisch-okkulte Geheimgesellschaften bis an die Wende zum 20.Jahrhundert*, I and II, Graz 1975 and 1978.

Gadalla, Mustafa, *Egyptische kosmologie* (Egyptian Cosmology), Deventer 2000.

Garbers, K. and J. Weyer (eds.), *Quellengeschichtliches Lesebuch zur Chemie und Alchemie der Araber in Mittelalter*, Hamburg 1980.

Gentile, Sebastiano and Carlos Gilly, *Marsilio Ficino e il ritorno di Ermete Trismegisto* (catalog of the combined exhibition of the Biblioteca Medicea Laurenziana and the Amsterdam Bibliotheca Philosophica Hermetica), Florence 1999.

Gibbons, B.J., *Spirituality and the Occult*, London/New York 2001.

Gilbert, R.A., *The Golden Dawn and the Esoteric Section*, London 1987.

Gilly, Carlos, "Das Bekenntnis zur Gnosis von Paracelsus bis auf die Schüler Jacob Böhmes" in Roelof van den Broek and Cis van Heertum (ed.), *From*

Poimandres to Jacob Böhme: Gnosis, Hermetism and the Christian Tradition, Amsterdam 2000, pp. 385–427.

———, "Die Überlieferung des Asclepius im Mittelalter" in Roelof van den Broek and Cis van Heertum (ed.), *From Poimandres to Jacob Böhme: Gnosis, Hermetism and the Christian Tradition*, Amsterdam 2000, pp. 335-369.

———, "Die Rosenkreuzer als europäisches Phänomen im 17. Jahrhundert" in *Rosenkreuz als europäisches Phänomen im 17. Jahrhundert*, Amsterdam 2002, pp. 19-57.

Carlos Gilly and Cis van Heertum (eds.), *Magia, Alchimia, Scienza dal '400 al '700; L'influsso di Ermete Trismegisto* (catalog of the combined exhibition of the Biblioteca Nazionale Marciana of Venice and the Biblioteca Philosophica Hermetica of Amsterdam in Venice 2002), 2 volumes, Florence 2002.

Giordano Bruno, De heroïsche mens in het oneindige universum (The Heroic Man in the Infinite Universe), Haarlem 2002.

Godwin, Jocelyn, Christian Chanel and John P. Deveney, *The Hermetic Brotherhood of Luxor, Initiatic and Historical Documents of an Order of Practical Occultism*, York Beach ME 1995.

———, *Athanasius Kircher, A Renaissance Man and the Quest for Lost Knowledge*, London 1979.

———, "Music and the Hermetic Tradition" in Roelof van den Broek and Wouter J. Hanegraaff, *Gnosis and Hermeticism; from Antiquity to Modern Times*, Albany 1998, pp. 183–197.

———, *The Theosophical Enlightment*, Albany 1994.

Graf, Fritz, *Magic in the Ancient World*, Cambridge MA 1997.

———, "Excluding the Charming: The Development of the Greek Concept of Magic" in Marvin Meyer and Paul Mirecki, *Ancient Magic and the Ritual Power*, Princeton 1999, pp. 29–43.

Graves, Robert, *Griekse Mythen* (Greek Myths), Houten 1990.

Grube, G.M.A., *Plato's Thought*, London 1980 (reprint of 1935 edition).

Gruenwald, I., *Apocalyptic and Merkavah Mysticism*, Leiden 1980.

Gundel, Wilhelm., *Neue astrologische Texte der Hermes Trismegistos. Funde und Forschungen auf dem Gebiet der antiken Astronomie und Astrologie*, Munich 1936.

———, *Dekane und Dekansternbilder*, Glückstadt/Hamburg 1936.

Gundel, Wilhelm and Hans Georg Gundel, *Astrologumena. Die astrologische Literatur in der Antike und ihre Geschichte*, Wiesbaden 1966.

Gündüz, S., "The Knowledge of Life. The Origins and Early History of the Mandaeans and Their Relation to the Sabians of the Qur'an and to the Harranians" in *Journal of Semetic Studies*, Supplement 3, Oxford 1994.

Guthrie, Kenneth Sylvan, *The Pythagorean Sourcebook and Library*, edited and introduced by David Fideler, Grand Rapids MI 1987.

Hak, Henri Johan, *Marsilio Ficino*, Amsterdam 1936.

Hall, Manly Palmer, *Twelve World Teachers*, Los Angeles 1937.

Hanegraaff, Wouter J., *Het einde van de hermetische traditie* (The end of the Hermetic Tradition) (Inaugural speech, 18 January 2000), Amsterdam 2000.

—————, "The New Age Movement and the Esoteric Tradition" in Roelof van den Broek and Wouter J. Hanegraaff, *Gnosis and Hermeticism; from Antiquity to Modern Times*, Albany 1998, pp. 359–383.

Hawking, Stephen, *Het Heelal. Verleden en toekomst van ruimte & tijd* (The Universe. Past and Future of Space and Time), Amsterdam 2002 (25th edition).

Heidegger, "Die Zeit des Weltbildes" (1938) in *Holzwege*, Frankfurt 1959.

Heindel, Max, "Het probleem der voeding, gezondheid en langdurige jeugd-wetenschappelijk beschouwd" (The Problem of Food, Health and Longevity from a Scientific Point of View) in Max Heindel, *Het Christendom der Rozekruisers* (Christianity of the Rosicrucians), Haarlem 1929.

—————, "De gave der genezing" (The Gift of Healing) in Max Heindel, *Rozekruisers Cosmologie* (Rosecrucian Cosmology), Amsterdam (not dated) pp. 539–545.

Henderson, Joseph L., "Oude mythen en de moderne mens" (Old Myths and Modern Man) in Jung c.s., *De mens en zijn symbolen* (Man and his Symbols), Rotterdam 1993, pp. 88–133.

Hermes Trismegistus; Pater Philosophorum, catalog of an exhibition in the Bibliotheca Philosophica Hermetica, Amsterdam 2002.

Hermetische geneeskunde, (Lectorium Rosicrucianum) (The Hermetic Art of Healing), Haarlem (not dated).

Hesiod, *De geboorte van de goden. Werken en dagen* (The Birth of the Gods. Their Labor and Days), translated and clarified by Wolther Kassies, Amsterdam 2002.

Hjärpe, J., *Analyse critique des traditions arabes sur les Sabéens harraniens*, (Dissertation), Uppsala 1972.

Hofmeier, Thomas, "Cudworth versus Casaubon: Historical versus Textual Criticism" in Carlos Gilly/Cis van Heertum (eds.), *Magia, Alchimia, Scienza dal '400 al '700; L'influsso di Ermete Trismegisto* I, Florence 2002, pp. 581–587.

—————, "Philology versus Imagination: Isaac Casaubon and the Myth of Hermes Trismegistus" in Carlos Gilly/Cis van Heertum (eds.), *Magia, Alchimia Scienza dal '400 al '700; L'influsso di Ermete Trismegisto* I, Florence 2002, pp. 569–573.

Holmyard, E.J., *Alchemy*, Northampton 1957.

Huart, C., (ed. and trans.), *Le livre de la création et l'histoire*, 4 Volumes, Paris 1899–1919.

Hurry, J.B., *Imhotep*, Oxford 1928.

Jackson, Howard M., *Zosimus of Panopolis on the Letter Omega*, Missoula MT 1978.

Jaffé, Aniela, *Jung over parapsychologie en alchemie—Jungs laatste jaren* (Jung about Parapsychology and Alchemy—Jung's Last Years), Rotterdam 1969.

Jasnow, R. and K.-T. Zauzich, *Proceedings of the Seventh International Congress of Egyptologists*, ed. C.J. Eyre, Leuven 1998, pp. 607–618.

Johnson, Paul, *The Masters Revealed: Madame Blavatsky and the Myth of the Great White Lodge*, Albany 1994.

Jong, Heleen. M.E. de, *Michael Maier's* Atalanta Fugiens; *bronnen van een alchemistisch emblemenboek* (Michael Maier's *Atalanta Fugiens*; Fountain Sources of an Alchemistical Book of Symbols), Utrecht 1965.

————, "Spirituele alchemie" in Marcel Messing (ed.), *Religie als levende ervaring* (Religion as a Living Experience), Assen 1988, pp. 167–197.

Jong, K.H.E. de, *De Griekse Mysteriën* (Greek Myths), The Hague 1943.

Josten, C.H., "A Translation of John Dee's *Monas Hieroglyphica*" in *Ambix*, Vol. XII, 1964, pp. 84–221.

Jung, C.G., *Psychologie und Alchemie*, Zürich 1952.

————, "Der Geist Mercurius" in C.G. Jung, *Symbolik der Geistes*, Zürich 1948.

————, *Herinneringen Dromen Gedachten* (Memories, Dreams and Thoughts), Rotterdam 1952.

————, *Droom en Individuatie* (Dream and Individualization), Rotterdam 1986.

————, *Verlossing in de Alchemie* (Deliverance in Alchemy), Rotterdam 1986.

————, *Paracelsica*, Zürich/Leipzig 1942.

————, *Alchemical Studies*, included in Collected Works, Volume XIII, London 1968.

Kaniok, Erich, "De grote ruimte" (The Large Universum) in *Giordano Bruno. De heroïsche mens in het oneindige universum* (The Heroic Man in the Infinite Universe), Haarlem 2002, pp. 58–71.

Kayzer, Wim, *Vertrouwd en o' zo vreemd. Over geheugen en bewustzijn* (Intimate but still so strange. About Memory and Consciousness), Amsterdam/Antwerpen, 1995.

Kerényi, Karl, *Hermes. Guide of Souls* (English translation of *Hermes der Seelenführer*, Zürich 1944), Dallas TX 1987.

Kingsford, Anna and Edward Maitland, *The Perfect Way or The Finding of Christ*, London 1882. (Dutch translation by A.B. van den Meer, *De ware weg of het vinden van den Christus*, Amersfoort, not dated.)

——————, *The Virgin of the World*, London 1885.

Kingsley, Peter, "An Introduction into the Hermetica: Approaching Ancient Esoteric Tradition" in Roelof van den Broek and Cis van Heertum (eds.), *From Poimandres in Jacob Böhme: Gnosis, Hermetism and the Christian Tradition*, Amsterdam 2000, pp. 17–41.

——————, *In the Dark Places of Wisdom*, Inverness CA 1999.

——————, "Poimandres. The Etymology of the Name and the Origins of the Hermetica" in Roelof van den Broek and Cis van Heertum (eds.), *From Poimandres in Jacob Böhme: Gnosis, Hermetism and the Christian Tradition*, Amsterdam 2000, pp. 41–77.

Klijn, A.F.J., *Edessa, de stad van de apostel Thomas* (Edessa, the City of the Apostle Thomas), Baarn 1962.

Knight, Christopher and Robert Lomas, *De sleutel van Hiram* (The Key of Hiram), Baarn, 1997.

Kristeller, Paul Oskar, *Studies in Renaissance Thought and Lettters*, Rome 1969 (reprint from 1956 edition).

Kristeller, Paul Oskar, 'The Scholastic Background of Marsilio Ficino, in Paul Oskar Kristeller, *Studies in Renaissance Thought and Letters*, Rome 1969, pp. 35-99.

——————, *Renaissance Thought I and II*, New York 1961.

Kybalion: A Study of the Hermetic Philosophy of Ancient Egypt and Greece by the "Three Initiates," Homewood (IL) 1912.

Langford, Garstin, E.J. (ed.), *The Rosie Crucian Secrets. Their Excellent Method Of making Medicines of Metals also their Laws and Mysteries*, Northamptonshire 1985.

Layton, Bentley, *The Gnostic Scriptures*, London 1987.

Leezenberg, Michiel, *Islamitische filosofie. Een geschiedenis* (Islamic Philosophy. A History), Amsterdam 2001.

Leijenhorst, Cees, "Fransesco Patrizi's Hermetic Philosophy," in Roelof van den Broek and Wouter J. Hanegraaff (eds.), *Gnosis and Hermeticism; from Antiquity to Modern Times*, Albany 1998, pp. 125–147.

Lennhof, E., *De Vrijmetselaren* (Freemasons), Zutphen 1931.

Letrouit, Jean, «Hermetisme et alchimie: contribution à l'étude du *Marcianus graecus 299 (=M)*" in Carlos Gilly/Cis van Heertum (eds.), *Magia, Alchimia, Scienza dal '400 al '700; L'influsso di Ermete Trismegisto* I, Florence 2002, pp. 85–113.

Letters of Marsilio Ficino, Volumes 1–6, London 1975–2001.

Lewis, Paul and Robert Margotta, *Ontwikkelingen van de Geneeskunde* (Developments in Medicine), Haarlem 1996.

Lindsay, *The Origins of Alchemy in Graeco-Roman Egypt*, London 1970.

Luckert, Karl W., *Egyptian Light and Hebrew Fire*, New York 1991.

Magie van het bloed op het altaar der Genezers (Lectorium Rosicrucianum) (Magic of the blood on the altar of the Physicians (Lectorium Rosicrucianum)), Haarlem (not dated).

Mahé, Jean-Pierre, "De weg naar de onsterfelijkheid" (The Way to Immortality) in G. Quispel (ed.), *De hermetische Gnosis in de loop der eeuwen* (The Hermetic Gnosis over the Centuries), Baarn 1992, pp. 27–53.

———, "Preliminary Remarks on the Demotic *Book of Thot* and the Greek *Hermetica*," *Vigilae Christianae* 50 (1996), pp. 353–363.

———, "La Renaissance et le mirage égyptien" in Roelof van den Broek and Cis van Heertum (eds.), *From Poimandres in Jacob Böhme: Gnosis, Hermetism and the Christian Tradition*, Amsterdam 2000, pp. 369–385.

———, "Fragments Hermétiques dans les Papyri Vindobonenses Graecae 29456 r°. et 29828 r°," in E. Lucchesis and H.D. Saffrey (ed.) *Mémorial André-Jean Festugière, Antiquité païenne et chrétienne*, Geneva 1984, pp. 51–65.

———, *Hermès en Haute-Egypte*, 2 Volumes, Québec 1978–1982.

Marschall, Peter, *Alchemie: de Steen der Wijzen* (The Philospher's Stone), Baarn 2001.

Ma'shar, Abu, *Kitab al-Uluf*, revised by Ibn Djuldjul, *Tabaqat al attiba*, 5 (written in 987–988 A.D.), Cairo 1955.

Massignon, M.L., «Appendix III: Inventaire de la Littérature Hermétique Arabe» in André-Jean Festugière, *La Révélation d'Hermès Trismégistes*, Paris 1950, pp. 384–400.

Masudi, *Kitab al-Tanbih*, ed. M.J. de Goeje, Leiden 1894.

Mathaeus Merian de Oudere (Matheus Merian, the Elder), catalog of exhibition with the same name, Frankfurt 1993.

McIntosh, Christopher, *The Rosicrucians. The History and Mythology of an Occult Order*, Wellingborough 1987.

Mead, G.R.S., *Fragments of a Faith Forgotten*, London 1900.

———, *Thrice Greates Hermes; Studies in Hellenistic Theosophy and Gnosis*, 3 Volumes, London 1906 new edition in 1 volume, York Beach 1992.

———, *The Hymns of Hermes*, Grand Rapids MI 1991 (1st edition, *Echoes from the Gnosis*, 1908).

Meade, Marion, *Madame Blavatsky; The Woman behind the Myth*, New York 1980.

Meer, A.E.G. van der, *The Harran of the Sabians in the first Millennium* A.D.; *Cradle of a Hermetic Tradition?* (publication pending).

———, "Zeven sleutels tot het werk van Marsilio Ficino, een introductie" (Seven Keys to the Work of Marsilio Ficino, an Introduction) in M.

Shepherd (ed.), *Marsilio Ficino. Een universeel mens* (Marsilio Ficino. A Universal Man), Deventer 2002, pp. 25–38.

Ménard, Louis, *Hermès Trismégiste*, Paris 1866.

Mendes da Costa, Charlotte, "Marsilio Ficino en de geneeskunde" (Marsilio Ficino and the Healing Arts) in M. Shepherd (ed.). *Marsilio Ficino. Een universeel mens* (Marsilio Ficino. A Universal Man), Deventer 2002, pp. 119–132.

Mendoza, Ramon G., *The Acentric Labyrinth. Giordano Bruno's Prelude to Contemporary Cosmology*, Shaftesbury/Rockfort/Brisbane 1995.

Mercurii Trismegisti, liber de potestate et sapientia dei, Corpus Hermeticum I–XIV, versione latina di Marsilio Ficino, PIMANDER, Treviso 1471.

Merkelbach, Reinhold, *Abrasax. Ausgewählte Papyri Religiösen und Magischen Inhalts*, Opladen 1992.

Merkur, Dan, *Gnosis. An Esoteric Tradition of Mystical Visions and Unions*, Albany 1993.

Meurs, Jos van, "William Blake and his Gnostic Myths," in Roelof van den Broek and Wouter J. Hanegraaff, *Gnosis and Hermeticism; from Antiquity to Modern Times*, Albany 1998, pp. 269-311.

———, "William Blake and his Gnostic Myths," in G. Quispel (ed.), *De Hermetische Gnosis in de loop der eeuwen* (The Hermetic Gnosis over the Centuries), Baarn 1992, pp. 539–580.

Meyer, Marvin and Paul Mirecki, *Ancient Magic and Ritual Power*, Leiden/New York/Keulen 1995.

Meyer, Marvin and Richard Smith (eds.), *Ancient Christian Magic. Coptic Texts of Ritual Power*, Princeton 1999.

Mills Harper, George, *Yeats's Golden Dawn*, Wellingborough 1987.

Moore, Thomas, "Marcilio Ficino, magiër en ziener (Marsilio Ficino, Magus and Seer)" in M. Shepherd (ed.), *Marsilio Ficino. Een universeel mens* (Marsilio Ficino. A Universal Man), Deventer 2002, pp. 101–108.

Mulisch, Harry, *De ontdekking van de hemel* (Discovery of Heaven), Amsterdam 1995.

Murfet, H., *When Daylight Comes*, Madras/London 1988.

Neugebauer, O. and H.B. van Hoesen, *Greek Horoscopes*, Philadelphia PA 1959.

Neymeyer, Ulrich, *Die Christlichen Lehrer im zweiten Jahrhundert*, Leiden/NewYork/ Copenhagen/Cologne 1989.

Oort, J., van, "Hermes en Augustinus," in G. Quispel (ed.), *De hermetische Gnosis in de loop der eeuwen* (The Hermetic Gnosis over the Centuries), Baarn 1992, pp. 287–312.

Overton Fuller, Jean, *Blavatsky and Her Teachers*, London 1988.

Pagel, Walter, *From Paracelsus to Van Helmont. Studies in Renaissance Medicine and Science*, London 1986.

———, *Paracelsus. An Introduction to Philosophical Medicine in the Era of the Renaissance*, Basel/New York 1958.

Paracelsiana, (Lectorium Rosicrucianum), Haarlem (not dated).

Paracelsus, *Selected Writings*, (Jolande Jacobi, ed.), London 1951.

Paracelsus, *The Hermetic and Alchemical Writings* (Vol. II), in an edition of Arthur Edward Waite, London 1894.

Pearce, Geoffrey, "Ficino and Astrology" in M. Shepherd (ed.), *Marsilio Ficino. Een universeel mens* (Marsilio Ficino. A Universal Man), Deventer 2002, pp. 108–119.

Peters, F. E., "Hermes and Harran" in M. Mazzaoui and V.B. Moreen (eds.) *Intellectual Studies on Islam: Essays Written in Honor of Martin B. Dickson*, Utah 1990, pp. 185–215.

Peukert, Will-Erich, *Panasophie; Ein Versuch zur Geschichte der weissen und schwarzen Magie*, Berlin 1976 (3rd edition, reprint of 2nd abridged edition).

Picknett, Lynn and Clive Prince, *Het geheime boek der Grootmeesters* (The Secret Book of the Grand Masters), Baarn 1998.

Pico della Mirandola, *Over de menselijke waardigheid* (About Man's Dignity) in the translation of J. Hemelrijk, Arnhem 1968.

Pingree, D., *The Thousands of Abu Ma'shar*, London 1968.

———, "Some of the Sources of the Gayat al-Hakim" in *Journal of the Warburg and Courtauld Institutes*, 43 (1980), pp. 1–15.

Plessner, M., *Studia Islamica* 2, Paris 1954.

Plotinus, *Enneads*, introduction and translation by Rein Ferwerda, Baarn/Amsterdam 1984.

Plutarchus, *Moralia*, (translation by F.C. Babbitt in the The Loeb Classical Library), Cambridge MA/London 1984.

Porreca, David, *The Influence of Hermetic Texts on Western European Philosophers and Theologians (1160–1300)*, Warburg Institute, London 2001.

Preisendanz, K. (a.o., eds.) *Papyri Graecae Magicae. Die Griechischen Zauber-Papyri*, 2 volumes, Stuttgart 1973–1974 (reprint of the original edition of 1928–1931).

Problematiek der Geneeskunde, (Lectorium Rosicrucianum) (The Problematic Nature of Medicine (Lectorium Rosicrucianum)), Haarlem (not dated).

Puliafito, Anna Laura, "Searching for a new physics: Metaphysics of light and ancient knowledge in Francesco Patrizi da Cherso" in Carlos Gilly/Cis van Heertum (eds.), *Magia, Alchimia, Scienza dal '400 al '700; L'influsso di Ermete Trismegisto* II, Florence 2002, pp. 255–267.

Quagebeur, Jan, "Lettres de Thot et Décret pour Osiris" in *Funerary Symbols and Religion* (dedicated to Prof. M.S.H.G. Heerma van Voss), edited by J. Kamstra, H. Milde and K. Wagtendonk, Kampen 1988, pp. 105–127.

Quispel, G., "Gnosis and Alchemy: the *Tabula Smaragdina*" in Roelof van den Broek and Cis van Heertum (eds.), *From Poimandres to Jacob Böhme: Gnosis, Hermetism and the Christian Tradition*, Amsterdam 2000, pp. 303–335.

————, *Asclepius, De volkomen openbaring van Hermes Trismegistus* (The Great Revelation of Hermes Trismegistus), Amsterdam 1996.

————, "Reincarnation and Magic in the Ascelepius" in Roelof van den Broek and Cis van Heertum (eds.), *From Poimandres to Jacob Böhme*, Amsterdam 2000, pp. 167–233.

————, "Hermes Trismegistus and the Origins of Gnosticism" in *Vigilae Christianae* 46 (1992), Leiden, pp. 1–19.

Quispel, G., (ed.), *De Hermetische Gnosis in de loop der eeuwen* (The Hermetic Gnosis over the Centuries), Baarn 1992.

Reitzenstein, R., *Die hellenistische Mysterienreligionen nach ihren Grundgedanken und Wirkungen*, Leipzig 1904.

————, *Poimandres, Studien zur Griechisch-Ägyptischen und Früh-christlichen Literatur*, Leipzig 1904.

Ricks, Stephen D., "The Magician as Outsider in the Hebrew Bible and the New Testament" in Marvin Meyer and Paul Mirecki, *Ancient Magic and Ritual Power*, Leiden/New York/Keulen 1995, pp. 131–145.

Rigo, Antonio, "From Constantinople to the Library of Venice: the Hermetic Books of Late Byzantine Doctors, Astrologers and Magicians" in Carlos Gilly/Cis van Heertum (eds.), *Magia, Alchimia, Scienza dal '400 al '700; L'influsso di Ermete Trismegisto*, I, Florence 2002, pp. 77–85.

Rijckenborgh, Jan van, *De Egyptische oer-gnosis en haar roep in het Eeuwige Nú* (The Egyptian Primeval Gnosis and her Calling in the Eternal Now), 4 volumes, Haarlem 1960–1965.

Rijnders, Henk, *De Golem ontsluierd. Over joodse mystiek en Kaballa* (The Golem Unveiled. About Jewish Mysticism and the Kabala), Deventer 1991.

Ritman, Joost R., "Geburt der Rozenkreuzerbruderschaft" in *Rosenkreuz als europäisches Phänomen im 17.Jahrhundert*, Amsterdam 2002, pp. 57–75.

————, "De Bibliotheca Philosophica Hermetica" in G. Quispel (ed.), *De Hermetische Gnosis in de loop der eeuwen* (The Hermetic Gnosis over the Centuries), Baarn 1992, pp. 644–662.

————, "Voorwoord" (Prologue) in M. Shepherd (ed.) *Marsilio Ficino. Een universeel men* (Marsilio Ficino. A Universal man), Deventer 2002, pp. 7–13.

Ritter, H., and M. Plessner (trans.), *"Picatrix," Das Zeit des Weisen von Pseudo-Magriti*, London 1962.

Robinson, John J., *Born in Blood*, London 1990.

Roep van het Rozenkruis, De. Vier eeuwen levende traditie (The Call of the Rosicrucian. Four Centuries of Living Tradition), Haarlem/Den Haag 2000.

Roob, Alexander, *Het Hermetische Museum; Alchemie & Mystiek* (The Hermetic Museum: Alchemy and Mysticism), Cologne 1997.

Rooijen-Dijkman, H.W.A. van, *Jamblichus/Porphyrius. Leven en leer van Pythagoras* (Iamblicus/Porphyrius. Life and Teachings of Pythagoras), Baarn 1987.

Rosenthal, F., *Das Fortleben der Antike im Islam*, Zürich 1965.

Rudolph, Kurt, *De Gnosis. Wesen und Geschichte einer spätantiken Religion*, Göttingen 1980.

Ruijling, J.A.G., *Hermippus; een als gnostisch en hermetisch te duiden verhandeling over astrologie* (Hermippus; an alleged Gnostic and Hermetic Treatise about Astrology), Arnhem 2002.

Runciman, Steven, *De val van Constantinopel 1453* (The Fall of Constantinople in 1453), Haarlem 1979.

Ruska, Julius, *Tabula Smaragdina; ein Beitrag zur Geschichte der hermetischen Literatur*, Heidelberg 1926.

Salaman, Clement, Dorine van Ooyen and William D. Wharton, *The Way of Hermes*, London 1999.

Santi, Bruno, *The Marble Pavement of the Cathedral of Siena*, Florence 1982.

Sauneron, Serge, *Les prêtres de l'ancienne Égypte*, Paris 1962.

Schaefer, Heinrich Wilhelm, *Die Alchemie. Ihr ägyptisch-griechischer Urs-prung und ihre weitere historische Entwicklung*, Wiesbaden 1967 (reprint of 1887 edition).

Schick, Hans, *Das ältere Rosenkreuzertum. Ein Beitrag zur Enstehunsgeschichte der Freimaurerei*, Berlin 1942.

Schitterend ongeluk, Een. Wim Kayzer ontmoet Oliver Sacks, Stephen Jay Gould, Stephen Toulmin, Daniel C. Dennet, Rupert Sheldrake and Freeman Dyson (A Brilliant Coincidence.Wim Kayzer meets Oliver Sacks, Stephen Jay Gould, Stephen Toulmin, Daniel C. Dennet, Rupert Sheldrake and Freeman Dyson), Amsterdam/Antwerpen 1995.

Scholem, Gershom, *Major Trends in Jewish Mysticism*, New York 1941.

Schuhmann, K., "Francesco Patrizi en de Hermetische filosofie" (Francesco Patrizi and the Hermetic Philosophy) in G. Quispel (ed.) *De Hermetische Gnosis in de loop der eeuwen* (The Hermetic Gnosis over the Centuries), Baarn 1992, pp.339–356.

——————, "Giovanni Picco della Mirandola en het Hermetisme" (Giovanni Pico della Mirandolla and the Hermetica) in G. Quispel (ed.) *De Hermetische Gnosis in de loop der eeuwen* (The Hermetic Gnosis over the Centuries), Baarn 1992, pp. 313–339.

Schuré, Eduard, *De grote ingewijden* (The Great Initiates), Amsterdam 1909.

Schwartz, M.A., *De gouden ezel* (The Golden Ass), Amsterdam 1996.

Scott, Walter, *Hermetica; The Ancient Greek and Latin Writings which contain Religious or Philosophic Teachings Ascribed to Hermes Trismegistus*, Boston 1993.

Scott Walter and A.S. Ferguson, *Hermetica* IV, Oxford 1936.

Sezgin, F., *Geschichte des Arabischen Schrifttums*, Vol. IV, Leiden 1972.

Shaw, Ian and Paul Nicholson, *British Museum Dictionary of Ancient Egypt*, Cairo 1996.

Sheldrake, Rupert, *De wedergeboorte van de natuur* (The Rebirth of Nature), Utrecht/Antwerpen 1995.

Sheldrake, Rupert and Matthew Fox, *Wetenschap en spiritualiteit* (Science and Spirituality), Utrecht/Antwerpen 1997.

Shepherd, M. (ed.), *Marsilio Ficino. Een universeel mens* (A Universal Man), Deventer 2002.

Sibley, E., *A Key to Physics and the Occult Sciences*, London 1801.

Siebert, G., "Hermes," *Lexicon Iconographicum Mytholigiae Classicae* 5.1 (1990), pp. 285–286.

Sinnett, A.P., *Esoteric Buddhism*, London 1872.

Slavenburg, Jacob, *Een sleutel tot gnosis. Inzicht in de betekenis van de Nag Hammadi- vondst voor de mens van nu* (A key to Gnosis. Insight into the meaning of the discovery of the Nag Hammadi codices for the present man), Deventer 2000.

——————, "Hermes op het breukvlak van twee eeuwen" (Hermes on the dividing line of two centuries) in G. Quispel (ed.), *De Hermetische Gnosis in de loop der eeuwen* (The Hermetic Gnosis over the Centuries), Baarn 1992, pp. 580–597.

——————, *De geheime woorden. Een ontdekkingsreis door vijfentwintig eeuwen verborgen kennis.* (The secret words. A journey of discovery through twenty-five centuries hidden knowledge), Deventer 1989, (3rd, fully revised edition with the title: The secret words. A journey of discovery through twenty-five centuries of Gnosis, Deventer 1996; 4th edition 1999).

——————, *Mystiek en Spiritualiteit; een reis door het tijdeloze* (Mysticism and spirituality. A journey through timeless space), Deventer 1994.

——————, "Paracelsus. De natuurlijke gezondheid van lichaam en geest" in *Kunst en Wetenschap* (Paracelsus. The natural health of body and soul in *Art and Science*), 10th annual., nr. 2, 2001, pp. 29–31.

——————, *H.P. Blavatsky, de theosofie en de meesters* (H.P. Blavatsky, Theosophy and the Masters), Deventer 1991.

——————, "Ficino en Hermes" (Ficino and Hermes) in M. Shepherd (ed.), *Marsilio Ficino. Een universeel mens* (Marsilio Ficino A Universal Man), Deventer 2002.

——————, *De oerknal van het christendom. Veelkleurig perspectief van een impuls* (The "Big Bang" of Christianity. Multi-colored perspective of an impulse), Haarlem 2003.

———, "*De 'euforie' van de 'New Age'*" (The Euphoria of the New Age) in *Bres*, 203 (Aug/Sep. 2000), pp. 4–14.

———, "*De 'verloren erfenis* (The lost inheritance), Deventer 1995[2].

Slavenburg, Jacob, De "logische" Jesus (The "logical" Jesus), Deventer 2002.

———, *Opus Posthuum; een onthullende blik op het vroegste christendom* (Opus Posthuum. A revealing glance at early Christianity), Deventer 2001.

Slavenburg, Jacob and W.G. Glaudemans, *Nag Hammadi-geschriften* I and II (Nag Hammadi Codices, Vol. I and II), Deventer 1994 and 1995. (respectively 5th edition in 2000 and 2nd edition in 1996).

Sleutels van Salomo, (The Keys of Salomon) by Rabbi Salomo, Dutch translation by J. Verschure, Amsterdam 1981.

Smit, Frans, "Bruno als voorloper van zijn tijd" (Bruno as a forerunner of his time) in *Giordano Bruno. De heroïsche mens in het oneindige universum.* (Giordano Bruno. The Heroic Man in the Infinite Universe), Haarlem 2002, pp. 25–31.

Spakman, J. "De voltooing van de Renaissance in het nu" ("The Fulfillment of the Renaissance in the Now") in *Ficino. Brug naar de Hermetische Gnosis* (Ficino. Bridge to the Hermetic Gnosis), Haarlem 2001, pp. 36–56.

Spierenburg, H.J., *De Philonische Geheime Leer. De kaballa van Philo van Alexandrië* (The Philonian Secret Doctrine. De Kabala of Philo of Alexandria), Deventer 2001.

———, *H.P. Blavatsky, On the Gnostics*, San Diego 1994.

———, *The Inner Group Teachings of H.P. Blavatsky*, San Diego 1995.

Stafleu, Dick, *En toch beweegt zij. Geschiedenis van de natuurkunde van Pythagoras tot Newton* (And yet she moves. History of Physics from Pythagoras to Newton), Meppel/Amsterdam 1992.

Stapleton, E.E., G.L. Lewis and F. Sherwood Taylor, "The Sayings of Hermes quoted In the *Mã Al-Waraqi* of Ibn Umail" in *Ambix: The Journal of the Society for the History of Alchemy and Chemistry*, Vol. III, April 1949, nr. 3 and 4, pp. 69–91.

Steuchus, Augustus, (Agostino Steuco da Gubbio), *De perenni philosophia*, Lyon 1654.

Stevelink, R., "De bevrijdende geneeskunst van Paracelsus" (The Liberating Healing Art of Paracelsus) *in Theophrastus Aureolus von Hohenheim, genaamd Paracelsus; geneesheer, wijsgeer, Godsverklaarder,* Theophrasus Aureolus von Hohenheim, called Paracelsus, Physician, Philosopher and proclaimed God-revealer), Haarlem 2001, pp. 29–39.

Stricker, B.H., *De brief van Aristeas; de hellenistische codificaties der praehelleense godsdiensten* (The Letter of Aristeas; the Hellenistic Codifications of the Pre-Hellenistic Religions), Amsterdam 1956.

Stufkens, H., *Gesprekken over Jung. Religie—gnosis—alchemie* (Conversations about Jung. Religion—Gnosis—Alchemy), Rotterdam 1993.

Subba Row, T., *Collected Writings* II, composition and commentary by Henk J. Spierenburg, San Diego 2001.

Tardieu, M., *Le Manechéisme*, Paris 1981.

——————, "Sabiens Coraniques et Sabiens de Harran," *Journal Asiatique*, 274, (1986), pp. 1–44.

Thomas, Keith, *De ondergang van de magische wereld. Godsdienst en magie in Engeland 1500–1700* (The Downfall of the World of Magic. Religion and Magic in England 1500–1700), London 1991.

Tröger, K.-W., *Mysterienglaube und Gnosis in Corpus Hermeticum XIII*, Berlin 1971.

Uchelen, N.A. van, *Joodse Mystiek; Merkawa, tempel en troon* (Jewish Mysticism; Merkawa, Temple and Throne), Amsterdam 1983.

Ullmann, M., *Die Natur-und Geheimwissenschaften im Islam*, Leiden/Keulen 1972.

Uxkull, Woldemar von, *Eine Einweihung im alten Ägypten. Nach dem Buch Thoth*, Wuppertal 1997 (reprint).

Velde, H. te, "Some remarks on the Mysterious Language of the Baboons" in *Funerary Symbols and Religion* (dedicated to Professor M.S.H.G. Heerma van Voss), edited by J. Kamstra, H. Milde and K. Wagtendonk, Kampen 1988, pp. 129–138.

Vere, Ketmia, *Der Compass der Weisen*, Berlin/Leipzig 1779.

Vermaseren, M.J. *Mithras, de geheimzinnige God*, (Mithras, The Secretive God), Amsterdam/Brussel 1959.

Versnel, H.S., "The Poetics of the Magical Charm: An Essay on the Power of Words" in Paul Mirecki and Marvin Meyer (eds.), *Magic and Ritual in the Ancient World*, Leiden/Boston/Cologne 2002, pp. 105–159.

Vliet, J van der, "Raising the *djed*: a rite de marge," *Akten München 1985 III* (ed. S. Schoske), Hamburg 1989, pp. 405–411.

Vries-Ek, P. de, "Hermes en de levende geest Mercurius" (Hermes and the living Spirit Mercurius) in G. Quispel (ed.) *De Hermetische Gnosis in de loop der eeuwen* (The Hermetic Gnosis over the Centuries), Baarn 1992, pp. 597–610.

Waddell, W.G., *Manetho*, Cambridge 1980[6].

Waszink, Jan H., *Die Seele ist ein Hauch*, Zürich/Müchen 1980.

Wilson, Colin, *Meester van de onderwereld; Jung en de twintigste eeuw* (Master of the Underworld. Jung and the Twentieth Century), Amsterdam 1985.

Wissen-Harkink, E.J. van, "De geboorte van de Rozenkruiserbeweging in de zeventiende eeuw" (The Birth of the Rosicrucian Movement in the Seventeenth Century) in John van Schaik (ed.), *De Rozenkruisers ontsluierd* (The Rosicrucians unveiled), Zeist 1994.

Wittkower, Rudolf and Margot, *Born under Saturn: The Character and Conduct of Artists*, New York 1969.

Wolfstieg, August, *Ursprung und Entwicklung der Freimauererei* (3 Vols.), Berlin 1920.

Yates, Frances A., *Giordano Bruno and the Hermetic Tradition*, Chicago/London 1991.

———, *The Theatre of the World*, London 1987

———, *De Geheugenkunst* (The Art of Memory), Amsterdam 1990.

———, *The Rosicrucian Enlightment*, London 1972.

———, *The Occult Philosophy in the Elizabethan Age*, London 1979.

Zandee, J., "Het Hermetisme en het oude Egypte" (Hermeticism in Ancient Egypt), in G. Quispel (ed.), *De Hermetische Gnosis in de loop der eeuwen* (The Hermetic Gnosis over the Centuries), Baarn 1992, pp. 97–175.

———, *Egyptische tempels en goden* (Egyptian Temples and Gods), Kampen 1965.

Zinguer, Ilana, "La lecture des manifestes rosicruciens en France' in *Rosenkreuz als Europäisches Phänomen im 17.Jahrhundert*, Amsterdam 2002, pp. 176–190.

Zirkoff, Boris de, 'The Sources of the Secret Doctrine" in Virginia Hanson (ed.) *H.P. Blavatsky and the Secret Doctrine*, Madras/London 1988, pp. 13–22.

Zitman, Wim H., *Sterrenbeeld van Horus* (Constellation of Horus), Baarn 2000.

Zweers, M.E.B., *Die Zauberflöte en de Gnosis* in G. Quispel (ed.), *De Hermetische Gnosis in de loop der eeuwen* (The Hermetic Gnosis over the Centuries), Baarn 1992, pp. 443–492.

Abbreviations Used

Asclepius	*Asclepius* (in the Dutch translation by G. Quispel, *Asclepius. De volkomen openbaring van Hermes Trismegistus* (The Great Revelation of Hermes Trismegistus), Amsterdam 1996).
CH	*Corpus Hermeticum* (in the Dutch translation by R. van den Broek and G. Quispel, *Corpus Hermeticum*, Amsterdam 1990 and the English translation by G.R.S. Mead, *Thrice Greatest Hermes*, London 1964).
CW	H.P. Blavatsky, *Collected Writings* Vol. II, Subba Row.
Giordano Bruno	Frances A. Yates, *Giordano Bruno and the Hermetic Tradtion*, Chicago/London 1991.
Gnosis and Hermeticism	Roelof van den Broek and Wouter J. Haanegraaf (eds.), *Gnosis and Hermeticism; from Antiquity to Modern Times*, Albany 1998.
Gundel/Gundel	Wilhelm Gundel and Hans Georg Gundel, *Astrologumena. Die Die astrologische Literatur in der Antike und ihre Geschichte*, Wiesbaden 1966.
Gundel, *Dekane*	Wilhelm Gundel, *Dekane und Dekansternbilder*, Glückstadt/Hamburg 1936.
Hermetic Gnosis	G. Quispel (ed.), *De Hermetische Gnosis in de loop der eeuwen* (The Hermetic Gnosis over the Centuries), Baarn 1992. A new edition appeared by the Rosicrucian Press in Haarlem, in 2004.
Il retorno di Ermete	Sebastiano Gentile, *Marsilio Ficino e il ritorno di Ermete Trismegisto*, catalog of the combined exhibition of the *Bibliotheca Medicea Laurenziana* and the Amsterdam *Bibliotheca Philosophica Hermetica*, Florence 1999.
Liber Hermetis	*Liber Hermetis* in W. Gundel, *Neue astrologische Texte der Hermes Trismegistos. Funde und Forschungen auf dem Gebiet der antiken Astronomie und Astrologie*, Munich 1936.
Magia, Alchimia I & II	Carlos Gilly/Cis van Heertum (eds.), *Magia, Alchimia, Scienza dal '400 al '700; L'influsso di Ermete Trismegisto*, catalog of the combined exhibition of the *Bibliotheca Nazionale Marciana*, Venice and the Amsterdam *Bibliotheca Philosophica Hermetica* in Venice 2002, 2 volumes, Florence 2002.

Mead, *Hermes*	G.R.S. Mead, *Thrice Greatest Hermes; Studies in Hellenistic Theosophy and Gnosis*, York Beach ME 1992. This edition is one volume containing the three seperate volumes printed in 1906.
NHG I and II	Jacob Slavenburg/W.G. Glaudemans, *Nag Hammadi-geschriften*, (Nag Hammadi codices), 2 volumes, Deventer 1996 and 2000.
PGM	*Papyri Graecea Magicae*
Poimandres-Böhme	Roelof van den Broek and Cis van Heertum (eds.), *From Poimandres in Jacob Böhme: Gnosis, Hermetism and the Christian Tradition*, Amsterdam 2000.
Révélation	A.J. Festugière, *La Révélation d'Hermès Trismégiste*,Vol. I, L'astrologie et les sciences occultés, Paris 1944.
Nock/ Festugière	Corpus Hermeticum, *Texte établi par A.D. Nock et traduit par A.J. Festugière*, 4 volumes, Paris 1945–1954.
Scott	Walter Scott, *Hermetica; the Ancient Greek and Latin Writings which contain Religious or Philosophic Teachings Ascribed to Hermes Trismegistus*, Boston 1993 (reprint of the 1st edition in 3 volumes in 1924–1936).
Stobeaus	Johannes Stobeaus, *Anthologium* (Hermetic fragments).

Chronology

+/- 3100 B.C. The Lunar God Thoth is worshipped as a baboon.

+/- 2700 B.C. Thoth with an Ibis-head is shown with a writing tablet.

+/- 1370 B.C. Amenhotep III installs large baboon statues at the temple of Thoth in Hermopolis. In the following era Thoth is worshipped as the Inventor of writing, composer of the calendar, physician, astrologer, the All-Wise, and Guardian of Souls.

800–332 B.C. Thoth is worshipped as Hermes by the Greeks in Egypt.

From +/- 400 B.C. Astrological, magical and medicinal treatises in the name of Hermes.

After 332 B.C. Thoth becomes more and more the Grecian Hermes and, with the title of Hermes Trismegistus, becomes the All-Wise Hermes as the "grandson" of Thoth.

+/- 200 B.C. Bolos (Demokritos) of Mendes writes the alchemical text *Physica et Mystica*.

+/- 100–275 A.D. Composition of the *Corpus Hermeticum*, probably compiled from older material, the Latin translation of *Logos Teleios* (*Asclepius*) derived from the *Tabula Smaragdina*.

+/- 300 Zosimus, the hermetic Alchemist.

+/- 150–500 Hermes is mentioned frequently in writings of Christian Church Fathers (Justinius, Clemens, Tertullianus, Arnobius, Lanctantius, Cyrrillius, Augustinus, Quodvultdeus) and the Neo-Platonists (Iamblichus and Proclus).

+/- 500 Johannes Stobaeus inserts into his collection of Greek texts thirty or more short and longer hermetic writings, among which is the *Koré Kosmou* (Virgin of the World).

+/- 800–1000 Arabs translate and edit a great amount of hermetic texts.

+/- 1600 In Constantinople Michael Psellus has in his possession treatises of the *Corpus Hermeticum*. Most of the (by his own hand?) classifications appear in the Renaissance. In the West the *Asclepius* is rediscovered.

From +/- 1060 Flourishing of (hermetic) magic in texts, among others like the "Book of Magic" called the *Picatrix*. The composition of the *Liber XXIV Philosophorum*. Hermes is frequently mentioned in the works of Alain van Rijssel, Thierry of Chartres, and Albertus Magnus.

1401–1464 Nicolas de Cusa (Cusanas) revaluates the *Asclepius*.

1458 In Florence, Cardinal Bessarion obtains a complete handwritten copy of the *Corpus Hermeticum*.

1460 or 1462 Cosimo de' Medici obtains the handwritten manuscripts of the *Corpus Hermeticum*, which are translated by Marsilio Ficino in 1463.

1471 First edition of Ficino's translation of the *Corpus Hermeticum*.

1486 Pico della Mirandola completes his 900 propositions, among which include some hermetic ones. Hermes also appears here in his famous speech about "The Dignity of Man."

1488 Giovanni di Stefano completes his floor mosaics in the Cathedral of Sienna, among which appears Hermes Trismegistus as time companion of Moses. At about the same time, Hermes is being painted on the ceiling of the Walburgis Church in Zutphen, Netherlands.

1506 Trithemius has his *Stenographia* printed. This alchemical priest, mentor of, among others, Agrippa and Paracelsus, is a staunch Hermeticist.

1511 Agrippa von Nettesheim teaches *hermetica* in Pavia. In 1533, his very influential paper called *De occulta philosophia* is published.

1493–1541 Paracelsus practices as a physician, philosopher and alchemist. Due to his admiration of the *hermetica*, he was called *Trismegistus Germanus* and *Hermes Secundus*.

1543 *De revolutionibus orbium coelestum* by Copernicus appears. Hermes is quoted in this "revolutionary" paper.

1564 John Dee publishes his very influential *Monas hieroglyphica* with the "Seal of Hermes."

1592 Fransesco Patrizzi teaches at the Papal University in Rome. A year prior he had recorded in his *Nova de universis philosophia* a great number of hermetic treatises.

1595 Heinrich Khunrath's alchemical *Amphitheatrum sapientiae aeternae* is published.

1600 Public burning of the visionary Giordano Bruno in Rome. In the same year the (hermetic) Platonic chair is withdrawn.

1614 Isaac Casaubon researches several texts from the *Corpus Hermeticum* and dates them to the 2nd/3rd century A.D.

1614–1616 The Rosicrucian manifesto appears in print, having also been inspired by Hermes.

1617 Publication of Michael Maier's *Atalanta fugiens*.

1619 René Descartes' vision of the "Angel of Truth" forms the introduction of a mechanical, soulless world view.

1574–1637 Robert Fludd—physician, alchemist, and admirer of Hermes Trismegistus.

1641 Robert Morey is admitted to one of the lodges of the Freemasons.

1646 The learned Elias Ashmole also enters a Freemason lodge.

1667 Amos Comenius establishes the *Collegium Lucis* in Amsterdam. He proposes a society in the spirit of Hermes Trismegistus.

17th–19th Century Numerous groups occupy themselves with the hermetic range of thought.

1757–1827 William Blake represents Hermes in his artistic oeuvre.

1791 Premiere of Mozart's *Die Zauberflöte*, which contains much hermetic symbology.

1875 Foundation of *The Theosophical Society*. Helena Blavatsky, one of the founders, urges for the recognition of the Hermetic Philosophy as one of the two oldest religious movements (described in her books *Isis Unveiled* and *The Secret Doctrine*).

1884 Anna Kingsford, a Theosophist, establishes a "hermetic lodge" that rapidly became the independent *Hermetic Society*.

1884 Founding of *The Hermetic Brotherhood of Luxor* by Max Theon.

1885 Publication of the *The Virgin of the World* by A. Kingsford, a translation of fragments of Stobaeus.

1888 Founding of the influential *Hermetic Order of the Golden Dawn*.

1906 Publication of *Thrice Greatest Hermes* by G.R.S. Mead (3 volumes, reprinted into 1 volume in 1992).

1912 Publication of the *Kybalion*.

1924–1936 New translation of the *Corpus Hermeticum*, *Asclepius* and the fragments of Stobaeus (together with other hermetic fragments later supplemented by A.S. Ferguson).

1942 Carl Gustav Jung holds lectures on *Die Geist Mercurius*.

1945 At Nag Hammadi in Egypt, three hermetic texts are found.

1944–1954 *La Révélation d'Hermès Trismégistes* by André-Jean Festugière.

1945–1954 *Corpus Hermeticum*, *Asclepius* and the fragments of Stobaeus in a critical dissertation by Nock and Festugière.

1956 First edition of the *Hermetische Definities* (Hermetic Definitions) translated from Armenian in a Russian translation (followed in 1976 by a French translation).

1960–1965 Dutch translation of the *Corpus Hermeticum* together with the *Tabula Smaragdina* by J. van Rijckenborgh in his *De Egyptische oer-gnosis* (Egyptian Archaic Gnosis).

1990 Exhibition of the *Bibliotheca Philosophica Hermetica* in Amsterdam of the documented history of the *Corpus Hermeticum* and the publication of a new Dutch translation of the *Corpus Hermeticum* by Roel van den Broek and G. Quispel, followed in 1996 by a new translation of *Asclepius* by G. Quispel.

1991 Publication of fragments of the Greek original of the *Hermetic Definitions*.

1999 Exhibition in Florence about Marsilio Ficino and the return of Hermes Trismegistus in Florence organized by the *Biblioteca Medicea* and the *Bibliotheca Philosophica Hermetica* in Amsterdam.

1999 Inauguration of a chair at the University of Amsterdam teaching Hermetic Philosophy.

2002 Exhibition in Venice about the influence of Hermes Trismegistus in the 15th to the 18th centuries organized by the *Biblioteca Nazionale Marciana* and the *Bibliotheca Philosophica Hermetica.*

2003 Publication of the 1st edition of *De Hermetische Schakel* (The Hermetic Link) by Jacob Slavenburg.

Illustrations

Page 156: Fortasse Licebit, Hermes chases away Evil, in the shape of the Devil, *Encyclopaedia ad Aram mysticam*, 1631, Bibliotheca Philosophica Hermetica, Amsterdam.

Page 179: Magical formula in the *Treatise of the Eighth and Ninth Heavenly Sphere*, *Nag Hammadi Codex VI*, Leiden 1972.

Page 220: Plate A: Hermes to Asclepius, *Asclepius* 24: "Or don't you know, Asclepius, that Egypt is the counter-image of the Heavens?" © W.H.Zitman, *Egypt: Image of Heaven*, Amsterdam 2006, back cover.

Page 221: Plate B: Wim Zitman showed that the constellation of Osiris (Scorpio) is right above the holy places along the Nile, © W.H.Zitman, *Egypt: Image of Heaven*, Amsterdam 2006, p. 230.

Page 231: The Corpus Hermeticum in probably the oldest Greek handwritten manuscript (from the collection of Cardinal Bessarion), Biblioteca Marciana, Venice, 15th century (Cod.Marc.Gr. 242).

Page 243: Tarot card of Mantegna showing Hermes Mercurius in hunting garb with caduceus, *Suite d 'estampes de la renaissance italienne dite Tarots de Mantegna*, Bibliotheca Philosophica Hermetica, Amsterdam.

Page 255: Portrait of Paracelsus, *Th. Paracelsus*, *Astrologia et astronomica*, 1567, Bibliotheca Philosophica Hermetica, Amsterdam.

Page 261: In the *Basilica Chymica*, famous alchemists from various nations are pictured, Oswaldus Crollius, *Basilica Chymica* (frontispiece), Frankfurt 1609.

Page 266: Drawing of a Magical Circle for the Wednesday from The Keys of Solomon, *Clavicula Salomonis*, 18th century manuscript M244, Bibliotheca Philosophica Hermetica, Amsterdam.

Page 268: *Liber Naturae Apertus*, Adam Michael Birkholz, *Die sieben heilige Grundsäulen*, Leipzig 1783.

Page 270: Monas hieroglyphica figure, John Dee, *Monas hieroglyphica*, Antwerp 1564.

Page 277: A cosmic scheme in Copernicus' *De Revolutionibus Orbium Coelestium*, 1543, Bibliotheca Philosophica Hermetica, Amsterdam.

Page 285: Statue of Giordano Bruno at the Campo dei Fiori in Rome.

Page 288: Page from Michael Maier's *Atalanta Fugiens*, Oppenheim 1618.

Page 289: The words of Epigram X put to music in the shape of a fuga.

Page 290: Hermes Trismegistus, Ruler of the four elements. Illustration from Michael Maier's *Symbola Aureae*, Frankfurt 1617.

Page 291: *Museum Hermeticum*, H. Kunrath, *Amphitheatrum*, 1609, Bibliotheca Philosophica Hermetica, Amsterdam.

Page 295: cover of Jacob Slavenburg's book "...and the two shall be one." Original coniunctio illustration from the *Rosarium Philosophorum*, 1550.

Page 318: Title page of *Ars Magna Sciendi* of Kircher, Amsterdam 1669.

Page 320: William Blake's drawing of Newton as the Creator of a mechanical world view, The Tate Gallery, London.

Page 331: Illustration of Secret Figures: The Hermetic doctrine. *Geheime Figuren der Rosenkreuzer*, 1785, Bibliotheca Philosophica Hermetica, Amsterdam.

Page 333: Amsterdam's Bibliotheca Philosophica Hermetica, Hermes Mercurius can be seen.

Page 355: Symbol of a Freemason Lodge with the two pillars—Jachin and Boaz, Adam Michael Birkholz, *Compass der Weisen* (frontispiece), 1779, Bibliotheca Philosophica Hermetica, Amsterdam.

Color Insert

Plate 1: One of two images of Hermes Trismegistus in the Medieval Walburgis' church in Zutphen, (Netherlands) (see page 222).

Plate 2: Above: Ficino's Introduction (Argumentum) to the *Corpus Hermeticum*, in which there is handwriting of Lorenzo de Medici, Biblioteca Medicea Laurenziana, Florence, 15th-century manuscript (Plut.21.8).

At right: View of Florence from the villa of de Medici, photo by author (see page 226).

Plate 3: Hermes in conversation with other philosophers, Guillaume de Tignonville, *Les ditz des philosophes*, 15th century manuscript (M205), Bibliotheca Philosophica Hermetica, Amsterdam (see page 255).

Plate 4: Illustration from Secret Figures with a personification of Sophia, wisdom, *Geheime Figuren der Rosenkreuzer*, 18th-century manuscript (M309), Bibliotheca Philosophica Hermetica, Amsterdam (see page 294).

Reference Notes

Introduction and Prolog

1 In 1945, several very important hermetical treatises were found at Nag Hammadi, among them *The Treatise of the Eighth and Ninth Heavenly Sphere*. It is very unique, giving the research into Hermes a new dimension.

2 Many splendid books have been written about the "Egyptian Hermes" and many more about the hermetic tradition from the Renaissance on. Studies of the hermetic influence during the Middle Ages and aspects of the *Hermetica* were published. (See Bibliography for a list of Literature.)

3 *Korè Kosmou* (The Virgin of the World) by Stobaeus (23.8). I made use of the translation of A.D. Nock and A-J. Festugière, the *Corpus Hermeticum*, 4 Volumes, (here: Vol. III, *Fragments extraits de Stobée* I-XXII and Vol. IV, *Fragments extraits de Stobée* XXIII-XXIX; *Fragments divers*). See also Carsten Colpe and Jens Holzhausen (eds.), *Das Corpus Hermeticum Deutsch*, 2 volumes (Vol. 2); Walter Scott, *Hermetica: The ancient Greek and Latin Writings which contain Religious or Philosophic Teachings ascribed to Hermes Trismegistus* (new edition of first publication in three volumes dd. 1924-1936); G.R.S. Mead, *Thrice Greatest Hermes; Studies in Hellenistic Theosophy and Gnosis* (new edition of the 3 volumes in one).

4 *Asclepius* 24. From the translation by G. Quispel.

5 See illustrations on p. 24.

6 Herodotus (450 b.c.), *Histories* 2, p. 67.

7 This is the Hypogeum of Hermopolis Magna, today called Tuna-el-Gebel, located several kilometers from the cult center of Hermopolis.

8 See illustrations on p. 24.

9 See p. 36.

Chapter I

10 Edward Schuré, *De grote ingewijden* (The Great Initiates).

11 According to the Egyptian priest-chronicler Manetho; Iamblichus, *Over de Mysteriën* (About the Mysteries), 8.1.

12 Clemens of Alexandria, see p. 40.

13 Plato, *Phaedrus*, pp. 274–275. The art of writing would dull their memory.

14 One eye symbolizing the Sun, the other the Moon.

15 For an elaborate description of all aspects of the deity Thoth, see Patrick Boylan, *Thoth, the Hermes of Egypt*.

16 Boylan, *Hermes of Egypt*, p. 101.

17 Boylan, *Hermes of Egypt*, pp. 147–148.

18 Garth Fowden, *The Egyptian Hermes, a historical approach to the late pagan mind*, p. 22.

19 Brian P. Copenhaver, *Hermetica, The Greek* Corpus Hermeticum *and the Latin* Asclepius *in a new English translation, with notes and introduction*, xiii.

20 The descriptor *Magna* is used because there was another Hermopolis in the delta region.

21 The name Hermopolis is Greek. It was previously called Chemnou (or Khemennu, place of the Eight-folded). The village now located at this place is called Achmounein. The renaming of this holy place occurred during the conquest of Egypt by the Greeks in 332 b.c. when Thoth was transformed into Hermes (Trismegistus). It is remarkable that the Greek writer Herodotus, who visited Egypt around 450 b.c., also uses the name Hermopolis (*Histories II*, p. 67).

22 This was common in cult centers of antiquity. Peter Kingsley describes the custom of the Greeks in *In the Dark Places of Wisdom*.

23 See H. ten Velde, "Some remarks on the Mysterious Language of the Baboons," in *Funerary Symbols and Religion*, pp. 129–138.

24 *The Egyptian Book of the Dead* is actually an incorrect title that dates back one and a half centuries. It contains several papyri describing rituals pertaining to the passage from one life to the other. Specifically, *The Papyri of Ani* (ca. 1420 b.c.), the one of Hoeffner (ca. 1300 b.c.), and those of Anhai (ca. 1100 b.c.) are important. In *The Book of the Dead* a continuous numbering of the various sayings of these papyri was used. These sayings have been taken from the *Egyptian Book of the Dead* translated by M.A.Geru.

25 *Egyptian Book of the Dead*, Aphorism 100.

26 *Egyptian Book of the Dead*, Aphorism 126.

27 Or the "*Gnosis of Rê*," see p. 133.

28 See A-J. Festugière, *La Révélation d'Hermès Trismegéstus*, Vol. 1, L'Astrologie et les sciences occultes (hereafter also called *Révélation)*, p. 68.

29 I will not comment on the aspects of, for instance, *ka*, *ba*, and *ach*, since that would take me outside the scope of this book.

30 Boylan, *Hermes of Egypt*, p. 101. This notation can also refer to the aspect of Thoth as knower of the hearts of people.

31 See *Egyptian Book of the Dead*, Aphorism 94: "...I have the writings of Thoth in my possession...."

32 *Corpus Hermeticum* (from now cited as *CH*) 16.1–2, in the Dutch translation of R. van den Broek and G. Quispel; G.R.S. Mead, *Thrice-Gretatest Hermes* 3 Vols.; B. Copenhaver, *Hermetica.*

33 Many variations exist regarding the opinions on the "Hereafter." These vary greatly depending on both time period and geographic location. Some rather

general characteristics are portrayed here—something we also encounter in various papyri and sacrophagus texts.

34 J.F. Borghouts, *Egyptische sagen en verhalen* (Egyptian Sagas and Stories), pp. 142–158.

35 Woldemar Uxkull, *Eine Einwendung im alten Ägypten. Nach dem Buch Thoth* (An Application in Ancient Egypt According to the Book of Thoth).

36 Fowden, *Egyptian Hermes*, pp. 5–7.

37 See Martin Bernal, *Black Athena Writes Back*, p. 389 and Serge Sauneron, *Les prêtres de l'ancienne Égypte*, pp. 133–169.

38 See J. Zandee, *Egyptische tempels en goden* (Egyptian Temples and Gods), pp. 49–53.

39 The *pir-ankh* of Sais was famous for its training of midwives. Nabil I. Ebeid, *Egyptian Medicine in the Days of the Pharaohs*.

40 Clemens of Alexandria, *Stromatis*, 6.4, pp. 35–37.

41 The term *Hermetica* will be used when the totality of hermetic works is meant.

42 R. Jasnow and K-T. Zauzich, *Proceedings of the Seventh International Congress of Egyptologists*, pp. 607–618. It pertains to fragment B 3/4, Jasnow/Zauz ich, p. 609.

43 Jasnow and Zauzich, *Proceedings*, fragment B 3/10.

44 Jasnow and Zauzich, *Proceedings*, fragment B 3/13–3/15.

45 *The Treatise of the Eighth and Ninth Heavenly Sphere* (hereafter referred to as *Eighth and Ninth Sphere*) is one of the three hermetic treatises found in the jar at Nag Hammadi in 1945.

46 Jean-Pierre Mahé, "Preliminary Remarks on the Demotic *Book of Thot* and the Greek, *Vigiliae Christianae*," pp. 353–363, 356.

47 *Eighth and Ninth Heavenly Sphere* , NHG I, pp. 398–404.

48 Jasnow and Zauzich, *Proceedings*, fragment B 6/5–7, pp. 611–612.

49 Jasnow and Zauzich, *Proceedings*, fragment C 4/6–12, p. 612.

50 Jasnow and Zauzich, *Proceedings*, p. 614.

51 Jasnow and Zauzich, *Proceedings*, p. 618.

52 Jasnow and Zauzich, *Proceedings*, p. 618.

53 Mahé, "Preliminary Remarks…," p. 359.

54 See the first treatise (*Poimandres)* of the *Corpus Hermeticum* (CH 1. pp. 25–26).

55 *Asclepius* 17, from the translation by G. Quispel (hereafter referred to as *Asclepius*).

56 "But this text is rather an exception. Due to the evolution of Hellenistic Cosmology and Beliefs concerning soul, the hermetic great Beyond is no longer underground but heavenly." Mahé, "Preliminary Remarks," p. 354.

57 Regina Schulz (ed.), *Ägypten, die Welt der Pharaonen*, p. 520.

58 Mahé, "Preliminary Remarks," p. 360.

59 Mahé, "Preliminary Remarks," p. 361.

Chapter 2

60 Herodotus was certainly not the first Greek to visit Egypt. The story goes that, before him, Thales of Milete, Solomon, and Pythagoras had all been there. The Greeks also possessed their own settlement in Egypt named Naucratis from the second half of the seventh century onward.

61 Herodotus, *Historiën* 2, p. 50.

62 Herodotus, *Historiën* 2, p. 51.

63 Herodotus, *Historiën* 2, p. 51.

64 Karl Kerényi, *Hermes, Guide of Souls*, p. 73.

65 Kerényi, *Guide of Souls*, pp. 64–65.

66 G. Siebert, "Hermes," *Lexicon Iconographicum Mythologiae Classicae* 5.1, pp. 285–286.

67 See among others Pausanias, *Graeciae descriptio*, 4.33.5, 5.27.5.

68 Kerényi, *Guide of Souls*, p. 65.

69 Homer, *Hymne op Hermes* (Hymn to Hermes), pp. 1–543. This hymn was created between the 7th and 4th centuries b.c.

70 Robert Graves, *Griekse Mythen* (Greek Myths), p. 66.

71 Graves, *Griekse Mythen*, p. 66.

72 The serpents represent polarity: the male serpent positive and the female serpent negative. Positive and negative here indicate plus and minus, and are not value based. The serpents stand as a symbol of the integration of opposites.

73 DNA is a protein molecule in the form of a double spiral and carrier of hereditary characteristics. (See, among others, Onno and Robert Docters van Leeuwen, *Tarot on herstelde orde* (Tarot in Reconstructed Order), p. 395, and Harry Mulisch, in his novel *De ontdekking van de hemel* (The Discovery of Heaven), p. 8.

74 Homer, *Hymne op Hermes*, p. 14.

75 Homer, *Hymne op Hermes*, pp. 175, 292.

76 Hesiod, *Opera et dies* (Birth of the Gods. Works and Days), p. 102.

77 Plato, *Cratylus*, pp. 407e–408a.

78 Hesiod, *Opera et dies*, p. 107–108.

79 Homer, *Hymne op Demeter* (Hymn to Demeter), p. 17; Apollodorus, *Bibliotheca*, 1, p. 5.

80 Robert Fitzgerld, *Odyssey*, Book XXIV, p. 445.

81 Citation by Franz Cumont, *Astrologie et religion chez les Grecs et les Romains*, p. 149.

82 Garth Fowden, *The Egyptian Hermes*, p. 23.

83 Diodorus Siculus, *Diodori bibliotheca historica*, 5, p. 75.

Chapter 3

84 Garth Fowden, *The Egyptian Hermes*, p. 1.

85 The division of "technical" and "philosophical" *Hermetica*, also used by Brian Copenhaver (*Hermetica*, xxxii et seq.), is progressive in comparison with the opinions of researchers at other times who made a sharp distinction between "vulgar," magical, and philosophical *Hermetica*.

86 Plato, *Philebus*, p. 18b.

87 Later footnoted text shows Hermes mainly as a man, if not a spiritualized man. Amminias Marcellinus sees him as a man gifted with an extraordinarily strong spirit (Fowden, *Egyptian Hermes*, p. 28).

88 This letter is announced in the manuscript of Syncellus (p. 72), as shown in the Greek written tradition of W.G. Waddell, *Manetho*, p. 208.

89 J.P. Mahé, "De weg naar onsterfelijkheid" (The Way to Immortality) in G. Quispel (ed.), *De Hermetische Gnosis in de loop der eeuwen* (The Hermetic Gnosis over the Centuries), pp. 28.

90 See Fowden. See also A.D. Nock and A-J Festugière, *Corpus Hermeticum* (hereafter cited as Nock/Festugière) Vol. 3, CLXV; and Festugière, *Révélation*, p. 75. See also p.101.

91 Peter Kingsley, "Poimandres. The Etymology of the Name and Origins of the Hermetica," in *From Poimandres to Jacob Böhme* (hereafter cited as *Poimandres-Böhme)*, p. 53.

92 *Asclepius* 37.

93 See libellus 12 of the *Corpus Hermeticum*. Here Hermes says he had heard of Agathodaimon and he finds it a pity that he never wrote it down. Agathodaimon's quote is: "*The ALL is One*, specifically the spiritual Being is One. We live by the power and the workings of the Eternal whose consciousness and true Self is good" (12.8.). In the same treatise, we find another citation by Agathodaimon: "Gods are immortal beings, humans are mortal Gods!" (12.1). In yet another citation: "the soul lies within the body, consciousness within the soul, the Logos within consciousness and God is the Father of them all." Here Hermes calls Agathodaimon "the glorious God" (12.13). Cyrillus of Alexandria also describes, in *Contra Julianum* (p. 553a), a dialogue between Hermes and Agathodaimon.

94 Iamblichus, *Over de Mysteriën* (The Mysteries), 8.5, 10.7.

95 Iamblichus, *Over de Mysteriën*, 8.4, p. 265.

96 *Korè Kosmu* (Isis to Horus), one of the *Fragments of Stobaeus* (23, p. 5.); see also Stobaeus fn. 319.

97 *Eighth and Ninth Heavenly Sphere, NGH* I, p. 403.

98 It was customary in Egypt to use the superlative great (*âa âa*) even for Thoth—in Greek *megas kai megas*. From Ptolemus IV Philopator (221–205 b.c.), we observe the Egyptian superlative translated, in this case pertaining to Hermes, by the Greek superlatives *megistos kai megistos kai megistos*, simplified to *trismegistos*.

99 M. Plessner, "Hirmis," in *The Encyclopedia of Islam*, p. 463. (See also the Interlog.)

100 In the *Corpus Hermeticum*, he is called "the grandson of God" (10.14).

101 The artist is Giovanni di Stefano, who finished it in 1488. See the colored illustration opposite the title page.

102 See Part II of this book.

103 Nock/Festugière, 1.v.

104 B.H. Stricker, *De brief van Aristeas; de hellenistische codificaties der praehelleense godsdiensten* (The Letter of Aristeas; The Hellenic Codices of the Pre-Hellenic Religions), p. 113.

105 See Patrick Boylan, *Thot, the Hermes of Egypt*, p. 150.

106 As is shown on the inner side of the walls of the temples attributed to him in the Open Air Museum in Karnak (at the old temple complex).

107 The division of the year into 12 Moon months of 30 days plus an extra 5 days is not exact. A Moon month consists of 29.53 days and not 30 days (Helmut Brunner, *Altägyptische Religion*, p. 16).

108 Plato, *Phaedreus*, pp. 274c–275b and *Philebus* pp. 18b–d, wherein he speaks about Theuth (Thoth). See also Festugière, *Révélation*, p. 69.

109 Jean-Pierre Mahé, *Hermès en Haute-Égypte*, (2 Vol.).

110 Fowden, *Egyptian Hermes*, pp. 24–25.

111 Casaubon; see pp. 258–259.

112 Roelof van den Broek, in his collection *Poimandres-Böhme*, p. 13.

113 Peter Kingsley, "An Introduction to the Hermetica: Approaching Ancient Esoteric Tradition," in *Poimandres-Böhme*, p. 21.

114 Kingsley, "Introduction to the Hermetica," p. 19.

115 Peter Kingsley, "Poimandres," in *Poimandres-Böhme*, pp.55–56.

116 Kingsley, "Poimandres," p. 70; see also in this collection "Introduction," p. 20. For reference to Casaubon, see pp. 258–259.

117 Iamblichus, *Over de Mysteriën*, 8, p. 4.

118 Kingsley, "Poimandres," p. 75.

Chapter 4

119 Wim H. Zitman, *Sterrenbeeld van Horus* (Constellation of Horus). See also primarily the very insightful website http://www.zitman.org.

120 *Asclepius*, see illustration on p. 77.

121 In the Jewish *merkawa* mysticism based on the vision of Ezechiël who observes the throne-wagon (*merkawa*) of the Unnameable, the soul of the Seer transverses the *heikalot*, heavenly palaces where guardians try to prevent their entrance (I. Gruenwald, *Apolcalyptic and Merkavah Mysteries* and N.A. van Uchelen, *Joodse Mystiek; Merkawa, tempel en troon* (Jewish Mysticism, merkawa, temple and throne).

122 See, among others, M.J. Vermaseren, *Mithras, de geheimzinnige god* (Mithras, The Secretive God).

123 See, for example, the Mandean hymn in the *Linker Ginza* 56, shown by J. Slavenburg, *De Geheime woorden*, p. 98.

124 Festugière, *Révélation*, p. 89.

125 How could this absurd doctrine arise, develop, spread, and force itself on superior intellects for century after century? There, in all its simplicity, is the historical problem that confronts us. Franz Cumont, *Astrology and Religion among the Greeks and Romans*, xiii.

126 *Asclepius* 24, here in the Nag Hammadi Codex, *NHG* I, p. 416.

127 R. Bauval and A. Gilbert, *The Orion Mystery* and Wim Zitman, *Sterrenbeeld van Horus* (Constellation of Horus), made clear on the website http://www.zitman.org.

128 Mustafa Gadalla, *Egyptische kosmos* (Egyptian Cosmos), p. 18.

129 R. van den Broek, *De taal van de Gnosis* (The Language of the Gnosis).

130 See the chapter "The Ring of Hermes."

131 See the chapter "The Mystery of the Self."

Chapter 5

132 Stobaeus, 29.

133 In modern astrology, one uses the word *decanate* (plural: *decanates*). I deliberately use *divine decanates* because it indicates that, in the first instance, we speak of "Gods" using decanates as their vehicle. The Latin *decanus* means "head of ten." Not only is each degree a deity (see further on), but one deity presides over each decimal.

134 Mercury was known among the Greeks as *ho astèr tou Ermou*, the star of Hermes. Venus was the star of Aphrodite. With the Chaldeans, Jupiter was considered the God Marmuk, Venus as Ishtar, Saturn as Nineb, Mercury as Nebo, and Mars as Nergal (Franz Cumont, *Astrologie et religion chez les Grecs et les Romains*, p. 15).

135 Wilhelm Gundel and Hans Georg Gundel, *Astrologumena. Die astrologische Literatur in der Antike und ihre Geschichte* (Astrologumena. The Astrological Literature in Antiquity and its History), cited hereafter as Gundel/Gundel.

136 According to most researchers, the astrological plaque in the dome of the chapel to Osiris in the temple of Hathor at Dendera dates to the 1st century a.d.

137 Gundel/Gundel, pp. 35–36; Festugière, *Révélation*, p. 77.

138 Gundel/Gundel, p. 28.

139 Gundel/Gundel, p. 254.

140 Gundel/Gundel, p. 4.

141 Festugière, *Révélation*, pp. 104–106.

142 Festugière, *Révélation*, p. 98.

143 Astronomical constellations and zodiacal signs do not have to appear together and in practice do not often do so. Moreover, all zodiacal signs have an equal size of 30 degrees, which is not so with astronomical phenomena.

144 Thereby also fixing the *imum coeli*—the opposite point.

145 Festugière, *Révélation*, pp. 77 and 117; Gundel/Gundel, pp. 36–40.

146 Gundel/Gundel, p. 15, and especially Wilhelm Gundel, *Dekanen und Dekansternbilder* (hereafter cited as Gundel, *Dekane*).

147 *Iatrology*, medical doctrine that was linked with astrology, practiced at first in a sacred surrounding, but later manifesting as "popular" medical practice.

148 Gundel/Gundel, p. 15.

149 Gundel/Gundel p. 16 and W. Gundel, *Neue astrologische Texte der Hermes Trismegistos. Funde und Forschungen auf dem Gebiet der antiken Astronomie und Astrologie* (hereafter cited as *Liber Hermetis*). For the concept of "Houses," see further on.

150 Referred to by Paulus of Alexandria, Gundel/Gundel, p. 16.

151 It is remarkable that, in the list of decanates—i.e. in *Liber Hermetis*—regions are included over which the specific astral God rules. In modern times, nations and cities are astrologically connected to zodiacal signs.

152 Firmicus Maternus, *Mathesis* 3.1.1.

153 Festugière, *Révélation*, p. 110.

154 Festugière, *Révélation*, p. 111.

155 Festugière, *Révélation*, p. 103.

156 Gundel/Gundel, p. 34.

157 Firmicus Maternus, *Mathesis* 3.1.1 and Gundel/Gundel p. 32.

158 Vettius Valens, *Anthologion* 6, p. 241 in Gundel/Gundel p. 30.

159 Gundel/Gundel, p. 30.

160 The so-called rule of Hermes has been used for centuries (even under Ptolemy) to correct a birth time. Without a proper birth time, no correct horoscope can be made, but time announcements often have been inaccurate up until our electronically controlled time. The rule probably was that the sign and degree in which the Moon stands at the time of conception becomes the Ascendant at birth for when the Moon waxed and the Descendant for when the Moon wanes.

161 See Gundel/Gundel, p. 33.

162 Festugière, *Révélation*, p. 122.

163 The work has been newly published in *Liber Hermetis*; see also Festugière, *Révélation*, pp. 120–121.

164 *Liber Hermetis*, p. 349 and Festugière, *Révélation*, p. 113.

165 The measurements of the printed pages are 21.5 x 28 cm, with type measuring 15.5 x 26.

166 Festugière, *Révélation*, p. 77 and Gundel, *Dekane*, Vol 1, "Die Altägyptische dekane."

167 O. Neugebauer and H.B. van Hoesen, *Greek Horoscopes*, p. 5.

168 Stobaeus 6.1–2; 7–8. This is the popular numbering as used by Scott and Nock/Festugière. G.R.S. Mead (*Thrice-Greatest Hermes*) numbers this excerpt 9 instead of 6.

169 *Liber Hermetis*, fol.1, r.I and II.

170 In modern astrology, the decanates are not much used anymore. The lists of rulers of the decanates differ. Often one proceeds from a succession of planets in the same group: In Aries—Mars, Sun, and Jupiter (being all rulers of fire signs), then Taurus—Venus, Mercury, and Saturn (all rulers of earth signs).

171 Ptolemy, *Tetrabiblos* 1, p. 12.

172 *Liber Hermetis*, fol. 34, v.I.

173 *Liber Hermetis*, fol. 14, r. I.

174 Data acquired from O. Neugebauer and H.B. van Hoesen, *Greek Horoscopes*, p. 8.

175 Thus the 6th House traditionally belongs to health and sickness (just as with Ptolemy), the 9th House to study and religion, and the 12th House to trials and isolation. Modern astrology makes use, in a general sense, of the classical meanings as we find them in the hermetic writings.

176 *Liber Hermetis*, fol. 28, v.II.

177 According to Firmicus Maternus, Hermes revealed to Asclepius the working of the 360 degrees in 12 books. He calls them *Myriogenesis* (*Mathesis* 5.1, p. 36).

178 *Liber Hermetis*, fol. 18, r.I.

179 *Liber Hermetis*, p. 136.

180 *Asclepius* 35; Mead, *Thrice Greatest Hermes*, Vol II, pp. 236–237.

181 *CH* 9.7, Mead, *Thrice Greatest Hermes*, Vol II, p. 85.

182 *CH* 3.3, Mead, *Thrice Greatest Hermes*, pp. 50–51.

183 *CH* 16.15, Mead, *Thrice Greatest Hermes*, p. 174.

184 Festugière, *Révélation*, p. 111.

Chapter 6

185 Gundel/Gundel, p.16.

186 "Holy" and "healing" stem from the same root. Healing is an "old-fashioned" word that indicates curing. It also holds the meaning of "to make whole again" within this context—the healers' goal.

187 Paul Lewis and Robert Margotta, *Ontwikkelingen van de Geneeskunde* (Developments of Medicine), p. 12.

188 Lewis and Margotta, *Ontwikkelingen van de Geneeskunde*, see *papyrus Ebers*.

189 Manetho calls him by his Greek name, Imouthes.

190 See especially J.B. Hurry, *Imhotep*. See also Ian Shaw and Paul Nicholson, *British Museum Dictionary of Ancient Egypt*, pp. 139–140.

191 How it was spread out in general during antiquity one can read in the fascinating study of Peter Kingsley, *In the Dark Places of Wisdom*.

192 *Sympatheia* means "connectedness."

193 *Liber Hermetis*, fol.2, r.l. The physical specifications have probably fallen away at the divine decanates of the first signs of the zodiac in this book. It is inconceivable that they were never in it.

194 August Bouché-Leclercq, *L'astrologie grecque*, p. 319.

195 Gundel, *Dekane*, p. 374 and Festugière, *Révélation*, p. 141.

196 See p. 130, the *Hermetic Definitions*, which states: "What is human? The immortal Idea of each human."

197 Meaning when planets are in a malevolent relationship to each other.

198 Citation by Festugière, *Révélation*, p. 130. See also Sebastian Gentile, *Il ritorno di Ermete*, pp. 136–138.

199 Citation by Gundel, *Dekane*, p. 374 and Festugière, *Révélation*, p. 141.

200 Festugière, *Révélation*, p. 139.

201 Festugière, *Révélation*, pp. 141–143 and Gundel, *Dekane*, pp. 374–379.

202 Festugière, *Révélation*, p. 144.

203 From Festugière, *Révélation*, p. 151, *Over de invloed van de planeten op planten* (About the Influence of Planets on Plants).

204 Festugière, *Révélation*, p. 154.

205 Gundel/Gundel, p. 19.

206 Gundel/Gundel, p. 20.

207 *Poimandres* (CH 1.26) shows the similarity to the ascending liberated soul meeting God.

208 The *Kyranides* shows up frequently in the legacy of Cardinal Bessarion (Vol. 2). A summarized history of its legend can be read in Antonio Rigo, "From Constantinople to the Library of Venice: The Hermetic Books of Late Byzantine Doctors, Astrologers and Magicians," in *Magia, Alchemia* I, pp. 77–85.

209 Festugière, *Révélation*, p. 205.

210 Festugière, *Hermetism et mystique païenne*, p. 32.

211 Festugière, *Révélation*, pp. 203–204.

212 I Festugière, *Révélation*, p. 207.

213 A part of literature describing the mystical-magical relationship between animals and plants.

214 Festugière, *Révélation*, p. 215.

215 Text and commentaries "*About the plant called peony*," see Festugière, *Hermètisme et mystique païenne*, pp. 181–202.

216 Somewhat compared to the description of God in the *Secret Book of Johannes* from the Nag Hammadi discovery (*NHG* I, pp. 93–129).

217 Text and commentaries *Over de plant, pioen genaamd* (About the plant called peony), see Festugière, *Hermètisme et mystique païenne*, pp. 181–202.

218 Or to Nero, we are not certain.

219 The text of Thessalon's letter is reproduced in Festugière, *Hermètisme et mystique païenne*, "L'expérience religious du médecin Thessalos," pp. 141–181.

220 Festugière, *Hermètisme et mystique païenne*, pp. 169–170.

Chapter 7

221 The *Korè Kosmou* by Stobaeus is shown as excerpt 23. *Korè* means "young girl" (sometimes "virgin")—also young woman, bride, daughter, little doll, pupil, apple of the eye. Together with Gilles Quispel, I chose the last translation: *Oogappel van de Wereld*. The Virgin of the World (=Isis) is used by the translator. (See Mead.)

222 Stobaeus 23.68.

223 *Papyri Graecae Magicae* (hereafter cited as PGM) I, p. 127.

224 Frits Graf, *Magic in the Ancient World*, I.

225 Dutch translation by M.A. Schwartz: *De gouden ezel* (The Golden Ass).

226 Xenophon, *Cyropaedia* 8.3, p. 11, as described by Fritz Graf, "Excluding the Charming: The Development of the Greek Concept of Magic," in Marvin Maeyer and Paul Mirecki, *Ancient Magic and Ritual Power*, pp. 29–43.

227 Among others, the classic Eliphas Levi, *Leer en Ritueel der Hogere Magie* (History of the Higher Magic) from 1856.

228 Check the Bibliography for literature accompanying this chapter.

229 These papyri date back to between the 2nd to 5th centuries b.c. The papyri (by the way, not only the papyri but also inscriptions in stone, bowls, pieces of ceramic, and tablets of gold, silver, lead, pewter, etc.) represent only a very small part of a great number of magical texts and magical incantations from antiquity. See in particular *Papyri Graecea Magicae. Die Griechischen Zauberpapyri*, 2 Volumes, K. Preisendanz et al (eds.), and *The Greek Magical Papyri in Translation (including the Demotic Spells)*, Hans Dieter Betz (ed.).

230 F.R. Dumas, *Histoire de la Magie*, 5.

231 Citation from the translation of J.F. Borghouts, *Ancient Egyptian Magical Texts*, 2.

232 Borghouts, *Ancient Egyptian Magical texts*, Citation 71, pp. 44–45.

233 Borghouts, *Ancient Egyptian Magical texts*, Citation 115, p. 80.

234 *Aan de afnemende maan* (To the Waning Moon), PGM IV, p. 2289.

235 *The Ring of Hermes*, PGM V, pp. 213 255.

236 H.S. Versnel, citation from "The Poetics of the the Magical Charm: An Essay on the Power of Words," in Paul Mirecki and Marvin Maeyer (eds.), *Magic and Ritual in the Ancient World*, p. 113.

237 *Hymne op Hermes*, PGM V, pp. 400–413 (see also PGM XVIIb).

238 *Liefdesspreuk van Astrapsoukos* (Love Spell of Astrapsoukos), PGM VIII, pp. 1–63. The title is rather misleading.

239 *Droomwens* (Dreamwish), PGM XII, p. 145. See also, for example, *Toverformule voor het zakendoen* (Magical Spell for Doing Business), PGM IV, p. 2359 et seq.

240 *Lamp-waarzeggerij* (Soothsaying by a lamp), PGM VII, pp. 540–578.

241 *Bezweringsformule voor verlegen mannen* (Soothsaying Spell for Shy Men), PGM V, pp. 304–369.

242 Plutarch, *Morelia*, (trans. F.C. Babbitt, Loeb Classical Library).

243 *Isis' klacht* (Isis' complaint), PGM IV, pp. 94–153.

244 *Geheime Boek van Johannes* (The Secret Book of John). A specific list of 365 gods or angels who are responsible for the physical body. See the list of angel names who, at the time of Creation, are assigned to a specific part of the body, NHG I, pp. 108–110.

245 R. Reitzenstein, *Poimandres Studien zur Griechisch-Ägyptischen und Frühchristischen Literatur*, p. 303.

246 Marvin W. Maeyer and Richard Smith (eds.), *Ancient Christian Magic. Coptic Texts of Ritual Power*, p. 85. See also Stephen D. Ricks, "The Magician as Outsider in the Hebrew Bible and the New Testament," in Marvin Maeyer and Paul Mirecki (eds.), *Ancient Magic and Ritual Power* I, pp. 131–145.

247 Maeyer and Mirecki (eds.), *Ancient Magic and Ritual Power* I, pp. 177–178.

248 Maeyer and Mirecki (eds.), *Ancient Magic and Ritual Power* I, pp. 206–207.

249 *PGM* I, pp. 1–42.

250 Reinhold Merkelbach, *Abrasax. Ausgewählte Papyri Religösen und Magischen Inhalts*, p. 138.

251 Maeyer and Smith, *Ancient Christian Magic*, p. 284. See also Marvin Meyer, "The Prayer of Mary Who Dissolves Claims in Coptic Magic and Religion," in Maeyer and Mirecki (eds.), *Magic and Ritual in the Ancient World*, pp. 407–416.

252 *NHG* II, p. 108.

253 See *CH* 16.2, in which is revealed that "the extraordinary sound and correct pronouncement of Egyptian words automatically gave the spoken word a magical power."

254 Peter Kingsley, *In The Dark Places of Wisdom*.

255 *NHG* I, pp. 400–401.

256 *NHG* I, p. 403.

Chapter 8

257 Festugière, *Révélation*, p. 215, which speaks about a "Pseudo-Science."

258 H.M.E. de Jong from Michael Maier's *Atalanta Fugiens; bronnen van een alchemistisch emblemenboek*, (Sources of an Alchemistical Emblem Book), p.15.

259 Plutarch, *About Isis and Osiris*, p. 364c (Loeb Library 82–83).

260 *CH* 1.26, G.R.S. Mead, *Thrice Greatest Hermes*, Vol II, p. 10.

261 See the last chapter of this book.

262 C.G. Jung, *Droom en Individuatie* and *Verlossing in de Alchemie* and, respectively, the 1st and 2nd part of *Psychologie und Alchemie*. Jung received from his friend Richard Wilhelm (well-known for his translation of the *I Ching*, which carried a foreword by Jung) a small book called the *Secret of the Golden Flower*. It contained an alchemical Taoist text of Chinese Yoga. Jung became fascinated by the similarities of the alchemistical symbology in it, which matched the result of his patients' symbolic language and drawings. This was the historical spiritual "link" he was looking for to support his theory of Archetypes in the collective unconsciousness of mankind. He proceeded to study alchemy very seriously and gave many lectures at the "Eranos Conferences."

263 Demokritos (Democritus) is the Greek philosopher who developed the so-called atom-theory in the 5th century b.c. In the context of science, the name "pseudo-Democritus" refers to Bolos of Mendes.

264 See, among others, Heinrich Wilhelm Schaefer, *Die Alchemie. Ihr ägyptisch-griechischer Ursprung und ihre weitere historic Entwicklung*, 2 et seq.

265 *35 kapittels van Zosimus aan Eusebia*, *Alch.Gr.* 175.12, citation by Festugière, *Révélation*, p. 245.

266 *Alch.Gr.* 188.7, *Révélation*, p. 242.

267 Olympiondorus, *Alch.Gr.* 84.12, Festugière, *Révélation*, pp. 252–253.

268 Anonymous, *Alch.Gr.* 408.4, Festugière, *Révélation*, p. 250.

269 *Aphorisms of Hermes*, *Alch.Gr.* 115.10, Festugière, *Révélation*, p. 242.

270 Olympiondorus, *Alch.Gr.* 84.12, Festugière, *Révélation*, pp. 252–253.

271 *The True Book of Sophè*, Festugière, *Révélation*, p. 261.

272 Festugière, *Révélation*, p. 228.

273 Citation by Garth Fowden, *The Egyptian Hermes*, p. 90.

274 We notice this very strongly with Trithmenius (see Part II of this book).

275 Manuel Bachmann and Thomas Hofmeier, *Geheimnisse der Alchemie*, pp. 11–12.

276 See, among others, Allison Coudert, *Alchemie* (Alchemy), p. 24.

277 See, among others, H.M.E. de Jong, *Atalanta Fugiens*, p. 41.

278 *Boek van het geheim der schepping*, in the translation by J. Ritman in "De Bibliotheca Philosophica Hermetica," in *Hermetisch Gnosis*, p. 650

653. See J. Ruska, *Tabula Smaragdina; ein Beitrag zur Geschichte der hermetischen Literatur* and Will-Erich Peuckert, *Pansophie*, p. 89.

279 A close parallel exists with the *Picatrix*, in which the Spirit of perfected Nature is revealed to Hermes. *Picatrix*, Volume III, Part 6, pp. 198–201 in H. Ritter and M. Plessner (eds.), *Picatrix. Das Ziel des Weisen von Pseudo-Magriti*. In this story, Hermes cannot see anything, and cannot light anything due to the wind. In a dream, a manifestation advises him to make a wind-cover. The answer to Hermes' question about his identity is answered by the beautiful manifestation: "I am your perfected Nature. If you desire to see me, call me by my name," p. 182.

280 Ruska, *Tabula Smaragdina*. He calls the *Tabula* not Greek, but Middle-Eastern (Syria, Iran), p. 37 et seq.

281 G. Quispel, "Gnosis and Alchemy: Tabula Smaragdina," in *Poimandres-Boehme*, p. 304.

282 E.J. Holmyard, *Alchemy*; Ruska, *Tabula Smaragdina*; G. Quispel, "Gnosis and Alchemy," p. 304.

283 Translation of Heleen M.E. de Jong in "Spirituele alchemia" (Spiritual Alchemy) in Marcel Messing (ed.), *Religie als levende ervaring* (Religion as a Living Experience), p. 173.

284 See, among others, Jacob Slavenburg, *Opus Posthuum, een onthullende blik op het vroegste christendom* (Opus Posthuum, a Revealing Glance of the Earliest Christianity).

285 CH 14.5.

286 See illustrationon on p. 408.

287 CH 16.5, G.R.S. Mead, *Thrice Greatest Hermes*, Vol. 2, pp. 171–172.

288 Mead, *Thrice Greatest Hermes*, "The Perfect Sermon" or "The Asclepius," II, 2, Vol. 2, p. 198.

289 Mead, *Thrice Greatest Hermes*, III, 1, p. 199.

Chapter 9

290 G.R.S. Mead, *Thrice Greatest Hermes*, XII, 3, pp. 209–210.

291 CH 16.2., Mead, *Thrice Greatest Hermes*, Vol. 2, p. 171.

292 Garth Fowden considers *Asclepius* to be a "compilation of material from various sources" (*The Egyptian Hermes*, p. 38). This is not certain, since the original text has perished and the Latin translation is not quite accurate and dated later, allowing interpolations to be inserted. Some extensive additions have been included.

293 Mead, *Thrice Greatest Hermes*, "The Perfect Sermon" or "The Asclepius," I Vol. 2, pp. 197–198.

294 Mead, *Thrice Greatest Hermes*, p. 237.

295 Mead, *Thrice Greatest Hermes*, p. 204.

296 Mead, *Thrice Greatest Hermes*, p. 241.

297 This is also the foundation of the theosophy in the *Corpus Hermeticum*, as in 10.14: "There are three levels of Being: 1. God... 2. The Cosmos... 3. Human."

298 Mead, *Thrice Greatest Hermes*, XL, 2.3, Vol. 2, p. 207.

299 *Hermetische Definities* (Hermetic Definitions), 7.7. See also Definition 1.1.

300 Mead, *Thrice Greatest Hermes*, XX, 2, Vol. 2, p. 217. See *Viennese Hermetic text*: "The only God has no name. Because being One, He-who-is is nameless (B 13-15)." Jean-Pierre Mahé, "Fragments Hermétiques dans les Papyri Vindobonenses Graecae 29456 r° and 29828 r°" in E. Lucchesis and H.D. Saffrey (eds.), *Mémorial André-Jean Festugière. Antiquité païenne et chréstienne*. pp. 51–65.

301 Mahé, "Fragments Hermétiques," XX, 2.3, Vol. 2, p. 217. See also J. Zandee, "Het Hermetisme en het oude Egypt" (Hermeticism and Ancient Egypt), in *Hermetische Gnosis* (Hermetic Gnosis), pp. 120–124.

302 Mahé, "Fragments Hermétiques," XXI, 1, Vol. 2, p. 217.

303 Mahé, "Fragments Hermétiques."

304 Mahé, "Fragments Hermétiques" (trans. G. Quispel); *Nag Hammadi Codex* VI, p. 65 (trans. J. Slavenburg and W.G. Glaudemans in *NHG* I, 414).

305 *Asclepius* 19.

306 *Asclepius*, 4.

307 CH 1.26, (trans. "God within himself, not God himself.")

308 *Asclepius* 23. "Yes, indeed, Asclepius, human is greater than all the Gods and fills us with awe…"

309 *Asclepius*, 22.

310 *CH* 1.12, Mead, *Thrice Greatest Hermes*, Vol II, p. 5.

311 *Hermetic Definitions* 7.1.

312 "Jodendom en gnostiek" (Judaism and Gnosticism), in R. van den Broek, *De taal van de Gnosis. Gnostische teksten uit Nag Hammadi* (The Language of Gnosis. Gnostic texts from Nag Hammadi Codex), pp. 166–177.

313 See p. 79.

314 *Asclepius* 6.

315 *Asclepius*, 29.

Chapter 10

316 Giovanni Corsi wrote this in *Vita Marsilii Ficini* (6). The *Vita* in Latin has been absorbed in total in the dissertation of Henri Johan Hak called *Marsilio Ficino*, pp. 178–186. It seems strange that Ficino thanks Cosimo in a letter dated September 4, 1462 for the gift of the villa at Carregi (see Hask, p. 40, fn 1), but this is just about the time Ficino started the translation of the *Corpus*. The transaction of house ownership, however, is dated April 18 1463, immediately after the completion of the translation (Sebastiano Gentile, "Ficino ed Ermete," in *Il ritorno di Ermete*, p. 27). Would Cosimo have promised Ficino the villa before the *Corpus*' translation was done—something he so eagerly anticipated—and handed it over to him when it was finished? (He had two short years to live.)

317 Stobaeus 23.8.

318 B.H. Stricker, *De brief van Aristeas; de hellenistische codificaties der praehelleense godsdiensten* (The Letter of Aristeas; The Hellenic Codices of the Pre-Hellenic Religions), p. 113.

319 In *Anthologium* (Anthologies), Johannes Stobaeus (5th century a.d.) records some citations from hermetic writings, such as tracts 2, 4, and 10 of the *Corpus Hermeticum*, *Asclepius* 3 and 29, and many others that we can study only due to his collection. In modern translations, the excerpts are divided from 1 to 11 (Hermes to Tat); 12 to 17 (Hermes to Ammon); 18 to 22 (Hermes to an unknown pupil); and 23 to 26 (Isis to Horus, with the *Korè Kosmou* (23), The Virgin of the World). The last three excerpts—2, 28, and 29—are small fragments from citations or scripts of Hermes' writings.

320 See, among others, J-P. Mahé, "The way to immortality," in *Hermetical Gnosis*, pp. 51–52.

321 Symphorien Champier, *Liber de quadruplici vita*, 1507, with the Latin translation of the *Definitiones Asclepius*.

322 See, among others, Brian P. Copenhaver, *Hermetica*, xlix et seq. and Walter Scott, *Hermetica*, pp. 33–35.

323 G. Quispel describes the 18th treatise as being "of real spiritual historical value," since it announces that Love moves the Universe. He connects it with John's saying: "God is Love," *Corpus Hermeticum*, p. 197.

324 See Jacob Slavenburg, "Ficino en Hermes," in Michael Shepherd (ed.), *Marsilio Ficino. Een universeel mens* (Marsilio Ficino. A Universal Human), pp. 153–170.

325 Peter Kingsley, "Poimandres: The Etymology of the Name and the Origins of the Hermetica," in *Poimandres-Böhme*, pp. 41–77.

326 Kingsley, "Poimandres," primarily the 2nd treatise, *A general conversation of Hermes with Asclepius*.

327 For this material, see primarily Jacob Slavenburg, *De geheime woorden. Een ontdekkingstocht door vijfentwintig eeuwen gnosis* (The Secret Words. A Journey of Discovery of Twenty-Five Centuries of Gnosis).

328 See, for instance, the previous chapter: "God is capable of both."

329 *Hermetische Definities* (Hermetic Definitions), 9.4.

330 *Evangelie van Thomas* (Gospel of Thomas), logio 67.

331 *CH* 5.2.

332 Alexandrian Libraries, R. van den Broek, *Bibliotheken en geleerden in de Oudheid* (Libraries and Scholars in Antiquity).

333 Eusebius, *Kerkgeschiedenis* (Church History), 5.10, pp. 1–4.

334 Ulrich Neymeyr, *Die Christlichen Lehrer in zweiten Jahrhundert*, (The Christian Teachers in the Year 200), pp. 40–45.

335 Clemens of Alexandria, *Stromateis* 1.71.6.

336 Roelof van den Broek, "Hermes en zijn gemeente in Alexandrië" (Hermes and his Community in Alexandria), in *Hermetische Gnosis* (Hermetic Gnosis), pp. 9–27.

337 H.J. Spierenburg, *De Philonische Geheime Leer. De Kaballa of Philo of Alexandrië* (The Secret Doctrine of Philo. The Kabala of Philo of Alexandria).

338 Spierenburg, *De Philonische Geheime Leer*, pp. 123–128.

339 van den Broek, "Hermes en zijn gemeente in Alexandrië" (Hermes and his Community in Alexandria), in *Hermetische Gnosis*, p.10.

340 Bentley Layton, *The Gnostic Scriptures*, p. 143.

341 *Asclepius* 24.

342 Konrad Dietzfelbinger, *Mysteriescholen. An het oude Egypte via het oerchristendom tot aan de rozenkruiser in deze tijd* (Mystery Schools. from Ancient Egypt via Primeval Christianity to the Rosicrucians of our Time).

343 van den Broek, "Hermes en zijn gemeente in Alexandrië," in *Hermetische Gnosis*, pp. 9–27, and also "Religious Practices in the Hermetic 'Lodge': New Light from Nag Hammadi" in *Poimandres-Böhme*, pp. 77–97.

344 Specifically treatise 13, but also 1 and 11, in which the Spirit speaks to Hermes directly.

345 *CH* 10.1, 10.7, and 13.1.

346 Stobaeus 3 (Scott's 4a.1) and 6.1.

347 Fragment B, in the 10th treatise: "*...In the General Teachings, O' Tat, I often spoke of...*" (Greek text of this fragment: 54).

348 See p. 40.

349 Clemens of Alexandria, *Stromateis* 6.4, pp. 35–37.

350 CH 16.1, G.R.S. Mead, *Thrice Greatest Hermes*, Vol II, p. 170.

351 *Eighth and Ninth Heavenly Sphere*, NHG I, p. 399.

352 NHG I, pp. 399–400.

353 NHG I, p. 403.

354 NHG I, p. 404.

355 Modern theories can hardly hold ground after the discovery of *The Treatise of the Eighth and Ninth Heavenly Sphere* in the Nag Hammadi manuscripts. This pertains to the hermetical mysteries being *Lesser Mysteries* or "reading mysteries" (Reitzenstein, *Die hellenistische Mysterienreligionen nach ihren Grundgedanken und Wirkingen*, pp. 51 and 61; K.W. Tröger, *Mysterienglaube und Gnosis in Corpus Hermeticum* XIII, pp. 52–53 and 167).

356 See, among others, Jacob Slavenburg, *Mystiek en Spiritualiteit; een reis door het tijdloze* (Mysticism and Spirituality; A Journey through Timelessness).

357 Garth Fowden, *The Egyptian Hermes*, p. 160.

358 CH 9.1, Mead, *Thrice Greatest Hermes*, Vol II, p. 80.

359 CH 10.1, Mead, *Thrice Greatest Hermes*, p. 91.

360 *Eighth and Ninth Heavenly Sphere.*

361 Jacob Slavenburg, *Opus Posthuum. Een onthullende blik op het vroegste Christendom (30–70 b.c.)* (Opus Posthume. A revealing glance at earliest Christianity 30–70 b.c.). Roelof van den Broek confirms sacred meals were very common in antiquity. His vision on two different meals is interesting—the communal and the private one, taken immediately after initiation, just as Justinus Martyr and Apuleius described independently ("Hermes and His Community in Alexandria" in *Hermetic Gnosis*, p. 19).

362 This was also happening in the Jewish *merkawa* mysticism. N.A. van Uchelen, *Joodse Mystiek, Merkawa, tempel en troon*, (Jewish Mysticism, Temple and Throne).

363 Roelof van den Broek, "Religious Practices in the Hermetic 'Lodge'" in *Poimandres-Böhme*, pp. 77–97.

Chapter 11

364 Clement Salaman, Dorine van Oyen, and William D. Wharton, "The Way of Hermes," *Corpus Hermeticum* (see CH 1.1–7) *Nous* is used, translated by scientists mostly as "spirit" and also sometimes as "consciousness." In Latin, we recognize therefore *spiritus, human,* and *daemon*—in English, "spirit," "mind," and "ghost." The translators left *Nous* untranslated in the above. In this fragment, instead of the translation of "the Word" at some places, the original *Logos* has been brought back. See also for the "issue *Nous*" p. 161.

365 CH 1.27, G.R.S. Mead, *Thrice Greatest Hermes*, Vol II, p. 10.

366 In 1906, Mead, a theosophist within the circle of H.P. Blavatsky, also made a magnificent translation of the Hermetic writings (*Thrice-Greatest Hermes*). A separate small bundle called *The Hymns of Hermes* appeared in 1907.

367 CH 2.14, Mead, *Thrice Greatest Hermes*, Vol II, p. 44.

368 *Asclepius* 34.

369 Stobaeus 28.

370 CH 11.19, 20, Mead, *Thrice Greatest Hermes*, Vol II, pp. 118–119.

371 CH 10.4, Mead, *Thrice Greatest Hermes*, p. 92.

372 CH 5.2, Mead, *Thrice Greatest Hermes*, p. 66.

373 CH 11.22, Mead, *Thrice Greatest Hermes*, p. 119.

374 CH 12.21–22, Mead, *Thrice Greatest Hermes*, pp. 133–134.

375 CH 11.2, 15–16, Mead, *Thrice Greatest Hermes*, pp. 112, 117.

376 *Hermetic Definitions* 3.1.

377 See, among others, J. Slavenburg, *Een sleutel tot gnosis. Inzicht in de betekenis van de Nag Hammadi-vondst voor de mens van nu* (Key To Gnosis. Insight in the Importance of the Nag Hammadi Codex Discovery for the Human of Today).

378 As in CH 10.12.

379 See, for instance, the 7th treatise of the *Corpus Hermeticum*.

380 Read on for an outline on "Human."

381 Specifically in the Valentinian writings of the *Gospel of Phillipus* and Jacob Slavenburg, *De geheime woorden* (The Secret Words).

382 See, for instance, CH 7.

383 "Everything emanates from the One and returns to the One. No words exist to define its Being, nor can one place it anywhere. As soon as one describes it, one is facing a predicament for it stops being One..." Thus says Rein Ferweda in his introduction of the translation of Plotinus' *Enneads* (20). During the 1st century b.c., Eudorus of Alexandria had stated that the One emanates matter, in comparison to Plato, who puts both independently next to each other.

384 CH 1.12–14, Mead, *Thrice Greatest Hermes*, Vol II, pp. 5–6.

385 *CH* 10.22, Mead, *Thrice Greatest Hermes*, Vol II, p. 111.

386 *Asclepius* 12: "...It's so delightful to rejoice its richness..."

387 Stobaeus 5.2. See also *Asclepius* 39, in which *Heimarmenè* (Fate) is named the second God.

388 Stobaeus 23.27–29.

389 *CH* 10.14: "and so the Cosmos becomes the Son of God and Human the Son of the World, so to speak God's grandchild."

390 *CH* 12.2–3, Mead, *Thrice Greatest Hermes*, Vol II, pp. 127–128.

391 *CH* 12.4, Mead, *Thrice Greatest Hermes*, p. 128.

392 *CH* 16.10, 13–14, Mead, *Thrice Greatest Hermes*, pp. 173–174.

393 *CH* 12.23, Mead, *Thrice Greatest Hermes*, p. 134.

Chapter 12

394 *Asclepius* 16.

395 *CH* 18.16, G.R.S. Mead, *Thrice Greatest Hermes*, Vol II, pp. 212–213.

396 *Hermetic Definitions* 10.4.

397 *CH* 4.8, Mead, *Thrice Greatest Hermes*, Vol II, p. 58.

398 *CH* 14.9.

399 *CH* 14.7, Mead, *Thrice Greatest Hermes*, Vol II, p. 166.

400 *CH* 1.27, Mead, *Thrice Greatest Hermes*, p. 11. See also 7.1: "Whither stumble ye, sots, who have sopped up the wine of ignorance unmixed, and can so far not carry it that ye already even spew it forth?"

401 *CH* 12.11, Mead, *Thrice Greatest Hermes*, Vol II, p. 130.

402 *CH* 18.22, Mead, *Thrice Greatest Hermes*, p. 219.

403 *CH* 4.4, Mead, *Thrice Greatest Hermes*, p. 56.

404 *Asclepius* 27.4, Mead, *Thrice Greatest Hermes*, Vol II, p. 226.

405 *CH* 8.1, Mead, *Thrice Greatest Hermes*, Vol II, p. 80.

406 *CH* 11.14, Mead, *Thrice Greatest Hermes*, p. 117.

407 *CH* 12.15, Mead, *Thrice Greatest Hermes*, pp. 131–132.

408 See fn. 364.

409 See G.M.A. Grube, *Plato's Thought*. In chapter 4, "The Nature of the Soul" (pp. 120–150), he describes (based on text fragments) the development of Plato's thoughts regarding the three-fold soul, which are identical to Aristotle's teachings. Origines divides the soul into *Nous* (higher principle of understanding), *kardia* (the heart as guiding principle of the soul), and *sars* (the embodiment of the soul). Origines also recognizes the *pneuma* (spirit) as the highest part of the ladder, and the *soma* (body) as the lowest.

410 See fn. 364.

411 CH 10.17, Mead, *Thrice Greatest Hermes*, Vol II, pp. 96–97.

412 *Hermetic Definitions* 7.4.

413 CH 12.2, Mead, *Thrice Greatest Hermes*, Vol II, p. 127.

414 CH 12.4, Mead, *Thrice Greatest Hermes*, p. 128.

415 *Asclepius* 25.2, Mead, *Thrice Greatest Hermes*, Vol II, p. 223.

416 CH 12.8, Mead, *Thrice Greatest Hermes*, Vol II, p. ?.

417 CH 10.7, Mead, *Thrice Greatest Hermes*, p. 93.

418 Stobaeus 23.31–37.

419 NHG II (Dutch translation), pp. 397–411.

420 CH 10.15, Mead, *Thrice Greatest Hermes*, Vol II, p. 96.

421 Stobaeus 4.8 (with Fustugière; with Scott, 3.5).

422 Stobaeus 24.10.

Chapter 13

423 A.P. Sinnett, *Esoteric Buddhism*.

424 Mead's biographical data is scarce. See J. Slavenburg, "Hermes op het breukvlak van twee eeuwen" (Hermes on the dividing line of two centuries), in *Hermetische Gnosis*, pp. 580–597.

425 Part II of this book discusses the Theosophical Movement.

426 G.R.S. Mead, *Thrice-Greatest Hermes*, Vol. I, Prolegomena, xvi and p. 481; Vol. II, excerpts and fragments, xii and p. 371, Index; Vol. III, Sermons, xi and p. 403. I use the 1992 edition that combines the 3 parts in one volume.

427 Marion Meade, *Madame Blavatsky; The Woman behind the Myth*, p. 458.

428 *Asclepius* 12.1, Mead, *Thrice Greatest Hermes*, Vol II, p. 209.

429 CH 4.8, Mead, *Thrice Greatest Hermes*, Vol II, p. 58.

430 In Stobaeus, *Korè Kosmou*, 23.9, reincarnation into an animal is discussed if the human has lived an animalistic life. It is difficult to determine if this is meant literally or metaphorically (trans: "After disintegration of the body all its atoms (not the soul) will disperse to the appropriate kingdoms").

431 CH 10.19–20, Mead, *Thrice Greatest Hermes*, Vol II, pp. 97–98.

432 Specifically in Stobaeus, we find the hermetic opinion that not every soul has consciousness—that is, if Consciousness stands for spiritual knowledge or self-consciousness. This looks like the ideas in some gnostic writings saying that not all souls have *gnosis*, meaning divine insight or self-knowledge). This looks very much like the doctrine of predestination. In most cases, however, it means "self-consciousnes" and *gnosis* is ignored by some people or has not been developed as yet.

433 Stobaeus 23.40.

434 *Asclepius* 28.3, Mead, *Thrice Greatest Hermes*, Vol II, p. 283.

435 *Asclepius* 29.1–2, Mead, *Thrice Greatest Hermes*, pp. 228–229.

436 *Asclepius*, 28 and 29, Mead, *Thrice Greatest Hermes*.

437 As, for instance, in the *NHG* I: *Openbaring van Paulus* (Revelation of Paul), pp. 254–257.

438 *Hermetic Definitions* 6.3.

439 *CH* 13.13, Mead, *Thrice Greatest Hermes*, Vol II, p. 143.

440 *CH* 13.14, Mead, *Thrice Greatest Hermes*, p. 144.

441 See previous chapter.

442 *Asclepius* 11.3, Mead, *Thrice Greatest Hermes*, Vol II, p. 208.

443 Stobaeus 4a, 5–8. Although one speaks first of all about various kinds of souls, ultimately it seems to give an impression of various differences within one soul.

444 *CH* 16.15, Mead, *Thrice Greatest Hermes*, Vol II, pp. 174–175.

445 *CH* 12.13, Mead, *Thrice Greatest Hermes*, p. 131.

446 *CH* 12.14, Mead, *Thrice Greatest Hermes*, p. 131.

447 *CH* 10.13, Mead, *Thrice Greatest Hermes*, p. 95.

448 As translated by G. Quispel, also in the same passage of the *Corpus Hermeticum*.

449 *CH* 1.26, 10.13, 16, 17, p. 10 and *Asclepius* 28.1, p. 227.

450 Sinnett, *Esoteric Buddhism*, p.19.

Chapter 14

451 *CH* 1.24–26, G.R.S. Mead, *Thrice Greatest Hermes*, Vol II, pp. 9–10.

452 *CH* 13.7, Mead, *Thrice Greatest Hermes*, p. 141.

453 Pierre Courcelle, *Connais-toi toi-même. De Socrate à St. Bernard* (Know Yourself. From Socrates to St. Bernard). Contains a great source pertaining to self-knowledge.

454 *Hermetic Definitions* 9.4.

455 *Evangelie van Thomas* (Gospel of Thomas), p. 67,

456 NHG I, *Lessen van Sylvanus* (Lessons of Sylvanus), p. 326.

457 NHG I, *Boek van Thomas de Kampvechter* (Book of Thomas, The Camp Fighter), p. 219.

458 *Pseudo-Clementines*, *Homiliae* 3.56. See also *Recognitiones* 1.39.

459 *CH* 1.19, Mead, *Thrice Greatest Hermes*, Vol II, p. 99.

460 *CH* 1.21, Mead, *Thrice Greatest Hermes*, p. 8.

461 A handful of characteristics like the ones found in the *Hermetica*.

462 The word "hating" is really a short translation of the Greek word *miseoo*. In "Miseoo" in *Theologogisches Wörterbuch zum Neuen Testament* (Theological

Dictionary of the New Testament), IV, pp. 689 and 694, O. Michel speaks of "Das Hassen in der Nachfolgeforderung: Es handelt sich nicht um Hass im psychologist Sinn, sondern um bewusste Absage, Abkehr und Ablehung..., ähnlich dem Sprachgebrauch der atlichen Weisheidsliteratur."

463 CH 4.6, Mead, *Thrice Greatest Hermes*, Vol II, p. 57.

464 The image of meeting one's own Self we find regularly in archaic antiquity. The Mandeans recite in a hymn: "I am going to meet my own likeness. He caresses me and kisses me as if I had returned from far away lands." (Check Kurt Rudolph about the Mandeans in *Die Gnosis, Wesen und Geschichte einer spätantiken Religion*). In the "Song of the Pearl" in *Handelingen van Thomas* (Discourses of Thomas), 112, the meeting with the Self is portrayed as an encounter with the "Cloth." Mani calls the Self his twin (Soul): "I recognized him and saw that it was my own Self" (*Keulse Mani Codex* (Cologne's Mani Codex)).

465 CH 10.24, Mead, *Thrice Greatest Hermes*, Vol II, p. 99.

466 K.H.E. de Jong, *De Griekse Mysteriën* (The Greek Mysteries), p. 7.

467 NHG I, *Eighth and Ninth Heavenly Sphere*, pp. 399–405.

468 CH 13.15, Mead, *Thrice Greatest Hermes*, Vol II, p. 114.

469 NHG I, *Eighth and Ninth Heavenly Sphere*, pp. 400–401.

470 NHG I, p. 401.

471 CH 13.3, Mead, *Thrice Greatest Hermes*, Vol II, p. 140.

472 CH 13.11, Mead, *Thrice Greatest Hermes*, p. 143.

473 NHG I, *Eighth and Ninth Heavenly Sphere*, pp. 401–402.

474 CH 13.8-9, Mead, *Thrice Greatest Hermes*, Vol II, p. 142.

475 CH 4.11, Mead, *Thrice Greatest Hermes*, p. 59.

476 NHG I, *Eighth and Ninth Heavenly Sphere*, pp. 402–403.

477 Dydimus, the *Trinitate*, 757b: "of the third teaching of Hermes to Asclepius."

478 CH 13.13, Mead, *Thrice Greatest Hermes*, Vol II, p. 143.

479 Jesus also spoke "Secret Words" along with public teachings. J. Slavenburg, *De "logische Jesus"* and *Opus Posthuum* (The "Logical" Jesus and Opus Posthuum).

480 Garth Fowden, *The Egyptian Hermes*, p. 215: "At the heart it was a spiritual way, the way of hermetical *gnosis*."

481 Stobaeus 16.6.

482 Stobaeus, 10.3.

Interlog

483 Citation from *The Large Letter About the Spheres of Hermes of Dendera*, reproduced by Risala al Falakiya al-kubra.

Chapter 15

484 See p. 118.

485 A remarkable fact is that we know of many prominent female alchemists of this time, the most well-known being Maria the Jewess and Cleopatra (see also Jack Lindsay, *The Origins of Alchemy in Graeco-Roman Egypt*, especially pp. 240–278).

486 Marie-Louise von Franz, *Alchemy, an Introduction to her Symbology and Psychology*, pp. 20 and 199.

487 Garth Fowden, *The Egyptian Hermes*, p. 125.

488 Citation from Marcellin Berthelot and Charles-Émile Ruelle, *Collection des Anciens Alchimistis Grecs*, translated here by H.M.E de Jong in *Atalanta Fugiens*.

489 Carl Gustav Jung, Collected Works, Vol. XIII, *Alchemical Studies*, pp. 57–60.

490 *CH* 4.5–6, G.R.S. Mead, *Thrice Greatest Hermes*, Vol II, p. 57.

491 Fowden, *Egyptian Hermes*, p. 121. "The man of copper gives and the moist stone receives; the metal gives and the plant receives; the stars give and the flowers receive; the Heaven gives and the Earth receives; the thunderbolts give the fire which shoots from them. Everything is entwined together and separated, and all is blended together and dissolved, everything is moistened and everything is dried, and things carry flowers and blossom in the altar having the form of a bowl." (This is a citation from Allison Coudert: *Alchemy; the Philosopher's Stone*, translated by H.K. Engelmoer, pp. 96–97).

492 K.H.E. de Jong, *De Griekse Mysteriën* (The Greek Mysteries), p. 20.

493 *Regarding apparatus and ovens; authentic commentaries on the letter Omega*, pp. 3–5. This is what the Stoics called *apatheia* or, as the Gnostic Theodotus (2nd century b.c.) expressed it: "By initiation you are not prone to Fate, the Stars have no more influence on you." (Clemens of Alexandria, *Excerpta ex Theodoto*, 87.1).

494 Zosimus, *Final Liberation* and Fowden, *Egyptian Hermes*, pp. 122–123.

495 Lindsay, *Origins of Alchemy*, p. 324.

496 Probably 28 in total.

497 *Regarding apparatus and ovens*, 1. This treatise is referenced by Berthelot (III, XLIX. pp. 4–12), by Scott-Ferguson (*Hermetica* IV, pp. 104–112), by Ruska (*Tabula Smaragdina*, pp. 24–31), and by Howard M. Jackson (*Zosimus of panoplies on the Letter Omega*). This edition is not complete. A wonderful edition (with Greek text, French translation and commentary, and black-and-white and color pictures of the manuscript) is found in the catalog *Magia, Alchimia: Jean Letrouit, "Hermétime et alchimie: contribution à l'étude du Marcianus graecus* 299, pp. 85–113. Also see the commentary of part of the text by C.G. Jung, *Liberation in the Alchemy* (Vol. II of *Psychology and Alchemy*), pp. 132–138.

498 *Regarding apparatus and ovens*, 5 (Jackson 7).

499 *Regarding apparatus and ovens*, 5 (Jackson 13).

500 *Regarding apparatus and ovens*, 5 (according to the index by Jean Detroit). This paragraph and the following are not shown anymore by Jackson, who considered it not to be included in his work (Jackson 7).

501 *Regarding apparatus and ovens*, 16.

502 *Regarding apparatus and ovens*, 16. Allison Coudert calls this numerical series the "crab-formula" and deciphers it (*Alchemie*, p. 63).

503 Citation from Berthelot and Ruelle, *Anciens Alchimistis Grecs*, translated here by H.M.E de Jong, *Atalanta Fugiens*, p. 20. See the illustration on p. 119.

504 Probably out of fear that alchemists would make Egypt rich and the nation would revolt against the Romans.

505 J. Slavenburg, *De oerknal van het Christendom. Veelkleurig perspectief van een impuls* (The Big Bang of Christianity. Multicoloured perspective of an impulse). It points out the definite decree of the *Canon* of the New Testament in the 39th Easter proclamation of Athanasius in 367 b.c.

506 Roelof van de Broek, *Bibliotheken en geleerden in de Oudheid* (Libraries and Scholars in Antiquity).

507 *Asclepius* 24, Mead, *Thrice Greatest Hermes*, Vol II, pp. 221–222.

Chapter 16

508 A.E.G. van der Meer, *The Harran of the Sabians in the first Millennium a.d.; Cradle of a Hermetic Tradition?*

509 In present-day Turkey, close to the Syrian border.

510 F. Rosenthal, *Das Fortleben der Antike im Islam*, p. 25; E.J. Holmyard, *Alchemy*.

511 M. Bachmann, T. Hofmeier, *Hermes-Vater der Alchemie* in M. Bachmann and T. Hofmeier, *Geheimnisse der Alchemie*, p. 24: *Die Herkunft Hermes*, p. 25. For a summary of the Arab *Hermetica*, see Festugiére, *Révélation I*; M.L. Massignon, *Astrologie et les Sciences Occultes, avec un appendice sur l'Hermétisme Arabe*, "Appendix III: Inventaire de la Littérature Hermétique Arabe," pp. 384–400; F. Sezgin, *Geschichte des Arabischen Schrifttums*, Vol. IV, pp. 38–41, which gives a list of alchemical, astronomical, astrological, and magical-hermetical texts); M. Ullman, *Die Natur- und Geheimwissenschaften im Islam*, which gives a summmary of hermetic Arab writings about alchemy, astrology, and magic).

512 The scientific research is focussed on certain issues, of which the most important is: Did the Arabs strictly copy the texts or did they compose them? See fn. 512 and the historical summary by F. Sezgin, pp. 31–38. The greatest problem when one tries to retrace the Arabic fragments to Greek sources is that most researchers know Greek but not Arabic. A second problem is that few archaic Greek sources are available; we know that the Greek *Hermetica* is

much more elaborate than the current available texts (i.e. Clemens of Alexandria speaks about 42 Books). Sezgin (p. 38) maintains that the largest part of Arabian alchemical texts attributed to Hermes belong to the era of Zosimus. Most of them, however, are proven copies and adaptions of Greek originals. Szegin (p. 35, fn. 4) refers to literature that indicates that alchemical and astrological Arabian books can be traced directly to the *Catalogus codicum astrologorum Graecorum* (compare to Ullman, p. 148). While opinions still differ, we no longer speak with contempt about the Arabian *Hermetica* being "corrupt"; those days are past.

513 As Part I shows, this author does not make any distinction between the so-called "technical" and "philosophical" *Hermetica*. The indication here is strictly a distinction.

514 Bachmann and Hofmeier, *Geheimnisse der Alchemie*, p. 25.

515 Ullman, *Die Natur- und Geheimwissenschaften im Islam* p. 370.

516 *Risala al Falakiya al-kubra*. Citation by Ullman, *Die Natur- und Geheimwissenschaften im Islam*, p. 166 (fn. 4 refers to the manuscripts).

517 See further on in this chapter.

518 Manetho (Part I of this book); also *Asclepius* 37 and Cicero, *De natura decorum*, 3.56.

519 Abu ma' Shar's report arrived in several Latin translations in the West, influencing other writings like the *Summa philosophiae* of Robert Grosseteste. The written tradition in the Hebrew literature has been investigated by M. Plessner, *Studia Islamica* 2.53 f. (see summary in Plessner, *Encyclopaedia Islamica*, p. 464 and M. Bachmann and Th. Hofmeier, *Geheimnisse der Alchemie*, p. 25). Part of the report, Abu ma'Shar wrote around 845 a.d. has been included in the sources describing the primordial beginning of humanity in the *Fihrist* of Ibn an-Nadim. Ullmann (*Die Natur- und Geheimwissenschaften im Islam*, p. 372) suggests the original text was lost, but that since the text was so thoroughly quoted by others, reconstruction of it is possible. Ullman follows up that claim by showing five resources. M. Plessner indicates these as Ibn Juljul, Said al Andalus, Ibn al-Kift, and Ibn Abi Usaybi'a in "Hirmis," *Encyclopedis Islamica* (2nd edition), Vol. 3, pp. 463. For additional information, see M. Plessner, "Hermes Trismegistus and the Arab Science," *Studia Islamica* 2 (1954), pp. 45–49.

520 E.J. Holmyard, *Alchemy*, p. 100. Stories are written about this first Hermes having lived for a long time with Adam. (C. Huart (ed. and trans.), *Al-Maqdisi*, *The Book of Creation and History*, *Le livre de la création et de l'histoire*, Vol. II, pp. 83 and 137. See also Scott-Ferguson, *Hermetica* IV, pp. 251).

521 M. Plessner, *Studia Islamica*, 2, p. 56; M. Ullman, *Die Natur- und Geheimwissenschaften im Islam*, fn. 1.

522 M. Ullman, *Die Natur- und Geheimwissenschaften im Islam*, p. 373.

523 Ibn an-Nadim started his *Fihrist* with this version of the archaic history of humanity with the second Babylonian Hermes. He wrote it in 987–988 and

died in 995 a.d. It is the book of the catalog, or rather the first Arabian encyclopaedia (*The Fihrist of Al-Nadim, a tenth century survey of Muslim culture*, B. Dodge (ed. and trans.), Vol. 1 and 2). One notices that an-Nadim describes several colorful Hermes, showing him in various time periods and under different disguises.

524 M. Ullman, *Die Natur- und Geheimwissenschaften im Islam*, p. 373.

525 Meaning also Thrice (Thrice-Greatest).

526 Bachmann and Hofmeier, *Geheimnisse der Alchemie*, p. 25.

527 From now on called *Kitab al-Fihrist*.

528 "We already mentioned him. His books regarding the Stars were first: *The Width of the Key to the Stars* and secondly *The Length of the Key to the Stars*" (*Fihrist*, Book 7, Vol. II).

529 Al- Nadim, *Kitab al-Fihrist*, Book 7, Vol. III.

530 Al- Nadim, *Kitab al-Fihrist*, Book 8, Vol. II, p. 733. He mentions *The books of Hermes about incantations, special possessions and charms* and *The book of Hermes regarding resuscitation, amulets and magical spells*.

531 Al- Nadim, *Kitab al-Fihrist*, Book 10, Vol. II, 353.19 and introduction pp. 843–844. It contains many alchemistic writings of Hermes: *The Book of Hermes to his son about the Art (Alchemy), Running Gold (mercury); To Tat about the Art; Making of knots; Secrets; Al-Haritus; Al-Malitus (possessed by demons); Al-Astmakhus (about opening the stomach); Al-Sulimatis; for Armenius, the pupil of Hermes; for Biladus, the pupil of Hermes; about the vision of Hermes; Al-Arkhayqi (probably derived from the Greek word archaikè, origin, as 'In the Beginning…'*; and *for Damanus by Hermes*, (*Fihrist*, Book 10, Vol. 2, pp. 353, 9–13).

532 In Jean Letrouit, *Magia, Alchimia*, fn. 497.

533 E.E. Stapleton, G.L. Lewis, and F. Sherwood Taylor, "The sayings of Hermes quoted in the *Mã'Al-Waraqi* by Ibn Umail," in *Ambix; Being the journal of the Society for the Study of Alchemy and Early Chemistry*, Vol. III, April 1949, no. 3 and 4, pp. 69–91.

534 J. Slavenburg, *Opus Posthuum*.

535 "...First was the saying, then came the story," G. Quispel in "Hermes Trismegistus and the Origins of Gnosticism," in *Vigilae Christianae* 46 (1922), Leiden, pp. 1–19.

536 E.E. Stapleton, "Sayings of Hermes," p. 70.

537 E.E. Stapleton, "Sayings of Hermes," pp. 70–71; see also K. Garbers and J. Weyer (eds.), *Quellengeschichtliches Lesebuch zur Chemie und Alchemie der Araber im Mittelalter*, p. 94.

538 E.E. Stapleton, "Sayings of Hermes," p. 75.

539 E.E. Stapleton, "Sayings of Hermes," p. 80.

540 E.E. Stapleton, "Sayings of Hermes," p. 72.

541 E.E. Stapleton, "Sayings of Hermes."

542 These concepts have been gratefully used by C.G. Jung and his followers.

543 E.E. Stapleton, "Sayings of Hermes," pp. 76–77.

544 E.E. Stapleton, "Sayings of Hermes," p. 76.

545 F.E. Peters, "Hermes and Harran," in *Intellectual Studies on Islam: Essays Written in Honor of Martin B. Dickson*, M. Mazzaoui and V.B. Moreen (eds.): "The Arabs had on the testimony of the *Fihrist* a wide variety of *Hermetica* which included versions of the Hermes myth as well as works of Theology, Cosmology and Physics which were the substance of the Hermetic 'revelation'," p. 195.

546 Ullmann, *Die Natur- und Geheimwissenschaften im Islam*, p. 373, fn. 7.

547 M. Ullmann, *Tabaquat al-attiba* 9.1 and 10.2, p. 373.

548 Ullmann, *Tabaquat al-attiba*, 6.10.

549 Ullmann, *Tabaquat al-attiba*, 10.5.

550 Such as the Persian Sufi mystic Suhrawardi. See Mehdi Aminrazavi, "The significance of Suhrawardi's Persian Sufi writings in the Philosophy of Illumination," in *The Heritage of Sufism* I, Leonard Lewisohn (ed.), pp. 259, 285, 260. See also Michiel Leezenberg, *Islamitische filosofie. Een geschiedenis* (Islamic Philosophy. A History), p. 203. Dr. H.J. Witteveen highlighted several points during his lecture "De innerlijke bron" (The Inner Fountain-Source) during a symposium *Back to the source*, on May 10, 2003 at Bilthoven, Netherlands.

551 M. Ullmann, *Light thrown on Hermes of all Hermesses, for whoever so desires*, p. 168. See also fn. 5.

552 It is self-explanatory. "Science" meant something different at the time than it means today, with the materialistic scientific concept including all its divisions.

553 H. Ritter and M. Plessner (trans.), *Picatrix. Das Ziel des Weisen von Pseudo-Magriti*, Book 3, Vol. 6, pp. 198–201.

554 Compare to *Poimandres*, Part I of this book, pp. 116–118.

555 Fragments of the above variations are found in numerous texts. M. Ullmann gives a summation in *Die Natur- und Geheimwissenschaften im Islam*, p. 373, fn. 6.

556 *Fihrist*, Book 7, Vol. I, p. 757: "...Seven for the seven Gods, one for the God of the Djinni and one for the Lord of the Hours." See alsoRitter and Plessner, *Picatrix*, Book 3, Vol. 7, p. 239. In it is a discussion of a calf being sacrificed to Hermes.

557 "The Sabians from Harran have temples carrying the names of intellectual substances and Stars. These temples are: The Temple of the First Cause and Intelligence—I do not know however whether is meant the first or the second intelligence—and also the temple of World Order and one of Fate. The temple of the soul is shaped round, Saturn's is six-pointed, Jupiter's is

a triangle, Mars' is right-angled and long, the Sun's is a square, Venus' is a triangle within a square, Mercury's a triangle within an elongated square and the Moon octagonal. The Sabians have in there temples symbols and mysteries." (al-Masudi, *Murug*; D. Chwolsohn, *Die Ssabier und der Ssabismus. Die Entwicklung der Begriffe Ssabier und Ssabismus und der geschichte der harranischen Ssabier oder die syro-helenistischen Heiden im nördlichen Mesopotamien und in Baghdad zur Zeite der Califats*, p. 367.

558 S. Gündüz, "The Knowledge of Life. The origins and Early History of the Mandaeans and Their Relation to the Sabians of the Qur'an and to the Harranians," *Journal of Semitic Studies*, Supplement 3, p. 210.

559 F.E. Peters, "Hermes and Harran," p. 190. He remarks that the Iranian librarian of Harun, Abu Sahl al-Fardi al-Nawbakhti, being familiar with Hermes does not mention this identification.

560 Peters, "Hermes and Harran," gives as reference Jahiz, *Tarbi'*, *CH.*, Pellat (ed. and trans.), Vol.1. p. 55.

561 Abu ma'Shar, *Kitab al-Uluf*, revised by Ibn Djuldjul, *Tabaqat al attiba*, 5 (written in 987–988 a.d.)

562 Ullman, *Die Natur- und Geheimwissenschaften im Islam*, p. 371, fn. 2. He gives a series of Arabian authors who quote Abu ma'Shar and repeat his information.

563 S. Gündüz, *The Knowledge of Life*, pp. 132–133.

564 M. Tardieu, "Sabiens Coraniques et Sabiens de Harran," *Journal Asiatique*, p. 274 (1986), p. 18, fn. 6 and 7.

565 J. Hjärpe, *Analyse critique des traditions arabes sur les Sabéens harraniens*, pp. 35–40.

566 *Fihrist*, Book 9, Vol. I, pp. 751–753.

567 D. Chwolsohn, *Die Ssabier und der Ssabismus*, I, pp. 406–407.

568 Prior to being called Sabians, they were called Nabateans.

569 Gündüz, *The Knowledge of Life*, p. 17. It pertains to Sura 2:62, 5:59, and 22:17.

570 "As long as they did not create too much trouble, some witnesses say, even if they would sacrifice people and children" (*Fihrist*, Book 9, Vol. I, pp. 759): "...one day in August they slaughtered a boy and boiled him till nothing was left of him." Ad-Dimasqi tells another horrific tale about a mother and child (Chwolsohn, *Die Ssabier und der Ssabismus*, Vol. II, text III, par. 3, p. 387). We all know that similar accusations were used in all ages by various religions.

571 Hjärpe, *Analyse critique*, pp. 38–41.

572 See, among others, F.E. Peters, "Hermes and Harran," p.190.

573 Compare Sura's 19:56–57 and 22:85. D. Pingree, *The Thousands of Abu ma' Shar* (for date identification and parallel stories in other sources, 1, fn.3).

574 Koran, Sura 19, pp. 57–58.

575 Ullmann, *Die Natur- und Geheimwissenschaften im Islam*, p. 373, fn. 4, gives references to other sources.

576 As-Sahrastani, *Book About Religious and Philosophical Sects*, p. 9. See also D. Chwolsohn, *Die Ssabier und der Ssabismus*, I, pp. 415–450.

577 As-Sahrastani, *Book About Religious and Philosophical Sects*, p. 9.

578 As-Sahrastani, *Book About Religious and Philosophical Sects*, p. 28. See also the parallels of the Hellenistic hermetic practices as described in Part I of this book.

579 Nabateans formed a nomadic tribe living in northwest of the Arabian peninsula during antiquity. Their capital was Petra (current Jordan). Nabatean's agriculture is described in *Picatrix*.

580 F.E. Peters, "Hermes and Harran," p. 194: "...the purpose in the Nabataen agriculture remains obscure, but it is obviously Hermetic. Almost all of the material is pre-Islamic and appears to be Greek, with some traces of Mesopotamian lore...."

581 See also D. Pringee: "Some of the sources of the *Gayat al-Hakim*," in *Journal of the Warburg and Courtauld Institute*, 43 (1980), p. 1.

582 As-Sahrastani, *Book About Religious and Philosophical Sects*, p. 8.

583 As-Sahrastani, *Book About Religious and Philosophical Sects*, p. 34.

584 Masudi, *Kitab al- Tanbih*, ed. M.J. de Goeje, p. 161; D. Chwolsohn, *Die Ssabier und der Ssabismus* II, pp. 378–379.

585 Biruni, *Al-Altar*, pp. 205, 20, and 318: "They have various prophets, the majority being Greek philosophers such as Hermes the Egyptian, Agathodaimon, Wallis, Pythagoras, Baba and Solon the maternal grandfather of Plato and similar figures"; Hjärpe, *Analyse critique*. Compare this with As-Sahrastani, who calls Agathodaimon, Hermes, Ayana (?), Awadi (possible corruption of Arani), and Solon.

586 W. Scott and A.S. Ferguson: *Ibn Hazm al Qorthobi* (died 1064), pp. 256–257. D. Chwolsohn, *Die Ssabier und der Ssabismus*, Vol. II, p. 526.

587 J. Hjärpe, *Analyse critique*, p. 166.

588 *Fihrist*, Book 9, Vol. I, p. 750.

Chapter 17

589 See Color Plate 1.

590 R. van den Broek, "Hermes en Christus" (Hermes and Christ): 'Pagan' Witnesses to the Truth of Christianity," in F.G.M. Broeyer and E.M.V.M. Honée (eds.), *Profetie en godspraak in de geschiedenis van het Christendom; studies over de historische ontwikkeling van een opvallend verschijnsel* (Prophecy and Divine Revelation During the History of Christianity; studies about the development of a remarkable phenomena), pp. 214–238; see also Roelof van den Broek, *Poimandres-Böhme*, pp. 115–145.

591 Roelof van den Broek, "A Dutch Painting of Mercurius Hermes," in *Ésotérisme, Gnosis en Imaginaire Symbolique* (Mélanges offerts à Antoine Faivre), pp. 3–17.

592 Sebastiano Gentile. During the Middle Ages, other works attributed to Hermes with collected citations circulated besides the *Liber XXIV Philosophorum*, including the *Liber Alcidi*, which was frequently used and referenced by Ficino in his translation notes of the *Corpus Hermeticum* (*Il ritorno di Ermete*, XIX, pp. 83–85).

593 Stobaeus 28. Socrates as well as Hermes asks who God is.

594 *Asclepius*, pp. 232–233.

595 Antoine Faivre, *The Eternal Hermes. From Greek God to Alchemical Magus*, pp 133, 149 (Illustration).

596 See below.

597 Such as Iamblichus (Part I of this book).

598 See Part II of this book.

599 Clemens of Alexandria, *Stromateis* 1.21, p. 134.

600 Justinus Martyr, *Apologie* I, 21.1–2, translated by G.J.M. Bartelink in *Twee apologeten uit het vroege christendom: Justinus en Athenagoras* (Two Apologetics of Early Christianity: Justinus and Athenagoras).

601 Bartelink, *Twee apologeten*, 22.2.

602 W. Scott and A.S. Ferguson, Cyprianus, *Quod idola dii non sint* 6, p. 6.

603 Tertullianus, *Contra de Valentinianen* 15 (Contra the Valentines).

604 Tertullianus, *De anima* 2.

605 A Platonic philosopher from the 2nd century b.c.

606 Tertullianus, *De anima* 28 (translation of Jan H. Waszink in *Die Seele ist ein Hauch*) (The Soul is a Sheath).

607 Tertullianus, *De anima* 33.

608 Arnobius, *Adversus nationes* 2.13.

609 Check Part II of this book.

610 Arnobius, *Adversus nationes* 2, pp. 14–15. See J. van Oort, "Hermes en Augustinus," in *Hermetische Gnosis* (Hermetic Gnosis), pp. 295–296.

611 *Asclepius*, Humani vero, qui medietate generis sui contenti sunt, 5.

612 See Scott and Ferguson, Cyprianus, pp. 9–28.

613 Carlos Gilly, *Poimandres-Böhme, Die Überlieferung des Asclepius im Mittelalter* (The Tradition of Asclepius in the Middle Ages), pp. 337–339.

614 Lactantius, *Divinae instutiones* 4.9.3.

615 Lactantius, *Divinae instutiones*, 1.6, pp. 3–4.

616 Lactantius, *Divinae instutiones*, 1.7.2 and 4.13.2.

617 Lactantius, *Divinae instutiones*, 4.8, pp. 4–5.

618 Lactantius, *Divinae instutiones*, 7.13.3. See the parallel with *Asclepius* 8.

619 See the previous chapter about the Sin-temple in Harran.

620 See Roelof van den Broek, *Bibliotheken en geleerden in de Oudheid* (Libraries and Sages in Antiquity).

621 Aurelius Augustinus, *De stad van God* (The City of God), introduced and translated by Wijdeveld.

622 See T. Tardieu, *Le Manichéisme*, pp. 22–24, (See also fn. 7 there).

623 Augustinus, *Contra Faustum*.

624 Citation by J. van Oort, "Hermes en Augustinus," in *Hermetische Gnosis* (Hermetic Gnosis), pp. 287–312, 300.

625 Aurelius Augustinus, *The City of God*, 18.39, by Wijdeveld, p. 901.

626 There is a story that indicates the translation of the *Asclepius* was done by Apuleius. It appeared in the collected writings of Apuleius in Florence in 1512 a.d. (See *Hermes Trismegistus; Pater Philosophorum*, catalog of the exposition in the Bibliotheca Philosophica Hermetica in Amsterdam (1990), p. 46.

627 Aurelius Augustinus, *The City of God*, 8.23, by Wijdeveld, pp. 390–391.

628 *Asclepius* 23–24.

629 Aurelius Augustinus, *The City of God*, 8.23, by Wijdeveld, p. 392.

630 Aurelius Augustinus, *The City of God*, 8.23, by Wijdeveld, p. 393.

631 Aurelius Augustinus, *The City of God*, 8.23, by Wijdeveld, p. 392.

632 Almost the entire chapter 37.

633 *Asclepius* 37, G.R.S. Mead, *Thrice Greatest Hermes*, Vol II, p. 238.

634 van Oort, "Hermes en Augustinus," p. 305.

635 van Oort, "Hermes en Augustinus."

636 Aurelius Augustinus, *The City of God*, 8.24, by Wijdeveld, p. 397.

637 Aurelius Augustinus, *The City of God*, 8.24, by Wijdeveld, p. 395.

638 Aurelius Augustinus, *The City of God*, 8.26, by Wijdeveld, p. 399.

639 Aurelius Augustinus, *The City of God*, 8.26, by Wijdeveld, p. 401.

640 van Oort, "Hermes en Augustinus," p. 305.

641 Carlos Gilly, *Poimandres-Böhme*, "Die Überlieferung des Asclepius im Mittelalter" (The Tradition of Asclepius in the Middle Ages, later to be indicated as Gilly, *Asclepius*). It is remarkable that there are many references to this document while the one of his contemporary Cyrillus, Bishop of Alexandria (412–444) is forgotten. He points diverse times to Hermes (Scott and Ferguson, *Cyprianus*, pp. 191–227).

642 Citation in a commentary on a poem *Philosophy's Consolation* by Boëthius. Adabold, Bishop of Utrecht (1010–1026) quotes from the "alternative" *Asclepius* by Quodvultdeus (Gilly, *Asclepius*).

643 See G. Quispel, *De Receptie van de Asclepius in de Middeleeuwen* (The Reception of Asclepius in the Middle Ages), *Asclepius*, pp. 227–251, 231–232).

644 See the doctoral thesis by David Porreca, *The Influence of Hermetic Texts on Western European Philosophers and Theologians* (1160–1300).

645 No other person but Boccacio copied the *Cosmographia.*

646 Gilly, *Asclepius*, p. 339 and Sebastian Gentile, "Ficino ed Ermete," in *Il ritorno di Ermete*, pp. 19–35, especially 28–29.

647 Gilly, *Asclepius*, p. 348.

648 Gilly, *Asclepius*, p. 348.

649 Gilly, *Asclepius*, p. 353.

650 J. Slavenburg, *Mystiek en Spiritualiteit, een reis door het tijdeloze* (Mysticism and Spirituality; A Journey through Timelessness), pp. 51–52.

651 Gilly, *Asclepius*, p. 364.

652 CH 4.4, G.R.S. Mead, *Thrice Greatest Hermes*, Vol II, pp. 56–57.

653 Antoine Faivre, *The Eternal Hermes. From Greek God to Alchemical Magus*, p. 19.

654 Wouter J. Hanegraaf, *Het einde van de hermetische traditie* (The End of the Hermetical Tradition), as an antithesis against Frances Yates (*Giordano Bruno and the Hermetic Tradition*).

655 Faivre, *The Eternal Hermes*, p. 21: "The Mercury of the alchemical literature belongs to an uninterrupted tradition...."

Part II

656 From a poem by the American poet Henry Wadsworth Longfellow (1807–1882).

Chapter 18

657 Citation of Jean-Pierre Mahé in "La Renaissance et le mirage égyptien'," in *Poimandres:Böhme*, pp. 371–372. See P.O. Kristeller, "Marsilio Ficino e Lodovico Lazzarelli: Contributo alla diffusione delle idee ermetiche nel Rinascimento," in *Studies in Renaissance Thought and Letters*, pp. 230–231. See also K. Schumann, "Giovanni Pico della Mirandola and the Hermetica," in *Hermetische Gnosis* (Hermetic Gnosis), pp. 316–317.

658 According to K. Schumann (*Pico della Mirandola*, p. 316), Corregio thought himself to be the reincarnation of Hermes. This cannot be concluded from the text. In his pupil Lazzarelli's work called *Crater Hermetis*, it is written that it was Poimandres and he was to be reincarnated as Jesus Christ (see the end of this chapter).

659 See Kristeller, *Studies in Renaissance Thought and Letters*, pp. 249–261.

660 See Antonio Rigo, "From Constantinople to the Library of Venice: The Hermetic Books of Late Byzantine Doctors, Astrologers and Magicians," in catalog *Magia, Alchimia* I, p. 81.

661 See Roelof van den Broek and G. Quispel, *Corpus Hermeticum* (Introduction), p. 19 and specifically Sebastiano Gentile and Carlos Gilly, *Il ritorno di Ermete*, pp. 181–183.

662 Recently, a Dutch translation has been published by J.A.G. Ruijling, *Hermippus; een gnostisch en hermetisch te duiden verhandeling over astrologie* (Hermippus; a Gnostic-Hermetical Treatise About Astrology).

663 Namely treatises 1.4.10 and specifically 16 (Check Antonio Rigo, "From Constantinople to the Library of Venice," p. 77.

664 Rigo, "From Constantinople to the Library of Venice," p. 78.

665 Flavius Josephus, *De joodse oorlog en Uit mijn leven.* (The Jewish War and Taken from my Life.)

666 Steven Runciman, *De val van Constantinople 1453* (The fall of Constantinople in 1453), p. 82.

667 Runciman, *De val van Constantinople*, p. 8.

668 Joost Ritman, preface to Shepherd, *Marsilio Ficino. A Universal Man*, p. 7.

669 Ritman, preface to *Marsilio Ficino*.

670 Bessarion, *In calumniatorem Platonis*.

671 Ficino was born on October 19, 1433.

672 Sebastiano Gentile, "Ficino ed Ermete," in *Il ritorno di Ermete*, p. 27.

673 Mercvrii Trismegisti, *liber de postate et sapientia dei*, *Corpus Hermeticum I-XIV, versione latina di Marsilio Ficino*, *Pimander*, Treviso 1471.

674 See, for instance, J. Slavenburg, "The 'Euphoria' of the 'New Age,'" in *Bres* (203-Aug/Sep 2000), pp. 4–5.

675 J. Slavenburg, "Ficino and Hermes," in Shepherd, *Marsilio Ficino*, p. 175, fn 1.

676 According to Giovanni Corsi: *Vita Marsilii Ficini* 6, Henri Johan Hak, *Marsilio Ficino*, pp. 178–186). See specifically fn. 316 in this book.

677 See description of this manuscript by Carlos Gilly in the catalog *Magia, Alchimia* II, pp. 14–16 (index no. 1).

678 The writing, however, is mentioned by Festugière in his index of writings (*Ven. Venetus Marcianus*, p. 242, 15th century, Nock-Festugière I, xii), but he does not draw any further conclusions from it.

679 With this donation in 1468, the Library of the Republic of Venice obtained the largest collection of Greek manuscripts.

680 See also the description of this in *Magia, Alchimia* II, pp. 17–19 (index. no. 2).

681 See the *Kyranides* version of Bessarion, located in the Bibliotheca Marciana (Antonio Rigo, 79; *Magia, Alchimia* II, pp. 57–59).

682 See p. 222.

683 See pp. 233–237.

684 See, for instance, J. Slavenburg: *De verloren erfenis* (The Lost Inheritance).

685 By "Materialistic scientific method," I mean the manner used after the Enlightment to investigate everything and try to explain it based on the pure science of matter and not from the point of view of something intangible like spirit (or a derogative version of spirit like intuition or inner knowing).

686 As we noticed before, Festugière considered "the Hellenic Astrology as a mixture of an appealing philosophical doctrine, a foolish mythology and of wrongly applied methods" (*Révélation*, p. 89) and Franz Cumont asked himself out loud how on earth this absurd doctrine could have been created, developed, and spread among the intelligentia and continued on for centuries. (Franz Cumont, *Astrology and Religion Among the Greeks and Romans*, viii).

687 See Preface.

688 "Humanist" is derived from the Latin *humanitas*. "The Latin term is ambiguous since it stands both for the human race as well as for humane feeling being a personal virtue. This ambiguity reflects the ancient Roman Stoic ideal of *humanitas* combined with standards of cultural refinement, like having high respect for other persons as well as fellow human beings" (Kristeller, *Renaissance Thought* I, p. 132).

689 Kristeller, *Renaissance Thought* II, p. 98: "There also existed—long before Plato—an ancient pagan Philosophy and Theology represented by the teachings and writings of Hermes Trismegistus, Zoroaster, Orpheus and Pythagoras. The Hermetic writings, the *Chaldaic Oracles*, the Orphic hymns, the *Golden Verses of Pythagoras*, writings which modern scholars consider as apocryphal products of late antiquity, but were for Ficino authentic witnesses of an ancient wisdom which was antecedent to Plato, though in basic agreement with him." See also pp. 35–99.

690 So it is with Ficino; even someone such as the Apostle Paulus could occupy an important place in the colorful unity. See, among others, Annine van der Meer, *Zeven sleutels tot het werk van Marsilio Ficino, een introductie* (Seven Keys to the Writings of Marsilio Ficino, an Introduction), in Shepherd, *Marsilio Ficino*, p. 35.

691 From this circle, the new *Academia* sprouts forth. See Annine van der Meer, *Zeven sleutels tot het werk van Marsilio Ficino, een introductie* (Seven Keys to the Work of Marsilio Ficino, an Introduction), p. 29.

692 The manuscript with Greek commentaries from Ambrogio Traversari can be found at the *Bibliotheca Riccardiana* (*Il ritorno di Ermete*, pp. 66–68).

693 *Il ritorno di Ermete*, pp. 69–70.

694 Quodvultdeus, *Adversus unique hearses* (see the Interlog of this book).

695 Ficino in his *Argumentum*, the introduction to his Latin translation of the *Corpus Hermeticum*, to be found in his *Opera*, 1836. Primarily from the translation of C.L. Heesakkers in *Hermes Trismegistus; Pater Philosphorum*, p. 29.

696 See Ficino's commentary on Plato's *Philebus* from 1469.

697 Ficino, *De christiana religione*, p. 22.

698 At a later date, this transfer of tradition *philosophia perenis* (eternal philosophy) was called for the first time *De perreni philosophia* by Augustus Steuchus (Agostino Steuco da Gubbio).

699 The six days of Creation, the six sub-spaces between the seven planets, the number of Jupiter and the sum of 1 and 2 plus 3. See, among others, Michael J.B. Allen, *Synoptic Art, Marsilio Ficino on the History of Platonic Interpretation*, p. 25.

700 Proclus, *Theologia Platonica (Il ritorno di Ermete)*, pp. 76–80.

701 Ficino possessed a copy of this book: *Il ritorno di Ermete*, pp. 76–80.

702 *Logos*, (The teachings) of the Gods, see footnote below (Logos, metaphysically meaning Word (Latin, *Verbum*) or "manifestation of a deity," esoterically speaking.)

703 Iamblichus, *The Life of Pythagoras and his disciples*, p. 146.

704 Iamblichus, *The Life of Pythagoras*, taken from the Dutch translation of H.W.A. van Rooijen-Dijkman in *Iamblichus/Porphyrius: Leven en leer van Pythagoras* (Life and teachings from Pythagoras), p. 64.

705 Iamblichus, *Life of Pythagoras*, p. 199 (v. Rooijen-Dijkman, p. 80). Philophaus appears many times in antique literature as a Pythagorean sage. In Plato's *Phaedo* (61), Socrates speaks to several of his pupils.

706 Porphyrius, *The Life of Pythagoras*, p. 45, (Dutch translation by Rooijen-Dijkman, *Iamblichus/Porphyrius*.

707 Laertius indicates as his source of information Heraclitus of Rome (*Life of Pythagoras*, p. 4).

708 After this, he had been Euphorus and, during his life, he remembered his previous life as Aethalides. After Euphorus, his soul transmigrated to Hermotinus and, when he died, he became Pyrrhus, a Delphian fisherman. Finally, he returned to Earth as Pythagoras (Diogenes Laertius, *Life of Pythagoras*, p. 4, inserted in Kenneth Sylvan Guthrie's, *The Pythagorean Sourcebook and Library*, edited and introduced by David Fideler, p. 142).

709 Iamblichus, *Over de Egyptische Mysterien* (About the Egyptian Mysteries), 8.4.265.

710 Eusebius, *Preparatio Evangelica* 9.27.6. Later, Ficino quoted in *De christiana religione* (Ficino, *Opera*, 29) that Artapanus remarked that Hermes' acts were identical to Moses.

711 See frontispiece of this book.

712 Bruno Santi, *The Marble Pavement of the Cathedral of Sienna*, pp. 13–14.

713 Augustinus, *The City of God*, 18.8.

714 For example, Diodorus of Sicily (*Diordori bibliotheca historica*, 5.75) and the previously mentioned Artapanus, who identifed Hermes with Moses.

715 J.P. Mahé, "La Renaissance et le mirage égyptien'" in *Poimander-Böhme*, p. 377.

716 Mahé, *Poimander-Böhme*.

717 Lazarelli wrote his *Crater Hermetis* shortly before 1494, the year this text was published. See Kristeller, *Studies in Renaissance Thought*, pp. 221–249.

718 Sebastiano Gentile, "Ficino ed Ermete," in *Il retorno di Ermete*, p. 27.

719 Brian P. Copenhaver, *Hermetica*, xlviii.

720 Augustinus, *The City of God*, 8.24, about *Asclepius*, p. 37.

721 It has now been included as the sixteenth treatise. In modern editions, the *Corpus* counts 17 libelli, but numbered to and including 18. Number 15 is missing, since a publisher inserted fragments of Stobaeus here, which in recent editions are published separately with many other fragments. See Walter Scott, *Hermetica; The Ancient Greek and Latin Writings which contain Religious or Philosophic Teachings ascribed to Hermes Trismegistus*, pp. 33–35.

722 Symphorien Champier, *Liber de quadruplici vita*, 1507 with the Latin translation of the *Definitiones Asclepii*.

723 Not all editions would be able to withstand the critical scientific scrutiny of today. For instance, Lefèvre had made rather a few notes underneath some passages about magic. These personal notes had been made to enable him to justify himself before the Church, but were seen later by translators as being notes of Ficino himself, which gave them more justification than they deserved.

724 See W.J. Hanegraaff, *Het einde van de hermetische traditie* (The End of the Hermetical Tradition), p.12.

Chapter 19

725 Antoine Faivre, *The Eternal Hermes* (translated by Jocelyn Godwin), p.

90. See also illustration on p. 68.

726 CH 1.26, G.R.S. Mead, *Thrice Greatest Hermes*, Vol II, p. 10.

727 See Botticelli and the *Primavera*. See also, among others, Yates, *Giordano Bruno*, pp. 67–77 and Faivre, *Eternal Hermes*, p. 28.

728 Francis Yates, *Giordano Bruno*.

729 Geoffrey Pearce ("Ficino and Astrology," in Shepherd, *Marsilio Ficino*, p. 109) attributes Ficino's knowledge to *Picatrix*, while Frances Yates is not so sure (*Giordano Bruno*, p. 73). The *Picatrix* is an original Arabian book of magic by Magrito or Madjriti, probably dating to the 10th century and a celebrated medieval text, translated into Latin in 1256 at the command of King Alphonsus of Castile, according to Jocelyn Godwin.

730 CH 7.2, Mead, *Thrice Greatest Hermes*, Vol II, p. 77.

731 See Part I of this book.

732 Rudolf and Margot Wittkower, *Born Under Saturn: The Character and Conduct of Artists*.

733 Annine van der Meer, "Zeven sleutels..." (Seven keys...), p. 28. See also F. Spakman, "De voltooing van de Renaissance in het nu" (The perfection of the Renaissance in the now) in Ficino, *Brug naar de Hermetische Gnosis* (Bridge to Hermetic Gnocism), p. 45.

734 Yates indicates these images are not derived from *Picatrix*, but from Petrus of Albano (*Giordano Bruno*, p. 71, fn. 8).

735 *Picatrix*, quoted by Frances Yates, *Giordano Bruno*, pp. 52–53.

736 Mercurius is in this tarot card (XXII; Faivre, *Eternal Hermes*, p. 27). The so-called hermetical tarot has nothing whatsoever to do with the Thrice-Greatest. It concerns new pictures of a certain Godfrey Dawson from the school *Hermetic Order of the Golden Dawn*.

737 The book consists mostly of passages from hermetical writings, especially *Asclepius* (G. Quispel, *Poimandres-Böhme*, p. 222), and on the works of Plotinus.

738 The work dates to 1489, the last edition being published in 1647 (Charlotte Mendes da Costa, "Marsilio Ficino and the Healing Arts," in Shepherd, *Marsilio Ficino*, pp. 120–121.

739 Thomas Moore, "Marsilio Ficino, Magician and Seer," in Shepherd, *Marsilio Ficino*, pp. 1044–105.

740 *The Letters of Marsilio Ficino*, Vol. 1–6, letter 4.46.

741 *Letters of Marsilio Ficino*, Vol. 1–6, letter 4.46.

742 Ficino, *De vita colitis comparanda*, p. 20. An English translation by Ch. Boer, *Marsilio Ficino: The Book of Life*.

743 Ficino in his *Disputatio contra iudicium astrologorum*, dated 1477.

744 Geoffrey Pearce, "Ficino and Astrology," in Shepperd, *Marsilio Ficino*, p. 115.

745 See Mendes da Costa in Shepherd, *Marsilio Ficino*, p. 125.

746 This means "Harmonious connections (corners) to other planets."

747 Music played an important role in the life of Ficino. See p. 292 of this book.

748 Zoroaster is placed ahead of Hermes as head of the chain of sages by Ficino in the *Commentarium in Philebum* (1469), as well as in *christiana religione* and in *Theologica Platonica*.

749 It is important to note that, a century later, Francesco Patrizi—also in charge of a version of the *Corpus Hermeticum*—wrote in his *Nova de universes philosophia* that Zoroaster was the first-known philosopher. The geneaology is as follows: Zoroaster is a grand-son of Noah's son Cham; Cham founded colonies in Egypt and was the father of Osiris; a priest of Osiris was Hermes

Trismegistus; a grandson of this Hermes Trismegistus, also called Hermes Trismegistus, lived in the time of Moses and was the second philosopher here on earth; Hermes was therefore influenced by Zoroaster. Orpheus learned the wisdom religion from priests of Hermes in Egypt. After him came Pythagoras, and Plato attended his school (Francesco Patrizi, *Nova de universes philosophia*, 1591, in K. Schumann, "Francesco Patrizi en de Hermetische Filosofie" (Francesco Patrizi and the Hermetic Philosophy), in *Hermetische Gnosis* (Hermetical Gnosis), p. 343.

750 From the *Boek der vierentwintig wijsgeren* (Book of twenty-four philosophers). See the Interlog.

751 Ficino in his commentaries, *Commantarium Convivium* and *Theologica Platonica*, 18.3.

752 Hermes, in fact, is not the author of the "Book of twenty-four philosophers" and Ficino knew that.

753 See also Michael J.B. Allen, "Marsilio Ficino, Hermes Trismegistus and the *Corpus Hermeticum*," in his *Plato's Third Eye, Studies in Marsilio Ficino's Metaphysics and its Sources*, XII, pp. 38–47 (Article in *New Perspectives on Renaissance Thought. Essays in the History of Science, Education and Philosophy: In Memory of Charles B. Schmitt, ed. John Henry and Sarah Hutton*, p. 47.

754 The *Asclepius* and the lost *Panaretos* (See Schuhmann, "Pico della Mirandola," pp. 318 and 328).

755 See Schumann, "Pico della Mirandola."

756 Antoine Faivre, *Access to Western Esoterism*, p. 60.

757 Pico died in 1494. For this short biography, I consulted William G. Graven, *Giovanni Pico della Mirandola, Symbol of his Age, Modern Interpretation of a Renaissance Philosopher*, and Schumann, "Pico Mirandola."

758 Schumann, "Pico della Mirandola," pp. 323–327.

759 Pico della Mirandola, *Over de menselijke waardigheid* (About The Nobility of Human), trans. J. Hemelrijk, p. 9.

760 Pico della Mirandola, *Over de menselijke waardigheid* (About The Nobility of Human), compiled by Frances A. Yates in *De Geheugenkunst* (The Art of Memory), p. 160.

761 Yates, *Giordano Bruno*, see chapter: "Cabbalistic Magic," p. 84 et seq.

762 Yates, The Art of Memory, p. 158.

763 Faivre, *Access*, p. 60.

764 Yates, *Giordano Bruno*, p. 86.

765 NHG I, pp. 398–407.

766 CH *Book I*, *Poimandres*, p. 25.

Chapter 20

767 See p. 221–221.

768 Yates calls it "applied Magic, or power Magic," (*Giordano Bruno*, p. 145).

769 A letter to a good friend in Gent (Belgium) ended up into the wrong hands, which lead to ungrounded accusations against him for practicing malevolent magic. See, among others, Noel L. Brann, *The Abbott Trithemius (1462–1516); The Renaissance of Monastic Humanism*, pp. 18–19; and Klaus Arnold, *Johannes Trithemius (1462–1516)*, pp. 182–183.

770 Arnold, *Johannes Trithemius*, p. 182; Will-Erich Peuckert, *Pansophie; Ein Versuch zur Geschichte des weissen und schwarzen Magie*, p. 82; Brann, *Trithemius and Magical Theology*, pp. 86, 137.

771 Peuckert, *Pansophie*, p. 92.

772 Peuckert, *Pansophie*, p. 111.

773 See Yates, *Giordano Bruno*, for a short discussion of the three separate volumes, pp. 130–144.

774 Yates, *Giordano Bruno*, p. 141.

775 Derived from para-Celsus (literally, beyond Celsus). Celsus was the Greco-Roman medical writer from the 1st century. Paracelsus literarily followed in his footsteps. Walter Pagel does not exclude that it could also mean that Celsus was "the enemy of Christianity" (against whom the Church Father Origines wrote an antithesis). See Walter Pagal, *Paracelsus. An Introduction to Philosophical Medicine in the Era of the Renaissance*, p. 5).

776 See J. Slavenburg, "Paracelsus. The natural health of body and mind," in *Kunst en Wetenschappen* (Art and Sciences), 10th annual, no. 2, summer 2001, pp. 29–31.

777 Pagel, *Paracelsus*, pp. 8–9.

778 C.G. Jung, *Paracelsica.*

779 Paracelsus, *The end of birth and contemplation of the stars*, recorded in *The Hermetic and Alchemical Writings* (Vol. II, from an edition by Arthur Edward Waite, p. 300).

780 Paracelsus, in *Paracelsus: Selected Writings* (Jolande Jacobi, ed.), p. 149.

781 Slavenburg, "Paracelsus," pp. 29–30.

782 See, among others, Carlos Gilly, "Das Bekenntnis zur Gnosis von Paracelsus bis auf die Schüler Jacob Böhmes,"in *Poimandres-Böhme*, p 397; G. Quispel, "De belijdenis van de Gnosis in het Westen. Van Paracelsus tot Gottfried Arnold" (The Confirmation of Gnosis in the West. From Paracelsus to Gottfried Arnold), in *Hermetical Gnosis*, p. 396; R. Steve-link, "De bevrijdende geneeskunst van Paracelsus" (The Liberating Medicine of Paracelsus), in *Theophrastus Aureolus von Hohenheim, genaamd Paracelsus, geneesheer, wijsgeer and Godsverklaarder*, p. 30.

783 Slavenburg, "Paracelsus," p. 30.

784 See, among others, Hans Carl, *Hermetische heilkunde; Paracelsus und die Alchemie* (Hermetical Healing Art, Paracelsus and Alchemy), p. 23.

785 Carl, *Hermetical Healing Art*, p. 24.

786 "Was wir mit Alchemie bezeichnen, war im Grunde nichts anderes als das, was wir heute mit Chemie bezeichnen" (Carl, *Hermetical Healing Arts*, p. 13.

787 See especially Walter Pagel, *From Paracelsus to Van Helmont. Studies in Renaissance Medicine and Science.*

788 He developed a technique to extract laudanum from the poppy, which could be used as a pain-killer and is still used as one today.

789 Quotation by R. Stevelink, "De bevrijdende geneeskunde van Paracelsus" (The liberating Medicine of Paracelsus), p. 35. In the first volume of *De Natura Rerum* (De Generationibus Rerum Naturalium), Paracelsus describes the rotting process as "mother" of transmutation. That which is healthy is transformed into poison by decomposition, but if you reverse the process in laboratories, you will accomplish the ultimate greatest miracle, the "divine mystery, the ultimate secret and miracle, revealed by God to mortal human." This means practically that it should be possible to create an artificial human being in a test tube, a *homunculus* as the ash from a bird. See also Pagel, *Paracelsus*, p. 117.

790 See, among others, Pagel, *Paracelsus*, pp. 88, 129.

791 This shows a parallel with the Hindu *prãna* (life vitality) or ether concept as the fifth element.

792 See, among others, Pagel, *Paracelsus*, p. 105 and onward.

793 Paracelsus, in his introduction to *Organon der Heilkunde*.

794 Peukert, *Pansophie*, p. 212.

795 Peukert, *Pansophie*, p. 196.

796 Paracelsus, *Dawn of Philosophers*, inserted in *The Hermetic and Alchemical Writings* (Vol. I), in an edition of Arthur Edward Waite, p. 65.

797 Paracelsus, *Dawn of Philosophers*, in Waite, p. 70.

798 Paracelsus, *The Book about the tincture of philosophers*, in *The Hermetic and Alchemical Writings* (Vol. I), p. 21. In this manuscript, Paracelsus speaks about a "Revelation of Hermes' attributed to him. According to Waite (p. 23), this was apparently used by Benedictus Figulus in one of his works.

799 Paracelsus, *About the Nature of things*, in *The Hermetic and Alchemical Writings* (Vol. I), p. 125.

800 In the chapter about the Arabian Hermes, mentioned earlier, one speaks of known conditions like black, white, and red (nigredo, albeno, rubedo).

801 Paracelsus, *About the spirits of the Planets* in *The Hermetic and Alchemical Writings* (Vol. I), p. 72.

Chapter 21

802 Paracelsus, *About the spirits of the Planets* in *The Hermetic and Alchemical Writings* (Vol. I), p. 85.

803 Karl Schumann, "Francesco Patrizi and the Hermetical Philosophy," p. 344.

804 Cees Leijenhorst, "Francesco Patrizi and the Hermetical Philosophy," in *Gnosis and Hermeticism*, pp. 140–141.

805 Anna Laura Piliafito, "Searching for a new Physics: Metaphysics of light and ancient knowledge in Francesco da Cherso," in *Magia, Alchimia* II, p. 255.

806 Newspaper *Trouw* (Netherlands), Wednesday March 6, 2002: "Nog vóór de Campo stomgeslagen" (Even before the Campo silenced into dumbness).

807 Keith Thomas, *The Downfall of the World of Magic. Religion and Magic in England 1500–1700*, p. 253.

808 See Frances A. Yates, *The Occult Philosophy in the Elizabethan Age*.

809 Carlos Gilly, "Between Paracelsus, Pelagius and Ganellus; Hermeticism in John Dee," in *Magia, Alchimia* I, pp. 286–295. For John Dee as a hermeticist, see "John Dee and the Hermetic Philosophy," chapter 4 of Peter J. French, *John Dee. The World of an Elizabethan Magus*, pp. 62–89.

810 See Sebastiano Gentile, *Il ritorno di Ermete*, pp. 136–138; Festugière, *Révélation*, p. 130; and Carlos Gilly, "Hermeticism with John Dee," p. 286.

811 Gilly, "Hermeticism of John Dee," p. 287.

812 Frances A. Yates, *The Theatre of the World*, p. 12. See also French, *John Dee*, pp. 40–62.

813 Gilly, "Hermeticism of John Dee," p. 287.

814 Gilly, "Hermeticism of John Dee," p. 290.

815 Gilly, "Hermeticism of John Dee," p. 291.

816 The Latin used was not yet used by the Humanists.

817 *The Keys of Solomon*, pp. 21–22.

818 Keith Thomas, *The Downfall of the World of Magi*, p. 203.

819 Gilly, "The Hermeticism of John Dee," p. 287.

820 H.M.E. de Jong, *Atalanta Fugiens*, p. 6.

821 John Dee, *Monas Hieroglyphica*, theorem XIV.

822 A. Kircher, *Obelisci Aegyptiaci*, Rome 1666, according to Alexander Roob, *Het Hermetische Museum; Alchemie en Mystiek*, (The Hermetical Museum; Alchemy and Mysticism), p. 598.

823 Dietrich Donat, "Sakrale Formeln in Schrifttum des 17.Jh.," in *Slavische Barock literature I* (Slavic Baroque Literature I), citation by Roob, *Het Hermetische Museum; Alchemie en Mystiek*, (The Hermetical Museum; Alchemy and Mysticism), p. 598.

824 C.H. Josten, "A Translation of John Dee's *Monas Hieroglyphica*," in *Ambix*, Vol. XII, 1964, p. 100.

825 E.J. Langford Garstin (ed.), *The Rosie Crucian Secrets. Their Excellent Method of making Medicines of Metals also their Lawes and Mysteries* (note the old spelling).

826 J. Slavenburg, *De geheime woorden. Een ontdekkingsreis door vijfentwintig eeuwen van gnosis* (The Secret Words. A Journey of Discovery throughout twenty-five centuries of Gnosis).

827 See the chapter "Hermes and the Rosicrucians" about the Rosicrucian movement.

828 Frances A. Yates, *The Rosicrucian Enlightenment*, 1972.

829 For Johann Valentinus Andrea, see the chapter "Hermes and the Rosicrucians."

830 Gilly, "Hermetism with John Dee," p. 292.

Chapter 22

831 Hegel, about Giordano Bruno.

832 Wouter J. Hanegraaff, "The New Age Movement and the Esoteric Tradition," in *Gnosis and Hermeticism*, p. 374.

833 M. Shepherd (ed.), *Marsilio Ficino; Ficino: Brug naar de Hermetische Gnosis* (Bridge to the Hermetical Gnosis); *Giordano Bruno: Italian Dialogues; Jacob Böhme: "A very bright morning star arose."*

834 *Giordano Bruno, De heroïsche mens in het oneindig universum* (The Heroic Human in the Infinite Universe).

835 Frans Smit, The Heroic Human in the Infinite Universe, p. 28.

836 Various dialogues in *Aswoensdagmaal* (Ash Wednesday Meal) have been copied in Giordano Bruno's *Italiaanse dialogen* (Italian Dialogs), pp. 29–75 ("Herein Bruno defends the heliocentric theory of Copernican doctrine").

837 See the Interlog in this book.

838 Fifth dialog from *Over de oorzaak, het beginsel en het ene* (About the Cause, Principle and the One), *Italiaanse Dialogen* (Italian Dialogs), p. 101.

839 *Italiaanse Dialogen* (Italian Dialogs), pp. 101–102.

840 *Geheime Boek van Johannes* (Secret Book of John) 7, *NHG* I, pp. 93–129.

841 Giordano Bruno, *De immense VIII, x* (by Ramon G. Mendoza, *The Acentric Labyrinth, Giordano Bruno's Prelude to Contemporary Cosmology*, p. 135).

842 Copernicus, *De Revolutionibus Orbium Coelestium*, 1543. Copernicus also quotes in this "revolutionary" work Hermes Trismegistus, who seems to have called the Sun, "the visible God." See Copernicus' world view in Dick Stafleu, *En toch beweegt zij. Geschiedenis van de natuurkunde van Pythagoras tot Newton* (And Still She Moves. History of Physics from Pythagoras to Newton), pp. 95–110.

843 Ramon Mendoza gives a very handy summary of Bruno's ideas about the Universe in *The Acentric Labyrinth*, pp. 133–136, which I gratefully use here. See here also the references to the relevant parts of texts in Bruno's oeuvre.

844 *Asclepius* 30.

845 Bruno, *Italiaanse Dialogen* (Italian Dialogs), *Spaccia della bestia trionfante* (The driving away of the triumphant beast), p.190.

846 *CH* 5.2, G.R.S. Mead, *Thrice Greatest Hermes*, Vol II, p. 65.

847 Mendoza, *Acentric Labyrinth*, p. 134.

848 *Asclepius* 26.

849 Compare the fifth element (*quinta essentia*) by Paracelsus.

850 *Asclepius* 33.

851 Mendoza, *Acentric Labyrinth*, p 134.

852 Mendoza, *Acentric Labyrinth*, p. 135.

853 Erich Kaniok, "De grote ruimte" (The Big Space), in *The Heroic Human in the Infinite Universe*, p. 63.

854 Frances A. Yates, *Giordano Bruno and the Hermetic Tradition*, p. 215.

855 The best edition of the time is Francesco Patrizi's *Nova de universis Philosophia* from 1591 (see previous chapter) dated seven years after Bruno's dialog. However, in Antwerp in 1575, an edition appeared of the *Fragments of Stobaeus* by Christoffel Plantijn. See *Hermes Trismegistus, Pater Philosophorum; textgeschiedenis van het Corpus Hermeticum* (Hermes Trismegistus, Pater Philosophorum; text history of the *Corpus Hermeticum*), p. 28 (description 17).

856 For Momus, see, among others, Mead, *Thrice-Greatest Hermes* III, pp. 114–115.

857 Bruno, Clarification of *Italiaanse Dialogen* (Italian Dialogs), *Spaccia della bestia trionfante* (The driving away of the triumphant beast), pp. 167–168.

858 *Asclepius* 26.

859 See, among others, Yates, *Italiaanse Dialogen* (Italian Dialogs), in *Giordano Bruno and the Hermetic Tradition*, p. 215.

860 *Asclepius* 24–26 in *Italiaanse Dialogen* (Italian Dialogs), *Spaccia della bestia trionfante* (The driving away of the triumphant beast), pp. 196–197.

861 Yates, *Giordano Bruno and the Hermetic Tradition*, p. 211.

862 Bruno, *Italiaanse Dialogen* (Italian Dialogs), *Spaccia della bestia trionfante* (The driving away of the triumphant beast), p. 206.

863 Yates, *Giordano Bruno and the Hermetic Tradition*, p. 223.

864 See *Hermes Trismegistus, Pater Philosophorum*, p. 83 (at the *Bibliotheca Philosophica Hermetica*, Exhibition catalog no. 48).

865 *CH* 16.3, 4, 5 and 17, Mead, *Thrice Greatest Hermes*, Vol II, pp. 171–172, 175.

866 Mendoza, *Acentric Labyrinth*, p. 135.

867 CH 11.4, Mead, *Thrice Greatest Hermes*, Vol II, p. 113.

868 CH 5.5, Mead, *Thrice Greatest Hermes*, Vol II, p. 66.

Chapter 23

869 See, among others, Henk Rijnders, *De Golem ontsluierd. Over joodse mystiek en Kabbala* (The Golem Unveiled. About Jewish Mysticism and Kabala), pp. 23–27.

870 In reality, Paracelsus described in his first book *De Natura Rerum* (De Generationibus Rerum Naturalium) how it should be possible to culture in a phial an artificial human, a *homunculus*, from a bird's ashes. See also W. Pagel, *Paracelsus*, p. 117.

871 Biographical information on Michael Maier taken primarily from H.M.E. de Jong, *Atalanta Fugiens*.

872 Maier, *De Circulo Physico Quadrato*, 1616 a.d.

873 H.M.E de Jong, *Atalanta Fugiens*, p. 6.

874 See also *De Lapide Philosophico Libellus* of Lambsprinck, 1625 a.d.

875 Roob, *Het Hermetische Museum* (The Hermetic Museum), p. 332—a magnificent collection of beautifully printed illustrations, although his information is not always as accurate as it should be.

876 Carlos Gilly, "The *Amphitheatrum Sapientiae Aeternae* of Heinrich Khunrath," in *Magia, Alchimia* I, p. 342.

877 Gilly, "*Amphitheatrum Sapientiae Aeternae*," in *Magia, Alchimia* I, p. 342.

878 John Stuart Alitt, "Music and Marsilio Ficino," in Michael Shepherd (ed.), *Friend to Mankind. Marsilio Ficino (1433–1499)*, pp. 133–142.

879 Michelangelo did not agree with this; he thought such an idea too static.

880 See illustrations on pp. 288–289.

881 On the title page of the first edition of *Atalanta Fugiens* from 1617, Maier dedicates these fuga's to "the ears and the enrichment of the soul." Two voices stand in harmony opposite a single-tone melody "suitable for the singing of two line strophes" (H.M.E de Jong, *Atalanta Fugiens*, translation of the title page).

882 See, among others, Jocelyn Godwin, "Music and the Hermetic Tradition," in *Gnosis and Hermeticism*, p. 191.

883 Yates, *The Art of Memory*, p. 326.

884 From 1667 on, they had the same publisher in Oppenheim called Matthaeus Merian who also decorated the writings of Fludd. Merian was, moreover, married to Maria Magdalena de Bry, daughter of the Bry publisher in Oppenheim (see, among others, *Matthaeus Merian the Elder*, p. 9).

885 Robert Fludd, in an unpublished alchemistical treatise quoted by Coudert, *Alchemie* (Alchemy), pp. 95–96.

886 Yates, *The Art of Memory*, p. 326.

887 Robert Fludd, *Utriusque Cosmi, majoris silicet et minoris, metaphysica, atque technica historia*, Volume I, p. 11.

888 Yates, *Giordano Bruno, and the Hermetic Tradition*, p. 441.

889 Yates, *Giordano Bruno*, p. 443.

890 See, among others, Thomas Hofmeier, "Philology versus Imagination: Isaac Casaubon and the Myth of Hermes Trismegistus," in *Magia, Alchimia I*, pp. 569–573, and Yates, *Giordano Bruno*, pp. 398–403.

891 See primarily Peter Kingsley, "Poimandres," in *Poimandres-Böhme*, p. 73 et seq.

892 See, among others, Yates, *Giordano Bruno*, p. 403 and *The Art of Memory*, p. 326.

893 The 1st, 4th, and 13th. See Thomas Hofmeier, "Cudworth versus Casaubon: Historical versus Textual Criticism," in Gilly, *Magia, Alchimia* I, p. 583.

894 Kingsley, "Poimandres," p. 73; Hofmeier, "Cudworth versus Casaubon," pp. 584–585.

895 Hofmeier, in Gilly, *Magia, Alchimia* I, p. 586.

896 *Asclepius* 24, quoted by Bruno (*Italian Dialogs*, pp. 196–197).

897 Michael Sendivogius, *Novum lumen chemicum* (The new alchemistical Light).

898 Sendivogius, *Novum lumen chemicum*, citation by Peter Marschall, *Alchemie: De Steen der Wijzen* (Alchemy, the Philosopher's Stone), p. 318.

Chapter 24

899 J. Slavenburg, *De geheime woorden. Een ontdekkingstocht door vijfentwintig eeuwen verborgen kennis* (The secret words. A journey of discovery through twenty-five centuries of hidden knowledge).

900 *De roep van het Rozenkruis. Vier eeuwen levende traditie* (The Call of the Rosicrucian. Four centuries of living tradition), p. 24.

901 The most impressive Asklepion (at least their ruins) I found in Pergamum (now Turkish Bergama) where there is a subterranean tunnel leading to the healing areas, which are still completely intact.

902 See, among others, Herbert Erkelens, "De tempelslaap bij Asclepius (The sleep in the temple of Asclepius), in *Prana* 99 (Feb/Mar 1997) p. 44, and Peter Kingsley, *Verborgen plaatsen van wijsheid*, (Hidden places of wisdom), p. 86.

903 See Part I of this book.

904 All citations out of *Fama* are from *Fama Fraternitatis. Oudste manifest der Rozenkruisers broederschap bewerkt aan de hand van teruggevonden manuscripten*. The oldest manifesto of the Rosicrucians Fraternity, it was compiled out of rediscovered manuscripts by Pleun van der Kooij, pp. 73–112.

905 *Fama*, p. 75. Damcar is now called Damascus.

906 *Fama*, p. 85.

907 *Fama*, p. 91 (in the year 1604, as calculated in *Confessio*).

908 See *Asclepius* 33: "...emptiness does not exist at all, it could not have existed in the past and will not exist in the future."

909 *Asclepius*, pp. 93–95.

910 See Part I and Interlog in this book.

911 J.F. Borghouts, *Egyptische sagen en verhalen* (Egyptian legends and stories), pp. 142–158.

912 Various scholars identify it is the large barren inscription "mastaba 3518," but no certainty has been reached about it.

913 See the chapter "Hermes in England."

914 The 7 "days" stand for the 7 phases of the classical Path of Initiation.

915 Notice the symbology: nine times nine.

916 The Dutch translation of the writing of Johann Valentin Andrea, *De Chymische Bruiloft van Christian Rozenkreutz anno* 1459 (The Chemical Marriage of Christian Rozencreutz anno 1459, totals an impressive seventy-six pages—too many for a detailed copy of all the described events. Therefore, I will only point out the most outstanding ones.

917 The "mercurial" water; see the many alchemical illustrations in which King and Queen make love in a lake, like in the *Rosarium Philosophorum*.

918 Stripped of a materialistic point of view.

919 Andrea, *Chemical Marriage*, p .74.

920 Andrea, *Chemical Marriage*, p .76.

921 *Fama*, p. 101.

922 *Hermes princips post tot illiata generi humano damna dei consilio; artisque asminiculo medicina salubris factus heic fluo. Bibat ex me qui potest, lavet, qui vult: turbet qui audet; bibite fraters, et vivite. Chemical Marriage*, p. 41.

918. The Dutch translation on page 42 reflects a rather wooden style. More fluid translations are found in *De roep van het Rozenkruis* (The Call of the Rosicrucian), p. 80, and Konrad Dietzfelbinger, *Mysteriescholen* (Mystery schools), pp. 290–291. These are more freely rendered than Carlos Gilly's "Das Bekentniss zur Gnosis von Paracelsus bis auf die Schüler Jacob Böhme" (The Confirmation toward Gnosis from Paracelsus up to the scholar Jacob Böhme), in *Poimandres-Böhme*, p. 413, in which he correctly translates "Hermes, the Monarch."

923 Ilana Zinguer, "La lecture des manifestes rosicrucians en France" (The Lecture of the Rosicrucian Manifestos in France), in *The Rosicrucian as a European phenomena*, p. 182.

924 In the above article, Carlos Gilly mentions, among others, Heinrich Nollius, Christoph Besold, and Andreas Libavius (pp. 414–416) who emphasize the hermetical origin.

925 Daniel Mögling, *Speculum Sophicum Rhodo-Stauroticum*, 1618.

926 Gilly, "The Confirmation toward Gnosis," in *Poimandres-Böhme*, pp. 413–414.

927 *Confessio* by Frances A. Yates, the *Rosicrucian Enlightment*, p. 252 (Appendix). Besold adds to this later: "And that Science is nothing else then the her-metical Philosophy" (Gilly, "The Confirmation toward Gnosis, p. 415.

928 Joost Ritman calls Christian Rozencreutz a "representative of the Hermetical-Christian Philosophy" (Joost R. Ritman, "Geburt der Rosenkreutzerbruderschaft," in *Rosenkreuz als europäische*, p. 66. See also Karl R.H. Frick, *Die Erleuchteten Gnostisch-theosophische and alchemistische-rozenkreuzerische Geheimgesellschaften bis zum ende des 18. Jahrhundrets—ein betrag zur Geistesgeschichte der Neuzei*, (The enlightened Gnostic-Theosophical and Alchemistical-Rosicrucian Secret Societies during the end of the 18th Century—a study of the spiritual history of the new age), p. 151. Christopher McIntosh does not speak specifically about the hermetical tradition, but rather about the occult tradition whose roots are buried in antiquity. (Christopher McIntosh, *The Rosicrucians. History and Mythology of an Occult Order*, p. 24). Roland Edighoffer points at several elements indicating Hermes as the source ("Hermeticism in Early Rosicrucianism," in *Gnosis and Hermeticism*), pp. 197–217.

929 E. J. van Wissen-Harkink, "De geboorte van de Rosenkruisersbeweging in de zeventiende eeuw" (The Birth of the Rosicrucian movement in the 17th Century), in John van Schaik (ed.), *De Rosenkruisers ontsluierd* (The Rosicrucians Unveiled), p. 18.

930 van Wissen-Harkink, "De geboorte van de Rosenkruisersbeweging, p. 18. Mrs. Van Wissen is a member of A.M.O.R.C.

931 See the exceptional position Tobias Hess had, in Gilly, *The Rosicrucian as European phenomena*, pp. 19–57.

932 *De roep van het Rozenkruis* (The Call of the Rocicrucian), p. 30.

933 Martin Brecht, "Der alte Johann Valentin Andreae und sein Werk- eine Anzeige," in *The Rosicrucian as European phenomena*, pp. 75–85.

934 McIntosh, *Rosicrucians*, p. 46.

935 See, among others, *Cimelia Rhodostaurotica. Die Rosenkreuzer im Spiegel der zwischen 1610 und 1660 enstandenen Handschriften und Drucke* (Focus on Rosicrucians in existing writings and publications between 1610–1660), p. 32; and Adam Haslmayr, *Antwort an die lobwürdige Brüderschafft der Theosophen von RosenCreutz* (Answer to the honorable Rosicrucian Fraternity), 1612.

936 *De roep van het Rozenkreutz* (The Call of the Rosicrucian), p. 32.

937 Fludd, *Tractatus Apologeticus*, Leiden 1617; see McIntosh, *Rosicrucian*, p. 62.

938 McIntosh, *Rosicrucians*, p. 72.

939 Edighoffer, Hermeticism in Early Rosicrucianism, p. 211. Edighoffer uses the terminology of Antoine Faivre, "Renaissance Hermeticism and the Concept of Western Esotericism," in *Gnosis and Hermeticism*, pp. 109–125, making a distinction between hermeticism as it pertains to and is based on the archaic *hermetica* and hermeticism as it reflects other aspects of Western esotericism, like Kabala, alchemy, and similar forms of speculation.

940 Most historians believe that Christian Rosencreutz was a mythical figure and not a historical one. See, among others, Jean-Pierre Bayard, *De Rozenkruisers, Historie, traditie and rituelen* (The Rosicrucians, History, tradition and rituals), p. 23, and *The call of the Rosicrucian*, p. 36.

941 Frances Yates, *The Rosicrucian Enlightenment*, p. 49.

Chapter 25

942 Citation from M. Dierickx, *De vrijmetselarij. De grote onbekende. 1717–1967* (Freemasonry. The Great Unknown. 1717–1967).

943 John J. Robinson, *Born in Blood*, p. 199.

944 Robinson, *Born in Blood*. The Scottish nobleman, Michel de Ramsay (1686–1743), member of French Freemasonry, was of the opinion that the Templars were not the only source, but also other sections of medieval knighthood, specifically the Knights of St. John who guarded the Holy Grail. At a later date, a German Freemason, Freiherr Karl Gotthelf von Hund (1722–1776), became leader of the Masonic Templar's Bond, which is a continuation of the Knights Templar whose secrets allegedly had been preserved and passed on to the Scottish Freemasonry.

945 Michael Baigent and Richard Leigh, *The Temple and the Lodge*. By "best-seller," I refer to *The Holy Blood, the Holy Grail.*

946 Most researchers show indisputable links between the Rosicrucians and Freemasonry, but do not go so far as to state that the rise of Freemasonry in the 17th century originated solely from the Rosicrucian movement. See, among others, A.F.L. Aubel, *De vrijmetselarij. Oorsprong, wezen en doel* (Freemasonry. Origin, Essence and Goal), p. 14 et seq.

947 *De roep van het Rozenkruis* (The Call of the Rosicrucian), p. 54.

948 Hans Schick, *das ältere Rosenkreutzertum. Ein Beitrag zur Entstehungsgeschichte der Freimaurerei*, p. 155.

949 *The Call of the Rosicrucian*, p. 46. Earlier, Comenius had put down the fundamentals in his *Via Lucis*. See *Via Lucis -De weg van het licht* (The Path of the Light).

950 Comenius was later honored with the name "Spiritual Father of the Order of Freemasonry." Bayard, *De Rozenkruizers* (The Rosicrucians), p. 102.

951 Citation from Bayard, *The Rosicrucians*, p.103.

952 E. Lennhoff, *De Vrijmetselaren*, (The Freemasons), p. 48; Yates, *The Rosicrucian Enlightenment*, p. 211.

953 See, among others, Dierickx, *De vrijmetselarij* (Freemasonry), p.174, and McIntosh, *Rosicrucians*, pp. 148–150.

954 C. McIntosh, *Rosicrucians*, p. 89.

955 Yates, *Rosicrucian Enlightenment*, pp. 209–210.

956 Lynn Picknett and Clive Prince, *Het Geheime boek der Grootmeesters* (The Secret Book of the Grand Masters), p. 114.

957 These most wild speculations are, sadly enough, not often supported by trustworthy research. They are taken from many sources and the fragments are glued together in the most incongruous places.

958 Frick, *Erleuchteten* (The Enlightened), p. 171.

959 Frick, *Licht und Finsternis* I (Light and Darkness I), p. 293.

960 Karl W. Luckert, *Egyptian Light and Hebrew Fire*, p. 157.

961 J.R. Clarke, "A New Look at King Solomon's Temple and the Connection with Masonic ritual," in *ARS Quator Coronatorum*, November 1976.

962 Frick, *Light and Darkness I*, p. 295.

963 A.F.J. Klijn, *Edessa, de stad van de apostel Thomas* (Edessa, The City of Thomas the Apostle), pp. 44–63. These odes can still be read in the Gnostic *Pistis Sophia*. See verse 34.4–5 of the Odes. "The similarity to what is below is what is above" seems to me to refer to the hermetical axiom, as the *Tabula Smaragdina* phrases it.

964 Frick, *Light and Darkness I*, p. 313.

965 See the title page of "The Constitutions of Free-Masons" which reads: "In the Year of Masonry 5723, Anno Domini 1723."

966 The *Matthew Cooke Manuscript* can be seen in the British Museum (Additional M.S. 23.198). It is a transcription of a much older document (probably from around 1400). For a long time, the manuscript was in the possession of George Payne, Grand Master of the London Lodge in 1718. See August Wolfstieg, *Ursprung und Entwicklung der Freimaurerei* (Origin and Development of Freemasonry), Vol. I, pp. 228–232 and Vol. 2, pp. 22–24.

967 Christopher Knight and Robert Lomas, *The Key of Hiram*, pp. 194–195. The Inigo Jones manuscript probably dates from 1607, but some dispute this and assign it to one of his pupils some fifty years later (*The Key of Hiram*), p. 340.

968 *Key of Hiram*, p. 29.

969 *Key of Hiram*, p. 35.

970 *Key of Hiram*, p. 112 et seq.

971 *Key of Hiram*, p. 193.

972 Frick, *Light and Darkness I*, p. 293.

973 William A. Albright, *Archaeology and Religion of Israel*, and J. van der Vliet, "Raising the *djedd*: A rite de marge," in *Akten München 1985* III (ed. S. Schoske), pp. 405–411.

974 S. Clarke and R. Engelbach, *Ancient Egyptian masonry: the building craft*, pp. 136–150 and D. Arnold, *Building in Egypt; pharaoic stone masonry*, pp. 46–47.

975 Frick, *Light and Darkness I*, p. 337.

976 Frick, *Light and Darkness I*, p. 297.

977 Gershom Scholem, *Major Trends in Jewish Mysticism.*

978 Antoine Faivre, *Eternal Hermes*, p.140; Frick, *Light and Darkness II*, p. 149.

979 Antoine Faivre, *Eternal Hermes*, p. 141.

980 Frick, *Light and Darkness II*, pp. 105–151.

981 Karl R.H. Frick *Die Erleuchteten. Gnostisch-theosophische und alchemistisch-rosenkreutzerische Geheimgesellschaften bis zum Ende des 18.Jahrhundrets - ein Betrag zur Geistesgeschichte der Neuzeit* (The Enlightened, Gnostic-Theosophical, Alchemistical-Rosicrucian Secret Societies until the 18th Century—a report on the spiritual movement of the New Age), and Light and Darkness I and II.

982 J. Slavenburg, *De geheime woorden* (The Secret Words), pp. 168–172.

983 W. Chr. Kriegsman, *Conjectaneorum de germanicae gentis originae*. See among others Faivre, *Eternal Hermes*, p. 43.

984 Joscelyn Godwin, *Athanasius Kircher. A Renaissance Man and the Quest for Lost Knowledge.*

985 Carlos Gilly, "Hermetism for Tourists: Athanasius Kircher makes a museum piece out of Hermes," in *Magia, Alchemia* I (Magic and Alchemy I), pp. 504–505.

986 See the illustration on p. 318.

987 Rupert Sheldrake and Matthew Fox, *Science and Spirituality*, pp. 22–23.

988 Rupert Sheldrake, *The Rebirth of Nature*, p. 52.

989 Sheldrake, *Rebirth of Nature*, p. 54.

990 William Blake, *Jerusalem*, edited by Morton D. Paley.

991 See the fascinating tributes by Jos van Meurs in "William en zijn gnostische mythen" (William Blake and His Gnostic Myths), in *Hermetische Gnosis* (Hermetical Gnosis), pp. 539–580 and "William Blake and His Gnostic Myths," in *Gnosis and Hermeticism*, pp. 269–311.

992 See Color Plate 4 and the illustration on page 331.

993 Carlos Gilly's descriptions of the manuscripts M309 and M228 in *Magia, Alchemia* II, pp. 237–253.

994 See, among others, Bastiaan Blomhert, *Mozart in de tempel. Raadvlakken tussen componist en vrijmetselaar* (Mozart in the Temple. Correspondences between Composer and Freemasonry).

995 M.F.M. van der Berk, *Die Zauberflöte; een alchemistische allegorie* (The Magic Flute; an alchemistical allegory).

996 See the clarifying picture of Johann Emanuel Schikaneder presented by M.E.B. Zweers, *Die Zauberflöte en de Gnosis* (The Magic Flute and Gnosis) in *Hermetische Gnosis* (Hermetical Gnosis), p. 489–491.

997 Duet of Pamina and Papageno in *Die Zauberflöte* (The Magic Flute).

Chapter 26

998 H.P. Blavatsky, *Isis Unveiled I*, xii.

999 H.P. Blavatsky, *Isis Unveiled* and *The Secret Doctrine*.

1000 J. Slavenburg, *H.P. Blavatsky, de Theosofie en de meesters* (H.P. Blavatsky, Theosophy and the Masters).

1001 The most important modern biographies of Blavatsky are Marion Meade, *Madame Blavatsky—The Woman behind the Myth*; Sylvia Cranston, *HPB. The extraordinary Life and Influence of Helena Blavatsky*; H. Murphet, *When Daylight Comes*, xix-xxvi. A more elaborate description of her life (especially after 1873) has been included in H.P. Blavatsky's *Collected Writings* (hereafter cited as *CW*), I, xxv–lxvii; II, xxv–xxxvii; III, "Chronological Survey"; IV, xxviii–xxxii; V, xxiv–xxix; VI, xxiv–xlviii; VII, xxiv–xxx; VIII, xii–xxiv; IX, xxiv; X, xxiv–xxix; XI, xxiii–xxvii; XII, xxiii–xxvi; XIII, xxiii–xxvii.

1002 These postulates are written down, among other places, in many magazines and booklets of all branches of the Theosophical Society, including *Theosofia* of the Adyar branch of the Theosophical Society; *Sunrise*, magazine of the International Theosophical Society at Pasadena CA (USA); and *Theosofie*, UTL, Belgium.

1003 A. Trevor Barker (ed.), *The Mahatma Letters to A.P. Sinnett*. For "The Masters" (*Mahatma's*), see, among others, Slavenburg, *Blavatsky, Theosophy and the Masters*, chapter 6, pp. 106–125 and Paul Johnson, *The Masters Revealed: Madame Blavatsky and the Myth of the Great White Lodge*.

1004 Synopsis in Slavenburg, *Blavatsky, Theosophy and the Masters*, p. 72–73.

1005 Prolog of *The Secret Doctrine* I. A synopsis as included in the introductory comments of a branch of the Theosophical Society, the Theosophical center Post Nubila Lux (a citation on the back cover of *Arjuna*).

1006 Stobaeus 1 (based on the numerology of Festugière). Blavatsky quotes part of this saying in the *The Secret Doctrine* I, p. 286. The learned Dr. Anna Kingsford collaborated with Edward Maitland to make the Stobaeus fragments available in *The Virgin of the World*.

1007 Blavatsky, *The Secret Doctrine* I, p. 281, citation from Kingsford and Maitland, *Virgin of the World*, pp. 133–134. The Stobaeus fragment is no. 5 by G.R.S. Mead and no. 9 by Scott and Festugière.

1008 Blavatsky, *Secret Doctrine* I, p. 74.

1009 Blavatsky, *Secret Doctrine* II, p. 236, see fn.

1010 Blavatsky, *Secret Doctrine* II, pp. 488–489.

1011 Blavatsky, *Secret Doctrine* II, p. 97.

1012 Blavatsky, *Isis Unveiled* II, p. 50.

1013 *CH* 1.6, G.R.S. Mead, *Thrice Greatest Hermes*, Vol II, p. 4.

1014 Blavatsky, *Secret Doctrine* I, p. 286.

1015 Blavatsky uses "Pymander" as a title—following Ficino's tradition—and as a collective name for the *Corpus Hermeticum*.

1016 *CW* XI, p. 549, as described by H.J. Spierenburg, *H.P. Blavatsky, On the Gnostics*, pp. 5–6. Much research for references of Hermes Trismegistus and the Hermetic Tradition has been provided by the learned theosophist Henk Spierenburg.

1017 Blavatsky, *Secret Doctrine* II, p. 267, see fn.

1018 Blavatsky, *Secret Doctrine*, p. 491.

1019 Blavatsky aims here at the Stobaeus fragments and others as they were shown in *The Virgin of the World* by Anna Kingsford and Edward Maitland.

1020 Blavatsky, *Secret Doctrine* I, p. 285.

1021 Blavatsky, *Secret Doctrine* I,.

1022 Blavatsky, *Secret Doctrine* I, p. 236.

1023 Blavatsky, *Isis Unveiled* I, p. 444.

1024 See the diverse citations by Blavatsky in Spierenburg, *Blavatsky, On the Gnostics*, pp. 3–40.

1025 Regarding *Asclepius*—in the latest translation of Anna Kingsford's book, Blavatsky says: "This is quite philosophical and in accordance with the spirit of Eastern esotericism... It must be so, since the esoteric teachings in Egypt and India were identical" (*Secret Doctrine* I, p. 672).

1026 Blavatsky: "This is quite consistent with the vedantic teaching... There are many passages in the Hermetic Fragments which belong in totality to the Secret Doctrine" (*Secret Doctrine* I, p. 287).

1027 Prior to the publication of *The Secret Doctrine*, we already found that link in theosophical literature. In *The Solar Sphinx* by T. Subba Row, there is an extensive commentary on Kingsford's publication of *The Virgin of the World* and he links the *Fragments of Stobaeus* with "the teachings of the *Vedanta* and Buddhistic systems of religious thought" (T. Subba Row, *Collected Writings* II, pp. 365–390).

1028 Anna Bonus was born in 1846, and married at the age of twenty-one to her cousin Algemon Godfrey Kingsford, on the condition that she was allowed to live her own independent life. Originally, a journalist for a magazine, she established her own paper: *The Lady's Own Paper*. In addition to her medical studies, she became engrossed in esotericism together with Edward Maitland. In 1880, she received her doctorate in medicine. Her lectures, based on lucid dreams and information derived from them, she verified by her own independent study of philosophy. In 1882, she published them in *The Perfect Way or The Finding of Christ*. The following year, she applied her studies to a great number of Platonic, Gnostic, and hermetic writings with Edward Maitland in the British Museum. At the instigation of Blavatsky—who was still living in India—she was chosen the same year as Chairman of the London lodge of the Theosophical Society. Anna Kingsford suffered from asthma and bad health all her life. She passed away at the age of forty-one.

1029 A. Trevor Barker (ed.), *The Mahatma Letters to A.P. Sinnett.*

1030 See, among others, Sylvia Cranston: *HPB, The extraordinary Life and Influence of Helena Blavatsky*, p. 237.

1031 Cranston, *HPB*.

1032 Barker, *Mahatma Letters*, Letter no. 85, p. 444.

1033 Barker, *Mahatma Letters*, Letter no. 85, p. 444.

1034 Barker, *Mahatma Letters*, Letter no. 85, p. 445.

1035 Daniël van Egmond, "Western Esoteric Schools in the Late Nineteenth and Early Twentieth Centuries," in *Gnosis and Hermeticism*, p. 323.

1036 Oscar Wilde was a very welcome guest. See, among others, Joscelyn Godwin, *The Theosophical Enlightment*, p. 344.

1037 Kingsford and Maitland, *The Virgin of the World.*

1038 Treatises 16–18, *Corpus Hermeticum.*

1039 For her book *Isis Unveiled*, Blavatsky used citations from the French translation of the *Corpus Hermeticum* published in 1866 by Louis Ménard, with the title *Hermès Trismégiste*. For her book *The Secret Doctrine*, she used Everard's newly reprinted edition from 1884, *The Divine Pymander of Hermes Mercurius Trismegistus in XVII Books; Translated formerly out of the Arabic into Greek and thence into Latin and Dutch and now out of the Original into English by the learned divine Doctor Everard* (1st edition: London, 1650). Everard did not follow Ficino's division; i.e. *Poimander* is the 2nd treatise. See also Frank van Lamoen, *Hermes Trismegistus; Pater Philosophorum*, p. 136.

1040 The advertisement was placed in the reprinted edition of Everard's *The Divine Pymander.*

1041 Jocelyn Godwin, Christian Chanel, and John P. Deveney, *The Hermetic Brotherhood of Luxor; Initiate and Historical Documents of an Order of Practical Occultism*, p. 3.

1042 Godwin, et al, *The Hermetic Brotherhood of Luxor*, pp. 6–7; R.A. Gilbert, *The Golden Dawn and the Esoteric Section*, p. 6.

1043 Egmond, "Western Esoteric Schools" p. 318.

1044 Daniel H. Caldwell and Henk Spierenburg, *A Historical Introduction* in *The Inner Group Teachings of H. P. Blavatsky* by Henk J. Spierenburg, vii–xxix; also Jean Overton Fuller, *Blavatsky and her teachers*, pp. 226–228.

1045 Spierenburg, *Inner Group Teachings.*

1046 Westcott and Mathers were also active in the Hermetic Society of Anna Kingsford (Joscelyn Godwin, *The Theosophical Enlightment*, p. 362) and Westcott continued to be a member of the Theosophical Society—passive in the Esoteric Section, but active in the Inner Group (Spierenburg, *Inner Group Teachings* and J.H. Dubbink, *Nieuw materiaal betreffende de Esoterische School*, in *Geheime Leer* III; *Esoterische opstellen en instructies* (New information regarding the Esoteric School in The Secret Doctrine III; Esoteric postulates and instructions), p. 710).

1047 Blavatsky did not agree to these multiple memberships to both movements.

1048 Included (as Appendix S.) in George Mills Harper, *Yeats' Golden Dawn*, pp. 290–305.

1049 Edouardo Schuré, *Les Grands Initiés*, Paris 1889.

1050 Manly Palmer Hall, *Twelve World Teachers*.

1051 J. Slavenburg, "Hermes op de breukvlak van twee eeuwen' (Hermes on the dividing line of two centuries," in *Hermetische Gnosis* (Hermetic Gnosis), pp. 580–597.

1052 G.R.S. Mead, *Thrice-Greatest Hermes*.

Chapter 27

1053 See fn. 1056.

1054 *Kybalion: A Study of the Hermetic Philosophy of Ancient Egypt and Greece*, by "The Three Initiates."

1055 The *Kybalion* has been published many times and translated in various languages. I am quoting here from a Dutch private translation of H.L. van Draanen, distributed by the Rosicrucian organization A M O R C (Groothertoginnelaan 36, 2517 EH, The Hague, The Netherlands).

1056 The Stanza's are reflections of wisdom from the so-called *Book of Dzyan* (see Boris de Zirkoff, "The Sources of the Secret Doctrine," in Virginia Hanson (ed.), *H.P. Blavatsky and the Secret Doctrine*, pp. 13–22.

1057 The seven hermetical principles from *Kybalion* (author's free translation).

1058 Anna Kingsford-Bonus and Edward Maitland, *The Perfect Way or the Finding of Christ*, London 1882 (used in the Dutch translation by A.B. van der Meer, *De Ware weg of het vinden van de Christus*, pp. 343–344).

1059 A section of the *Advaita Doctrine* can be recognized in it.

1060 C.G. Jung, *Herinneringen Dromen Gedachten* (Memories, Dreams, and Reflections), p.175.

1061 The *Codex Jung* is the first of the 13 codices rediscovered near Nag Hammadi in 1945. It was named after Jung, because his Institute was originally going to finance the purchase of this first codex (including the famous *Gospel of Truth*). Gilles Quispel eventually bought it in 1952 and, on November 15, 1953, it was handed to Jung and named the *Codex Jung*. See specifically the contribution of Giles Quispel to the collection of C. Aalders, J.H. Plokker and G. Quispel, *Jung—een mens voor deze tijd* (Jung—a man for this time).

1062 Colin Wilson, *Master of the Underworld; Jung and the 20th Century*, pp. 96–97.

1063 C.G. Jung, *Psychologie und Alchemie* (Psychology and Alchemy).

1064 Aniela Jaffé, *Jung over parapsychologie en alchemie—Jung's laatste jaren* (Jung, about parapsychology and alchemy—Jung's last years), p. 80.

1065 Joseph L. Henderson, "Oude mythen en de moderne mens" (Old myths and the modern human), in Jung, *De mens en zijn symbolen* (Man and his Symbols), p. 131.

1066 C.G. Jung, *Herinneringen Dromen Gedachten* (Memories, Dreams and Reflections), pp. 150–151; Dan Merkur, *Gnosis. An Esoteric Tradition of Mystical Visions and Unions*, p. 39.

1067 The two lectures were printed in the *Eranos-Jahrbuch* 1942 and have been included in "Der Geist Mercurius" (The Spirit Mercurius), in Jung's *Symbolik des Geistes* (Symbology of the Mind), pp. 71–153. These pages belong to this publication.

1068 R. Reitzenstein, *Poimandres*.

1069 C.G. Jung, "Der Geist Mercurius," p. 87.

1070 C.G. Jung, "Mercurius und Der Gott Hermes," in "Der Geist Mercurius," p. 120 et seq.

1071 Jung, "Der Geist Mercurius," pp. 128–129.

1072 H. Stufkens, *Gesprekken over Jung. Religie-gnosis-alchemie* (Conversations about Jung. Religion-Gnosis-Alchemy), p. 67.

1073 Antoine Faivre, *The Eternal Hermes*, p. 65.

1074 Jung, Memories, Dreams, and Reflections, pp. 21–23.

1075 See, for instance, P. de Vries-Ek, "Hermes en de levende geest Mercurius" (Hermes and the living spirit Mercury), in *Hermetic Gnosis*, pp. 599–600.

1076 See Part I of this book.

1077 Jean Shinoda Bolen, *Goden in elke man* (Gods in each Man), pp. 245–286.

1078 *Corpus Hermeticum. Texte établi par* A.D. *Nock et traduit par* A-J. *Festugière* (4 volumes).

1079 F. van Lamoen, *Hermes Trismegistus; Pater Philosophorum*, p. 143.

1080 Festugière, *Révélation*.

1081 See specifically Part I of this book.

1082 R. van den Broek en G. Quispel, *Asclepius. De volkomen openbaring van Hermes Trismegistus* (The Complete Revelation of Hermes Trismegistus); Brian P. Copenhaver, *Hermetica* (The Greek *Corpus Hermeticum* and the Latin *Asclepius* in a new English translation, with notes and introduction);

Carsten Colpe en Jens Holzhausen (ed.), *Das Corpus Hermeticum Deutsch* (The German Hermeticum), 2 volumes (Vol. 3 in progress).

1083 Jan van Rijckenborgh, *De Egyptische oer-gnosis en Haar Roep in het Eeuwige Nú*, (The Egyptian Archaic-Gnosis and her Call in the Eternal Now). According to Frank van Lamoen, Van Rijckborgh used a 1706 German translation by Van Beyerland en Patrizi (*Hermes Trismegistus; Pater Philosophorum*, p. 144). Lex van den Brul shows as his source the translation by the German J. Scheibe and Englishman G.R.S. Mead: "Jan van Rijckenborgh—ein moderner Rosenkreutzer und hermestitcher Gnostiker" (Jan van Rijckenborgh—a modern Rosicrucian and hermetical Gnostic), in *Rosenkreuz als europäisches Phänomen im 17. Jahrhundert*, p. 395.

1084 In the late thirties, a series of booklets were published by the Lectorium Rosicrucianum: *De Hermetische Geneeskunde*, *De Problematiek der Geneeskunde Paracelsiana*, *De Magie van het bloed op het altaar der Genezers, etc*. (The Hermetic Art of Healing, The Problematic Nature of the Paracelsian Art of Healing, The Magic of Blood on the Altar of Physicians, etc). The Lectorium knew, moreover, a practical form of healing, completely in the style of the old secret fraternities (see, for example, the *Genezingswerk der Rozekruisers* (The Healing Task of the Rosicrucians)). This was also the case in Max Heindel's *Rosicrucian Fellowship*. See "De gave der genezing" (The Gift of Healing), in his *Rosicrucian Cosmologie*, pp. 539–545.

1085 Understandably, rules of a good diet (were) and are part of the healing process ("The problem of food, health and long lasting youth—as seen scientifically," in Max Heindel, *Het Christendom der Rozekruisers* (Christianity of the Rosicrucians).

1086 Rijckenborgh, *Egyptian Archaic-Gnosis*.

1087 P.A. Dirkse, J. Brashler, and D.M. Parrott, *Nag Hammadi Codices V, 2–5 and VI with Papyrus Berolinensis 8502, I and 4*, NHS 11, Leiden 1979. See also J.P. Mahé, *Hermès en Haute Égypte* (Hermes in Upper Egypt), Vol. I, which contains a publication of *The Treatise of the Eighth and Ninth Heavenly Sphere*.

1088 Mahé, *Hermès en Haute Égypte*; Garth Fowden, *The Egyptian Hermes*; Peter Kingsley, "An Introduction to the Hermetica: Approaching Ancient Esoteric Tradition," in *Poimandres-Böhme*.

1089 Specifically, the one in Florence in 1999 and in Venice in 2002. This was quoted several times earlier in this book.

1090 R. van den Broek and G. Quispel, *Corpus Hermeticum*.

1091 *Asclepius*.

Epilog

1092 *Korè Kosmou* (The Virgin of the World), Stobaeus 23.8.

1093 *Asclepius*.

1094 *Asclepius* I.

1095 CH 13.1-2, G.R.S. Mead, *Thrice Greatest Hermes*, Vol II, pp. 139–140.

1096 Wim Kayzer, *Vertrouwd en o zo vreemd. Over geheugen en bewustzijn* (Familiar yet very strange. About Memory and Consciousness), pp. 418–419.

1097 Daniel C. Dennett, an American philosopher.

1098 *Een schitterend ongeluk* (An Amazing Coincidence): *Wim Kayzer meets Oliver Sacks, Stephen Jay Gould, Stephen Toulmin, Daniel C. Dennett, Rupert Sheldrake and Freeman Dyson*, p. 348.

1099 Rupert Sheldrake (1942), an English philosopher and natural scientist.

1100 Stephen Jay Gould (1941), an American biologist.

1101 *Een schitterend ongeluk* (An Amazing Coincidence), pp. 348–349.

1102 William Paley (1743–1805), an English researcher.

1103 Heidegger, "Die Zeit des Weltbildes" (1938), in *Holzwege*, by Herman Berger, *Metaphysica, een dwarse geschiedenis* (Metaphysics, a Slanted History), p. 176.

1104 Stephen Weinberg (1933), an American physicist.

1105 Citation by Berger, *Metaphysica* (Metaphysics), p. 147.

1106 Berger, *Metaphysics*, p. 146, (The term "Theory of Everything" is originally from Einstein, who worked on it prior to his death. It is the title of one of the books by Ken Wilber, an American biologist, philosopher, and author.

1107 Ernest Rutherford (1871–1937), an English physicist who discovered that atoms in matter possess an inner structure.

1108 Niels Bohr (1885–1962), a brilliant Danish physicist, the "discoverer" of the Complementary Principle.

1109 Alexander Friedmann, a Russian physicist who stated a non-static Universe in 1922, prior to Hubble's observation.

1110 Stephen Hawking, *Het Heelal. Verleden en toekomst van ruimte & tijd* (The Universe. Past and Future in time and space), 25th edition, p. 233.

1111 David Filkin, *Stephen Hawking's universum* (Stephen Hawking's Universe), p. 252.

1112 Hawkings, *Het Heelal* (The Universe), p. 224.

1113 Tjeu van den Berk, *Mystagogie. Inwijding in het symbolisch bewustzijn* (Mystagogue. Initiation into the Symbolic Consciousness). On the cover of this book, we see a fascinating Hermetic illustration from the 12th century.

1114 David Bohm (1917–1992), an American quantum physicist who developed a theory that the whole Universe can best be understood as a kind of gigantic streaming hologram ("holo-movement").

1115 van den Berk, *Mystagogie*, p. 39, (Quoted from Fritjof Capra, *De tao van de fysica* (The Tao of Physics), pp. 132–133. See also J.J.W. Berghuys, *Mens en kosmos—een groot verband. Uitweg uit de crisis in rationeel denken* (Human and Cosmos—a Great Connection. The Way Out of the Crisis in Rational Thought), "Holisme" (Holisticism), p. 91 et seq.

1116 Rupert Sheldrake and Matthew Fox, *Wetenschap en Spiritualiteit* (Science and Spirituality), pp. 26–28.

1117 Sheldrake and Fox, *Science and Spirituality*, p. 27.

1118 See Herbert van Erkelens, "Het spanningsveld tussen mystiek en natuurwetenschap" (The field of resonation between Mysticism and Physics), in *Encyclopedie van de mystiek* (Encyclopedia of Mysticism), p. 313.

1119 Copra, *Tao of Physics*.

1120 See, among others, Herbert van Erkelens, *Het spel van de wijsheid. Pauli, Jung en de menswording van God* (The game of wisdom. Pauli, Jung and the becoming human of God.), p. 47.

1121 Sheldrake and Fox, *Science and Spirituality*, p. 29.

1122 *Een schitterend ongeluk* (An Amazing Coincidence).

1123 Leonard Cohen, "Anthem," from the CD: *The Future*.

1124 See diagram 5 in J. Slavenburg, *Een sleutel tot gnosis* (A Key to Gnosis), p. 109.

Index

About the Author

Jacob Slavenburg is a resident of the Netherlands. He holds a Ph.D. in cultural history and is the author of numerous books on the Hermetic Tradition and Gnostic Wisdom. In particular, he has done extensive work with the Nag Hammadi Library

His website is:

www.jacobslavenburg.nl/